"New Mecca, New Babylon"
Paris and the Russian Exiles, 1920–1945

"New Mecca, New Babylon"

Paris and the Russian Exiles, 1920 – 1945

ROBERT H. JOHNSTON

McGill-Queen's University Press
Kingston and Montreal

© McGill-Queen's University Press 1988
ISBN 0-7735-0643-8

Legal deposit 2nd quarter 1988
Bibliothèque nationale du Québec

Printed in Canada on acid-free paper

This book has been published with the help of a grant
from the Social Science Federation of Canada, using
funds provided by the Social Sciences and Humanities
Research Council of Canada.

Canadian Cataloguing in Publication Data
Johnston, Robert H. (Robert Harold), 1937–
New Mecca, new Babylon : Paris and the Russian exiles,
1920–1945

Includes index.
Bibliography: p.
ISBN 0-7735-0643-8

1. Russians – France – Paris – History – 20th century.
2. Refugees, Political – France – Paris. 3. Soviet Union
History – Revolution, 1917–1921 – Refugees. I. Title.

DK269.J64 1988   944′.361004917I   C88-090010-5

Contents

Preface

Refugees are an overwhelming reality of our age. Together with the nuclear issue and international terrorism, they demand attention and provoke reactions. Indeed, judging from the clamorous headlines, it may be argued that refugees excite more visceral reactions than even nuclear disarmament. This latter cause has its passionate proponents, to be sure. Yet its apocalyptic visions and technical complexities leave many citizens shrugging in ignorance, helplessness or apathy. Are not these vital matters best left to presidents and general secretaries?

Not so the issue of refugees. On the immediate, highly charged matter of their admission and presence, especially in the favoured lands of Western Europe and North America, virtually everyone has a vociferous opinion to offer. In this century repeated waves, from yesterday's Russians and Armenians to today's Haitians and Sri Lankans, have had to endure both the rigours of refugee life and the strains caused by their presence within a larger alien community. The experience has rarely been pleasant for anyone.

In focusing upon the Russian Civil War exiles in Paris, I have sought to present the collective biography of a community which, while experiencing these refugee ordeals to the full, saw itself as the brain and heart of a unique, worldwide phenomenon. This was the anti-Bolshevik Russian diaspora of the twenties and thirties, known to its senior members at the time as "Russia Abroad" and to history, more prosaically, as the first emigration from Soviet Russia. The experience of exile for the Russians, the reactions they provoked from their hosts, their image of themselves and their lost country, and their relationship to other refugees movements, including two later waves from the USSR, form a part, even an important part, of the twentieth-century refugee record. I venture to suggest that these matters also have their place in the history of Russia.

It remains for me gratefully to acknowledge the several obligations I have incurred while working on this book. I wish first to thank the Canada Council and McMaster University for their generous support during my protracted labours over the past several years, and the Social Sciences and Humanities Research Council of Canada for its assistance in the publication of this book. I also acknowledge with gratitude the help provided by the staffs of the Hoover Institution on War, Revolution and Peace, Stanford University; the Rare Book and Manuscript Library, Columbia University; the YMCA Historical Library, New York; the Library of the Royal Institute of International Affairs, Chatham House, London; and the Bibliothèque de Documentation Internationale Contemporaine, Université de Paris-X, Nanterre. I thank the Columbia University Libraries for permission to use and quote from the Paul N. Miliukov and Vladimir M. Zenzinov Papers in the Bakhmeteff Archive, Rare Book and Manuscript Library, Columbia University. I thank also Mr. Maynard Brichford, University Archivist, University of Illinois at Urbana-Champaign, for permission to cite from the Paul B. Anderson Papers. I wish too to acknowledge the courtesy of the *Russian Review* and *Canadian Slavonic Papers* in giving me permission to publish material previously published in slightly different form in their journals.

I take pleasure in recording also the kindness in submitting to interviews of three distinguished *émigrés* who appear in these pages, the late Pierre Kovalevsky, Wladimir Weidlé and Zinaida Schakovskoy. They were extremely patient in answering my questions, which I fear at times must have struck them as rather naïve. Colleagues in Canada have given aid and comfort. Here I have to thank André Liebich of the Université du Québec à Montréal, and Harvey Levenstein, Louis Greenspan, and George Thomas of McMaster University. Finally, I must record a particular and immeasurable debt to John Keep of the University of Toronto. His good humour in reading a manuscript unexpectedly presented to him and the impeccable scholarship of his suggestions for its improvement are here most gratefully acknowledged.

A NOTE ON TRANSLITERATION

The transliteration of Russian names always presents problems, which are compounded in the case of *émigrés* whose names assume various forms in Western exile. Without making any claims whatever for consistency, I have adopted certain spelling practices in the case of Russian proper names. The -ii ending in many male personal names is rendered in the narrative by the -y form more familiar to English-speaking readers. Most (but not all) first names are given in their English equivalents, while the soft sign, rendered in English by an apostrophe, has been entirely omitted throughout the narrative. The soft sign and the -ii ending have, however, been retained in the notes for the names of authors and titles of sources cited in the bibliography. Where Russian authors have written in both Russian and French and these works are cited in the bibliography, the Russian form only of the author's name is given there. In the narrative, where particular Russian names are more familiar in a Western form (Chagall, Chaliapin, Wrangel, Weidlé), this latter version has been employed. Titles of *émigré* journals and newspapers have been transliterated throughout from their original Russian form. Unless they themselves changed to the new style (a rare event), their spelling has not been brought into full conformity with Soviet-amended Russian orthography.

ON CURRENCY VALUES

The value of the French franc fluctuated widely between the two World Wars. In 1921 the official rate of exchange stood at around 13.5 francs to the us dollar. Over the next five years the franc then fell steadily, attracting throngs of American tourists to France. In July 1926 the dollar touched almost 50 francs. Two months later, the Union nationale government effected a drastic devaluation, which, though wiping out savings, had some success in stabilizing the international value of the franc. In December 1926 the new, gold-backed "Poincaré franc" stood at around 26 to the dollar. It remained in that vicinity until the 1934 devaluation of the dollar put the rate of exchange at 15.2 francs. The French currency then commenced a free fall. Against a background of collapsing cabinets (eleven between January 1934 and April 1938) and a growing menace of war, the franc slid through further devaluations and the abandonment of the gold standard. In December 1936 $1.00 bought 21 francs; in December 1937, 29 francs; in January 1939, 40 francs.

"New Mecca, New Babylon"

Introduction

In what may well be his most frequently quoted line of verse, W.H. Auden reminded those caught up in the passionate crusade of the Spanish Civil War: "History to the defeated may say Alas, but cannot help or pardon." Auden wrote as the first wave of the defeated in Spain was making its painful way northward toward French exile. Unconsciously the refugees followed the example set some sixteen years earlier by another migration of vanquished from their homeland, also torn by civil war. Between 1918 and 1921 perhaps as many as a million refugees poured out of Russia in a human tidal wave which had no equal in European history until the Spanish Calvary that touched the poets of Europe and America with its tragic suffering.

The Russian exodus, the first and largest of three from that country since 1918, was prompted by revolution and civil strife. Those who fled found no foreign poets to hymn their ordeal: they did not expect to. They arrived abroad with no thought of asking anyone's pardon, least of all history's, nor indeed of remaining long. Yet history decreed that, for all but a few, their stay would be permanent. How they responded to this circumstance, how they and their children reacted to life in an alien environment and confronted their principal concerns are the major themes of this book.

Who were these Russian refugees? The answer that most readily comes to mind is the stereotype common in the 1920s and not unfamiliar in later decades. This envisaged the Russian community which suddenly appeared in Western Europe as made up of impoverished aristocrats. All were deemed wildly impractical, exotic, and frenetic. To this mixture might be added a brace of Cossacks, a mournful choir, two or three onion-domed churches, ex-grand dukes driving taxi-cabs, and more than a touch of the suffering Slav soul. This was the world that French readers enjoyed in, for example, Joseph Kessel's highly popular novel *Nuits de princes* (1928). Kessel, himself of Russian descent, presented a multicoloured cast: nobly born taxi drivers, nightclub dancers, gypsies, and assorted hangers-on flash like birds of paradise through bourgeois Paris, embodied in Mademoiselle Mesureux and her slightly seedy, thoroughly respectable boardinghouse. That the image did not invariably correspond to the reality of exile life was just one more liability the refugees were obliged to endure. Count Vladimir Kokovtsev's definition in 1930 of his fellow refugees, made to a sympathetic French journalist, seems a half-ironic, half-resigned acknowledgement of the features commonly assigned in the West to his exiled compatriots: "nostalgia, fatalism, balalaikas, lugubrious songs of the Volga, a crimson shirt, a frenzied dance – such is the Russian emigration."[1] Insistence that the *émigrés* were more than this, that they represented a different image and "[were] not all ardent Cossacks, the prestige-laden personification of the steppe,"[2] usually failed to make headway against the clichés. And yet the clichés, for all their irritating superficiality, were not wholly inappropriate. There were indeed Russian nightclubs, grand dukes, Cossack taxi drivers, choirs, and expensive restaurants in most large European cities between the two world wars. German and French residents, to say nothing of visiting tourists, saw and judged accordingly. But this was very far from the whole; still less was it the image of the Russian community favoured by those who belonged to it.

It is in attempting to get away from the stereotype that the difficulties of definition begin. There was, to be sure, a legal statement of the exiled Russians' corporate identity. In 1926 representatives in the League of Nations of states sheltering Russians hammered out a formula to the effect that a Russian refugee was "any person of Russian origin who does not enjoy, or who no longer enjoys, the protection of the Government of the Union of Soviet Socialist Republics and who has not acquired another nationality."[3] Seemingly terse enough: can anything be added? One detail relevant to their condition might be emphasized: the circumstances of their departure from Russia. In the struggle that followed the collapse of the tsarist and provisional governments the Russian Civil War exiles represented the defeated, the first of twentieth-century Europe's political lost causes. From monarchists to Mensheviks, with all the infinitely complex, quarrelsome variations in between, they had all been bested by the Bolsheviks. The act of flight acknowledged defeat, a temporary one they hoped, but a defeat all the same.

A common citizenship, a common catastrophe, for most a common language – these features admitted, the historian falls back on those over-worked words "majority," "many," "some," "a few." The vast majority of the *émigrés* left Russia in the months immediately preceding and following Wrangel's collapse. Their departure, whether motivated by considerations of personal safety, political choice, or family cohesion, in theory presumed a degree of free will in deciding to leave, though this probably did not seem the case at the time. All objected to the Bolshevik regime and what it was doing, or was thought to be doing, to Russia. Many of the pre-October political and cultural leaders who got away tended to see themselves, in the early years at least, as constituting a "Russia Abroad" (*zarubezhnaia Rossiia*), the temporary guardians of their country's interests until the Bolshevik perversion had run its brief, murderous course.

A small minority would have none of this. A trickle of refugees through the 1920s and 1930s regretted their decision to leave Russia, or else resolved that nothing could be worse than continued exile; they went back home. Others, like the Mensheviks and Left Socialist Revolutionaries flung out of Russia against their will, arrived in the West announcing they were expellees, not *émigrés*. They wanted nothing to do with the emigration, whether as "white Russians," "Russia Abroad," "Russian No.2," or any other variant of anti-Soviet purpose. Of course it was easier for the exiles to appreciate these distinctions than it was for their non-Russian hosts. From the outside it appeared that whatever the reasons for their departure, the Russian refugees all shared the ordeals common to their outcast state. Did not this fact impose its overriding unity? Foreign bureaucrats might think it did, or should; however, the history of the Civil War emigration suggests otherwise.

At this point some explanation is necessary of the limitations placed upon this study of the Russian exiles in France between the world wars. The first has to do with its geographic focus. The Russian diaspora was scattered to every part of the globe from Paraguay to Manchuria; within this "Russia Abroad" there was a continual ebb and flow in all directions. But no one had any doubt where their "capital" was to be found. From the Versailles peace conference onward, Paris took its place as the political centre of the Russian emigration. Here the all too numerous anti-Bolshevik factions vied with each other to win the ear of sympathetic foreigners, even as they denounced each other for past and present sins. Then came the best part of a decade during which exiled Russian politicians planned their country's post-Soviet structures upon the certain day of Russia's liberation. By the middle twenties the French capital had taken over from Berlin primacy of place in the *émigré* cultural world. Indeed, Professor Marc Raeff has recently affirmed, in introducing Vassily Yanovsky's "book of memory" of the interwar years, that "the culture of the Great Russian Emigration must be identified with Russian Paris."[4] But beyond the artists and writers, though partly in response to their presence, there came to France, to her capital in particular, tens of thousands of utterly uncelebrated Russians, who had slowly to accustom themselves to the drab rigours of exile existence. Some sense of their lives and fortunes is as much a part of the history of this emigration as are the activities of its prominent figures.

This requirement immediately raises the critical issue of sources. How many of the 120,000 or so Russians who settled in France left easily visible traces for the historian? Comparatively few. The large majority figured anonymously in statistical tables and political speeches; rarely did the refugee "man in the street" emerge from his obscurity. This circumstance can hardly surprise one. The ordinary *émigré*, who had not been prominent in old Russia and who showed no particular talent in exile, was preoccupied with the sheer task of surviving. For each Paul Miliukov, known to all, there were thousands like Paul Brunelli, would-be poet in Russia, "boiled in the factory furnace" in France. Above all there was the fact of their outcast condition. Defeat by the Bolsheviks seemed to condemn the losing side to a degree of historical oblivion which Vladimir Nabokov saw eventually engulfing even the *émigré* intelligentsia, its best known component. Introducing his novel of *émigré* life, *Dar* (The Gift), to Western readers in the 1960s, Nabokov explained the apparently archeological nature of his inquiry: "The tremendous outflow of intellectuals that formed such a prominent part of the general exodus from Soviet Russia in the first years of the Bolshevist Revolution seems today like the wanderings of some mythical tribe whose bird-signs and moon-signs I must now retrieve from the desert dust."[5] It is my hope that this book may brush away some of the dust burying that part of the Russian diaspora which found refuge in France.

The history of the Russian emigration is more than a record of what the politicians of old Russia were devising in exile for the happy day of their country's restoration. Indeed, I contend that this dimension merits the least attention from the historian attempting a collective biography of the Russian emigration in France or elsewhere. The efforts of the exiled intelligentsia to defend Russian values abroad and to assess the nature of the regime governing Russia are much more deserving of attention. But the largely silent mass has also left its own "bird-signs and moon-signs" which can be retrieved from accessible, if dusty repositories. The *émigré* press is a particularly rich source. In any case, the distinction between élite and mass is somewhat artificial. It breaks down in one important area of exile life: relations with the host community and the struggle to survive. Employers, and Frenchmen generally, cared nothing for the Russian refugee's antecedents. To his neighbour, a Russian in France was less the innocent victim of Bolshevik persecution, possibly with a lifetime of distinction behind him, than he was just "le Russe" down the hall or further along the assembly line. His foreignness might be overlooked but was never forgotten and would be recalled in moments of stress. These occasions were not lacking and were never pleasant for the guests.

On the issue of *émigré* élite and mass one further point must be made. The literary intelligentsia believed, more strongly than anything else, that in exile it defended the best of Russia's spiritual, artistic, linguistic, and historical traditions which, woven together, constituted their country's cultural legacy. In what ways and how successfully this inheritance was cherished in the penury of exile is a significant part of the record of the emigration. This is not only because of the refugee intellectuals' image of themselves vis-à-vis their lost homeland; it was also relevant to their life in France with its thousand alien temptations. In assessing this work of cultural defence, however, no attempt has been made to evaluate the place in Russian literature of the many writers who contributed to the effort, nor have I attempted to judge their creations. Such an enterprise lies beyond the scope of this study and, more to the point perhaps, has already been undertaken by literary historians such as Edward Brown and Gleb Struve. The latter's pioneering study, first published in 1956, has recently been republished in a revised edition. [6]

Some comment is also necessary regarding terminology. Throughout the book I have used the words *"émigré," "exile,"* and *"refugee"* interchangeably to describe the status of the subjects of the former Russian empire who fled abroad from Soviet power in the years during and immediately following the Russian Civil War. Of these terms, *émigré* was the one most favoured by the Russians themselves. It evoked memories of the French exodus of 1789, a precedent very much in the mind of older Russians, while the collective noun emigration suggested an underlying cohesion within their far-flung ranks. The word *exiles* summoned up its own reassuring memories of those individual Russians of the nineteenth-century, who also chose to remove themselves from a disagreeable political climate at home and acquired, in some cases, historical merit as a result. But the term which most accurately describes what the Russians in fact were is *refugees.* They furnish an early example of the twentieth-century refugee phenomenon analyzed in Michael Marrus's wide-ranging examination of "awkward, confused, powerless, and often utterly demoralized [masses who] presented the international community with the by-now stock figure of the unwanted suppliant." [7] Unlike many later refugees, however, they were not driven primarily by the impulse to improve their economic well-being in more prosperous lands elsewhere. Fear of Bolshevism and what it might mean for them and Russia played a much greater part in their exodus. Still, almost all the difficulties faced by later waves of refugees were first experienced by the Russian Civil War exiles from their country in the grip of victorious Bolshevism. In this they were "pioneers."

Some elaboration is also in order of what Paul Tabori has called "the semantics of exile": a definition, or at least the hallmarks, of the exile/refugee condition. Tabori acknowledged that it was no easy task. He found himself, he tells us, "somewhat like a far from saintly Sebastian, riddled with arrows" from commentators whose suggestions he had invited as to definitions of his terms. Tabori finally settled on certain "fundamental points" in defining his subject. The first of these applies to Russians who quit their country during the Revolution and Civil War: "An exile is a person who is compelled to leave his homeland – though the forces that send him on his way may be political, economic or purely psychological. It does not make an essential difference whether he is expelled by physical force or whether he makes the decision to leave without such an immediate pressure."[8] Tabori's further "fundamental points" concern the exile's attitude toward his homeland, his adaptability and contribution to his country of refuge, and the factors which promote or prevent his ultimate assimilation. These are considered in the course of the book.

CHAPTER ONE

Exodus

On Sunday, 14 November 1920, late in the afternoon, the French cruiser *Waldeck-Rousseau* set sail from the Crimean port of Sebastopol. She brought up the rear of a 126-ship flotilla of mostly Russian vessels, still defiantly flying the St Andrew ensign, all bound for Constantinople. On board the fleet were some 150,000 refugees, the wreckage of General Petr Nikolaevich Wrangel's White army, accompanied by his civilian staff and anyone else who had managed to beg, bribe, or fight his way up the gangplank. Behind them lay the Crimea and all Russia, now in vengeful Bolshevik hands; ahead, unperceived, loomed a life of exile and an exile's eternal "what ifs" and "if onlys." As *Le Temps* and the *Times* of London fired salvos of reproachful regrets in their wake, the refugees packed on deck were prey to a turmoil of emotions. Apprehension about the future mingled with pain over the immediate past, while thankfulness at their escape competed, often across generations, with grief at leaving Russia in such dire condition.[1] And no doubt some devotees of the late imperial regime felt an especial bitterness at being cast out as suppliants on the shores of the Bosporus, in the city promised to Russia five years earlier by the victorious powers now in temporary possession of it.

The human cargo of Wrangel's fleet was a major component of a population shift then unmatched in recent European history. The tide began gathering inside the fracturing Russian empire in 1918 with the opening stages of the Civil War. In the immemorial manner of all such wars the tide grew in volume as the conflict raged on, with the former empire's seceding peripheral regions taking the brunt. By the autumn of 1920, with Bolshevik victory imminent, the swelling crest of the refugee wave began to break over southeastern and central Europe. The spring of 1921 saw the tide reach full flood, pouring out in every direction from a Russia that seemed, to its fleeing citizens, to be governed by madmen. Subsequent inundations would, in the not so distant future, inure Europe to such sights, but in the aftermath of "the war to end wars" the sheer size of the exodus was novel. The Russian refugees, together with Armenians in flight from Turkish genocide, presented the continent with human tragedy on a colossal scale and its legislators with a series of complex socio-administrative problems for which they had no ready solutions.[2]

It is appropriate to consider at this stage a point made from time to time within the emigration, particularly from its right wing, concerning the émigrés' collective nature. This proclaimed their historical uniqueness to the peoples into whose midst they had come. Early in 1922 the orientalist Vasily Nikitin offered a detailed analysis of émigré political nuances for readers of the *Revue des sciences politiques*. He began with a firm denial that the sudden Russian influx into Western Europe then underway resembled an earlier, much invoked precedent, the French aristocratic exodus of 1789. Rather than a repetition of Koblenz, the Russian emigration was, Nikitin insisted, a new, more significant social and political phenomenon. Extrapolating from some partial statistics, submitted from British sources, of Russian refugees in Egypt and Cyprus, Nikitin declared that all social classes were represented in the emigration, with the prerevolutionary privileged class not much more than a quarter of the whole.[3] Eight years later the poet Zinaida Hippius returned to the same theme. She wrote at a time when the prospect of a return home, invoked by Nikitin as certain, must have seemed dim even to the most optimistic. Her essay confirmed the view of the uniqueness of the emigration. It had no parallel, not even in the Jewish diaspora two millennia before. In one respect only were these two alike: each was the expulsion of a people. From the highest to the lowest, all social elements of the nation were represented in exile. To Hippius it therefore seemed logical that they should consider and call themselves a nation.[4]

Hippius's theory that the emigration represented Russia, that it in fact was Russia in miniature, comprising the best of the nation's creative élite, became a central conviction among many émigrés, by no means all of whom can be dismissed as elderly reactionaries. The finest elements of Russian society, supported by a million loyal, suffering citizens, had temporarily left Russia but would assuredly return before long to restore the legitimate, natural order. Had not Belgium and Serbia given the example in the Great War? In the early years of exile the sheer mass of numbers, among whom could be counted figures prominent in every walk of Russian life and culture, seemed to lend substance to the vision of Russia Abroad. In spite of disappointments the vision never entirely dissipated. As late as 1984 the prolific émigré writer Roman Gul, neither politically reactionary nor of the older exile generation between the wars, still proclaimed his conviction that he had "carried Russia" with him into emigration.[5] Certainly in the 1920s the notion of Russia Abroad seemed more defensible than the image presented in Koblenz 130 years before of *la France extérieure*.

The heterogeneity of the Russian emigration distinguished it from the French exodus of 1789. But the two did resemble each other in a common, general conviction that their exile would be, must be, brief. "The first *émigrés* had faith in the future," wrote Ernest Daudet of the French aristocrats of 1789. "They saw themselves home before long. This conviction explains why they left so quickly, without settling their most urgent affairs, without assuring themselves of the resources to live in exile longer than a few weeks. The certainty of a speedy return characterized the emigration in its beginnings."[6] In the same spirit, the former editor of the Constitutional Democratic party's daily newspaper *Rech*, Iosif Hessen, crossed the Finnish frontier in January 1919 to remove himself from the upheavals in Petrograd. Years later he wrote that it did not in the least occur to any of them that they were leaving their country for many years, "the oldest among us possibly for ever." Hence there had been no need to take much luggage.[7] Unlike their French predecessors, however, not all Russian exiles wished to go back to the good old days of monarchical abolutism. In that sense, Koblenz was, indeed, an inappropriate precedent. Still, the zeal displayed by Nikitin, Hippius, and others to establish the uniqueness of their exodus suggests a sensitivity to charges that the Russians' proper place was in some limbo alongside others who had resisted the tidal sweep of progress.

How many fled from Russia? A precise figure can never be known; even the approximate estimates vary impressively. Statistics advanced by *émigré* organizations convey only a rough idea. The major relief agencies such as the Russian Red Cross and the Union of *Zemstva* and Towns (*Zemgor*) performed heroic feats of assistance but had neither the means to collect accurate data on a world scale, nor the material and political resources to keep on at the task.[8] An illustration of these complexities was furnished by the "Central Information Office" set up in May 1920 in Constantinople by Countess Tatiana Bobrinskaia. Its function was to compile figures on the number of Russian refugees passing through the city's several camps and to serve as a clearing house for statistics of *émigré* movements. Her office published a set of figures purporting to show that as of New Year's Day 1921 a little over one million Russian refugees now lived in Europe and the North African colonies of the European great powers.[9] Bobrinskaia's estimate may well have been more realistic than other figures offered; nevertheless her committee was obliged to wind up its operations in April 1921.[10]

Difficulties also lay in wait for non-Russian bodies and individuals who set about enumerating the refugee wave during the 1920s. The first to attempt it in a systematic way was the infant League of Nations. Three months after Wrangel's armies and their civilian protégés were rescued from the Crimean beaches the League Council took up the problem, destined to become wearyingly familiar, of what to do about the Russian refugees. Their main camps at Constantinople and Gallipoli were desperately overcrowded, epidemics threatened, the Turks did not want them, while the French government, hitherto the main source of financial support, made clear its desire to cut its losses from having backed the wrong side in the Civil War.[11] Elsewhere, the Baltic republics, the Balkan monarchies, and Poland, all very shaky states, contemplated with alarm the spectacle of tens of thousands of indigent Russians pouring across their brand new frontiers. In short, it was just the sort of international emergency calculated to test the willingness of member states to match with deeds the promises made in setting up the League of Nations.

The initial response was encouraging. After cautiously affirmative answers to the Council's enquiry whether action would be appropriate, member states resolved in June 1921 to appoint a High Commissioner for the Russian refugees. The Council resolution in this sense expressed the pious hope that its appointee's responsibility would lie less in direct relief than in helping to disperse the refugees to countries "where the cost of living is small and where there is a good chance of their obtaining productive employment." The Council allotted a niggardly £4,000 to assist in the realization of this hope. The challenge was overwhelming, and it is small wonder that the Council heard before long the recommendation from its High Commissioner that in the long run "the final and satisfactory solution" to the problem of the Russian refugees was their repatriation. He did concede that the step did not appear feasible at the time, given Russia's current condition.[12] Other obstacles stood in the way of this convenient answer. The Soviet authorities would hardly have permitted a massive, unrestricted return; more to the point, the refugees themselves expressed their general intention not to go back voluntarily to a Bolshevik-ruled Russia.[13]

The man who accepted the League's invitation to assume what promised to be an arduous charge was the Norwegian polar explorer, Dr Fridtjof Nansen. In the first grim years of exile Russians came to find in him and his officials a source of real help in the complications of their new existence: documents, movement, jobs, settlement, and the like. Even so, approaches he made to the Soviet government and his talk of repatriation earned Nansen considerable abuse from conservative émigré politicians.[14] It may certainly be doubted whether, even with his Nansen passports, the High Commissioner for Russian refugees had any precise knowledge of how many Russians were in his charge at any specific moment. The statistical evidence was, and is, dense; it is also conflicting. It comes from a variety of sources, no single one of which is to be trusted above all others. Private relief agencies, émigré and other, saw only a part of the refugee flood, while Nansen's own office, international though it was, still depended on individual governments for its statistical computations. These did not tell the whole tale. The continual ebb and flow across frontiers defeated efforts to maintain accurate, up-to-date records of refugee movements; such efforts were likely to be quite perfunctory in Eastern Europe, the Near East, and China. Moreover, talk among League officials of ultimate repatriation hardly encouraged anti-Soviet Russians to cooperate with foreign bureaucrats trying to enumerate them.

Surveys of the Russian emigration between the world wars reflected, and at the same time contributed to, the confusion about numbers. In 1924 a German scholar, Hans von Rimscha, published the first volume of a study which remains the best general account of the emigration's early years.[15] Rimscha quoted figures advanced by the American Red Cross in December 1920 on the number of Russians it was supporting, added to the 130-150,000 evacuees from the Crimea. He came up with a European total of 2,094,000 which did not include Bulgaria or Rumania, both countries of heavy Russian settlement. To this he added 350,000 or so that he judged lived outside Europe, mainly in the Far East, as well as the twenty percent he estimated as not supported by the Red Cross. This made a grand total of just under three million Russian refugees.[16] Within half a dozen years this figure came under challenge. A subcommittee of private relief agencies attached to the High Commissioner's Office published statistics which found that between 405,427 and 495,427 Russian refugees were in Europe on 1 January 1930. The imprecision of the estimate, caused largely by doubt as to Russian numbers in the first two European countries of refuge, France and Germany, lessened its reliability. This had already been questioned by a second set of figures, published under official auspices a short time before. This set came from the High Commissioner's Office itself and was drawn up on the basis of data received from national governments. According to this source, 828,946 Russian refugees were in Europe at the end of the 1920s.[17]

A more authoritative voice on the question spoke out a few months before the outbreak of the Second World War. Sir John Simpson reviewed the several sets of figures submitted on Russian refugee numbers, along with material contributed by his *émigré* research assistant from the principal archive of Russian exile history in Prague. His researcher's estimate, even after Simpson revised it upward, was still lower than those of Rimscha, Nansen, and the American Red Cross. Simpson calculated that between 668,000 and 772,000 "unassimilated" Russian refugees were in Europe and the Near East on 1 January 1922. He also raised estimates submitted to the League in 1936-7 by a Nansen Office investigator and concluded that the "unassimilated" Russian exile population of Europe and the Near East at that moment amounted to a figure somewhere between 345,000 and 386,000.[18] Simpson's statistics were produced some years after the others and were in part based on now unavailable archival data. Even so, his figures still offered a wide range of minimum and maximum totals. Occasionally these were at variance with nationally produced totals. In the French case, for example,

Simpson's estimated national total of Russian refugees in the late thirties was as much as double the figure advanced at the time by French authorities.[19] Short of throwing up one's hands, perhaps the wisest solution to the dilemma is to endorse Michael Marrus's conclusion "that the refugees from Bolshevik Russia probably numbered close to a million at the highest point"; the total then fell substantially in the late 1920s.[20]

Where did they all go? Ultimately almost everywhere. The first brunt of the exodus fell upon the successor states of the Russian, German, and Austro – Hungarian empires because they were the closest. Bulgaria, Rumania, Turkey, and China received their large shares of the flood for the same reason. Since very few refugees were able to bring out much in the way of material assets, they were all more or less dependent on the goodwill of foreigners. The Slavic lands offered what seemed the surest refuge, where readjustment might require the least wrench and Russia was not far off. Bulgaria, Yugoslavia, and Czechoslovakia, especially the two latter, gave the Russians a warm welcome in spite of their own manifest difficulties. King Alexander and President T.G. Masaryk became in a sense patrons of particular sections of the Russian emigration. Right-wing monarchist groups were well represented in Yugoslavia. They cherished the King's ties to the Romanovs and his strong aversion to Russia's post-October rulers. In Prague the Czechoslovak government gave generous aid to the exiles and their children. Refugee Russian academics found in Prague a particularly hospitable welcome. Masaryk himself was a close friend of the Constitutional Democratic (Kadet) party leader P.N. Miliukov, and knew Russia, her history and culture intimately. Russian liberals and democratic Socialists venerated the Czechoslovak president, nowhere more than in the pages of the diaspora's most widely read "thick journal" and chief cultural monument, *Sovremenniia zapiski* (Contemporary Notes).[21] This mutual regard had historical consequences. With Masaryk's encouragement and the financial backing of the foreign ministry, an archive was established in Prague to serve as repository for the records of the worldwide Russian exile community. In one of the bitter ironies of which *émigré* history has had more than its share, a *Sovremenniia zapiski* editor, Vadim Rudney, in 1937 urged fellow *émigrés* to contribute their papers to this archive. In so doing, he wrote, they would help it to become a leading centre for historical studies of the Revolution, Civil War, and emigration at a time when the richer sources in Moscow were politically controlled and inaccessible.[22] Eight years later Eduard Benes, who as Czechoslovakia's foreign minister had authorized the help given in setting up the Russian Historical Archive Abroad (*Russkii zagranicheskii istoricheskii arkhiv*) and had later incorporated it into his own ministry, as president offered it to the Soviet government in a gesture of pan-Slav gratitude to Czechoslovakia's liberators. The gift accepted, fifteen freight cars transported the collection's irreplaceable documentary materials to Moscow. They have remained there out of bounds ever since.[23]

The most powerful magnets to the refugees, particularly to their political and cultural leaders, were not the Slav capitals, but the metropolises of continental Europe, Berlin and Paris. Berlin held the inside track in the early twenties. The city stood at the crossroads for those who poured out of Russia through its secessionist border regions, Finland, Poland, and the Baltic states; its cultural attractions exerted a strong pull on the old intelligentsia in their flight westwards. The city's size and proximity to East European borders attracted the anonymous thousands seeking shelter, jobs, security, and the company of an established Russian community. Not all were satisfied, but at least postwar Germany was, for a few years, cheaper to live in than its neighbours, even if living conditions in the larger cities were often arduously primitive.[24] Just how many arrived to take up residence is, as usual, uncertain. Simpson's maximum figure, based on his researcher's investigation of the Prague archive during the 1930s, is 250,000 "unassimilated" Russian refugees in Germany on 1 January 1922. Eight years later the total had fallen to a point between 90,000 and 100,000, and by 1937 to 45,000. However, the German government reported at the end of 1922 that as many as 600,000 Russians were then in Germany.[25]

Russian Berlin of the twenties found its most vivid memorialist in Vladimir Nabokov. His novel *Dar* catches the city and its Russian population of the moment as a fly in amber. The novel's central protagonist, Fedor Godunov-Cherdyntsev, struggles to hold off the alien world around him in a manner endlessly duplicated by his real life compatriots in exile. Perhaps not all the concessions necessary to survival were hateful. Nabokov's English lessons to Berlin businessmen and tennis lessons to "their tanned bob-haired daughters" were a lot less onerous than the jobs undertaken by most of his refugee countrymen, if they had employment at all.[26] The collapse of the mark in 1923, followed by Dr Schacht's drastic currency reforms, wiped out jobs and savings, drove prices upward and forced thousands of vulnerable Russians out of Germany. The great days of Russian Berlin were over.[27] Mensheviks and Left Socialist Revolutionaries (SRS) continued to live mainly in the German capital until Hitler's coming to power; but by late 1923 the centre of the Russian exile world had moved from the banks of the Spree to the Seine. Vadim Belov, an early Soviet observer of the *émigrés*, may well have been right, from his particular viewpoint, when in 1923 he described Paris as "an archeological museum of Russian reaction."[28] From the opposite Russian vantage point, however, the French capital was preparing to assume its sixteen-year long role as brain and heart of the Russian exile world.

The appeal of the City of Light to expatriate Russians was nothing new. Aristocratic travellers from St Petersburg had long staked their claim to the city's delights. Peter I had twice led the way; his "fledglings" were quick to follow. For gentry Russia Paris remained through the eighteenth and nineteenth centuries primarily the arbiter of taste and fashion, the uncontested centre of all that Europe had to offer in the way of amusement and style. Periodic crises between the two countries proved no lasting barriers. After each nadir – 1815, 1856, 1870 – the capital again saw its Trubetskois, Gagarins, Shuvalovs, and their friends, to say nothing of Romanovs, who made *la tournée des grands-ducs* a recognized part of the city's tourist attractions. Even in adversity these old habits were to die hard. The Grand Duke Alexander Mikhailovich, brother-in-law of the last tsar, arrived in Paris in January 1919 and made like a homing pigeon for the Ritz hotel. The fact that he was now a homeless refugee, owning as material resources nothing but a bundle of tsarist rubles and a rare coin collection, meant only that one day he would come down to earth hard. Until then life should go on as of old.[29] Another favoured Romanov haven was the Côte d'Azur. Nicholas I's wife had found the congenial climate much to her liking. Alexander II's tubercular eldest son also found a refuge in Nice, dying there in 1864. His fiancée married his younger brother, the future Alexander III, and she, as Empress Maria Fedorovna, visited Nice with her tubercular son. Imperial favour brought a large aristocratic contingent to the region during the empire's waning years. Many of them paraded in strength on 18 December 1912, along with an imposing French delegation, at the consecration in Nice of the Orthodox cathedral of St Nicholas.[30] As matters turned out, the ceremony was as much a requiem over its Russian celebrants as it was a dedication of their splendid new church.

Although freely spending nobles have left the more notorious name, they were far from being the only Russian tourists in France during the half century before 1914. There were also the political critics and men of letters. They arrived with serious purpose in mind, to view the capital of bourgeois or, more hopefully, of revolutionary Europe. After the failure of the 1848 revolutions Alexander Herzen bequeathed some sharp sketches of a particular *bête-noire*, the philistine Parisian bourgeois.[31] His memoirs convey an initially jaundiced impression of the French. He drew attention to traits which later Russian exiles would remark on in their turn. Herzen "particularly disliked the tone of condescending superiority which Frenchmen assume with Russians." But then he was a refugee in their country. "To get on a different footing with them one would have to impress them with one's consequence; to do this one must possess certain rights, which I had not at that time."[32] Unlike most of his postrevolutionary compatriots, Herzen was eventually able to make good this deficiency. Less committed travellers were, it seemed, more easily satisfied. Russian visitors flocked to the city in the last decades of European peace. Among them was a bevy of artists, including Marc Chagall, who congregated noisily in their "beehive" on the rue Dantzig.[33] Though their poverty was extreme, they would probably have been willing to echo Anton Chekhov's enthusiastic verdict, delivered in May 1898, "what a town it is, my God, what an admirable town!"[34]

While personal impressions and tastes were decisive in shaping individual Russians' views of France, the political and diplomatic atmosphere of the day added an important dimension to the relationship. Privileged Russia, soon to be so richly represented in exile, had good reason to look with warmth upon the Third Republic, quite apart from the opportunities it afforded the well-to-do for personal distraction. This was, after 1893, the heyday of the Franco-Russian alliance, with French funds contributing their notorious share to keeping tsardom afloat. Differences of regime were obvious enough but the governments in Paris and St Petersburg had no difficulty in maintaining their intimacy, in spite of critical views of this "unnatural" alliance held by Socialist politicians in the first capital or by conservative diehards in the second. Maurice Paléologue, France's elegant ambassador in Russia during the Great War, could not have been more at home in court circles had he been born to the purple. The toasts exchanged in July 1914 between Nicholas II and President Raymond Poincaré testified to a mutual satisfaction at a relationship profitable to both sides.

Neither aristocratic and bourgeois enjoyment of life in France, nor official pleasure at ties with the French Republic, tell the whole tale of the prewar Russian relationship with their nation's principal ally. Another, perhaps ultimately more significant, aspect concerned those Russians most dedicated to destroying the world of Poincaré's hosts. Russian revolutionaries too had been drawn to Paris, though their reasons tended to the practical and political, rather than the tourist or literary. They soon attracted critical notice. The police, in unconscious anticipation of their postwar refrain, from time to time remarked upon the presence in the city of an uninvited Russian population. In December 1907 the Paris police prefect submitted a lengthy report to Premier Clemenceau on the subject of "Russian revolutionary schemings" in France. His analysis began with the flat assertion that "Paris has always been the preferred refuge of expatriates from the Russian empire." In past years this had not posed any problems. "Rebellious Poles, pitiable Israelites, even nihilists" had managed to find some kind of welcome.[35] But more recently, in the aftermath of the Russo-Japanese war and unsuccessful revolution in Russia, the numbers had increased and, with them, police difficulties. Paris was now the capital, "or, more precisely, the grand headquarters of Russian revolutionaries" throughout Europe. They numbered, as a minimum, perhaps 25,000 in the capital, "mostly anarchists and Jews." Any greater accuracy was elusive, "[as] concierges are usually quite unable to indicate the number of tenants in lodgings occupied by Russians." They met from time to time in locations known to the authorities but conversed in Russian. This made police supervision "very difficult." These sessions, Clemenceau read, had no other aim "but to keep up refugee passions [and] make [their] propaganda more effective."[36]

Ilia Ehrenburg confirmed these rueful judgments. Arriving in Paris in 1908 at the age of seventeen, a not very hotly pursued fugitive from the tsarist political police, he settled into a single room on the avenue Denfert-Rochereau, not far from the city's southern fringe. He became a minor participant in the polemics of the Russian revolutionary colony. Vladimir Ilich Lenin was briefly one of that number: half a century later Ehrenburg, "shaggy Ilia" to his friends, was still properly awed by his memories. He found Paris a city where "everything seemed unexpected and everything was possible," often provincial but still widely considered the capital of the world. In those easy, far-off days, Ehrenburg lived in France without passport or identity card. When some kind of proof became necessary for the police, friendly neighbours attested to his good standing. Their aid sufficed.[37] Had no other differences existed, this circumstance alone was enough to mark Ehrenburg and his friends off from their post-1917 compatriots in exile.

What did French and Russians see in each other at this time? The answer depended upon the individual's standpoint and inevitably drew upon stereotypes. To that small group of Russians who knew much about France or who were interested in her, she stood for one or several of the features already enumerated: an agreeable society, the source of the glorious or fearful principles of 1789, 1793 and 1848, the generator of new ideas, culture and capital, or, as in the case of "anarchists and Jews," simply a place to survive in and dream dreams. The French view of Russia and the Russians was not markedly more sophisticated. Educated liberal opinion in the quarter-century or so before 1890 would have begun by disliking the autocratic oppressor of so many peoples; on the other hand the spectacle on an unforgettable July day in 1891 of the Russian autocrat bareheaded and at attention for the Marseillaise tended to sweep reservations aside in a public frenzy of pro-Russian enthusiasm.[38] Thereafter, imperial visits, Russian novels, theatre and ballet, and, far from least, an outpouring of French gold, kept Russia very much to the fore in the public consciousness. Of course this awareness did not at all mean that the larger reading public was genuinely knowledgeable about their country's new partner. It is probably more accurate to say that the staple ingredients of the Russian image that anti-Bolshevik refugees would later encounter were firmly in place, indeed grew stronger, during the period of official intimacy and alliance.

Russians in France were frequently irritated by the notions which Frenchmen entertained about Russia.[39]

Literary and academic figures did what they could to enlighten their countrymen on serious Russian matters. One especially assiduous zealot was the diplomat and critic Eugène-Melchior de Vogüé. Briefly stationed in St Petersburg during the last years of Alexander II's reign, and married to a lady-in-waiting of the Empress Maria Alexandrovna, de Vogüé conceived an intense interest in Russia, above all in her literature, then scarcely known in France. Indeed, Parisian salons and the French reading public had not thought there was much in Russia worth their serious attention through most of the century.[40] A humiliating defeat in 1871, followed by diplomatic isolation, changed this perception, lifting French eyes to what lay beyond Germany. De Vogüé's five articles in the *Revue des deux mondes*, published as a single volume in 1886,[41] sang the glories of Russian literary culture to a public much more willing than hitherto to believe in Russia's European credentials and, more hopefully, in her potential as an anti-German ally. His judgments may have been more confident than profound, but de Vogüé seems to have been "the vulgarizer that the hour required."[42] His volume on the Russian novel made a deep impression and improbably became, in Charles Corbet's words, "one of the cornerstones of [the public's] faith in Russia."[43] Academic worthies such as Albert Vandal, Alfred Rambaud, Anatole Leroy-Beaulieu, and Louis Leger contributed tomes on Russian history and literature,[44] complementing lectures on these subjects at the Sorbonne. In 1910 one of the professors involved in the teaching effort, Emile Haumant, published a study of Franco-Russian cultural relations which enjoyed success with the critics.[45] Couched in occasionally patronizing tones, a few of Haumant's judgments have an ironic ring to them in the light of what lay just over the horizon. "It is in any case certain," Haumant concluded, "that we have given them the taste, which-they hardly had before us, for unfettered thought, we have inspired in them the love of beauty in literature and, from this, a revulsion against the crude and uncivilized in books and perhaps elsewhere." True, traditional francophile elements were not as important as they once had been. In their place Haumant perceived new, popular elements moving to the fore. But France had nothing to fear from the Russia of the people: "easy communication" would come, sympathy would follow. Foreseeing danger to French intellectual pre-eminence from "elected majorities," Haumant reminded his readers that the French role in civilizing the world had been a great one. "Foreigners always come to us, above all from immense Slavdom. The day is still far off when [Russian] youth will no longer be seen on the roads to France."[46]

A few years later, as if to justify his confidence, the greatest wave ever of Russian youth, with their parents, broke over France. It included many of those to whom Haumant had looked for easy communication and sympathy.

WHERE TO GO?

On 23 May 1919, in the evening, the thirty-six-year-old Socialist Revolutionary Mark Vishniak arrived in Paris from Odessa via Marseilles. Behind him lay the furnace of Russia in civil war, ahead stretched half a century of exile on two continents. His mood that evening was as gloomy as the cavern of the Gare de Lyon, his doorway into refugee life. What could the future bring to a man deprived of his country, possessing little capacity for physical labour or for life in alien surroundings? What had he to offer? And what of Russia? What sort of fate lay in store for her? When and how would he return? Every adult Russian who quit his country during the Civil War felt, or would feel, the same anguished doubts.[47]

The summer of his arrival in the West remained a vivid memory to Vishniak. Looking back many years later on his first days in emigration he remembered how Paris had then seemed, "a new Mecca, a new Babylon," the focus of the hopes, the faith, and the calculations of the world. The peace conference underway at Versailles when he arrived would remould the nations of the earth and place them all, Russia foremost among them, on new and juster foundations.[48] So thought Mark Vishniak, devout disciple of Woodrow Wilson, so too hoped several score Russian politicians who managed to make their way to Paris. Desperate to tell the peacemakers the truth about Russia, as they saw it, they hurried unbidden to the temporary capital of the world. For the remaining thousands of Russians who did not have a case to plead at Versailles, the choice of Paris was not as instinctive as it was for Vishniak and the other political exiles. Any of at least five reasons could be a factor in resolving where to settle. Financial resources were obviously one, availability of employment another, the willingness of governments to permit their entry, residence, and work a notorious third. The existence of an already established Russian community and the political-cultural attractions of specific cities added their powerful inducements. Overall, the French capital's claims were hard to deny, as the prewar police and Emile Haumant, in their separate ways, had acknowledged.

It was highly unlikely that any Russian refugee saw Paris or France as an inexpensive shelter and moved there for that reason alone. Without aid from the League, the French government, or some relief agency, very few émigrés would have got to France from the overcrowded camps of Constantinople or penurious exile life in the Balkans or Poland. Later on small savings might help refugees arriving from Germany, but most began life anew with nothing. How many, after all, were in a position to follow the Grand Duke Alexander Mikhailovich's example in remembering to bring out his rare coin collection, or to copy Prince Felix Iusupov's foresight in smuggling out of Russia his wife's jewels and their favourite Rembrandts?[49] Life was cheaper in Eastern Europe and, for a while, in Berlin. If the cost of living had been the sole criterion, Paris would not have remained for one-and-a-half decades the headquarters of the Russian diaspora.

A stronger incentive to move and settle was the availability of employment. At least until the Depression, the industrialized, urbanized nations of Western and Central Europe had more to offer than the agricultural, still largely feudal economies that prevailed in the Balkans and Poland. As the largest urban conglomerations of the continent, Berlin, then Paris offered the best chances of keeping body and soul together. The Germans and the French also proved relatively liberal in the matter of papers. In the early postwar years the French government was willing, in fact eager, to recruit foreign labour to rebuild the war-devastated regions of northeastern France. Russians benefited from this. Yet they too came to appreciate the truth of the old proverb that a man is born with a body, a soul, and a passport. There could be no doubt which of these three was the most important in the eyes of officials.[50] All the same, it should be remembered that on a per capita basis France ranked first among countries accepting postwar refugee immigrants. Russians were a part of this influx, though eventually exceeded in numbers by Italians and Spaniards.[51]

The lure of France, Paris in particular, was least resisted by the prerevolutionary political and cultural élite that was so heavily represented in the emigration. Even if they did not actually all live in the capital or its environs, the onetime leaders of old Russia, along with the would-be leaders of a new, non-Bolshevik state, came to see their community's capital there. The peace conference encouraged this view. Countless émigré groups and individuals busied themselves with the complexities of "the Russian Question" in the hope of gaining a hearing by the Big Four under the tapestried triumphs of the Sun King. Some got their audience, but to no discernible advantage for their cause.[52] There then occurred "a noticeable ebb" in the number of Russians coming to Paris, the consequence of the city's high cost of living compared to that of Berlin.[53] This was a brief interruption. By late 1923 Berlin was in economic slump; Prague, Sofia, and Belgrade, all hospitable to their Russian guests, could not match Paris's assets as an international magnet. The city could boast a wide and varied range of newspapers and journals. It was here that the conviction was most stubbornly defended that the emigration must represent, indeed that it embodied, genuine Russian values and that it had a clearly recognized identity and purpose. Jean Delage, a French journalist and assiduous champion of the Russian exiles, wrote in 1930 of his certainty that "real Russia, civilized Russia, friend of order and liberty, is in exile. She is scattered all over the globe but all her heads, all the control levers, are in Paris."[54] With reservations about the reality of the "control levers," one may take Delage's assessment as a depiction of a favourite image of themselves held by many older *émigrés* during the first decade of their life outside Russia.

Paris attracted Civil War refugees for material, ideological, and personal reasons. To outcast anti-Bolsheviks who had been prominent in old Russia the city held out a front row seat on the spectacle of world politics, the best place to organize, propagandize and, so it was devoutly hoped, influence decisions about the subject closest to their hearts, Russia's post-Bolshevik future. They could also debate in Europe's most politically sophisticated capital Russia's past and present condition in the knowledge that their ideas would reach an extensive, attentive audience. The literary intelligentsia was more likely to find readers through the pages of the daily newspaper *Posled-niia novosti* (Latest News) and the periodical journal *Sovremenniia zapiski*, both published in Paris. Then too, above all this, there was the fact of Paris itself, the city where no topic was forbidden, no fashion unexplored. Surrounded by what he called "the special French air of freedom," Vassily Yanovsky felt seized by the sentiment "that everything may be thought or said, on the spiritual as well as the everyday plane, everything may be weighed anew, overhauled and understood in a new way," one which owed nothing to church, revolutions or mythologies. "Freedom in an everyday sense, pragmatic, comfortable, poetical freedom in an uninterrupted flow. This is France, this is Paris ... where ethnic Gauls and *sales métèques* converged not by accident from the entire world, as if invited to a picnic."[55]

The intensity of these feelings and the range of cultural creativity which they produced made Paris a special place for Russian exiles between the wars, one remembered always by those who lived there and took part in its life. The writers and artists who contributed so much, along with a galaxy of commentators on every aspect of *émigré* life, formed the so-called "active" emigration, in effect the community's apex. But the existence of an apex presumes a broader base beneath. Paris, and France, also attracted tens of thousands of "passive" exiles, men and women without prominence, political past, important social contacts, or literary gifts. Paris to them meant anonymity, a possibility of employment, the presence of Russian cultural institutions and of fellow countrymen in whose company current difficulties might sometimes be set aside in favour of talk about Russia.

How many refugees arrived in France? The question is even more difficult to answer satisfactorily than it is to establish the exile total in all of Europe. The estimates for France range from 60,000 to 400,000. One fact is sure. Nobody really knew for certain how many Russians were in the country at any moment. The statistical data is most profuse and contradictory for the period 1919 to 1923, when the refugees were most mobile. This constant flux made it difficult for national authorities to keep track of who lived where; moreover, it was not until 1926 that national origin was included on the census as a question to be answered by foreign-born respondents. Until then, therefore, bureaucratic estimates of the number of Russians in France were only marginally more trustworthy than other figures offered. It is also not improbable that the Russians who arrived in France under irregular circumstances would be disinclined to co-operate with official efforts at enumeration, lest these be the prelude to some new vexation. Then, too, there was the known Russian tendency to proliferate from the smallest beginnings. If, in the settled days before the war, authorities had found it impossible to pinpoint the number of Russians in French boardinghouses, how much greater was the confusion fifteen years later with Russians pouring into the country in unprecedented numbers! Mademoiselle Mesureux's ordeal illustrated the problem clearly. Her first Russian boarder had no sooner taken up residence when, "by a mysterious multiplication, by a kind of massing together which left Mademoiselle Mesureux stunned and bewildered, there were three, then five, then ten, until finally every vacant spot in her house was occupied by persons who registered themselves with the police [as holders of a] Nansen passport."[56]

An additional complicating factor in the enumeration tangle is the question of defining nationality. Just who counted as Russian? "Those who considered themselves to be Russian" is one obvious reply which, however, fails to satisfy. What of the non-Russian subjects of Nicholas II, Ukrainians, Azerbaijani, Georgians, and other minority elements in the emigration? French landladies might see them all as *Russes*, but officials in Geneva and Paris wavered, as did the statistical tables they compiled.[57] There is also the companion problem of how and when *émigrés* and their children ceased being regarded and recorded as Russian. This point raises a network of interrelated questions about legal status, assimilation, naturalization, and so forth that will be considered elsewhere.[58] It is sufficient here to emphasize the point that the calculation of Russian numbers in France is not simply a matter of conflicting statistics, though that is a major source of confusion. Problems of definition, *émigré* mobility, bureaucratic error and inertia contributed their share to the discrepancy of the data.

Three broad sets of figures have been offered of the Russian colony in France. The top figure is 400,000; it has some respectable sponsors. The estimate appears to have originated in information from a French source to League officials. In 1924 Dr Nansen reported to the League Council that 400,000 Russians were then in France; six years later this same total, now including Armenians, was still being passed to the Council.[59] *Émigré* leaders, with no means of collecting reliable data, seem to have accepted it, as did two interwar French monographs on foreign immigration into France.[60] Soviet studies of the subject begin by quoting much lower totals but more recent figures repeat this Nansen estimate.[61]

The next set of figures halves this estimate, putting the number of Russians in France at between 150,000 and 200,000. In November 1920 the American Red Cross cited this range as its guess at refugee numbers; it was also, confusingly enough, the estimate ten years later of a subcommittee of organizations reporting to the Nansen Office. The marked variation – 400,000 versus 150,000 – in two sets of figures reported under League auspices at only one year's interval between them provoked a terse footnote from Sir John Simpson to the effect that "the official figures are contradictory concerning the number of [Russian] refugees in France."[62] He himself advanced totals for "unassimilated Russian refugees in France" which ranged from 70,000 in 1922 to a maximum of 175,000 in 1930, then down to 110,000 by 1937.[63]

The third set of estimates puts the maximum number of Russians in France at some point under 150,000. Pierre Kovalevsky, the diaspora's principal *émigré* historian, chose the 100 – 150,000 range as the most realistic in his 1971 survey of the interwar years.[64] The French census of 1936 reported a precise total of 91,577 Russians, naturalized and not, then in France. A post-World War II study commented, however, that even this apparently authoritative figure must be regarded as approximate since it included only those who had entered France with official stateless papers, the famous Nansen passports, instituted in July 1922.[65] Those who had arrived earlier, or who had presented other travel documents, or who had entered France illegally, would not have been included. Finally, in 1943, bureaucrats in occupied Paris published statistical tables of alien immigration which offered the lowest estimate yet of Russian residents in France. These claimed a total of 32,300 Russians in the country in 1921; this number then doubled within five years to reach a maximum of just under 72,000 by 1931. Five years later, according to the same source, the number of Russians had fallen to 64,000.[66]

What can usefully be made of this statistical welter? One point seems reasonably certain. In spite of its impressive backers, the figure of 400,000 is far too high. Kovalevsky dismisses it out of hand as fantastic; he is surely right to do so.[67] How it started can only be surmised. Simpson suggested that it originated with a French delegate at Geneva; how he got it is unknown.[68] League officials, including the Nansen Office, initially accepted it, and the figure remained persistently in tables for years thereafter. Just why it should have done so is a mystery. Even if all nonethnic Russian refugees from the former Russian empire were included, and no allowance were made for those refugees who, having arrived in France, died, were naturalized, or evaded enumeration, the 400,000 figure would still seem excessive.

Even with this extreme estimate excluded, the effort to arrive at a firm number of Russians is not greatly assisted. It seems reasonable to suggest a considered view that the maximum number of Russians in France probably did not much exceed 120,000 and that this total was reached by the early 1930s. While this estimate is larger than the figures offered in 1943 and is smaller than Sir John Simpson's maximum number in 1938, it falls between Kovalevsky's minimum and maximum figures and is not incompatible with the 1936 census in spite of the latter's noted deficiencies. The figure of 120,000 in 1930 also accords with a police estimate in May 1938 of 63,000 Russians then in France,[69] allowing for an annual average attrition rate of between seven and eight percent over the eight year period.

The estimated size of the Russian colony in Paris presents fewer obscurities. The capital and its surrounding districts certainly harboured more onetime subjects of Nicholas II than did any other region of France. In 1930 Jean Delage reported that 43,250 Russians lived in the twenty *arrondissements*, plus a further 9,500 in the suburbs.[70] In 1932 Georges Mauco, an authority on immigrant labour questions, stated that 36,964 Russians lived in the Seine *département*, with 3,503 more in the adjacent Seine-et-Oise.[71] By 1939 the figure had probably dropped to the neighbourhood of 20,000.

Though to say so contradicts the clichés referred to earlier, all social conditions were represented in the Russian influx. Boris Aleksandrovsky, an *émigré* physician for twenty-five years until his post-1945 return to the USSR, noted of his former fellow refugees that "they [were] not all princes, bankers and landlords." That element, according to his impression, comprised less than one percent of the total. Most of the remaining "active" emigration consisted of military officers from the White armies, failed students, petty and middle rank bureaucrats, traders, commercial and industrial figures, and "some members of the intellectual professions."[72] Mostly failures or former exploiters – perhaps Aleksandrovsky's categories were a little too arbitrary, an unsubtle acknowledgement of his own changed fortunes by the time he came to write his memoirs. All the same, his account admitted the genuine heterogeneity of the Russian exile world.

An observer with less at stake than Aleksandrovsky was the French journalist André Beucler. In 1937 this friend of the Russian refugees looked back on the years of postwar Russian settlement in France and decided that it was time to remind his countrymen of the circumstances under which the refugees had arrived and who, collectively, they were. Mercifully Beucler did not allow himself to become lost in the statistical maze. In fact, he let the question of Russian numbers pass with the entirely safe remark that "between 100,000 and 400,000 Russians" had come to France.[73] He distinguished four groups within the Russian community. One consisted of Soviet citizens who were not now part of the emigration. A second, chronologically earlier element was the old guard, members of the prerevolutionary colony who had not returned to Russia following the tsar's overthrow. In Paris this strand included Russian Jews long established in their own district of the ancient Jewish quarter in the fourth *arrondissement*. Outside the capital, strongly different in most respects from their compatriots there, was the corporal's guard of Russian aristocrats on the Riviera. Their doyenne, Alexander II's morganatic widow Princess Iurievskaia, died in 1922. Few in this diminishing band would have linked themselves to the post-1917 political emigration, if only because the association placed them in company they roundly despised. To most French contemporaries this distinction between the pre- and post-1917 arrivals was probably much less noticeable than to Russians or to Beucler.

Beucler's third group, the core of the Civil War influx, was its military component: Wrangel's army and some veterans of the Russian brigades that had served on the Western and Balkan fronts. These ex-warriors remained, for the most part, tight knit in their loyalty to their several chiefs. They became in consequence favourite bogeys for Soviet and French Communist allegations of "White Guardist conspiracies." The fourth and last of Beucler's categories was the amorphous mass he labelled the "non-military emigration." It was the most difficult to define precisely, as it was composed of several elements. One was the political and cultural leadership of old Russia; another consisted of men from the business and professional strata who saw no future for themselves in Soviet Russia. Then came those whose class background or associations made continued residence in Russia a hazardous proposition, along with those of every class who had simply been caught up in the whirlwind of defeat and evacuation.[74]

Beucler's classification, though accurate as far as it went, was as open to qualification as every other generalization about the *émigrés*.[75] At any rate, once in Paris, they lived where they could regardless of their antecedents. Ilia Ehrenburg told his readers that the post-1917 exiles who reached the city settled in the fashionable districts of Passy and Auteuil,[76] far from the virtuously proletarian regions occupied not so long before by himself and other refugees from tsarist misrule. He was propagating a myth. The Civil War exiles lived where they did for reasons that apply to refugees everywhere they settle: where they could afford, where they were allowed, close to their place of employment if they had any. To be sure, a few were able to choose the *beaux quartiers* of the sixteenth *arrondissement*; the overwhelming majority necessarily looked elsewhere. A favourite location was the rue de Vaugirard in the fifteenth, the capital's longest street. Others gathered in the seventeenth around the place and avenue des Ternes, within reach of the Orthodox cathedral of St Alexander Nevsky on the rue Daru. The cathedral was the uncontested heart of Russian Paris. Around it, on the rue Pierre-le-Grand and rue de-la-Neva, sprang up a profusion of teashops and other small commercial enterprises, all forming an enclave where Russian was heard more frequently than French. Further out from the centre, Vincennes on the city's eastern edge and Issy-les Moulineaux and Boulogne-Billancourt on its southwestern, attracted large numbers of Russians. The two latter suburbs proved particularly enticing because of the presence nearby of the Renault automobile plant, the biggest single employer in France of immigrant labour. Not so employed but also resident in Boulogne, on the rue Gutenberg, was Prince Felix Iusupov, Rasputin's assassin. His activities through the 1920s provided much grist for journalistic mills.[77]

One district of Russian Paris enjoyed a special, if transitory notoriety. This was Montparnasse, more properly "Russian Montparnasse" of the early and middle 1920s. Half a dozen cafés and restaurants – Le Dôme, La Rotonde, La Closerie des Lilas, Le Petit Vavin chief among them – furnished the meeting ground for expatriate Russian artists and political exiles just as they had in prerevolutionary times. A historian of the district's great days observed of its pre-1917 Russian visitors that the "revolutionaries" were much the more preferable customers, being cultured people, "as opposed to the artists."[78] Ehrenburg, still then in the revolutionary category, never lost his nostalgia for these encounters. The opening sentence of his first novel, published in 1922, evokes their memory and the atmosphere of the moment: "On 26 March 1913 I was sitting, as always, in the café La Rotonde, on the boulevard Montparnasse, in front of a cup of coffee, emptied long before, waiting in vain for someone to free me by paying the patient waiter six sous."[79]

In 1917 there was a complete change of cast. One set of émigrés, including Ehrenburg, went home and was replaced in Montparnasse, as elsewhere, by another. Even so, a measure of continuity was preserved. The new arrivals, upon entering La Rotonde, "sat down in the still warm seats vacated by the Bolsheviks."[80] Poetry readings, political arguments, and heated discussion about current cultural gods furnished the stuff of these sessions. Vassily Yanovsky has given us the most detailed portrait of Russian Montparnasse and its "only important basic entertainment; passionate, inspired talk." The intensity fed upon the feverish atmosphere of the time and place, when Montparnasse briefly became, for all nationalities in Paris, "the latest outpost of the avant-garde," the place to see and to be seen.[81] The budding poet and writer Zinaida Shakhovskaia lived in the midst of this "jungle," next to La Rotonde and Le Dôme. She went to them as to a performance, "not as a participant but as a spectator" of the rich, passing scene.[82]

In the provinces the area of greatest Russian concentration remained the *département* of Alpes-Maritimes, specifically Nice. The city had, of course, been a long-standing favourite with Russians and it continued to draw them in the years following the revolution.[83] As in Paris, their centre was the Orthodox cathedral, situated close to the point where the boulevard-du-Tzarewich meets the avenue-Nicolas-ΙΙ. The names, if nothing else, reminded resident Russian aristocrats of happier times. Another major area of settlement, albeit involuntary, was created by the French decision in December 1920 to intern the vessels of the Wrangel fleet, with their crews, in the port of Bizerta, near Tunis. Several thousand Russian sailors languished in unhealthy conditions and mounting discontent in eight primitive camps as French, *émigré*, and Soviet spokesmen argued over the fleet's rightful ownership and disposition.[84] In metropolitan France every major city acquired its Russian colony. Numbers ranged from 3 – 4,000 in Lyons and Marseilles to a few hundred in Bordeaux, Lille, and smaller towns. It is worth noting that in Lyons the resident *émigrés* maintained cordial relations with the city's Radical mayor, Edouard Herriot, in spite of the distinctly cooler opinion held of him by Russian political figures in Paris.[85] The capital's Russian-language press reported regularly on these "Russian corners" in France, even the least significant, thus keeping the exile "nation" informed of what was going on throughout its various French segments.

Of the several groups listed by Beucler, Stupnitsky, and other demographers of the Russian emigration, the one which historiographically dominates the rest, to the point where it is easily assumed to be synonymous with the whole, is the emigration's most visible top layer, its "active" minority of writers, journalists and cultural figures. It was, after all, their presence in the Paris of the 1920s that conferred upon the city its preeminence within the worldwide Russian community. This is not to say that political activity and artistic creativity were to be found only in the Parisian sector of the emigration. Political argument went on wherever two or three Russians were gathered together, and none of the larger cities of Russian settlement – Berlin, Prague, Sofia, or Harbin – was without its Russian newspapers, churches and cultural societies. But Paris counted the most.

The French capital did not owe its rank in the Russian exile world to luxurious nightclubs or extravagent eccentrics. *Émigré* reality was something different, with other preoccupations. One concern, earning enough money to survive, was common to refugees of every stripe. But this frequently unpleasant imperative was only fractionally more compelling than a second concern of overwhelming importance to the prerevolutionary intelligentsia now in exile. The defence and propagation of a certain idea of Russia against and in place of the detested Soviet reality obsessed all *émigré* politicians and writers – in emigration the two professions were synonymous. And nowhere in "Russia Abroad" was this defence more passionate and varied than in the French capital. The participants and audience were disputatiously present; the intellectual traditions of the city, to say nothing of their own, spurred the combatants on. Underlying all the polemics was a determination to preserve an individual and collective Russianness. The *émigré* intelligentsia was convinced that its country's interest required it to remain fully Russian, ready to defend with both tongue and pen the values which had fallen to its charge since the catastrophe of October 1917. *Sovremenniia zapiski*'s editorial board put the task succinctly in its introduction to the first of its seventy volumes. The new journal was to be dedicated "above all to the interests of Russian culture ... as in Russia itself there is now no place for free, independent expression."[86] This self-imposed responsibility rested on the editors' conviction that it was their duty, and, by extension, that of every articulate Russian, to defend the best of Russia's heritage while abroad. "You may temporarily have Moscow," the exiled intelligentsia said in effect to the Soviet regime, "but we have Russian culture."

The defence of historic Russian values while in exile absorbed much intellectual energy. The campaign focused on beliefs about the nature of Russia, her history, people, arts, and future. Unanimity on these matters was not to be expected from a community as fractious as the Russian *émigrés*. But it is fair to assert that an essential aspect for those who thought about the matter was an acceptance of Russia's necessary communion with Europe. With rare exceptions, the poets, writers, journalists, and other "active" members of the intelligentsia were, in the Russian historical sense, Westerners. They did not, of course, all speak French or feel at home in the West. That was the case with very few. Intensely Russian in feeling, memories, and instinct, most refugee intellectuals saw their country as both a beneficiary of and a mighty contributor to the stock of European culture. They were certain that Russia's further progress depended on their continual reaffirmation of this fact. The two loyalties need not conflict. Had not Fedor Dostoevsky himself acknowledged, even as he reproached his countrymen for their servility towards Europe, that Russia's links with European culture had been beneficial to their country? "Active" *émigrés* of the older generation would, by and large, have confirmed the tribute that the great writer paid in January 1881, shortly before his death, to Russia's debt to the West: "Europe, like Russia, is our mother, our second mother. We have taken much from her; we shall take again, and we shall not wish to be ungrateful to her."[87] But Russia's newest rulers were proving far worse than ungrateful.

It needs to be stressed that *émigré* outrage at Bolshevik rule in Russia was not just a case of the dispossessed shrieking in impotent fury at their supplanters, even though that emotion was undeniably present in exile ranks. It also stemmed from a genuine grief at seeing a regime in control of their lost homeland which appeared bent upon the eradication of Russia's European links, and which notoriously denied the standards of morality and humanity deemed to form part of European civilization. The European veneer that Russia had so painfully acquired over the preceding two centuries, a veneer which those now in exile in large measure personified, was ripped away, cast aside in favour – so it seemed – of barbarism. To Russian refugee intellectuals it was plain that men who slaughtered the innocent, burned churches, and sold off the treasures of the Hermitage could have nothing to do with the Russia of Pushkin, Tolstoi, or the Rights of Man. They were, in fact, its antithesis. In Roman Gul's robust phraseology, a re-ordering of the new state's name, their lost homeland was now a "Union of Sons of Bitches of the Revolution," governed by "the pseudonyms": Lenin, Trotsky, Stalin, and the rest.[88]

The exiles' struggle to preserve their personal and collective Russianness, as they simultaneously defended the interests of historic national values, stimulated an intense, ultimately exhausting effort that lasted the better part of two decades. The campaign was concentrated in Paris. A recent survey of the Russian press in the city during the 1920s reveals the zeal with which the two related tasks were undertaken.[89] Of course, not all refugees could contribute. The larger "passive" mass, worn out after eight to ten hours labour in factory, farm, or mine, might only manage a glance at *Poslednia novosti* or its rival, *Vozrozhdenie* (Resurrection). Even so, their membership in the Russian community and interest in its concerns were no less authentic than those of the more visible articulate minority. Both "active" and "passive" *émigrés* were, in any case, relegated to the sidelines when it came to those matters which interested them the most. They were all spectators of Russian events between the wars, not participants in them. Their Russia lay in the past and, so they desperately hoped, in the future as well. Until the day of vindication Paris remained the centre of their world. It was a city new to almost all and intimidating to most. Yet it was one which for a while seemed, in the words of its least typical, most notorious Russian resident, "full of promises and possibilities."[90]

CHAPTER TWO

Elusive Unity

Lev Dmitrievich Liubimov was one of those who decided, after experiencing more than a year of Bolshevik rule in Petrograd, that he had had enough. A nineteen-year old graduate of the Alexander *Lycée* and scion of a family at the highest level of the bureaucratic élite, he took the Finnish exit from Russia in the summer of 1919, choosing refuge abroad until a Bonaparte should emerge to restore order in his demented country. Until the saviour appeared, Liubimov waited and wandered: south through Poland and the Balkans, into Germany, where he studied in Berlin, to arrive finally in Paris in 1924. There he was able, probably thanks to his family connections, to secure a position on the new, conservatively oriented newspaper, *Vozrozhdenie*, which began to appear on Paris streets in June 1925. For the next fifteen years his was one of the most strident voices on the *émigré* right recalling prevolutionary times, extolling tsarist institutions, and damning everything that had happened in Russia since February 1917. Unimagined by any of those who read his nostalgic vituperation was Liubimov's eventual abandonment of the *émigré* cause, his return to Moscow, and his apologetic, informative memoir of life in alien parts.[1]

Liubimov's anti-Soviet indignation, while it lasted, drew its basic sustenance from his conviction that the natural order of things in Russia had been overturned. Nothing could go right until that order had been restored and the Liubimovs of the emigration had returned to resume their customary place. This sentiment was widespread among conservative exiles, particularly those who had been something in pre-February days. In a more general sense, the certainty of their return to a de-Bolshevized Russia provided the refugees with a raft to cling to in the first bewildering phase of exile life. Russians, including Liubimov, held to this perception with tenacity. Twenty years after the October Revolution, a sympathetic observer of the Russians in France saw many of the surviving *émigrés* "even today ... psychologically in the position of railway passengers sitting on their trunks and waiting for the signal to depart." But he went on to add that "for the greater number it has been necessary to look around for some place to 'dig themselves in.'"²

The need to "dig in," while impatiently looking for the signal to leave, imparted a duality to the early years of exile life. Yakobson's metaphor defined the refugees' chief preoccupations: to organize for an uncertain and, so it was universally hoped, brief sojourn abroad, even as they maintained an all-absorbing interest in Russia. This included both the Russia they had lost and the one they hoped to regain and, for a few, remodel.

The French years of the first emigration may be divided for historiographic purposes into successive periods when the note of "next week / month / spring in Russia" vied with the pressures of refugee existence. Until 1924 the second of these claimed distinctly less attention from the exiles than did the first; thereafter, as the prospect of a return faded, the imperatives of exile became more difficult to ignore. Nevertheless, though impatience to go back to a post-Bolshevik Russia loomed large in *émigré* minds, it should not be allowed to obscure the efforts of individuals and organizations concerned with the gigantic tasks of the here in France and the now of the refugee present. In material terms – and these did matter – they achieved more than the myriad speeches and articles about how things had been in old Russia and would be in the new once the Bolshevik incubus were shaken off.

The Russian diaspora had no leader, either in France or elsewhere, no figure around whom all sections of the emigration could unite. Paris was its recognized capital, but not because any acknowledged chief or government resided there. In a legal sense, whatever that was worth, pride of place in the list of those who claimed the mantle of leadership belonged to the men of the defunct Provisional Government. Any examination of the political "names" of Russian France should therefore begin with that regime's last official representative in Paris, the dean of the Russian emigration in France, Vasily Alekseevich Maklakov. Aged fifty-one in 1920, Maklakov had behind him a front-rank reputation as parliamentary orator and lawyer. A prominent Duma member, speaking from a Right Kadet position,³ he added fresh lustre to his name with his speeches on behalf of those deputies charged after the Vyborg manifesto in 1906. His role in the defence of Mendel Beilis, a Jewish tailor wrongfully accused in 1911 of the murder of an Orthodox child, enhanced his reputation still further.⁴ A major public career seemed not improbable. But like so many others of his background and character, he was a casualty of the events following upon the fall of the monarchy. His creed was reason and intelligent scepticism; he had a profound veneration for legal form and he instinctively preferred organic evolution to the more violent confrontations predicted by those on his political left, beginning in his own party. To the bottom of his soul he feared the destructive potential of Russian society's lower depths.⁵ By the middle of the revolutionary summer Maklakov's world was coming apart. He fervently supported General Kornilov; when that would-be saviour vanished, Maklakov went off to gilded exile in the West to replace Alexander Izvolsky at the Paris embassy. Izvolsky, the living embodiment of the secret diplomacy of the bad old days, had resigned some months before. His successor proceeded to his post only to discover, when he presented himself at the Quai d'Orsay, that the government he represented had disappeared into history, taking with it the official reason for his presence in France.[6]

The ambassador did not long remain unemployed. He assumed control of the Conference of Ambassadors, an informal gathering of senior Russian representatives who watched over their country's diplomatic interests in the West. These were, it need hardly be said, firmly anti-Bolshevik. The Conference summoned into existence the Russian Political Conference, an umbrella organization of exiled politicians and diplomats.[7] Its membership ranged from Popular Socialists to veteran servants of the fallen autocrat. As such, its existence must be regarded as something of a miracle in the heated climate of the anti-Bolshevik camp, where suspicions among rival factions almost matched its common animosity against Lenin. In any event the cacophony of voices claiming to speak for Russia's future did not manage to attract much attention from the peacemakers of Versailles. Protests at the slighting of allied Russia's representatives went the same way as all the pamphlets which these dispossessed Russians rained down upon the statesmen of Europe and America.[8]

Even before this point had been reached, Maklakov existed in a sort of diplomatic limbo. On the one hand, he continued to occupy the splendid mansion in the rue de Grenelle which housed the Russian embassy. He had correct, even cordial relations with several French political leaders, much better than those enjoyed by P.N. Miliukov and A.F. Kerensky. As far as the Western bourgeois public was concerned, the embassy and its chief represented Russia, or at least the Russia which that public preferred to any other. Letters flowed in through 1919 and 1920 inquiring about opportunities inside Russia once matters had returned to normal. Could the embassy provide details as to trade possibilities for Walden Worcester Wrenches of Worcester, Massachusetts? was one example, typical of several less alliterative others.[9] All this was well enough and testified, if to nothing else, to the public's continuing difficulty in grasping what was going on in Russia. Yet the fact remained that Maklakov no longer represented a functioning government. Whom did he represent? The Quai d'Orsay seemed unsure. A minor incident illustrated their perplexity. On 3 March 1919 the embassy received an acknowledgement of congratulations sent to Premier Clemenceau on his escape from an assassin. This missive was sent to *Son Excellence Monsieur Maklakoff Ambassade de Russie*, but clearly visible still are the lightly erased letters *ur* at the end of *Ambassade*.[10] He was not included in the diplomatic list, nor was he invited to major state occasions. This provoked indignation in certain émigré circles: had not pre-Bolshevik Russia proved her loyalty to France at ruinous cost to herself? But Maklakov saw matters more dispassionately. "I was like a newspaper placed on a chair to show it was occupied" he commented some years later to an inquiring French journalist.[11] Whatever the ambiguities of his status in the eyes of French protocol officials, Maklakov's occupancy of the embassy, with his innumerable French contacts and organizational gifts, made him an obvious intermediary between French bureaucrats and the refugee mass in France. Recognition of the Soviet regime by the Cartel des Gauches government in October 1924 forced Maklakov to vacate the premises on the rue de Grenelle but did not lessen his responsibilities. On the contrary, it intensified them to the point where for a quarter century he was to represent the Russian exile community to the French authorities, all the while seeking to guide, in a noncompulsory way, his fractious flock through the difficulties of refugee life.

The two names from the political emigration most familiar to the French public and, simultaneously, the most disliked by their compatriots in exile, belonged to "the father and son of the March Revolution,"[12] Paul Nikolaevich Miliukov and Alexander Fedorovich Kerensky.

"What is to be done with you? You have no soul, only glass: clear, transparent, deep as crystal, not to be warmed by hands or tears, just glass!"[13] Fedor Rodichev's furious reproach as Miliukov prepared in 1921 to tear the remnant of their party in two rather than compromise his latest certainty was one more complaint in a long litany going back two decades. In exile many additions would be made. No non-Bolshevik Russian aroused more passionate feelings, usually hostile, from émigrés. In part this came from Miliukov's manner, in part from his political record. Cool to the point of hauteur, professorial, unable to hide impatience with those who would not, or could not, follow his doctrinaire reasonings, he rarely unbent or gave evidence of any warm humanity. His political actions since 1917 showed little consistent purpose. He began that fateful year a firm proponent of Russia's alliance with Britain and France, the incarnation of war to victory, notoriously in favour of Russian annexation of Constantinople and the Dardanelles, a defender of the monarchy, if not of the monarch. He served a brief, inglorious stint as foreign minister in the Provisional Government; a year later came a short-lived flirtation with the Germans that badly damaged his reputation in the West.[14] He arrived in Paris in December 1920, hard upon the final ruin of the White armies, to press upon consternated colleagues his "new tactic," a re-alignment of what remained of their Constitutional Democratic party (Kadets) leftward toward the Right SRS.[15] He did not get his way uncontested. Nevertheless, in July 1921, obdurate to all appeals, Russia's most eminent liberal led a minority group out of the party he had done so much to inspire. The sundered larger fragment of those who resisted Miliukov's arguments continued to face right. It spent the next few years listening in small rooms to reports from one another on Bolshevik crimes and from recently arrived refugees on, among other topics, the monarchical longings of Russia's oppressed masses.[16]

The man responsible for the Kadet party's final disruption devoted his energies thereafter to political comment, journalism, and party organization. The last of these was the least. It had to do with his Republican-Democratic Association (RDO), the political expression of his latest views. He never ceased to urge its ideas on his fellow exiles old and young, and claimed some success in his efforts.[17] Generally, however, his vision of a republican Russia, organized as a parliamentary, democratic federation with Socialists very much to the fore, all inspired by Professor Miliukov, late of the Provisional Government, was not one that the émigré mass found the least enticing.

Miliukov made his major contribution to émigré history as political commentator, historian, and editor. Whether the subject was the Bolsheviks, Russian history, or issues affecting their lives in France, everything from Miliukov's pen bore the stamp of its author. This was most apparent in the editorial columns of his newspaper Posledniia novosti where he pointedly disregarded the advice he elsewhere offered his exiled compatriots that "one must not build political programmes on personal tastes and preferences which are clearly unrealizable."[18] Editorials aside, Miliukov's paper became the most widely read and distributed organ of the entire emigration, perhaps even "from Tahiti to Australia, from Norway to South Africa" as its editor claimed toward the end of Posledniia novosti's life.[19] Its daily appearance through almost twenty years of arduous exile was certainly a tribute to Miliukov's energy and will. Thanks in the main to him, Posledniia novosti is arguably the richest source of information on the life of the Russian community in France between the two world wars.

None of this spared Miliukov the animosity of almost every sector of the emigration. His intellectual certainties, the manner of their delivery, his political gyrations, and his prominence in 1917 combined to create a formidable indictment against him in the minds of the large émigré majority to his political right. The fusillade of shots aimed at Miliukov in Berlin in March 1922 by a pair of Fascist thugs, missing him but killing his colleague V.D. Nabokov, expressed this hatred in shockingly violent action.[20] But it existed in milder form in countless words of criticism. The gentle Peter Struve, for instance, deplored Miliukov's willingness to bring further division into an émigré body whose most urgent requirement was so clearly unity. Not content with breaking up what remained of his party, the Kadet chieftain did so in a manner deeply offensive to those who had made such sacrifices for the principles Miliukov now disdained.[21] Posledniia novosti's lesser rival, *Vozrozhdenie*, first under Struve, then more venomously under Iuly Semenov, never wearied in its criticisms. Ivan Nazhivin, a quixotic disciple of Leo Tolstoi and fierce reactionary, devoted a large part of his considerable literary output to abuse of "poor, old babbling Miliukov."[22] The so-called postrevolutionary movements in the younger *émigré* generation also saw in the former foreign minister a natural target. None of this induced Miliukov to soften his views or adopt a less conspicuous profile. Rather the contrary.

His 1917 rival and colleague, Alexander Kerensky, also had few admirers and many critics. In 1929 he told Charles Ledré, then compiling his account of the Russian community in France, that "in general I am detested by the emigration." Yet he had the consolation of knowing "that all Russia is behind me" in his ideas.[23] The remark hints at Kerensky's most striking characteristic: an utterly unshakeable confidence in the correctness of his principles, in their widespread popularity in Russia, and their eventual, certain triumph there. Optimism was not uncommon among *émigré* political figures, at least in the early years of exile, but none held it longer, expressed it more volubly, or went out on more limbs in predicting the course of Russian events than did the former head of the Provisional Government. His invariable error reinforced the burden he already carried from the fact that his cabinet had capitulated to Lenin and his Bolsheviks: "he let the enemy into the besieged fortress and then shamefully abandoned his post."[24] His reputation as a vacillating, posturing loser clung to him wherever he travelled among Russians. All the same, it is probably fair to say that, though *émigrés* with particularly fond memories of tsarism continued to heap insults upon him,[25] he did not excite quite the same degree of distaste as Miliukov. His was a much warmer personality than that of *Poslednia novosti*'s coldly unemotional editor.[26] Politically the two men pursued very similar paths in exile, particularly after Miliukov's "new tactic" brought him closer to the Right sr position. That very prospect proved an especially bitter pill for Kadet critics of the new line demanded by Miliukov.[27]

The editor of *Posledniaia novosti* stood fractionally to the left of that point in the political emigration where the basic division occurred between a democratic minority, pledged to some form of republican, federative Russian democracy, and a conservatively inclined majority which ranged from moderate constitutional monarchists to antisemitic reactionaries and imitators of Italian and German Fascism. Other than the Republican-Democratic Association, the democratic sector included a handful of Right srs. Mark Vishniak was of their number. Until his death in New York in 1976 this *Sovremenniia zapiski* editor remained, with Kerensky, the Soviet regime's most irreconcilable enemy on the exile left. More stubbornly than any other Russian Socialist, he personified the unforgiving loathing of Communism held by those who had once, a lifetime before, shared the left end of the Russian political spectrum with the Bolsheviks. Mensheviks and Left SRS had their headquarters in Berlin from where they levelled occasional criticism at their Russian democratic comrades in Paris.[28]

The image presented by the far larger portion of the emigration – Miliukov spoke of eighty-five percent[29] – that did not belong to the democratic camp was confusingly varied. Other than Vasily Maklakov, who shared the views of that part of the Kadet party opposed to the "new tactic" but whose position demanded a degree of political neutrality, there was no individual whose prestige or notoriety among Russians and French approached that of the two Provisional Government ministers. Among moderate conservatives perhaps the outstanding figure was Peter Struve. Active in pre-1905 days in the Union of Liberation and during the Civil War in the Denikin and Wrangel "governments," Struve was to experience more than most the often harsh truth that many of exile's worst disappointments are received at the hands of fellow refugees. Other prominent names from an era vanished in Russia continued to appear in the emigration's early years of political activity: Anton Kartashev, Vasily Kokovtsev, Fedor Rodichev, the irrepressible Vladimir Burtsev, among others. To their right stretched a noisy spectrum of monarchical legitimists, antisemitic reactionaries and Fascist grouplets that made a greater impact in the Far Eastern and Balkan areas of Russian refugee settlement.[30]

A flurry of attempts in the first half-dozen years of exile pursued the elusive goal of political cohesion among émigrés or at least a large portion of them. None deserves more than passing attention. In January 1921 a gathering was held in Paris of thirty-two members of the defunct Constituent Assembly out of the fifty-six then in exile. The session was organized by an SR-Left Kadet alliance, the embodiment of Miliukov's "new tactic"; he himself was much in evidence throughout. Their aim was to devise a set of democratically inspired proposals for the organization of post-Bolshevik Russia; they duly published their conclusions. Refugees paid little heed and *Posledniia novosti* (not yet Miliukov's) acknowledged that "Oh Lord, not again!" was their more likely response to news of the meeting.[31] A few months later Vladimir Burtsev cobbled together an émigré "National Congress," dominated by Right Kadets, which advanced its own, more conservative views on the same subject. These undoubtedly commanded more sympathy from refugees than anything suggested by Miliukov and his friends, but they had only marginally deeper impact.[32]

An echo from the supposedly buried past was next to be heard in September 1924, when the Grand Duke Cyril Vladimirovich, a cousin of Nicholas II, proclaimed himself emperor and called upon loyal Russians to rally to his cause. Though he was the nearest surviving male claimant, his announcement was not endorsed by either of the two senior Romanov representatives, the Dowager-Empress Maria Fedorovna and the Grand

Duke Nicholas Nikolaevich. It also much embarrassed moderate monarchists like Struve, who did not wish any precipitate act of that sort to decide in advance so important a question affecting Russia's future. The pretender continued nonetheless to issue proclamations from his "court" at St-Briac, on the Breton coast; he decorated the faithful and was generally ignored by left and right in France until oddly taken up by the Young Russia movement in the 1930s.[33] Finally, in April 1926, came the most ambitious effort yet in the convocation of a "Congress of Russia Abroad." This was a larger, more intensive attempt than hitherto of the moderate right to fashion some representative, organized nucleus around which exiled anti-Bolsheviks might rally, to become at last "a unified body of active Russian forces [that might] free Russia from the yoke of the Third International."[34] This sentiment and the identity of its framers sufficed to keep the left away, jeering.[35] The ultraright, on the other hand, was represented. Its chief spokesman during the sessions in the Hotel Majestic in Paris was N.E. Markov II, a vociferous hater of intellectuals and, in Richard Pipes's trenchant phrase, "a thug who had acquired notoriety with his antisemitic tirades in the Duma."[36] His involvement could only harm the conservative cause. The Congress wound up its deliberations with a series of resolutions and to a fanfare of hopeful editorials in Struve's *Vozrozhdenie*.[37] Not one was to be justified.

In reviewing the political passions of the first decade of the Russians' exile, their historian is armed with the knowledge of how meaningless to Russia and the world were the endless plans and profusion of articles attacking the Soviets, looking forward to better times in a post-Bolshevik Russia freed by someone else's efforts and organized in any one of a dozen ways. *Emigré* politicians of the day saw something of this but usually preferred to identify local rivals as the ones pursuing a hopeless political cause, rather than the anti-Soviet camp as a whole. The mutual criticism, often degenerating into open vituperation, between Russian democrats, conservatives, and reactionaries on every issue to do with Russia was a reminder that hatreds could be as unforgiving against fellow refugees in another political camp as they were against distant, inaccessible Bolsheviks. The "Russia Abroad" congress in 1926 of "old, mangy, rheumatic and gouty lions … the united Russian counterrevolution," to cite one not untypical democratic critic,[38] offered the last grand-scale opportunity for attack. But even without public meetings, intra*émigré* hostilities and the invective these engendered raged on. Between the democratic sector and its taunts at the "Russia Abroad" congress, the moderate right with its disdain for Miliukov and his allies, and the far right lost in its restorationist obsessions, no compromise in the name of unity was ever attainable. This fact remained a basic feature of the emigration. It strengthened the inclination of non-Russians to ignore *émigré* political pretensions, just as Vladimir Burtsev had warned in the days of the final defeat of the White armies.

If politics excited divisions among exiled Russians, the will-o'-the-wisp of unity seemed to become more substantial in the common concern of refugees to maintain their national identity. On such matters *émigrés* might meet as Russians, with political differences never forgotten but at least subordinated to the greater interest. Or so it sometimes turned out.

The preservation of Russianness demanded great effort at every moment of refugee life. It was easier for some than for others. Exiles who arrived in the West already middle-aged or elderly had no difficulty in knowing and feeling themselves to be thoroughly and unchallengeably Russian. Their preoccupations, memories, experiences, loyalties, and language left no other possibility and conferred on them almost total immunity to alien cultural penetration. Those under forty might not feel so secure, while adolescents were likely to drift uneasily between the new country and the old. [39] These important generational distinctions in the experience of exile are explored elsewhere in this biography. [40] Certainly refugees of all ages shared a common love of Russia and a profound interest in those features of Russian life which contributed most to their country's and their own unique national identity. In exile these sentiments were strongly nurtured by the *émigré* press, the Orthodox church, and Russian culture.

THE PRESS

In fleeing Russia, the Civil War refugees abandoned, they believed only briefly, any direct part in Russia's affairs. Hopes that their spokesmen might influence European statesmen when they conferred on Russian matters vanished at Versailles and the subsequent Allied conferences which eventually led to general recognition of the Soviet regime. But though *émigrés* could neither determine nor influence, they could certainly comment. Virtually from the moment that the first shipload of refugees landed at Constantinople, the first newssheets appeared. Parading their defiance of Bolshevism, they proclaimed another Russian presence to the world. Every component part of the refugee wave wanted its say, though only one or two individuals might do the actual work in the name of a wider constituency. War veterans, aristocrats, Guards' officers, engineers, Cossacks – all had their mouthpieces; there were even organs claiming to speak on behalf of Caucasian highlanders (editor Prince Elmurza Bekovich-Cherkassky) and "the 150-million strong Russian peasantry." [41] Where the Soviet press was uniform, dull, politically monochromatic and reflected authority, the *émigré* press, in its early years at least, was varied, noisy, argumentative, full of notions, and utterly powerless. Most were unable to put down lasting roots. In Gleb Struve's phrase, Russian newspapers sprang up everywhere like mushrooms, but like mushrooms their lifespan proved brief. [42]

The most respected, widely read, and longest lived organ of the *émigré* daily press was *Posledniia novosti*. The newspaper's first editor, the former

Kiev lawyer M.I. Goldstein, declared in its first issue that he hoped to show the facts from Russia as they were, without any tendentious interpretation.[43] A year later his successor, Miliukov, defined his own approach. At a time when many of his party colleagues were still furiously reviling him over his "new tactic," he announced that his paper also was going to defend the new line. Armed struggle was over. The old tactic of attempting to impose change on Russia from the outside, using foreign help, had failed. Russia's emancipation would surely come, but the means must be new, generated from inside the country. Natural evolutionary pressures would play their part. Implacably hostile to Bolshevism, *Posledniia novosti* ardently supported the popular endeavour to regain liberty, which could not rest on other than democratic foundations.[44] What Miliukov's admirer, the writer Don Aminado, called *Posledniia novosti's* "informed neutrality" was abandoned; the newspaper proceeded to assume a distinct ideological cast. "The quite insignificant fact that the recently formed Republican–Democratic direction [of the paper] was far from corresponding to the views and tastes of the *émigré* majority in no way disturbed the new editor."[45]

After the shattering disappointment of the Kronstadt rising, Miliukov's newspaper settled into its role of chief *émigré* critic of Soviet reality. This remained its major function beyond 1924, when recognition of the USSR by the European powers brought what its editor acknowledged was a new stage in the history of Russia and the emigration.

Seven months after French recognition a challenge to *Posledniia novosti* presented itself with the appearance in Paris of another Russian daily, *Vozrozhdenie*. Peter Struve was its editor; financial backing was provided by the prerevolutionary oil magnate A.O. Gukasov. Struve placed his newspaper firmly in the moderate conservative-nationalist sector of exile opinion. His first editorial dedicated *Vozrozhdenie* to the best of Russia's liberal traditions, as exemplified in the civil structures of Catherine the Great, the reforms of Alexander II, and "the great reforms" of 1905. The nation's best conservative values were to be equally inspirational; Struve invoked the names of Dmitry Donskoi, Peter I, Pushkin, and Speransky.[46] The new journal got off to a good start with an impressive group of contributors to its first issue.[47] For the next two years Struve struggled to hold the newspaper to his initial editorial promise, but his situation grew increasingly unhappy. Gukasov's high-handed interference led to the editor's humiliating dismissal in August 1927.[48] Under his replacement, Iuly Semenov, *Vozrozhdenie* descended into an ever shriller, more obsessive anti-Sovietism. Its readership declined steadily; in July 1936 the paper went from daily to weekly publication at a tripled price.

None of the remaining Russian newspapers in Paris equalled these two in longevity. Vladimir Burtsev's *Obshchee delo* (Common Cause) appeared irregularly in short bursts. He favoured an emotional, declamatory style.

In mid-November 1920, as exile began, he went further than any other refugee in his professed devotion to France, "every Russian's second fatherland"; but his fervour cooled before long.[49] In any case Burtsev's excitable disposition – "as naive now [at near 70] as at 15!" – diverted serious attention from him.[50] Alexander Kerensky transferred his *Dni* (Days) from Berlin to Paris in 1926. It made a generally feeble impression. Its political line of democratic socialism found few supporters, while its editor was no asset in courting readers. In exile Kerensky clamorously insisted on the rightness of his course in 1917 and continually injected his own opinions throughout his newspaper. No Russians were converted, but his reputation as an expert on Russia stood high among foreigners. *Dni* became a weekly in 1928. It also adopted the Soviet-amended orthography so as to emphasize its editor's seriousness in seeking to establish links with young Soviet democrats who were, Kerensky insisted, now turning toward the ideals of the February Revolution.[51] His useless apostasy on the spelling issue did nothing to postpone the journal's end. It finally came in 1933 after repeated financial crises. The ex-premier went on offering comment in other journalistic columns, forever hopeful of Russia's regeneration and the triumph of his political beliefs.

Lasting not quite as long as *Dni*, *Rossiia i slavianstvo* (Russia and Slavdom) was published weekly, or fortnightly when funds ran low, for six difficult years by Peter Struve and friends after his departure from *Vozrozhdenie*. Then there was *Illustrirovannaia Rossiia* (Illustrated Russia), also right of centre, which displayed pictures of *émigré* notables, including the winners of the occasional "Miss Russia" competition which it sponsored. Several organs were aimed at a specific readership. The most vociferous of these through the last half-dozen years before the war was probably *Bodrost* (Courage), the weekly journal of the Young Russia movement. At the opposite end, in lonely isolation on the far left, stood *Sotsialisticheskii vestnik* (Socialist Herald), published twice monthly in Berlin until Hitler's coming to power forced its Jewish, Menshevik editors to move to Paris. In the French capital they held aloof from other refugees, criticized everyone to their right, enrolled few, if any, recruits and exerted themselves to maintain a rigid ideological purity.[52]

Posledniia novosti stood first in this variegated throng. Its pre-eminence owed nothing to the paper's political allegiance to the February Revolution and the image of a democratic, republican Russia. It is indeed a tribute to the newspaper's quality that it remained the most widely read daily of the entire emigration in spite of these unpopular loyalties.[53] In 1938 Miliukov claimed a readership of at least 200,000 throughout the world diaspora, although the daily press run was then only 39,000 copies.[54] He also took pride in telling an inquiring French reporter that the Soviet government "buys several hundred copies every day."[55] The extent of its coverage of

Russia in exile, its literary and cultural range, and an unhysterical prose style all contributed to its appeal. Accusations by later returners to the USSR that the paper ignored French affairs were unjust and missed the point.[56] The journal's editor saw its function in France as that of loudspeaker for free Russian opinion and as a source of information for *émigrés* on matters that interested or concerned them. To have expected from the Russian press the same absorption in the minutiae of French political and social life as that displayed by the French dailies was plainly absurd. Comment on Russia past and present, reports on major European events, the life of the Russian community, French political and administrative decisions that touched their lives, news of cultural interest – these were the subjects that filled the paper's columns. Take, for example, the issue of 5 January 1929. As no story of overwhelming significance dominated the news, it may be seen as an average day. The issue contained six pages. On page one a two-column editorial, covering two-thirds of the left half, commented on the bleak economic situation in Russia. The unsigned editorial was usually written by Miliukov. He judged it to be the paper's main feature, which gave guidance on questions of the day.[57] Moving his scrutiny to the centre of the page, the reader could skim the latest bulletins from world capitals: had Leon Trotsky been kidnapped?; George V was ill; the Bulgarian minister in London had written his memoirs (a synopsis followed); some details of French political manoeuvres on the eve of a new parliamentary session. Longer reports followed on the right of the page about a political crisis in Yugoslavia and Communist machinations in French labour unions. Much of this carried over to page two, the bottom half of which was devoted to an examination of the role of the Orthodox church in Russian life in France. Page three presented a short story or essay, the traditional "feuilleton," along with some pictures of interest: Lenin in disguise and a cobbler giving a pair of shoes to the Prince of Wales. A detailed, pessimistic analysis of the Soviet economy followed on page four. It provided details of a flourishing black market in Vladivostok. Page five offered the latest installment of a historical novel, notices of forthcoming social events, stock exchange and sporting news, reviews and advertisements. These last extolled the attractions of Au Cosy Tea Shop Salon, Vodka Garçon Russe, and various pills for neurasthenics. The giant department store Au Printemps trumpeted its wares from the top of page six; underneath came classified announcements of the various services available to readers at modest price. Madame Rose, fortune-teller, made frequent appearances in this section.

Vozrozhdenie's format did not differ greatly, though its political line was a world apart. The calibre of its reporting was often markedly lower, with anti-Soviet gossip getting prominent mention. Both newspapers featured cartoons in which two themes predominated. Readers would often see depicted two or three *émigrés* comparing notes on their life in France. This could focus either on the difficulties with landladies, employers, and legal status, or on the rarer joys such as a lottery win. Alternatively, there might be a sketch of the Soviet leadership of the day. Stalin as a Caucasian bandit, Trotsky, Kaganovich, or Litvinov as obviously un-Russian malefactors tormenting a defiant Russian peasant or duping some credulous Herriot or Lloyd George. Reports from outlying districts of the Russian diaspora appeared frequently. Thursday editions featured essays on literature and literary criticism. The two newspapers were the target of occasional reproaches for their insufficient attention to serious literature and for their willingness to publish what some critics thought was superficial work. Yet, as Gleb Struve has pointed out, most readers came home after a day of fatiguing labour and preferred to relax with lighter fare. In any case, the literary quality of the novels and other popular material presented in the press was often quite high.[58]

THE CHURCH

The most visible sign of a Russian presence in the great cities of Central and Western Europe were the cupolas of an Orthodox church. These buildings, many inherited from earlier times, stood in striking contrast to French and German neighbours. They became a natural centre of Russian assembly and symbol of their lost country. But how the church in exile ought to be organized and how it should relate to Russia were questions which provoked passionate dissension. The arguments reflected divisions of appropriately Byzantine complexity.

At the heart of the problem was the issue of canonical obedience. Until the October Revolution foreign dioceses of the Russian Orthodox church, except those in North America, came under the jurisdiction of the Petrograd Metropolitan. The Civil War disrupted ecclesiastical unity and so Patriarch Tikhon in effect conferred autonomous status on dioceses outside Russia by a decree of 20 November 1920.[59] When they arrived in Constantinople, some refugee Russian bishops formed themselves into a Supreme Ecclesiastical Administration of the Russian Church Abroad and entered into relations with the Serbian and Constantinople patriarchs. The former dignitary invited the Administration to establish itself in the small Serbian town of Sremske Karlovtsy. This was done, and the Administration, headed by the Metropolitan Antony, proclaimed itself as acting in the name and with the blessing of the Moscow patriarchate. Some substance was in fact imparted to this claim by Tikhon's edict of 8 April 1921, confirming the Administration's action in confiding Orthodox dioceses in Western Europe to the pastoral care of the bishop of Volhynia, Evlogy, who resided in Paris.[60]

The apparent unity between the Moscow patriarch and his flock outside

Russia could only be illusory. It was not to be expected that fiercely anti-Soviet Russian believers could remain in communion with and owe obedience to an authority ultimately subject to Bolshevik control. As long as the church inside Russia remained persecuted, the exiled faithful might legitimately claim to be at one with it in resisting Bolshevism. Such was the assumption underlying a declaration in December 1921 by a gathering of clergy and laity in Sremske Karlovtsy. Since it lacked the temporal weapons to press its case, the meeting invited the Allies, due to meet in Genoa the following spring, to resume their anti-Soviet crusade.[61] The unfortunate Tikhon, squeezed between an atheist regime and anti-Soviet believers abroad, dissolved the Sremske Karlovtsy Administration and demanded that the clergy stay out of politics. Beyond changing the Administration's name to Synod, his flock in the West paid small heed to his admonitions.

The strain induced by these rival claims became unbearable as the church inside Russia began to move toward an uneasy co-existence with Soviet power. In July 1927 Tikhon's acting successor, Metropolitan Sergei of Nizhnyi Novgorod, enjoined upon Metropolitan Evlogy that neither he nor his clergy should permit themselves anything in their public or religious activity which might be taken as an expression of disloyalty toward the Soviet government. It was now Evlogy's turn to be pulled in different directions. He published Sergei's communication, so touching off intense debate. At the same time, Evlogy faced the suspicions of the Sremske Karlovtsy synod, which vied with him for the religious allegiance of the Orthodox laity in France. In 1927 the synod, with dubious authority, deposed Evlogy and replaced him in Paris with Archbishop Serafim. There were now two Orthodox hierarchies in the West.

Confusion continued to pile upon confusion. In March 1930, Evlogy participated in services held throughout England on behalf of Russian Christians suffering for their faith: he himself spoke out on the subject.[62] This act, in conjunction with requiem masses offered for the souls of Nicholas II and his family, provoked the long impending rupture between Evlogy and the Moscow patriarchate. Evlogy was again deposed, this time by Sergei, and his church was again entrusted to another cleric, Archbishop Vladimir. The latter refused to assume the charge. Evlogy thereupon convoked in Paris an assembly of bishops, who requested him to stay at his post. He agreed and resolved the question of canonical obedience by soliciting and receiving from the senior Orthodox patriarch, that of Constantinople, the title of Exarch of the Ecumenical Patriarch. This act of seeming submission to an authority renounced over four centuries before led to yet further schism. A small group renounced Evlogy and pledged itself instead to the Lithuanian metropolitan Eleftheros, still obedient to the Moscow see.[63]

Three ecclesiastical jurisdictions now competed for the loyalty of Orthodox Russians in exile. The Sremske Karlovtsy synod, presided over by Metropolitan Antony, drew most of its support from the Balkan and Far Eastern areas of Russian settlement, though it had its followers in Western Europe. Forty-two of the seventy Orthodox parishes in Western Europe were in France and French North Africa; the majority of these remained loyal to Evlogy. The pro-Moscow element was insignificant. In spite of attempts by churchmen and laity to bridge the gaps, the divisions persisted as a stand-ing reproach to the faithful.[64] Yet the schisms did not prevent those who sought a refuge in religion from finding it.

Divided though it was, the church remained unquestionably Russian. It was a link to the past and a consolation in the present. But for whom did it retain significance? Democratic opinion generally downplayed the church's role in the emigration. An editorial in *Posledniia novosti* on Sergei's effort in 1930 to depose Evlogy held that this was a matter of interest only to believers. The church was not a political institution; its future was thus up to its members alone.[65] The tone implied that this number was in significant; a suggestion a year earlier that it might comprise very many *émigrés* in the provinces prompted a second investigator to issue a firm denial. Of some 600 Russians in Grenoble "only twelve to fifteen," accord-ing to M. Kurdiumov, were interested in church affairs; of 2,000 Russians in Lyons only 200; in Besançon six out of 180. Kurdiumov claimed that this was the general pattern, though it did not mean that most *émigré* Russians were nonbelievers. He conceded that a convinced atheist was very rare. Every family went to church on major festivals. In most cases, however, their par-ticipation was passive. The real work of building churches and attracting congregations under very hard material conditions was done by a tiny minority.[66] Charles Ledré agreed that religion was important as a binding force in a community that had only anti-Bolshevism to cement it. But he saw at least the appearance of religious indifference in some *émigré* quarters. Ledré attributed this to the example of nonpractising French neighbours, the fatigues of the working week and even to the lack of good Sunday clothes.[67]

It was not surprising that the Russians who minimized the role of the church in *émigré* life came in the main from the left of the political spec-trum. Its members had the strongest memories of the ties between the hierarchy and the autocracy in prerevolutionary years, as well as of the Orthodox church's all too frequent reactionary part in public affairs. Given all this, was it possible for a Russian democrat to be an Orthodox believer? Or did fidelity to religion imply a preference for monarchical rule?[68] *Posled-niia novosti* seemed to suggest that the answers to these questions were respectively negative and positive. But this was not invariably the case. Decades of exile and nostalgia worked their effect upon, among others, Alexander Kerensky. He came to "lean on the church" whose rites consoled him, even if others disapproved of such backsliding.[69] Even Kurdiumov acknowledged that the church was important to *émigrés* as an emblem and link to Russia.[70] Whether or not they attended services regularly, participated in church affairs or felt anguish at its unedifying quarrels, they knew that it embodied, more than any other institution, a millennium of Russian history. And with the Soviet regime's continuing war on religion and the Russian past, culminating in the destruction in 1931 of Moscow's cathedral of Christ the Saviour, it seemed to most *émigrés* quite natural to stress Orthodoxy and anti-Bolshevism as essential components of genuine Russian patriotism. Furthermore, religion provided a barrier to the refugees' too rapid absorption into French life. This feature was particularly important to the postrevolutionary elements, especially Eurasianism, which attracted younger exiles who were disillusioned with their parents' political creeds and felt rootless in the West.

Orthodox churches were natural centres of Russianness, sanctuaries where a refugee's links to his native land were most apparent. Grandest of all was, and is, the Alexander Nevsky cathedral in Paris, a few steps from the clamour of the Champs-Élysées. Built in the 1860s with financial contributions from Alexander II and wealthy members of the resident Russian colony, its five golden cupolas dominate a corner of what still seems to be old Russia, rather than the heart of the French capital. The impression is much the same in the Russian corners of Nice, Cannes and, most strongly, at Sainte-Geneviève-des-Bois, forty kilometres south of Paris. Here, on land donated by an English benefactress, were built a retirement home for elderly Russians, a small, blue domed church, and a cemetery where tens of thousands of refugees have found their final rest. Their ranks include some of the greatest names of the nation's immediate pre-Soviet past; no spot in Europe evokes more powerfully the memory of old Russia. On a humbler scale churches and chapels proliferated wherever Russians settled, prompting Zinaida Shakhovskaia to write that no emigration in history had built so many.[71]

Churches require priests. The Orthodox Theological Institute, founded in Paris in 1925, existed in part to meet this need. It had associated with it eminent exile figures such as the philosophers VV. Zenkovsky and Father Sergei Bulgakov: their pupils went out to all corners of the Russian refugee world.[72] The impulse was pastoral and national. In Asnières, for example, on the capital's grimy northern edge, an Orthodox priest arrived in 1931 to minister to Russians there. He had, we are told, seventy-five centimes in his pocket. Five years later he had a church and his budget exceeded 40,000 francs. Hard, unremitting toil was the essential ingredient; small wonder that a British observer concluded in 1937 that "it is certainly no sinecure being a priest in the [Russian] emigration."[73] For *émigrés* anxious to preserve links to Russia and a Russian condition for themselves and their children, the priest, and the church he served, offered far more than any politician.[74]

CULTURAL ACTIVITIES

On 6 June 1926 Vasily Maklakov addressed a large group of distinguished Russians gathered at the Sorbonne. The day was the anniversary of Alexander Pushkin's birth; for that reason it had been selected the year before as an appropriate day annually to celebrate the glories of Russian culture. It was, Maklakov insisted, an occasion for rejoicing by the entire emigration. No other day, no other name could unite them so well. Separated now from Russia and living as stateless persons with many differences between them, they were nevertheless at one with each other and with those still in Russia in venerating their country's most national poet. The former ambassador contrasted Pushkin's intense humanity to the currently fashionable "superstition" of the omnipotent state. In Soviet Russia that state threatened Russian culture. It remained the emigration's vital task to protect and develop that culture, acquainting the world with its achievements. But Maklakov saw dangers in the emigration too. To begin with, émigrés were vulnerable to a host of outside, alien pressures. Moreover, if the culture they defended remained a purely émigré phenomenon, it could not expect to survive the first exile generation. Younger writers and artists would either return to Russia or fuse with Europe. But if those now abroad took care to preserve their nationality, the danger that they might not prove equal to their responsibility was less menacing. They would not be foreigners in a post-Bolshevik Russia, in spite of its certain differences to the country they had once known.[75]

The dean of the Russian community spoke at a moment when, in the words of P.N. Miliukov, the emigration stood at a crossroads. Miliukov meant the term politically; behind his metaphor was his hope that the hitherto conservative émigré mass might turn from outworn dreams of "a spring campaign" toward his own Republican-Democratic Association.[76] No rush of converts took place then or ever, but the exile dilemma was real enough. They were not going back in triumph; the Soviets were powerful, recognized and united; the emigration was weak, poor and divided. What purpose did it serve? Maklakov's remarks were addressed to these doubts.

His speech emphasized four central convictions. Russian culture mattered vitally; the Soviet regime could not protect it, but indeed was bent upon that culture's destruction; the émigré intelligentsia must take up the responsibility, resisting alien cultural pressures and the loss of contact with Russia; this commitment would preserve their nationality and make them useful to a later Russia freed from Bolshevism.

The culture that was of such importance to the older intelligentsia had both wide and narrow definitions. In a general sense it meant the achievements over past centuries of the creative Russian mind and hand. Together they had given the nation its identity. They included language, religion, and artistic and scientific accomplishments of every sort. More particularly, the term referred to literature and poetry of the nineteenth and early twentieth centuries, the spoken and written word whose free expression was now impossible inside Russia. To make up for this enforced silence in a manner worthy of the great traditions of the past became the intelligentsia's essential, self-imposed task. It was their duty to Russia and, equally, to the European culture that had given them much and received much in return.[77] They had little else. "For those of us who have lost our country," wrote Dmitry Merezhkovsky, "Russian literature is our final homeland, everything that Russia was and that Russia will be."[78]

Prose and poetry have remained for succeeding generations of Russian exiles central to their sense of identity and purpose. No little energy has gone into demonstrating this fact. Liudmila Foster's massive bibliography lists in over twelve hundred pages the contributions made to Russian letters by writers who were driven out of Russia or who refused to return there during the first half-century of Soviet rule.[79] In the first emigration the vital importance of Russia's literary culture found its most vigorous expression in the seventy volumes of *Sovremennia zapiski*. Published between 1920 and 1940 at intervals that grew longer as exile lengthened, every blue-covered volume, each of some 500 pages, offered a resounding proof of the tenacity with which the editors pursued their initially stated goal of serving "above all the interests of Russian culture." Its creators took their inspiration from the "thick journals" of nineteenth-century Russian literature; it may be argued, however, that their own journal was superior in achievement to its predecessors.[80]

Five men got the new publication off the ground and formulated its basic ambitions. M.V. Vishniak, A.I. Gukovsky, V.V. Rudnev, N.D. Avksentiev, and I.I. Fondaminsky were all from the right wing of the Socialist Revolutionary party and had been members of the Constituent Assembly for the seventeen hours of its single session.[81] Following the Assembly's abrupt closure, the five struggled unavailingly against the prevailing tide and eventually made their way to Paris. There, amid other preoccupations, they agreed on the need to explore the reasons why the democratic values they cherished had gone down to such overwhelming defeat inside Russia. Thence followed the obligation, as they saw it, to defend abroad those same values on behalf of the oppressed Russian people. With an initial press run of 2,000 copies, the first issue proclaimed the editors' intention of meeting these several responsibilities.[82]

It is improbable that the political dimension of *Sovremennia zapiski's* mission made any converts. But to the editors the defence of "the democratic programme of March 1917" was, in the beginning at least, only marginally less compelling than the cultural role. Certainly this was true for Mark Vishniak, the journal's secretary, treasurer, principal editor (until 1938), historian, main contributor, and longest-lived defender. Other contributors found him unyielding in his convictions, "the last iconoclast, irreconcilable, disinclined to bow to anyone, always with his own opinion, always in a minority, displeased with himself, unhappy with others ... the very last of the last Romans."[83] Nina Berberova was harsher than Don Aminado in recording what she saw as Vishniak's "violent character, lack of restraint ... [and] unbearable personality," even as she recognized the clarity of his view of Soviet reality.[84] Perhaps the strain of producing numerous volumes year after year, never certain whether financial crisis would overwhelm them, served to sharpen his temper.[85]

In ranging Sovremenniia zapiski on the side of the February Revolution, the editorial board also insisted that the journal should not be seen as a militant political organ capable only of uniting a narrow band of fellow thinkers. It sought rather to be a nonparty organ of independent judgment, which would decisively reject ideological sectarianism and dogmatism.[86] This proved more than mere verbiage. The journal welcomed contributions from authors whose loyalties spanned most of the émigré political spectrum. Only those on the far right were automatically excluded; they in turn would hardly have wished to contribute to a publication that championed the February Revolution and had Jewish Socialists on its board. At no time could any reader have been unaware that the five editors (four after Gukovsky's suicide in 1925) were all Right SRs who in 1917–18 had been active in support of the Kerensky regime and of the Constituent Assembly. All the same, in the sense – far from usual in Russian journalistic history – that it opened its pages to opinions often sharply differing from those of its editors, Sovremenniia zapiski could indeed be described as nonparty. This feature never prevented the editors from registering disapproval of politically unorthodox articles. But they printed them.

Inside the covers readers found a rich selection. Two-thirds of the volume was devoted to prose and poetry from émigré writers both familiar and less well known. Then followed articles on a variety of topics: current politics and diplomacy, extracts from memoirs and biographies, religious and philosophical essays. The section "Culture and Life" presented shorter pieces, often review articles and essays on lighter themes. Finally came short reviews of books that were of special interest to Russian readers.

Two issues ten years apart can serve to illustrate this range, Volume 29, published in 1926, drew heavily from the older generation of émigré writers. The literary contributors included Boris Zaitsev, Ivan Bunin, Mark Aldanov, and Dmitry Merezhkovsky. Dovid Knut, a younger poet of the

Paris-based intelligentsia, contributed a short poem. Then came half a dozen essays by senior figures. V.V. Zenkovsky wrote on philosophical issues and N. S. Timashev on Soviet nationality questions, while Vishniak himself presented a thirty-two page analysis of the contemporary political scene. "Culture and Life" offered lengthy reviews by the poet Vladimir Khodasevich and philosopher Fedor Stepun of two new émigré journals, *Versty* (Versts)[87] and *Put* (The Way). Shorter pieces followed on the new Judaism, Pushkin's legacy, and the teetotal movement in American politics.

Ten years later volume 60 retained the same format; however, the younger poets and writers were now making their mark. Boris Zaitsev still led off the literary section, but then came a chapter from *Invitation to a Beheading*, a new novel by the outstanding prose writer among the younger men, Vladimir Nabokov, under the pen name Sirin. Two more literary pieces followed, one by Nina Berberova, the other by Georgy (Gaito) Gazdanov, both writers who began their careers in emigration. The sections devoted to political and historical commentary remained the preserve of the veterans: Miliukov, Maklakov, Vishniak, Berdiaev, Fedotov, and Rostovtsev. Their articles examined subjects on a broad front, ranging from the economy of the ancient Hellenistic world to the politics of oil. It may be presumed that younger writers had as yet nothing useful to say on these matters.

The volumes of *Sovremenniia zapiski* published in the 1930s make it clear that the editors took very seriously their responsibility to encourage talented younger writers, who before long would take over the charge of defending Russian cultural interests abroad. This was a major reason behind the creation of Ilia Fondaminsky's "circle": gatherings of émigré writers, would-be writers, their friends and hangers-on, of all ages, every second Monday in Fondaminsky's apartment on the avenue de Versailles. There every subject was fair game and no émigré group or viewpoint was excluded. Vassily Yanovsky's evocative memoir gives an affectionate portrait of these sessions. The participants' freedom to range over every topic they owed to the tradition of the city and country where they lived; it is to this tradition of artistic freedom that Yanovsky attributes many of the cultural accomplishments of the first emigration. Vladimir Nabokov, who himself accomplished much, was an early beneficiary of these literary occasions. Fondaminsky first invited him to submit his work to the journal in 1930; he then suggested he take part in the meetings of his "circle." At 130, avenue de Versailles, in what seemed "like a spiritual center for the culture of the Russian diaspora," Nabokov met the leading personalities of Russian exile letters.[88]

No one can seriously challenge Gleb Struve's judgement on *Sovremenniia zapiski* that "it is difficult to exaggerate [the journal's] significance in émigré literature."[89] It was not difficult, however, to detect a defensive note in that journal's several discussions of that literature's enduring reality. Could a Russian literature truly exist outside Russia? How long could it survive?

How did it relate to Soviet literature? Could writers in exile compose away from Russia? Seventy volumes of *Sovremenniia zapiski*, to say nothing of many separately published works, testify that the answers to at least the first and last of these questions are positive. In the case of the older generation's best known writer, Ivan Bunin, it has been strongly suggested that his work in exile is at least as good as, if not actually better than, his earlier prose written in Russia.[90] The questions persisted nonetheless. Georgy Adamovich, literary critic and poet, took them up in a probing article in 1932. He observed that *émigré* literature was, after all, not founded on the reality of Russia, but on memories of her. Its main preoccupation had been to hold on until better days. These had not come. But the writer's original high purpose remained to speak the truth as he saw it, rejecting "tactical" considerations. It was fortunate, to the francophile Adamovich, that most writers found themselves in France, a country with a refined literary culture. Its excellence could help intellectuals develop their own gifts and tastes, in contrast to the barbarity and literary pretentiousness evident in Soviet writing.[91]

Adamovich offered rather meagre consolation, though his words received powerful reinforcement the next year when Ivan Bunin was awarded the Nobel Prize for literature. Still, absence from Russia weighed heavily. Edward Brown has noted a major casualty: the loss, save within a purely *émigré* circle, of the Russian language from everyday life.[92] France's "refined literary culture," not to mention her language, pressed all around.[93] Conscious of this and of his own fragility, the exiled Russian writer had in effect three avenues open before him. He might doggedly pursue his vocation, continuing to write in Russian for a diminishing audience, facing material hardships, hoping all the while that his contribution to Russian letters would one day be recognized in Russia. Most of the older writers followed this road. Alternatively, the Russian poet and novelist abroad might move into a new language and win a readership in France, Britain, and America. Several of the younger literary figures did this, Nabokov, Shakhovskaia, and Berberova among them. Henri Troyat, who arrived in Paris in 1920 as Lev Tarasian, an eight-year-old child, grew up in French and Russian, though he writes only in the former language. He is thus, at his own insistence and by general recognition, a French novelist, not Russian. His two worlds nevertheless remain intimately linked. In 1938, when he received the Prix Goncourt for *L'Araigne*, he won, along with the plaudits of literary Paris, the congratulations of several prominent *émigré* writers: Merezhkovsky, Hippius, Bunin, Remizov. They, one or two generations older, wholly Russian in culture and sentiment, rejoiced for their young compatriot. But he still recalled, some forty years afterward, their evident sadness that their talents were deprived of a comparable audience. "It seemed to me," Troyat remarked to an interviewer in 1976, "that they illustrated the tragic problem of exiled intellectuals who ... torn from the mass of their compatriots ... had abruptly lost their reason for being."[94]

Writers reluctant to accept either of these alternatives might consider a third choice, return to Russia. Alexei Tolstoi took this course in 1923, heaping scorn on those he left behind.[95] A longing for Russia undoubtedly played a part in his decision, but at least as strong, in the view of his distant cousin and biographer, was the prospect of favoured treatment by Russia's new rulers.[96] He was not disappointed: the "Soviet count's" gamble paid off in spectacular fashion. Two contributors to *Sovremennïia zapiski*, the writer Alexander Kuprin and poet Marina Tsvetaeva, went back in 1937 and 1939 respectively. Loneliness, family pressures, disenchantment with *émigré* life, perhaps in Kuprin's case, "to die in Russia," brought about their fateful resolution.[97] Tsvetaeva's husband, a Soviet agent within the emigration, and their daughter, had preceded her back to Russia; she returned with their son. Tolstoi apart, not one of these former *émigrés* was to find much happiness or a long life in the USSR. Return to Russia was not, in fact, an answer acceptable to more than a thin scattering of *émigré* intellectuals. It seemed too much like surrender.

On the eve of his return to Soviet Russia, Alexei Tolstoi predicted to Ilia Ehrenburg that no literature would come out of the emigration.[98] He was wrong. But it was a literature, or, rather, a part of Russian literature, all but unknown to the Russian people at home. Furthermore, the emphasis that the *Sovremennïia zapiski* editors and others placed upon full cultural freedom, their insistence that the exiled intelligentsia served Russia by nurturing her culture in freedom abroad, are not self-evident truths to all those Soviet writers who, in their turn, later ran afoul of the authorities. Edward Brown draws attention to this point, one that the Westernized élite of the first emigration would have rejected out of hand. When he took up residence in France in 1973, the dissident Soviet writer Andrei Siniavsky stressed that it was "there, and not here," that would be found the source of the future renewal of Russian literature. Alexander Solzhenitsyn, for his part, has declared with characteristic finality that "not in the emigration, with its luxury of so-called free expression, has literature been successful, but in our homeland, stretched upon the rack."[99]

The extent to which, during the interwar years, *émigrés* not part of the literary intelligentsia were impressed by *Sovremennïia zapiski's* contents or sense of cultural mission must remain a matter of conjecture. The Turgenev library, another shrine of Russian culture in Paris, one the German occupiers would destroy, reported in 1933 that the journal was more widely read by library users than any other. This should cause no surprise, as it had no real rivals in the Russian periodical press. It is likely that the general reader preferred its lighter offerings to its more ponderous political and philosophical treatises. The library revealed, for instance, that the most frequently borrowed books in 1932–33 had been the works of John Galsworthy (the Nobel laureate in 1932), Edgar Wallace, and Jack London. Of works by Russian authors the favourites were the historical novels of Ilia Ehrenburg and Mark Aldanov. The latter, a frequent contributor to *Sovremennia zapiski* and politically close to its board, was the most widely read author over the previous few years. Then came the novels of Dostoevsky and Leo Tolstoi.[100]

The effort on behalf of Russian literature lay at the core of the struggle to maintain a Russian cultural identity abroad. But that campaign involved more than literature alone and, for all the key role played by *Sovremenniia zapiski*, it was waged on a wider stage than the ever dingier offices of that journal.

In 1971 Michèle Beyssac, a French student of the Russian community in her country, published a chronicle of the culturally significant events that had occurred within the Russian colony during the decade 1920–1930. Her 300 pages, drawn from the Paris Russian press, convey strongly two particular impressions. One is the zeal with which expatriate Russians laboured to maintain a high level of cultural activity so as to preserve a sense of national cohesion. What impresses equally is the extent of that effort over the decade and its many forms and expressions. Lectures, concerts, theatres, study groups, clubs, and societies of every sort were available to the interested Russian *émigré* in the Paris region and, to a lesser extent, on the Riviera. Literary groups were well represented.[101] So too was the academic world. Professors from Petrograd and Moscow lectured on themes from Russian history and philosophy. The Russian Popular University played a central part in this. It was founded in 1921 in Paris by a group of refugee academics in imitation of the Petrograd original. It professed two aims. The first sought to provide for "the education of Russian youth in Russian conditions," the second looked to the creation of "an intellectual centre for Russians caught in the hard material struggle of *émigré* life." Classes were conducted on a shoestring budget dependent on the fees of students who often could pay nothing. Technical courses were popular, especially automechanics for those who aspired to drive a taxi.[102] But the main thrust was toward bringing Russian history and literature to Russian audiences. In October 1924, for example, Professor M.L. Gofman went to the Restaurant Franco-Russe in Billancourt to address local Russians on the psychology of Pushkin's works and on the poet's place in Russian literature. Another occasion saw Gofman and D.M. Odinets, a constitutional historian, appear at the town hall of the sixth *arrondissement* to lecture Russians gathered there on the Decembrists.[103]

The Religious-Philosophical Academy, transferred from Berlin, was a second centre of intellectual proselytizing. It offered somewhat heavier fare than the Popular University. Its lecture schedule was dominated by N.A.

Berdiaev's courses on contemporary religious and philosophical questions.[104] His collaborators included B.P. Vysheslavtsev, Father Sergei Bulgakov, Anton Kartashev, and V.V. Zenkovsky. Of this distinguished company it was Berdiaev who became best known to a foreign readership through his several books, all widely translated. But among fellow Russians he was a lonely figure, generally unpopular because of his willingness to see certain virtues in Soviet Russia. In contrast, he was prepared to acknowledge very few merits in Western society or in the emigration.[105]

The financial resources needed to sustain all this activity came mainly from Russian individuals and organizations, notably from Zemgor. But they had help. Governments offered some assistance, while a major, indeed vital source of support was the American YMCA. The Association had involved itself in Russian relief work during the Civil War; this continued in the camps of Constantinople and the Balkans after the final White débâcle. Much of the aid effort focused on what its secretary Paul Anderson ("Pavel Frantsovich" to his Russian charges) called "student Christian work" among youths of the diaspora, who might otherwise lose a precious component of their nationality.[106] But older refugees benefitted too. Academic figures received indispensable aid from one particularly valued YMCA body, its press. This was created in Prague in 1921 with the express purpose of helping Russian refugees to preserve their religious culture in exile. The press moved to Berlin in 1923; two years later it established itself in Paris. Thereafter, under Anderson's direction and in collaboration with Berdiaev and Vysheslavtsev, the YMCA Press published over 200 Russian titles in history, philosophy, theology, and *belles-lettres*. Berdiaev and his colleagues in the Religious-Philosophical Academy, novelists such as Bunin, Aldanov, Zaitsev, Remizov, and several others saw their books in print thanks to the YMCA Press. Two journals, *Put* and *Novyi grad* (The New City), both of religious-philosophical content, owed their lifespan to the same generosity. The small establishment on the rue-de-la-Montagne-Sainte-Geneviève has remained the oldest, most important publisher of Russian books outside Russia. Its services to expatriate Russian culture have been incalculable.

In addition to its services to the *émigrés*, the educated Russian mind offered much to the exiles' hosts. P.E. Kovalevsky devoted the larger part of his research energies to compiling records of Russians who gave of their talents to the non-Russian world.[107] His lists are extensive. In the physical and social sciences, from astronomy to zoology by way of botany, history, metallurgy, physics, sociology, and a dozen other disciplines, Kovalevsky reminded or, more accurately, told Russians and foreigners of the large contribution made to world culture by Russians who left their country in the early years of Soviet power. Men such as the historians Georgy Vernadsky and Mikhail Karpovich, the sociologist Pitirim Sorokin, the philosophers Nikolai Berdiaev and Lev Shestov, the archeologist Mikhail Rostovtsev led a galaxy of brilliant intellectuals. In Paris five émigré scholars became members of the Institut de France.[108]

Russian scholarly achievements had their impact in Western laboratories, conferences, and academic journals, if not on the broad mass of the European and American publics. This contrasted with those other areas of Russian culture where linguistic and intellectual barriers did not exist to limit appreciation by outsiders. The arts, in particular music and the dance, spoke an international language. By no coincidence, it was the great names in these two art forms which won the widest recognition from non-Russians.

One of these favoured individuals was Fedor Chaliapin. He, with the ballerina Anna Pavlova, had the greatest international popularity of any Russian living in the West. In his unsatisfying autobiographical sketch *Man and Mask*, the great basso has something to say about why he left Russia after a brief attempt at coexistence with the Soviet regime. Constant interference by officious bureaucratic hacks, the vulgarization of his art and of culture generally, and tempting offers from abroad, together induced Chaliapin to leave in 1921 with help from the sympathetic Commissar of Education, Anatoly Lunacharsky.[109] In going abroad, Chaliapin resolved to devote himself to his art, shunning politics entirely. Unfortunately, as his memoirs make clear, he was entering a world where such self-denial was unknown. A declaration in the Russian press announced Chaliapin's arrival in Paris: "rats [were] leaving the sinking ship" of Bolshevism. Had not the singer departed with the co-operation of the authorities, as a band blared the Internationale? His eminence did not spare him from the customary speculation as to whether he was one of "us" or "them."[110] The cabaret singer Alexander Vertinsky wrote of seeing leaflets calling on loyal Russians to boycott performances by Chaliapin.[111] In any case, whatever the suspicions entertained in the 1920s, the great singer's death in 1938 devastated an already much depleted community.[112]

If the term "Russian culture" evoked any image at all in Western minds, the first of these was, and probably still is, the dance. The debt that world ballet owes to émigrés remains very real, a subject of legitimate pride to those like Sergei Lifar, who left Russia in a hemorrhage of dance talent for life and work in the West.[113] He became choreographer in Diaghilev's Ballets Russes, working with Igor Stravinsky, Georgy Balanchivadze and others of scarcely lesser gifts. Diaghilev's innovative genius had an especially profound impact; in 1966, in symbolic acknowledgement of the debt, his name was given to a small square behind the Paris Opéra, at the heart of musical France. After Diaghilev's death in 1929 his company scattered to carry his techniques to the world. Lifar moved to the Paris Opéra, a few years later Stravinsky and Balanchivadze (now Georges Balanchine) moved to the United States. Then there were the incomparable dancers from pre-war days: Pavlova, Kshesinskaia (married to a Romanov), Preobrazhenskaia, Karsavina, all of whom inspired their successors with Russian standards and traditions. No other facet of Russian cultural creativity could marshal a comparable roster. It is surely here that the national culture made, and continues to make, its deepest impression upon the non-Russian world.

In surveying the names and activities presented by Beyssac and Kovalevsky, it is impossible to accept without challenge the frequent Soviet assertion that away from Russia the creative Russian mind is doomed to sterility and slow death. Some members of the literary intelligentsia feared this prospect, it is true, and literature always remains vulnerable. In other areas, however, the claim is demonstrably false. Igor Stravinsky, Sergei Kusevitsky, and Sergei Rakhmaninov, to name three eminent examples from music, had major reputations by 1914, which they went on to expand substantially in the years of exile ahead. In so doing, they did not become significantly less Russian than, say, Sergei Prokofiev, whose return to the USSR in 1932 prompted a Soviet biographer to exult at this proof that only in Soviet Russia could a Russian artist fully develop his art.[114] Certainly nostalgia for Russia was an ever present reality. Alexander Vertinsky, who returned to the USSR after World War II, made much of his homesickness in his account to Soviet readers of life in exile. Chaliapin and Karsavina both apparently confided in him their intense longing for Russia; even Pavlova told him how cold and alien she found England.[115] Just why, with such feelings, they did not follow Prokofiev and Alexei Tolstoi and go home, Vertinsky does not say. He himself evidently missed Paris greatly when he looked back later on his life in "that astonishing city." "One could not forget it, dislike it, or prefer another city to it, he assured his Soviet readers.[116]

Russians in France, as throughout the diaspora, could pride themselves on the artistic and intellectual accomplishments of their countrymen abroad. Insofar as anything brought them together, these did. To be a compatriot of Chaliapin and Pavlova was no mean thing. It was a condition much more likely to induce benevolent feelings in foreigners, to say nothing of a sense of common values among Russians, than did the knowledge of a nationality shared with Miliukov or Markov II. As the emigration neared the end of its second decade, *Vozrozhdenie's* assertive reporter, Lev Liubimov, felt that the French public ought to be reminded of some of this and of what it owed its Russian guests. He proceeded to give a list, less comprehensive than Kovalevsky's, in a seventy-five minute radio broadcast on New Year's Day 1939. His chronicle included the great names of literature and the arts, the world chess champion A.A. Alekhin, and V.N. Iurkevich, a member of the design team of the transatlantic liner *Normandie*.[117] Liubimov's address suggests too that in his final years as a champion of *émigré* values, he had come to enjoy a degree of official recognition. Zinaida Shakhovskaia, a few years younger than Liubimov and no admirer, was also concerned to identify the features in exile of her nationality. She saw Russia "gathered in and around churches, eating borshch and cutlets, in cheap and expensive [Russian] restaurants ... dancing at balls that are somehow always disorderly, attending lectures, creating disturbances at political gatherings, preferring protest to academic discussion. [*Emigré* Russia] founds churches, schools, universities, scout troops and literary associations; she waits and hopes, [and] with scarcely a murmur puts up with every ordeal."[118] They would thus be ready, still Russian, when the signal to depart finally was given. But until then, young and old had to look around for some place where they could "dig themselves in" and come to terms in some measure with the facts of their life in France.

CHAPTER THREE

Life in France

In seeking asylum in France, the Russian refugees found they had taken up residence in a country and among a people very different from their own. From the first moment of arrival these differences made themselves evident in a hundred ways. Some were disconcerting, others wounding. S. Vladislavlev arrived in Paris in the spring of 1923; at once he noticed the contrasts. The Russian "broad nature," expansiveness, impatience with regulation, and openness to friends stood at a polar opposite to French formality, reticence, preference for the golden mean, complex social gradations, and love of privacy. He also found, as all Russians did sooner or later, that their country's tragedy, so utterly absorbing to them, had much softer echoes outside the Russian exile world. A sympathetic Spanish fellow refugee interrupted Vladislavlev's recitation of the latest Soviet outrages with his own particular anguish: had the Russian read of the frightful wave of terror in Peru? The question struck Vladislavlev like a cold shower. He went on to record his gloomy feelings at the incredulous response of a French neighbour to his description of Russian conditions: "but that is quite barbarous!". Russia was so remote; her trials seemed as exotic as earthquakes in China and South America to a sedate French bourgeoisie.[1] All the same, since representatives of that class were responsible for shaping the conditions of the *émigrés'* new life, their goodwill, or at least nonhostility, was a vital factor in determining the degree of security enjoyed by refugees in France. Taken as a whole, relations between French hosts and Russian guests were neither the bleakly repressive tale suggested by Soviet and Soviet-returned Russians, nor the triumph of liberty invoked, more rarely, in the West.

When it came into contact with the French world, the *émigrés'* life in France existed on two levels. One had to do with the world of officialdom: the men who made the decisions affecting the foreign community and below them the bureaucrats who carried their decrees into effect, along with individuals who might intervene advantageously with those in authority. A second, more pervasive level of contact was to be found in the French relationship with the *émigrés* on a more personal basis as employer, foreman, landlady, neighbour, customer, or fellow worker.

The ability to make representations to influential Frenchmen on matters of urgent *émigré* concern was a precious asset, easily depleted and available to very few. The whole question was, in fact, extremely delicate. V.A. Maklakov never forgot that he and his charges were guests in France, dependent on their hosts for protection and succour. His approaches to French officials tended to be diffident, even defensive; he was in any case disinclined by temperament to indulge in confrontations. Though more self-righteously combative, Miliukov was occasionally ready to remind his readers that they ought to stay out of domestic French concerns. This did not unduly inhibit him in his own criticisms of policies he judged wrong. In the early years of exile any rumour of a Franco-Soviet rapprochement sufficed to bring out his protests. In due course *Vozrozhdenie* weighed in with ever sharper attacks, as successive cabinets in Paris moved from defiance, through recognition, to alliance with the detested regime in Moscow. Still, even *Vozrozhdenie* advised Russians to hold back from involvement in contentious local issues. For both organs the expression evidently meant any French concern that did not possess the slightest Russian dimension.

In the first phase of exile the public question which absorbed more *émigré* attention than any other, and which undeniably had the broadest Russian dimension of crucial importance to the refugees, was European recognition of the government responsible for their outcast condition. Using every lever at their command, the diplomats and politicians of old Russia struggled to prevent an outcome which they, and probably all *émigrés*, knew must be a lethal blow to confidence in the prospects for a non-Bolshevik Russia. Their complete failure forced the Russian community to face up to the fact of their powerlessness, as well as to a decisive new stage in their life in France.

On 25 November 1920, as Wrangel's legions streamed into the refugee camps of Constantinople and Gallipoli, a senior member of the Kadet party, Maxim Vinaver, issued a warning to colleagues gathered together with him in Paris. The danger now confronted them, he observed, of an Allied recognition of the victorious Bolsheviks. This would clearly be against the interests of National Russia. The emigration, or a substantial portion of it, must unite around a body which could defend these interests. Europe, he insisted, expected and desired no less of them, though the step would be very difficult.[2] Objections were immediate. Iu.V. Kliuchnikov, soon to proclaim, in the Change of Landmarks movement, an *émigré* heresy favourable to the Soviet regime, rejected all thought of rallying around the "human dust" of Wrangel's army. His epithet and the furore it provoked in his audience emphasized how remote unity was.[3] Meanwhile, the threat of recognition remained.

Powerless to affect decisions they saw as vital to Russia's future and to their own, *émigrés* in the West were limited to observer status in the recognition debates. Their only weapons were propaganda and warnings against doing business with the Bolsheviks. Had not Moscow's rulers already betrayed the Allies and Russia at Brest-Litovsk? How could anyone, even Lloyd George, think that dealings with Lenin's band might be profitable? In any event, his illegal regime was doomed. Its successor, soon to be in place, would not honour any commitment made by the Bolsheviks in Russia's name. The meeting in January 1921 of available Constituent Assembly members elaborated a series of resolutions incorporating these sentiments, which undoubtedly corresponded to overwhelming *émigré* opinion.[4]

The Anglo-Soviet commercial accord of 16 March 1921 was the first fall of pebbles heralding the avalanche of recognition. *Posledniia novosti's* new editor dwelt bitterly on the British eagerness to do business with the Bolsheviks over the corpses of the Kronstadt garrison, which had sacrificed itself for Russia's freedom.[5] Paying no attention to Miliukov's distress, the German, Norwegian, and Italian governments hastened to follow the British example. With the Soviets gradually moving away from the status of international pariah, *émigré* political leaders took comfort from French slowness to follow the lead from London. Two commanding figures on the French political stage of the early twenties, Aristide Briand and Raymond Poincaré, gave proof of heartening soundness on the subject of Russia. Poincaré, it is true, wondered aloud while out of office at the wisdom of allowing other states to get ahead of France in commercial dealings with Moscow – "hesitation is not a policy!"[6] – yet he did not change Briand's hard line upon becoming premier himself for the second time in January 1922. The distance maintained between Paris and Moscow had nothing to do with *émigré* protests,[7] but it suited their purposes well enough.

In 1922 two international conferences, one in Genoa, the other at the Hague, proved particularly trying to *émigré* nerves. Among the governments invited to discuss questions of European economic reconstruction was the one then ruling Russia.[8] *Émigré* politicians found this a portentous omen and mobilized their energies against it.[9] The meetings went ahead anyway. Though Russian issues and Soviet representatives played a large role in the two diplomatic encounters, no satisfactory solution emerged to the vexatious question of war debts, nor were Anglo-French hopes fulfilled of doing business with a "reasonable" Russian government. The most momentous news was, without a doubt, the thunderbolt on 17 April from Genoa that the two outcasts of Europe, defeated Germany and Bolshevik Russia, had met the day before at the Soviet residence in Rapallo to sign their diplomatic agreement. While the Allies erupted in angry speeches and editorials, Russian *émigré* attentions were fixed with equal intensity on other, related matters. When Soviet foreign commissar G.V. Chicherin arrived at the conference attired in a top hat and frock coat and then proceeded to deliver a cogent speech in French, the effect was distinctly reassuring to foreigners who had anticipated the uncouth Bolshevik savage of cartoon legend. Was this not another step toward respectability?[10] Ex-ambassador M.N. de Giers thought not. Through that spring and summer he kept in touch with Russian diplomats still at their posts, as he urged a coordinated propaganda effort and warned against a mass descent on Genoa. His agents sent back a mixed set of impressions. King Victor Emmanuel met the delegates and, so it was reported, conversed longer with Chicherin than with the other representatives.[11] Curiosity in high places was general. Giers heard that the Soviet visitors were objects of great interest, like some exotic marvel (*dikovinka*).[12] Their reception was cooler in the Hague. Queen Wilhelmina absented herself; the mayor "did not think it necessary to make the acquaintance of the Soviet delegation," nor was the Soviet flag flown over their hotel.[13] Noting these omissions and the lack of concrete results, Russian diplomats congratulated themselves that these first ventures of the Soviet regime on the international stage had been a failure.[14] That the Soviets assigned the blame for this mainly to Poincaré's stubbornness gave *émigrés* one more reason to esteem him above all other French politicians.[15]

On the face of things, the French government in 1922 seemed the least susceptible to pressures for recognition. Poincaré's *Bloc national*, resolutely anti-Bolshevik, retained a firm grip on power; President Millerand won Maklakov's private thanks for a public endorsement of the cabinet's hostility toward Moscow.[16] Soviet repudiation of Russia's debts encouraged strong anti-Soviet feelings among middle-class holders of now worthless tsarist bonds. But the shadows loomed. No government in the Third Republic could count on a lengthy tenure, even though Poincaré's second administration gave intimations of immortality by lasting over two years. Legislative elections were due in the spring of 1924 and it required no foresight to judge that Franco-Soviet relations might well play a role in the campaign. In the closing months of 1922 one political personality in particular moved to the forefront of those demanding a more realistic French policy toward the Soviet republic. This was Edouard Herriot, mayor of Lyons, its senior parliamentary representative, leader of the Radical party in the Chamber of Deputies, eloquent orator and writer, and *bête noire* of a large section of the Paris-based "active" emigration.

As early as January 1921 Herriot spoke out on the folly of French policy toward Soviet Russia. He kept up his criticisms through 1921 and 1922, as he insisted to the Chamber that, instead of snubs, France should extend her hand to Russia and help her to her feet. The mere suggestion set off pandemonium. Deputies of left and right screamed abuse at each other, forcing the session's temporary suspension.[17] Herriot's challenge came as a warning shot to his first major offence to *émigré* sensitivities on the subject of Franco-Soviet relations. In the late summer of 1922, accompanied by a party colleague, Edouard Daladier, Herriot journied to Russia to see things for himself. On his return he published an account of his impressions. In both excursion and book the mayor of Lyons set a style that would distress Russians in exile almost more than any other feature of their refugee life.

Herriot's trip to Soviet Russia in 1922 lasted a month. He visited Moscow, Petrograd, and Nizhnyi Novgorod. He met several Soviet notables: Trotsky, Kamenev, and Krasin, but not Lenin, then convalescing. He sent back articles for *Le Petit Parisien* that were in no way profound. He spoke not a word of Russian and had only the most superficial acquaintance with Russia's history. He returned to inform his countrymen about the new Russia, seeking "neither to flatter, nor to criticize, [but to] observe."[18] Whatever his intentions, however, Russians in France had no difficulty in seeing an excessive degree of flattery and far too little criticism in the Frenchman's comments on their country's government.

As he was completing his book about his voyage, Herriot gave his critics a taste of what he was going to say and a chance to rebut his arguments. Twice in November 1922 the Radical party chief addressed meetings attended by French and Russian political figures. His theme on these occasions was "Russia's present condition." Disclaiming any wish to discuss the merits of the Soviet regime, he proceeded to do precisely that, striding confidently across the minefield of *émigré* susceptibilities. He began by admitting there were features of the Soviet state which made the system unacceptable in France. These included the Soviet failure properly to separate legislative and executive powers or to provide for true liberty of thought. But positive signs were not lacking. The peasant was doing well under Lenin's New Economic Policy (N.E.P.). The "Russian government" [sic] had evolved and would continue to do so. Herriot found no trace of communism in Russia. The country resembled France under the Directory, as a new bourgeoisie emerged from revolutionary chaos. While industry was still in ruins and famine evident, the worst was over. Money was more plentiful, and Herriot, a veteran anti-clerical republican, ascribed this happy circumstance in part to the fact that the nation no longer needed to spend large sums on the imperial household or the church. The regime was stable: all Moscow observers agreed on that. Hence the speed with which other countries were becoming financially and economically involved with the Soviets, leaving France far behind. This injured the national interest. Trade contacts must be established at once, without anyone needing to worry about legal fine points or recognition. All that was the business of lawyers, Herriot soothingly advised.[19]

Comment from the Russians in his audience reflected their bitterness at Herriot's credulity. The lawyer A.A. Pilenko, who taught Soviet law at the Sorbonne, rose "as one of the Russians who did not sign Brest-Litovsk." He warned against French hopes of doing business with the Soviets under conventional legal protections. These did not exist. V.A. Maklakov also spoke with a guarded intensity. He would not comment on the policy France should adopt in Russian questions: that was for the French to decide. He doubted that the Bolsheviks could defend Russian interests at international conferences. They had not done so at Brest-Litovsk or Riga. They could not be serious allies, the Red Army was for parade purposes only. As for the stability of the regime, was not Lenin's government a decomposing entity doomed to fall, "even though we cannot predict the date of its collapse nor how it will happen?" No error was possible on this point. Herriot's other claims were equally erroneous. Soviet terror, class war, debt cancellation, and the absence of all law testified to the enduring reality of communism in Russia. It could only continue to survive with foreign help. The peasants had not greatly benefitted from the revolution; they had no share in the central power. Maklakov welcomed evidence that new life was developing inside his country. This would assist the process of internal evolution, as the Communist party dissolved.[20] Miliukov seconded his compatriots' reservations, adding his own. As his denunciations mounted, so too did his indignation to the point where he came close to accusing Herriot of lying. The no less volatile mayor reminded his audience that he had already done much for Russians in France, for intellectuals in particular. He knew his moral duty, "but I am not always certain that Mr Miliukov has always defended French interests."[21] The ironic reference to the Kadet leader's disastrous flirtation with the Germans was not lost on his hearers. Miliukov probably remained unrepentant. It is likely that Maklakov suffered the most during the exchange. It contained everything he most tried to avoid in his contacts with important Frenchmen.

Not long afterward Herriot published his book on the new Russia. Thanks to its author and subject, it sold well. The book announced the death of old Russia: religious, submissive, and peasant-oriented. The revolution, responsible for its end, had destroyed much, yet it was an event inseparable from Russian history. It had caused new forces to be born from a long oppressed people. By now, however, Communist ideology was largely irrelevant. Soviet Russia was at the stage of state capitalism, but "there are a hundred shades of red and a hundred different ways to wear them."[22] Europe and Russia needed each other. Intervention had been a mistake; what was wanted now was trade. The French and Russian republics must be reconciled. Otherwise other nations, Germany not the least among them, would solidly entrench themselves.[23]

Herriot's trip, articles, speeches, and book did more to familiarize Soviet

Russia's cause in France than did the efforts of any other individual French-man. His confident judgments about Russia old and new were among the first in an eventual flood of commentary on the subject from a wide variety of foreign observers. Very little of it was to give comfort to Bolshevism's Russian enemies in exile. Neither in 1922 nor in the two decades thereafter did they manage to mount an effective response to which significant numbers of non-Russians paid attention.[24] Herriot's labours were symptomatic in tone and result. The book was influential and his pleas in favour of normal, businesslike relations produced echoes in unlikely places. The commercial lure, so hotly denied by the émigrés, impelled even Joseph Noulens, the last French ambassador in Russia, fierce anti-Bolshevik, and chairman of the French bondholders association, to suggest that Poincaré dispatch a trade mission to Russia.[25] He got no immediate reaction, but pressures were clearly building that the émigrés could not match. A collection of essays on the recognition issue, published in 1923, signalled the way the wind was blowing. They were written by French and Russian authors and offered arguments for and against recognition. One contribution put the case in favour in frank, even brutal terms. The writer, Senator Anatole de Monzie, was one of Herriot's close political associates and in less than a year would be entrusted by the mayor of Lyons, newly elected as premier, to arrange the details of the recognition procedure. He went over to the offensive. "Is it asking too much," de Monzie inquired, "that we should wish to discuss Franco–[Soviet] Russian relations between Frenchmen, motivated solely by their concern for French interests, without the indiscreet interference of the Russian refugee party or parties in France?" De Monzie admitted he was "cynical" enough to believe that the émigrés' cause was not a French one, "and France has no debts to tsarism or the Kadets." The attacks on him in *Posledniia novosti* were annoying and, in fact, "the Russian emigration [was] becoming ever more active and imperious."[26] His dismissive tone brushed aside major Russian services in the Great War but de Monzie was not a man to dwell on the past when the future beckoned so imperatively.

Some, like de Monzie, might consider that the Russians in France were becoming unduly intrusive, but they had no role in the recognition debate other than that of an outside, intensely interested party. Miliukov admitted as much in a lengthy editorial early in 1924. European recognition of Soviet Russia was now at hand. Italy and Great Britain would, he thought, be the first to move toward Moscow; other states would follow. Their number might include France, especially if the issue became a trump card in the hands of the left bloc in the forthcoming elections. Again he rehearsed the reasons why democratic Russian opinion opposed recognition of "an illegal, non-national government." It would give an appearance of legality to acts of the newly respectable Soviet regime. These acts were dangerous and harmful to the Russian people. But émigrés did not despair. If foreign powers were not now convinced of the case against recognition, they would become so in time, even those now acting in the name of realism.[27]

Over the next ten months the scenario unfolded much as Miliukov foresaw. British and Italian recognition of the USSR came in early February; in France even Poincaré publicly softened his stance on the recognition issue.[28] More importantly, the *Cartel des Gauches* coalition under Herriot committed itself in its electoral programme to establishing full diplomatic relations with the USSR. The details would be determined in due course. The coalition's victory on 11 May removed the *émigrés'* hopes of a last-minute miracle; their disappointment was compounded a month later with the removal from office of President Millerand. It only remained for the new government to formalize the new diplomatic arrangements and in the wake of this to determine the legal status of the Russian community in France. Committees under de Monzie and Yves Delbos concerned themselves with these matters, while *Posledniia novosti* reported every rumour of difficulties in the way of Franco-Soviet relations.[29]

With recognition "inevitable and necessary,"[30] it was time that the refugees began thinking about their future in France. Desultory discussions had been going on under Maklakov's aegis since March, which produced the usual arguments between right and left. Should there be a representative exile body? If so, what powers should it have and what kind of political character might it possess? The right was generally in favour of a strong central agency capable of imposing some direction; the left dismissed any such notions. *Posledniia novosti* saw a representative organization as useful, but it was absurd to think that it might have legislative powers or a uniform political coloration. The French would never allow it, nor would the *émigré* world as a whole recognize it. Its function should be limited to business matters, to the day to day needs of the Russians in France, and to making their views known to the appropriate French officials.[31] The newspaper noted, rather sourly, the growth of pro-Soviet sentiments in the new government. Mark Aldanov conceded that, "as Europeans," Russian democrats might welcome the defeat of French right-wing parties. They had no reason to suppose, however, that Herriot, ever naive about Russia, would be particularly accommodating toward the exiles.[32]

Vasily Maklakov inevitably bore the brunt of *émigré* concern at impending French recognition of the USSR. Nervous rumours swept the Russian colony that recognition would mean the wholesale repatriation of Russians in France, or that they would be forced to choose between French and Soviet citizenship. Herriot soothed these fears and in fact displayed no little tact in his audiences with agitated exiles.[33] His government did reserve one heavy blow until the very moment of recognition in late October. Maklakov had always assumed, or hoped, that when recognition came, he would be able to hand the embassy over to French bureaucrats, thus sparing himself the unbearable necessity of having to deal directly with the representatives of the new order in Moscow. On 27 October he learned that the Quai d'Orsay refused to play any part in the building's transfer. This was a matter to be settled between Russians. [34] Maklakov was thus obliged, to his intense annoyance, to vacate the premises at 76, rue de Grenelle in something of a rush in order not to meet the incoming Soviet team headed by Leonid Krasin. With the building newly cleaned and its contents inventoried, Maklakov held a final mass, rolled up the Russian tricolor, rejected a suggestion that he save the embassy silver from the building's new owners, and paid his last official call at the foreign ministry. [35] His second career was over. His third, as defender of Russian exiles and their intermediary with those in authority, stretched ahead.

Acknowledging that "a new stage" had been reached in the emigration's existence, *Posledniia novosti*'s editor reminded his countrymen in France, five days after the Franco-Soviet exchange of telegrams, that their "all-national task" remained paramount. They must still stand for Russia's liberation from usurpers and bandits, and for the defence of that part of Russian culture, Russian knowledge and Russian free, independent thought, separated from the homeland but not destroyed by exile. What Miliukov termed the emigration's "general ... international significance" also endured. The existence and steady expansion abroad of a Russian refugee community testified to the real nature of Soviet power. "The time will come," he prophesied, "when the evidence will be accepted, when Western nations will realize [the nature of] the Soviet regime and grasp the phenomenon of the Russian emigration; when it will become clear that, just as in olden times when Russia absorbed the Asiatic invasion, protecting European culture, so now, in taking upon herself the Bolsheviks, she gives the West time to strengthen itself after the war and [time] to study the sickness born in the bloody chaos of world conflict." In the meantime *émigrés* hoped that the French would still see in their community that portion of the Russian people which had sacrificed everything in the name of its ideal and quit its native land, rather than be reconciled to its conquerors. [36]

Eventual justification was one thing, but the contemporary reality was another. As European powers competed to present official greetings to Moscow, the hope of final vindication assumed less importance for *émigrés* than their own immediate future. A legal statute formally defining their collective identity and rights was the ideal solution, but it was one that the Herriot government showed no eagerness to adopt. [37] At Delbos's prompting, Maklakov had presided over the formation, earlier that summer, of an *émigré* committee on refugee affairs, composed of representatives from a wide spectrum of Russian organizations. [38] Six of the committee's nine members were chosen from a "Committee of United Organizations," conservative and monarchical in allegiance, chaired by a devoted servant of the last tsar, Count V.N. Kokovtsev. The three remaining members represented minority democratic opinion, gathered together in a "Council of Public Organizations," presided over by Alexander Konovalov, Kadet minister of trade and industry in the first and last cabinets of the Provisional Government.[39] The joint committee's creation was, on paper, a step forward, but, given the sterile record of the past, only the most blindly optimistic émigré could have expected fruitful collaboration from its disparate elements. Its chairman would obviously play a crucial role; Maklakov was the leading, but not universally applauded candidate. He was, in fact, unenthusiastic about taking on the post and refused to do so if he were to be held accountable to an exile "parliament." This was not to be the case. The French government knew him and wished to continue working with him in Russian refugee matters. This was the key factor in inducing Maklakov to take on the responsibility.[40] His discretion and many contacts within French officialdom were the emigration's principal asset in its subsequent dealings with the host nation.

The refugees' legal position in France certainly required clarification. Soviet decrees of November and December 1921 had deprived anti-Bolshevik Russians abroad of their Russian citizenship, officially rendering them stateless (apatrides). The so-called Nansen passport, devised the following summer, was designed to confer upon them some form of internationally recognized identity and to permit them to cross borders legally, if they could get the requisite visas. Within individual countries the regulations were, of course, up to the host government. In France, before recognition of the USSR, courts applied tsarist Russian codes in civil cases between Russians in accordance with prerevolutionary agreements between the two countries.[41] With some exceptions, this remained true even after the disappearance of the tsarist and provisional governments and their replacement by a regime deeply hostile to French juridical procedures.[42] After recognition the authorities admitted the new reality to the point where they sequestered some Russian property, including churches.[43] The act caused consternation, but it may have been a precautionary measure to forestall any Soviet assertion of control in the days after Leonid Krasin moved into the rue de Grenelle.

The government moved slowly to correct these anomalies. A Ministry of Justice circular of 28 April 1925 established that all civil cases between Russians commenced since the previous 28 October would be settled according to French law, while tsarist codes would continue to be applied in cases underway before that date.[44] This latter category evidently included some contentious issues, for three years later a conservative émigré lawyer was still arguing that the invocation of tsarist law in French tribunals was absurd and should be completely abandoned.[45] The government also decided to invest Maklakov's émigré committee with a degree of legal personality. Instructions from the Interior Ministry to departmental prefects of 4 March and 9 May 1925 laid down that the "Central Office on Russian Refugee Affairs" (*Office central des réfugiés russes*) might intervene on behalf of stateless Russians before bureaucratic bodies and present attestations to which weight might officially be given (*dignes de foi*). This was a promising start, but a further five years were required before such opinions acquired legally binding effect in cases involving the *émigrés* in France and another six years beyond that until French ratification was completed of a League convention guaranteeing equal treatment of refugees and citizens of signatory countries.[46]

Strangers in another's land need highly placed friends to help smooth their difficult new path. Maklakov's contacts certainly helped a good deal, but his approaches were necessarily behind the scenes. Other patrons were more public. Inevitably, given the emigration's political origins, most French politicians and journalists who took up the Russian exiles' cause were firmly identified with the anticommunist right. This held true for the entire interwar period. A gala "Franco-Russian evening" at the Trocadéro in March 1935 found a representative company on full display. The occasion was lovingly recorded by *Vozrozhdenie*. Senator Gustave Gautherot presided over the celebration. A staunch conservative, "his convictions made him an ardent defender of order and traditional moral values," to cite the discreet words of his parliamentary biography.[47] He and the right-inclined political emigration were natural allies. A second senator, Henry Lémery, also attended. Representing Martinique in the upper chamber, he was from the conservative wing of the Radical-Socialists, a critic of the Soviet Union and of a foreign policy which relied unduly upon that state. In 1938 he took on the chairmanship of the newly founded Society of Friends of National Russia (*Société des amis de la Russie Nationale*) and was a proven source of aid to Russians in difficulties.[48] So too was the deputy Edouard Soulier, a former Protestant minister and member of Poincaré's *Bloc national*. Other guests included Joseph Noulens, the historian and politician Gabriel Hanotaux, two veteran generals of the Great War, Castelnau and Gamelin, and half a dozen deputies from the moderate and far right. The Russian contingent included two grand dukes, the Metropolitan Evlogy, Count Kokovtsev, and Maklakov. Speeches from both sides evoked prerevolutionary amity and paid tactful tribute to *émigré* stoicism in the face of present hardships.[49]

Conservative-nationalist *émigrés* reserved their warmest accolades for those Frenchmen who saw the Bolshevik menace most clearly, recognized the corresponding virtues of the Russian national cause abroad, and were able to offer it material encouragement. Four political grandees found special favour: Georges Clemenceau, Raymond Poincaré, Alexandre Millerand, and André Tardieu. The first, known to his admirers as The Tiger, was respected for his patriotism and inextinguishable scorn for the men who had signed the Brest-Litovsk peace.[50] The second and third, as premier and president, permitted the influx into France of anti-Bolshevik Russian refugees. Under Poincaré Paris became the capital of Russia Abroad.[51] Millerand, for his part, much disliked the Soviets and led an eventually successful legal effort to recover title to the properties sequestered by the Herriot government in 1924.[52] Tardieu was premier in January 1930 and May 1932, two bad moments in Franco-émigré relations. Moreover, he cast the sole negative vote in the Chamber of Deputies when it ratified the Franco-Soviet nonaggression pact of 1932.[53] A trio of valued allies came from the world of journalism. Jean Delage, Charles Ledré, and André Deuolor wrote at sympathetic length about the Russian colony in France and its ideals.

Friends on the left half of the political spectrum were understandably scarcer. Communist loathing of all Russian anti-Bolsheviks was only to be expected; men in Socialist and Radical ranks were ambivalent. On the one hand, the shrill anti-Soviet invective of the right-wing press provoked exasperation, nor was there much sympathy for the idea of a National Russia in exile. On the other hand, the two most notorious members of the political emigration, P.N. Miliukov and A.F. Kerensky, stood on amicable terms with the moderate left. In January 1930 the two men were invited to the Palais-Bourbon to address interested members of the Radical-Socialist and other groups on Stalin's forced collectivization campaign. Their condemnation of it was complete; their impact probably less so. An expression of thanks referred to "the need and intention" of the parliamentary party to study the Russian situation more fully in the light of "the moving declarations" made by their two guests. On his way out, Kerensky crossed swords with one French politician who clearly had not been moved. Marcel Cachin, a prominent Communist deputy from Paris, admitted no difficulties in the USSR other than "a discontent in certain landowners, otherwise known as kulaks, ... which perhaps has taken the form of some inclination toward revolt, strictly limited to a few villages." He invited the two Russians to produce documentary proofs of their contrary assertions at a public meeting he planned in Paris. The invitation was declined.[54]

The single most effective and hard working French intermediary on the émigrés' behalf came from the moderate Socialist ranks. This was Marius Moutet, a staunch member of the League for the Rights of Man, a pacifist, who later served in the Popular Front government and at all times remained an indefatigable champion of foreign minorities in France. He had visited Russia in 1917 with the official mission to stiffen the Socialist will to stay in the war; he owed a friendship with Kerensky to that occasion. He often intervened to assist troubled refugees and became an especially valued ally as the Depression began to bite. Pressures grew to reduce the number of alien workers in the labour market; foreign refugees, with no government to protect them, were vulnerable here. Moutet frequently accompanied members of Maklakov's committee on their pilgrimages to ministerial waiting-rooms, pleading for exemptions in the various draconian measures being devised to meet the emergency.[55] He spoke up in the Chamber and elsewhere in defence of exiles who faced the threat of expulsion with nowhere to go.[56] Conscious of the debt owed to him, *Posledniia novosti* adopted the proposal, which enabled many refugees to subscribe who had shown reluctance to join in anything suggested by Miliukov's newspaper.[57] Almost 18,000 signatures were collected and a celebratory banquet held at the Salle Lutétia. Maklakov presided, flanked by Metropolitan Evlogy and P.N. Miliukov.[58] Grudgingly in favour of the thanks, *Vozrozhdenie* chose to say little of their transmission to Moutet.

On one occasion when Moutet rendered his invaluable aid, *émigré* bickering negatively affected the community's relations with this important French benefactor. Among those who accompanied Moutet and Maklakov on their bureaucratic rounds in the summer of 1934 was a member of the democratic section of Maklakov's office, Iakov Rubinshtein. His politics and Jewish nationality did not endear him to *Vozrozhdenie*, which reacted with still greater displeasure when the government appointed him to the French section of the Nansen Refugees Office in Geneva. Semenov's attacks stung Moutet into a vigorous riposte, probably encouraged by the editor of *Posledniia novosti*. It seemed, Moutet wrote, that some far right segments in the Russian emigration had learned nothing and forgotten nothing. Their attacks and insults were adversely affecting French opinion of the *émigrés*. If the legal measures proposed or adopted did not fully meet Russian hopes, if they were obliged to submit to irksome new restrictions, these were, to a significant degree, the result of a particular newspaper's slanderous campaign. They should stop trying to discredit representatives and institutions which were trying to defend Russian refugee interests. After all, their position was difficult enough already.[59] This warning "from an old and present friend of Russia" was duly transmitted to *Vozrozhdenie* to the accompaniment of an approving editorial in that organ's chief Paris rival. At least publicly, the warning provoked only defiance in its intended target.[60]

Emigré comment remained restrained on matters which did not touch on Russian concerns. The major convulsions of French interwar life, the rise and fall of forty cabinets, were clearly the business of Frenchmen, not Russians. The single most violent domestic event of the two decades, the bloody Paris riots of 6 February 1934, elicited from *Posledniia novosti* a concerned editorial by Miliukov on France's "tragic days," with his hope that an outcome might be found worthy of the nation's republican structure. But it was not the business of a Russian newspaper to delve further into these possibilities.[61] *Vozrozhdenie* also regretted the violence, obviously the work of Communists.[62]

Moutet, Herriot and others of the moderate left might express occasional irritation at the Russian *émigré* right wing, but no Russian conservative had any justified cause for serious complaint on that score against the centre-left parties, including Socialists, in government or in opposition.[63] It is true that in the months leading up to French recognition of the USSR, the Radical-Socialist interior minister, Camille Chautemps, received reports on the mood of the Russian emigration, particularly its extreme right fringe. The calibre of the intelligence is unimpressive. Gossip, newspaper clippings, rumours, and details of the latest obscure polemics form the bulk of the material.[64] If the government derived its view of the Russians in France from sources such as this, clearly the republic had nothing to fear from Russia Abroad. Shortly after recognition Chautemps requested his prefects to provide him with profiles of their foreign residents. Among the points to which he desired answers was whether "seditious, revolutionary or Communist organizations" existed in their *départements*.[65] There was certainly nothing to fear from Russians on that score. The overwhelming majority of exiles undoubtedly preferred to see a government in Paris whose anti-Communist, anti-Soviet credentials were more vigorously evident than those of Chautemps and his colleagues.[66]

For those of the prerevolutionary intelligentsia who lived in exile by their pens, an important dimension to their labours in newspapers, journals, and lectures was the popularization of "a certain idea of Russia" among receptive French audiences. This was easiest at the academic level. The Sorbonne and the Institut d'Etudes Slaves assisted groups and individuals to offer lectures, in Russian and French, on a wide variety of topics.[67] One subject, for example, several times addressed by the literary critic and historian N.K. Kulman, was Russian Freemasonry, a highly sensitive topic to many *émigrés*.[68] Emile Haumant, "friend of Russia and Slavdom," was an honoured participant in occasional sessions; exiled Russian speakers included the literary commentator and philosopher A.Ia. Levinson and the ubiquitous Miliukov. As the decade ended, these university lectures were supplemented by periodic meetings between French and Russian writers to discuss literary questions of common interest. A half-dozen such encounters took place between the spring of 1929 and the end of 1930, organized by Robert Sébastien and Vsevolod Fokht under the name of "Studio Franco-Russe." These reunions drew important figures from both sides. Russian participants included Boris Zaitsev, Ivan Bunin, Mark Aldanov, Marina Tsvetaeva, Vladimir Weidlé, Nina Berberova and Nadezhda Gorodetskaia; their French interlocutors included figures of secondary rank, but also, upon occasion, Jacques Maritain, Georges Bernanos, André Malraux, and André Maurois.[69]

While these occasions may have served to increase mutual appreciation of each other's literature, it is unlikely that they did much, if anything, to enhance the image of National Russia among the Paris literati. To be sure, the faithful Ledré made extravagant claims,[70] Haumant remained a sympathetic ally, and prominent émigrés continued to enjoy their French friendships. But on the whole the émigré intelligentsia was swimming against a tide far stronger than itself; it had been condemned, moreover, to a place on the sidelines in Russian affairs. One of the sessions of the "Studio Franco-Russe," held on 25 February 1930, made these points with painful clarity. Leading members of the French and Russian literary élites were present, including Maurois, Malraux, Marcel Péguy, and a dozen others. The subject of the evening's discussion was the work of Marcel Proust; from the Russians present came resigned acknowledgement of the relevance of Proustian themes to their own condition. For the philosopher Boris Vysheslavtsev, his fellow exiles were as passive and contemplative of life as Proust, constantly tempted to seek consolation "in the remembrance of things past." Nadezhda Gorodetskaia, a voice from the younger generation of émigré writers, endorsed the analogy. She spoke of her age group's development outside a Russian atmosphere, without Russia. She felt they were all condemned to a Proustian existence as the only form of activity open to them. Other Russians present, pressed to contribute to the proceedings, had little to say. On the French side, the essayist and critic Benjamin Crémieux declared his reluctance to pronounce on such Russian opinions as had been offered, given the differences of culture and background he perceived between the two nationalities. He then emphasized his own difference in these realms by citing none other than Lenin as the supreme example of a man in whom action and life were one, the antithesis of Proust.[71] His reference must have given deep offence to his Russian audience. The whole session seems from its record to have been more notable for the polemics it engendered between the French participants than for any Franco-Russian celebration of mutually beneficial ties.

The émigré effort in France on behalf of non-Bolshevik Russian values undoubtedly registered its greatest failure in its campaign to combat two decades of Western intellectual approval, or at least justification, of the Soviet regime. On a popular level the struggle was equally barren of success. One recurrent complaint, for example, concerned the liberties taken with Russian history by popular novelists and dramatists. In December 1923 the Berlin Russkaia gazeta (Russian Newspaper) denounced a new film on Peter the Great. It had Russia's heroic emperor succumbing to a heart attack at the sight of his wife in the embrace of his best friend, Prince A.D. Menshikov.[72] Six years later, with equal indignation, N.N. Chebyshev reviewed Maurice Rostand's latest play, *Le dernier tzar*, for *Vozrozhdenie*. What to French spectators was just another exotic, tearful melodrama evoked pain and tragic memories for Russians in France. But there was nothing they could do about it. "We cannot interfere, still less prevent Mr Rostand from drawing his subjects from Russian history. He is at home. We are guests, and not always wanted guests." It gave Chebyshev little comfort to judge the play as one put on only for concierges.[73] Rostand's sentimental concoction appeared to suit both the public taste and a preferred public image of Russia, so that *émigré* sensitivities continued to be bruised. In October 1938 another *Vozrozhdenie* reporter recorded his distress on witnessing the filming of Maurice Tourneur's *Katia*, an imaginative account of the love affair between Alexander II and Ekaterina Dolgorukaia, starring a leading actress of the day, Danielle Darrieux. Nostalgia vied with outrage as the Russian watched the casual goings-on.[74] More detached about the matter, G.V. Adamovich passed on to *Posledniia novosti* readers a French comment he heard to the effect that, since Alexander II was hardly as important to history as Louis XIV or Napoleon, it was possible to "fantasize" about him.[75] *Émigré* intellectuals had little ammunition against this sort of condescension.

Questions of legal status, influential friends and the image of prerevolutionary Russia were concerns that interested most older *émigrés* to greater or lesser degree. But absolute priority of place, in terms of its claim upon their energies, went to the task of securing some means of keeping body and soul together. The jobs available ranged from the very few desirable possibilities to the far larger category of the onerous and unpleasant.

Finding employment for tens of thousands of its Russian charges was the earliest major preoccupation of Dr Nansen's Refugee Office. In 1924 this function was transferred to the International Labour Office in Geneva, directed by the French Socialist Albert Thomas. His selection was a happy one for the Russians. Like Moutet, he had visited Russia in 1917 and was on good terms with many in the *émigré* leadership. His office had a modest success in placing Russians in regular employment during the five years it held this responsibility.[76] The correspondence between Maklakov and Thomas contains references to one particularly vexing problem. Every holder of Nansen stateless papers was supposed to pay annual dues of twenty-five francs. This sum paid for a "Nansen stamp," which helped to defray expenses incurred in refugee relief work, but its collection provoked all kinds of complaints and caused Maklakov no little embarrassment.[77]

The difficulties of finding employment had to do with the nature of the Russian community, the economic facts of the day, and what was legally permissible. While no statistical breakdown by prerevolutionary occupation exists for the Russian colony in France, it is certain that few found positions in French life that corresponded either to their professional expertise in Russia or to their expectations. There was, of course, the rare luminary like Chaliapin whose appeal crossed international boundaries. On the national scale one Russian who briefly managed to win a large French following was the actor Ivan Mosjoukine (Mozzhukhin). Well known in prerevolutionary Russia, he enjoyed considerable success in the French cinema until the arrival of sound films. His ineradicable Russian accent then removed him from French screens and he died penniless in 1939.[78] His fate illustrated the inhibiting effect an alien background could have on *émigrés* who tried to continue professional careers in exile. On the other hand, to rely uniquely on Russians as patrons or customers was to court virtually certain penury. Ivan Bunin, the best known *émigré* writer of his generation and contributor to several Russian newspapers, longed desperately for the Nobel Prize that might lift him and his family from their dire material condition. Its award in 1933 was providential.[79]

Russians with professional qualifications who sought a French clientele faced formidable obstacles. To begin with, they usually confronted a thicket of regulations, which effectively shut them out. Lawyers and teachers had to have French nationality and state diplomas. Apparently more fortunate, physicians were formally subject only to the second requirement until 1933 when the rules were tightened. This latitude for doctors was illusory. Informal restrictions and financial difficulties permanently kept foreign numbers low in the medical, veterinary, and dental professions.[80] There were fewer barriers, apparently, to those who limited their practice to Russian patients.[81] One half-open door to a French practice was to offer one's services in the colonial empire. Eighty-one Russian physicians were so engaged in 1930; the number fell to forty-five three years later. A decree in 1936 extended the metropolitan ban to the colonies, but Moutet intervened to have the effect softened. There were never enough European doctors overseas.[82] Boris Aleksandrovsky, himself a doctor, estimated when back in Moscow that a maximum of only sixteen out of 400 members of the *émigré* Mechnikov Society of Russian Physicians succeeded in gaining French credentials.[83] Aleksandrovsky's tale is so full of horror stories that dwell on capitalist greed, the prostitution of medicine, and the despair of several Russian doctors that one wonders how the author himself managed to survive with his self-respect intact.

One theme that Aleksandrovsky sounds with vigour is the helpless vulnerability of the refugee to bureaucratic and police vexations. Even allowing for the rhetoric of a repentant sinner, his indignation may not necessarily have been artificial. Refugees are at all times sensitive to these pressures, and Russians in interwar France were no exception. The documentary complexities which confronted them brought a bewilderment that grew, rather than diminished, as the exile years lengthened. In 1935 Moutet publicly complained of the often badly thought-out, contradictory and illiberal regulations pouring out of Paris ministries.[84] That greater clarity resulted from his impatience is unlikely; the texts certainly became more restrictive in the final years of peace. Russian conservatives consoled themselves with the thought that the new codes were aimed at more recently arrived groups ("we always obey the law!"),[85] yet the general effect was dismaying. Handbooks published on the eve of the war give a dismaying description of what the foreign resident must have in hand. First in importance came his identity card. A nineteen-page booklet with details of the holder's civil status, it was normally granted for three years. Its color revealed at a glance what its owner might legally do. Green indicated a non-worker (*non-travailleur*), including those in the liberal professions, students, and the unemployed. Grey-blue cards belonged to industrial labourers; yellow ones to agricultural workers; orange to petty tradesmen and entrepreneurs (*commerçants*). Some of these documents might limit the owner's freedom of movement or his ability to seek a new job. To obtain one of these prizes, the applicant presented his case at the appropriate police station or prefecture. Naturally he needed supportive documents: a promise of employment, permission from the labour ministry (the notorious *avis favorable*), authentication from Maklakov's Office or one of its provincial branches, and local police permission. Armed with all this and possibly a friend to help in case of difficulties, the Russian petitioner flung himself on the mercy of a bureaucracy not celebrated for its generosity in such matters.[86] Before too long, it would all have to be done again.

Nansen passports were easier to obtain, though visas permitting entry into countries other than the one of residence were not.[87] In theory Russian holders of Nansen papers were supposed to benefit from lenient application of regulations governing alien refugees.[88] In practice, however, this circumstance did not make life significantly easier for Russian exiles. Military obligations were one troublesome issue, though not an actual reality until the late 1930s. A greater menace was the possibility of expulsion (*refoulement*) of Russians who, for whatever reasons, ran afoul of the authorities. With no country obliged to take them in, they could move back and forth across frontiers in a world of painful illegality. Aleksandrovsky has a characteristic story of a Russian engineer who, being questioned by a Paris traffic policeman for some minor infraction, replied in a mixture of Russian and broken French that "this law of yours is unknown to me." Unluckily, the Russian *vash* (of yours) sounded like the French *vache*, so that miscreant was duly expelled from France for insulting the police. Denied admission anywhere else, he ended by killing himself.[89] The tale sounds farfetched, even for the difficult years of the 1930s, but perhaps cannot be dismissed altogether. H.W.H. Sams noted in his sober report for Sir John Simpson's refugee study that the middle years of the decade saw a sharp increase in xenophobia after October 1934, when a Croatian terrorist assassinated King Alexander of Yugoslavia and French foreign minister Barthou in Marseilles.⁹⁰

Russians physically capable of employment thus entered the labour market with substantial liabilities. Inevitably, most of them, unskilled and speaking little French, found themselves either unable to get any regular work at all, or else compelled to take degrading, exhausting employment. In this they conformed to the iron law of refugee life. Necessity respected neither person nor class: bourgeois and aristocratic Russians submitted to a drastic proletarianization in exile. Even in their employment, however, there was a hierarchy. At its summit was the taxi.

The Russian taxi-driver, Vladimir Nabokov's "Colonel Taxovich," was, and is, a staple of Parisian lore between the two World Wars. Certainly for the *émigré* himself a job behind the wheel represented the best solution to his employment difficulties. It was one particularly attractive to military veterans. The job conferred a measure of independence, placing the driver in sole charge of his automobile; it took him out of backbreaking work in factory or farm, away from the impatient orders of a French overseer. It had the reputation of returning high wages. Yet these attractions did not tell the whole story. Andrei Sedykh, a journalist-chronicler of *émigré* life for *Posledniia novosti*, contributed a series of sketches of various exile categories: taxi-drivers were his first subject. He described the anonymous Russian in Billancourt saving his factory wages, cloistering himself with a map of Paris, and begging friends already in the business to drive him around the city. The police allowed would-be drivers six months to acquire complete familiarity with the capital's streets. Once hired, they worked like convicts for a twelve to fourteen hour day. Accidents, assaults, and stolen tires made life onerous. The driver's income, that winter of 1933, might amount to sixty francs a day, scarcely a fortune. Little extra could be expected from customers.Sedykh heard that provincial *curés* ("God will provide!"), elderly Englishwomen, and drunks tipped the least; fellow refugees, with better reason, were scarcely more generous.⁹¹ Nevertheless, in spite of all the drawbacks the taxi-driver's job retained its allure. One who succumbed, Prince Peter Dolgoruky, wrote later for Soviet readers of his delight when he managed to win employment with a Paris taxi company thanks to his command of English.⁹²

The profound political divisions within the upper, more vocal levels of the emigration reached down into the working mass. A brief report in *Posledniia novosti* a few days after French recognition of the USSR told of a meeting of Russian workers, mostly taxi-drivers and labourers in the automobile factories of Renault, Citroën, Delage, and Peugeot. Although the avowed purpose of the gathering was apolitical, it quickly witnessed a confrontation between "lefts" and "rights." Appeals for working class solidarity clashed with demands for an end to hostilities between workers and employers.[93] The polarization had the usual result of creating two rival representative bodies. One, the "Association of Russian Drivers and Automobile Workers," defended conservative political viewpoints; the second, the "General Union of Russian Drivers," took a democratic stance. In 1929 the latter group, much the smaller, claimed 700 members out of a total Russian taxi-driver population in the Paris region of some 4,000.[94] Through their respective newssheets the two associations kept up a sporadic fire at each other in the tradition of their larger exemplars *Vozrozhdenie* and *Posledniia novosti*.[95]

The anti-Soviet instincts of the overwhelming *émigré* majority often made for difficult relations between Russian and French workers. Whether or not they came from wealth and privilege, as popular leftist imagery had it, the Russian taxi-driver and his proletarianized compatriots were unlikely to feel any sympathy for those who looked favourably on the USSR. This meant pre-eminently the French Communist party, but the sentiment also extended to unions and labour agitation led by the left. On the other hand, by standing aloof, Russians risked alienating their French workmates, possibly with disagreeable personal consequences.

This dilemma was evident on major occasions of social turmoil. One such occurred in February 1934, coincident with but not caused by the riots of the 6th. Some days earlier all taxi-drivers in the capital went out on strike. Their grievances, vociferously backed by Socialists and Communists, concerned pay and working conditions. Most Russians drivers proved very reluctant to get involved. Garage owners, knowing this, informed their Russian employees that if new salary claims were met they would allow foreign-born drivers to comprise no more than ten percent of the work force. This would entail the dismissal of many hundreds of Russian drivers. French unions leaped to counter this "odious machination," but it probably encouraged defections from the common front, an aim supported by *Vozrozhdenie*.[96] A Soviet observer of the exciting events in Paris that February noted with satisfaction that Russian strike-breakers had their vehicles pushed into the Seine.[97]

Taxi-drivers were the aristocrats of the *émigré* work force. Under them, often struggling to rise, came refugees caught in every variety of employment. Many jobs were unpleasant and required a drastic change from the life of former times. One extreme example is presented in Felix Iusupov's memoir of exile. He himself lived mostly on the sale of family jewels and paintings, along with the occasional business venture. Constantly sued or suing, he figured often in the press in a context that reflected no credit on him or his community. The cumulative effect was unfortunate. In 1928 Janet Flanner, sharp-eyed observer of the Paris scene for the *New Yorker*, wrote after Iusupov's latest commercial fiasco that he had become "one of the most tragic, unromantic figures of the [Russian] refugee colony."[98] Iusupov told of a chance meeting in a Paris restaurant with a countess friend from St Petersburg days. She had since become a washroom attendant, while her husband looked after customers' coats. Iusupov kissed her hand and they chatted as toilets flushed around them.[99] Not all aristocratic ladies were reduced to such straits, however. William Wiser notes in his entertaining survey of Paris in the twenties that a vogue for things Russian saw "ruined countesses [and] fine boned Slavic models" engaged by Coco Chanel to launch her new, exclusively Russian line.[100] The fashion, as always, proved fleeting.

Two categories of employment had heavy Russian representation. One was the large mass of unskilled labour hired by the French government after the war to repair the nation's devastated northeastern regions. Thousands of male refugees in Balkan and Turkish camps signed up for this most demanding of all occupations, as it was a way of getting to France. But many were quite unequal to the strain once they arrived.[101] In any case, it was a form of labour quite without prospects. A job offering greater chances of permanency and marginally better working conditions might be had in one of the several automobile factories ringing Paris. According to Georges Mauco, an authority on French immigration and labour matters, 12,000 Russians were employed in metallurgy (largely car manufacturing) in 1930, making this by far the largest single form of employment of Russian labour.[102] One reason, according to an anonymously published guide, was that personnel managers were often military veterans sympathetic to brothers-in-arms down on their luck.[103]

An interesting feature of Mauco's report on alien labour in France is a series of statistical tables comparing the work habits and general desirability as employees of the several nationalities represented in the labour force during the 1920s. One of these tables, for instance, contrasts seven nationalities in 350 metallurgical enterprises employing a total of 60,000 foreign workers. The best were declared to be Belgians, eighty-five percent of whom were "good," fifteen percent "average," none unsatisfactory. Russians ranked second from the bottom on this scale, with forty-five percent "good," fifty percent "average," five percent unsatisfactory. Only North African Arabs scored lower.[104] More revealing, and today no doubt unthinkable, was a ranking in 1926 of thirteen national groups working for an unnamed Paris automobile manufacturer with 17,000 workers, 5,000 of whom were aliens. A dozen foremen judged their foreign workers on their physical appearance, regularity of attendance, daily output, quality of work, and competence in French. An average of these scores produced an overall mark. Russians were the second most numerous nationality after the Arabs. They scored high on physical appearance (8.7 out of 10), inferior only to Belgians and Swiss, both of whom achieved a perfect 10. Russians also did well in regularity, mental discipline, and quality of work. But their daily productivity was low and their ability in French weaker than any other group save the Chinese. Other nationalities, including Greeks, Armenians, Yugoslavs, and Czechs all achieved higher scores on the linguistic test; the Poles stood equal with the Russians. As a result, the Russian contingent dropped to sixth place in the final ranking (6.6 out of 10).[105]

Paul Briunelli may serve as a representative figure of those anonymous refugees who had been bourgeois, intellectual or aristocratic in Russia, but who were, in the words he chose as the title of his memoir of exile, "boiled in the factory furnace" as refugees. In the Russian community Briunelli played no part that attracted any particular attention; in everything except his apparent political allegiance[106] he seems to personify that shadowy individual, the typical Russian émigré. Evacuated from Russia to Constantinople with the debris of the White cause, Briunelli made his way to Paris in the early 1920s, his dream of becoming a poet in ruins. The battle to survive took precedence. A teaching post in the Berlitz language school was a stroke of good fortune; it lasted nine months. Then came chicken farming on a small property in Versailles. This took all his savings, but he had great hopes of prosperity. Unfortunately the chickens failed to co-operate and he lost everything. At this bitter point Briunelli was forced to seek employment in an automobile factory; he found it a fearful humiliation. The work was exhausting, his superiors were patronizing, and impatient with his assurance that he, as an intelligent man, could learn a skill as quickly as someone without any education. This job too turned out to be only temporary. Left with a worthless diploma, Briunelli nearly succumbed to despair. But his circumstances did not permit such an indulgence. Everyone had to contribute: his wife worked as a legal secretary; his daughter sewed shirts; his father-in-law, once a state councillor, now carved ornate wooden boxes that no one would buy. Next came a succession of factory jobs, interspersed with occasional outside work as messenger or postman. His only child died, mourning her absence from Russia. Through it all he clung to his dream of a taxi-driver's freedom. The preparation was arduous, but he persevered, spurred on by tales of the fortune to be made. Legal obstacles blocked his way for a while; until their removal Briunelli continued to take whatever work he could find. An unusually agreeable interlude was provided by the chance to sign on as an extra in a film about Joan of Arc. Several other Russians joined Briunelli in this adventure in which he was assigned the role of a cardinal, one of Joan's judges. But soon he was deposed from this eminence to the part of an attendant peasant, a fall mirroring his fortunes in real life. At length his taxi permit came through and he was able to step up to the summit of the émigré labouring world. His closing reflections about his new life reaffirmed his earlier resolution: to live, fight, and never give in. He took comfort from Hegel's famous assertion about the rationality of the real. Their struggles and dream of the Soviet usurpers' overthrow, all vividly real, were thus rational.[107]

Briunelli's memoir tells us much about *émigré* life. Difficulties of employment, proletarianization of middle and upper class exiles, bouts of despair, family tragedy, consciousness of futility and foreignness – such problems figure in stories of refugee life everywhere. One additional hazard for the Russians working in France was the reputation enjoyed among French workers by those now governing Russia. In all his jobs Briunelli came up against a veneration for Lenin and Soviet Russia that he could not shake. His own Russian hero, Leo Tolstoi, was unknown. Briunelli himself was assumed to be a count. If he were a genuine worker, why did he not live in the land of the proletariat to which he belonged? Generally, however, Briunelli found the French sympathetic. He was sure that, for all their admiration of things Soviet, French workers would not take to the system if they really knew anything about it. Yet nothing from him could convince them.[108]

If work in a Paris factory were impractical or unbearable, there was often the lure of the land to tempt the enterprising. The Paris suburbs and the Riviera saw a proliferation of Russian market gardens producing fruit, wine, honey, and flowers.[109] Other entrepreneurs might imitate Briunelli's efforts at raising chickens or other livestock on a small plot of dearly purchased or rented land.[110] But for those who wished to remove themselves far from the city, two main alternatives were at hand. Russians might be helped to find work or, better, a small property in rural France, or else encouraged to emigrate to the fertile, empty spaces of the New World.

During the early 1920s a trickle of Russians found their way to French farms, generally as agricultural labourers and sharecroppers (*métayers*). They might be prompted by nothing more complex than the wish for a healthier life than that available in large cities. Alternatively, as in the case of Cossacks who settled in the French countryside, they might find in a return to the land some ties to their old life in Russia. In either case, as in all forms of *émigré* *labour*, the work was hard and the initial return meagre. Welfare organizations, notably Zemgor, gave what material aid they could, supported by the ministry of agriculture and League refugee officials.[111] The effort was concentrated in the underpopulated rural southwestern *départements* between Toulouse and Bordeaux. In 1926 a committee chaired by A.I. Konovalov sent N.D. Avksentiev to inspect Russian settlements in the region. He reported positively on the whole, though he did observe difficulties between Russian workers and French farm owners. There were, for example, fears that the Russians were so backward that they might damage farm machinery unfamiliar to them; these proved groundless.[112] In February 1929 a conference in Toulouse between Russian farmers and French agricultural officials heard that seventy-eight farms in Gascony were being rented to Russians. The farms varied in size from twenty to one hundred hectares and average income approximated 24,000 francs a year. Half of this sum might go to pay off debts and rent. Still, the prospects seemed promising. One French academic participant was moved to state that France needed not only Russian working hands but also Russian farmers' brains and appeared to be finding them in the Russians he had met.[113] Unfortunately there were the usual complications. The Toulouse conference heard that there was little money, the Russian farm workers spoke little French, and their numbers were often divided by sharp internal quarrels. Something might be done about the first and second problems; nothing, it seemed, could assist in solving the third.[114] Kalmyk farm labourers who threatened to cast spells on their French employers were, no doubt, a difficulty more easily resolved.[115]

Those willing to try the open-air life but who found the going in France irksome might enlist in any of a number of schemes that promoted Russian emigration across the Atlantic. The destination was not Canada or the United States, where postwar restrictions excluded penniless immigrants from Eastern Europe, but South America. From time to time Russian newspapers in Paris examined the prospects open to adventurous Russians in the South American republics, while the customary stories of fortunes to be made did the rounds. Brazilian agents were among the first to tap the new Russian source of European migration. In 1921 about a thousand Russians left in a French steamer for Brazil: everything went wrong before they left the Old World. The Russians ended up in another camp, this one in Corsica, from which most were eventually transported back to the French mainland.[116]

In 1926 and 1927 further efforts were made to induce Russians, especially Cossacks, to move from France to the interior of Paraguay, Bolivia, and Peru. About 500 went off, followed by a thin stream in following years. Their reports were not encouraging. Some settlers made it back to Europe and told their fellow Russians to stay where they were. One of these, a Colonel Khapkov, contributed to *Posledniia novosti* a series of articles on "Why I returned from Paraguay." He complained that the reality of the General I.T. Beliaev *stanitsa* (settlement) in the Paraguayan interior vastly differed from the promise. This had caused many in the settlement's Russian population to desert it. Khapkov himself hoped to get his old taxi-driving job back and recommended Paraguay only if the sole alternative open to the *émigré* were "the Alexander III bridge," that is, suicide.[117] Bolivia, it appeared, was even worse, for another Russian who had been there counselled compatriots considering that country that they would do better to proceed directly to the cemetery.[118] Meanwhile a Cossack group of 160 returned *en masse* from Peru to hold a service of thanksgiving that they were still alive after months of battling snakes, vampire bats, and mosquitos.[119] No ordeals in France could be worse. As in Europe, the Russian colonies in South America concentrated in the major cities, Buenos Aires in particular.

Whether in mine, factory, restaurant, taxi, or farm, the lot of the Russian worker was hard. The "active" minority of writers and journalists also lived, with one or two exceptions, in materially difficult circumstances. But some might at least comfort themselves with the reflection that their poverty was no worse than that of most of their compatriots still in Russia and that exiled intellectuals were able, unlike their Soviet counterparts, to know they wrote freely in defence of their nation's eternal cultural interest.[120] The same thought offered no consolation to the army of those in humbler, less intellectually demanding occupations. Stoic endurance seemed their best response, as Briunelli concluded. George Orwell found this an admirable feature of the Russians he met during his days of Parisian squalor. Middle and upper class Russians, he felt, put up with adversity much better than their English opposite numbers would have done.[121] Tatiana Schaufuss, on the other hand, regretted the inability of Russian refugees to make a fuss. "To endure in silence seems to many Russians easier than to organize a group and make their grievances public," she wrote in 1939, clearly disapproving such reticence in her fellow exiles.[122] But perhaps there was an explanation. Nine years earlier Charles Ledré concluded in his sympathetic study of the Russians in France that "[they have] powers of resignation and forgetfulness which surprise us. These make exile less painful."[123] This apparent variant on the theme of the "suffering Russian soul" suggested what had become an evident reality of émigré life by 1930: the fact that it was going to go on. What alternative, other than endurance, did the Russian refugees have as they began their second decade of exile?

CHAPTER FOUR

Fathers and Sons in Exile

The year 1930 inaugurated a particularly difficult period for the Russians in France, one which saw more than the usual agonized introspection into their collective nature and purpose. Before the decade was a month old a sensational scandal burst over them, prompting the French press to turn its attention toward the nation's uninvited Russian guests. This proved a trying experience. Shortly thereafter, as if to extend their new notoriety, two French monographs appeared with the Russian community in France as their subject.[1] Generally sympathetic, each sought to acquaint the reading public with the Russians in their midst. "Nobody knows them here" asserted one of the two observers, not altogether accurately.[2] Two years later, as French memories of these events faded, the single most devastating episode in Franco-émigré relations put the Russians again under scrutiny, this time largely hostile.

Beyond these spasmodic bouts of French attention, the political and literary chiefs of the older generation faced their own difficult moment. Time was running out on them and their hopes of vindication. In 1930 Zinaida Hippius and Ilia Fondaminsky (the latter writing under his penname Bunakov) asked "What is the Russian emigration to do?" Their answers were, under the circumstances, understandably vague. Whether soon, as Hippius hoped, or at some possibly distant point in the future, as Bunakov predicted, they must be ready for the day of Bolshevik collapse. While they waited, they must organize. Hippius spoke of an "All-Russian National Union," Bunakov of economic and social bodies based on the refugee mass, not on the intelligentsia.[3] Nothing in the émigré past suggested that these ideas would be any more successful than any of the other myriad schemes proposed since their exile began. The authors seemed in fact to recognize this improbability.

In addition to the dream of effective organization, the Hippius-Bunakov essays also reflected their authors' hope in a second persistent mirage: that exiled intellectuals might yet serve the Russian people in their common homeland somehow freed of the Soviets. Jean Delage encountered this same brave thought in his interviews for his study of the Russians in France, Boris Mirkin-Getsevich, who lectured at the Sorbonne on the history of Russian law, evidently told the sympathetic Frenchman of his faith in the Russia of tomorrow, "reasonable, Europeanized, enriched by French intelligence, administration, justice [and] law."[4] Miliukov, for his part, saw the *émigré* intelligentsia performing the vital task of educating illiterate Soviet youth, "given over to the worst instincts." Certainly Bolshevism's days were numbered. In a prophecy where the wish was, almost palpably, father to the thought, Kerensky told Delage that the end was now sure in the light of "Stalin's new coup d'état. Perhaps the hand which will strike down the Bolshevik regime is close to the masters of the moment in the very heart of the Cheka."[5]

Publicly declared confidence in the intelligentsia's continued usefulness to Russia expressed the understandable wish of a displaced élite to maintain a sense of purpose despite its ordeals. The vast majority accepted that Bolshevism's brutalizing "anti-culture," to employ Weidlé's term,[6] made their return to and work in Russia all the more imperative. They had values which Russia still needed. Yet the security of this image undeniably depended upon its acceptance by younger *émigrés* into whose hands the faith must be transmitted. Here there loomed real danger. By the time Hippius and Bunakov came to compose their essays on the proper function of exiled Russians, there was sufficient evidence to alarm older intellectuals that this transmission might not, in fact, take place. As in all generations, but most particularly among those raised in exile, the faith of the fathers met challenge and rejection from within the ranks of the sons.

Several factors contributed to this disenchantment. One was the deepening economic crisis which gripped Western Europe, bearing down hard upon vulnerable refugees and turning the minds of more than a few younger ones toward new answers to old, apparently insoluble dilemmas. The endless, sterile polemics of the exile seniors, based on antediluvian quarrels, evoked only bored distaste. But above all this was the sheer fact of exile itself. A group of exiled academics faced this fact squarely in an appeal of 29 April 1930. "The years pass," they wrote, "and our physical isolation from our motherland is making itself felt, with special impact upon the rising generation. The very idea of [Russia] is becoming ever more abstract, the feeling for her is weakening and there is reason to fear that this phenomenon will grow stronger with every year. People of the older generation, having lived a good part of their lives in [Russia] and having had the good fortune to experience her directly, are gradually disappearing." What could be done? The best that the refugee professors were able to suggest was archival aid. "Those who still can must immediately, tirelessly transmit everything they have been preserving; all the information [they have] about our country and, in general, about everything Russian to young persons living abroad, [who are] now coming forward to replace them."[7]

The problem was, in a much used word, the denationalization of Russian émigré youth. Unfortunately the means to counter the threat were, as the professorial advice indicated, pitifully meagre.

All sectors of émigré opinion acknowledged the importance of the struggle against the loss of Russian national feeling in the young. Both for their own and Russia's sake, younger men and women of the emigration must not surrender to the alien culture around them, attractive though it might be, at least not without resistance. Mikhail Mikhailovich Fedorov, "father of the Russian student body abroad,"[8] personified, more energetically than any other intelligent, this determination to nurture the Russianness of the rising generation for service to Russia. In 1922 he had fashioned a "Central Committee for the Provision of Higher Education to Russian Youth Abroad," composed of delegates from all major relief and academic organizations active in the diaspora. It assumed as its main task "the preparation of cadres of Russian cultivated forces to relieve those crushed by the merciless Communist International, which has seized power in Russia." Once freed of her yoke, their country would require "well-prepared human material" for the gigantic job of restoration in all areas of the state and the national economy.[9] Given that Paris was the emigration's political centre and the place of residence of Fedorov's central committee, he and his colleagues looked to France for the most promising results.[10]

The impulse to educate the young in Russian conditions for ultimate service at home dominated the thinking of Fedorov's committee throughout the 1920s. Indeed, so pressing was the perceived urgency of the task that both conservative and democratic representatives collaborated in the committee's work.[11] Armed with his vision, Fedorov approached official French bodies with requests for assistance. It was, he told them, very much in the French interest to help needy Russian youth studying in France. These young men and women would soon proceed to Russia on Bolshevism's fall. There they would participate in the restoration of their country's structures and eventually play a prominent role in its post-Bolshevik government. Grateful for the aid given them in the West, they would strengthen Russia's ties to nations generous in their present assistance.[12]

Whether or not it was moved by the force of Fedorov's arguments, the government did funnel grants through his committee to Russian students in France. The aid offered was a drop in the bucket, or rather ocean, of Russian needs. From a level in 1922-3 of 575,000 francs, public subventions rose to approximately 675,000 francs in 1924-5. The Herriot cabinet's recognition of Soviet Russia raised the spectre that government aid to Bolshevism's enemies might be ended; with help from influential friends this threat was diverted.[13] All the same, the flow of French funds gradually ebbed. Grants, bursaries, and fee exemptions sank from a total of 527,000 francs in 1925-6 to 205,000 francs in 1931-2. The number of students supported wholly or partially on government stipends and exemptions reached a maximum of 201 in 1924-5, diminished to 42 in 1927-8, then rose marginally to 48 in 1931-2.[14] The general economic crisis undoubtedly played the chief part in bringing about the lessening of support; perhaps too Fedorov's mirage of post-Bolshevik Russian gratitude lost its power to open French purses. His committee made heroic efforts to win support from the Russian community and its foreign friends. By 1930-1 it was subsidizing 399 students in secondary and university level studies. This figure fell to 262 the following year.[15]

The bulk of Fedorov's campaign in France went toward the organization and maintenance of a Russian secondary school (*gimnaziia*) and the Popular University, both in Paris. Crèches and kindergartens were also started in the Paris suburbs, and in Bizerta, Nice, Marseilles, and Cannes. The Paris *gimnaziia* took form during the utterly chaotic conditions of 1920, when expectations of a quick return home were on everyone's mind.[16] Maria Maklakova, the ambassador's sister, had a major role in getting the institution going and in raising money from aristocratic friends, both French and Russian. Conditions were somewhat spartan in the premises finally acquired on the rue du Docteur-Blanche in the sixteenth *arrondissement*. In spite of support from the government and the city of Paris, the material burdens grew steadily heavier. In 1920 about fifteen percent of the student body made reduced or no financial contribution to their own education; seven years later the figure had risen to eighty percent.[17] In 1931 a munificent gift from the Russian colony's most generous foreign friend, the oil magnate Sir Henri Deterding, enabled the institution to move to more commodious quarters in Boulogne-sur-Seine. The new building, "the Princess Donskaia Russian School," bore the name of Deterding's second wife, an *émigré* ennobled by "Emperor" Cyril in recognition of her husband's generosity.[18]

The Popular University shared in these aims. It too stressed the need to provide Russian youth in exile with the opportunity to find intellectual stimulation and a Russian education while abroad.[19] An energetic couple, Nikolai and Sofia Denisov, gave support and offered their own apartment in the place du Palais-Bourbon. Sofia Denisova had been very active in relief work among *émigré* youth since the first terrible days in Constantinople.[20] In 1923 the university's headquarters were moved to slightly more spacious premises near Saint-Germain-des-Prés, though lectures continued to be given all over the city. Instruction was made available on a broad range of subjects that included automobile mechanics (popular with aspiring taxi-drivers), dressmaking, the manufacture of artificial flowers, and other skills which might bring employment. Along with these, the university offered courses in Russian history, language, literature, and religion. French language instruction, also popular, was the first subject offered when the university began its work in 1921. English lessons enjoyed a brief vogue until the United States imposed immigration quotas.[21] In its first ten years an annual average of some 420 students attended classes for diploma credit. About 1,300 sat in each year as auditors, and 8,894 heard at least one of the forty-three "conversations" on Russian cultural themes held during the decade.[22] Simpson reported that, of the Russian university students in France, half took "higher technical" subjects. The remainder chose political and economic sciences (17.6%), agriculture (14.3%), language and literature (7.4%), medicine and law (5.7%), natural sciences and mathematics (3.3%), other (1.7 %).[23]

The figures represent a valiant effort to realize a dream. The odds were impossibly long. Needs exceeded resources and the number of those who could be helped remained small. Meanwhile, outside pressures grew ever more insistent. In 1924, as the comparatively optimistic phase of *émigré* life was ending, a review of the Paris *gimnaziia's* first years admitted the insufficiency of the struggle against denationalization. Far more Russian children were attending French schools than were in Russian institutions.[24] Even in the *gimnaziia* French had established itself firmly. Beginning with the 1923-4 session, classes in French literature, language, and history had to be given in French, as did mathematics and chemistry to senior students.[25] The authors of the review saw the old certainties on the wane. "We do not know when, in what forms and how fully the external unity of the Russian people will be established within the framework of a Russian state." Yet the task to which they had dedicated themselves remained worthwhile.[26]

An important, even vital role in the campaign against denationalization was played by the YMCA and its independent Russian affiliate, the Russian Student Christian Movement (RSKhD). This latter body developed from Orthodox study circles in Czechoslovakia and in 1926 shifted its headquarters to Paris. Through discussion groups, lectures, youth camps, and propaganda work, the movement combatted the loss of religion and language by *émigrés* too young to have strong personal roots in Russia, who faced an uncertain, lonely life in the West. Religion in particular was seen as an integral part of Russian culture. It had to be preserved among Russian youth in exile, as it was being eradicated from their contemporaries in the USSR. The Student Christian Movement took over YMCA efforts in this direction.[27]

A second generous transatlantic donor to the cause of Russian education was the American Committee for the Education of Russian Youth in Exile. This was set up by Professor Thomas Whittemore, an archeologist and Byzantinist at Tufts College (now University) in Boston. His committee gave to the Russian Student Christian Movement and other *émigré* organizations concerned with education amounts which rose steadily from 60,000 francs in 1921-2 to 1,700,000 francs in 1926-7. The American subsidies then fell off to 150,000 francs in 1931-2 and vanished altogether as the Depression tightened its grip in the United States.[28] Adding all sources of aid together, Fedorov's committee estimated that from 1921 to 1932 there was spent on the education of Russian youth in France and its associated purposes the sum of 21.5 million francs. The figure seems impressive but is perhaps less so when compared to the corresponding totals in Czechoslovakia (120 million francs) and Yugoslavia (23 million francs).[29]

For all their good work, the Russian Student Christian Movement could not avoid one of the regular hazards of *émigré* life in the form of attacks from the political extremes. The movement's links with the YMCA, for instance, excited suspicions on the far right that Masonic influences were at work in the movement's evangelical activity. Support of this work from Metropolitan Evlogy failed to convince followers of Markov II on the furthest right fringe that Orthodox youth was not being corrupted.[30] The Masonic lodges excited almost, indeed as much, rancour among the likes of Markov II as did judaism and socialism. Professor N.M. Zernov, the RSKhD chairman, acknowledged the harmful effects of this hostility, inevitably made worse by the church splits of the 1920s.[31] Paul Anderson also met with difficulties in the YMCA's work with younger *émigrés*.[32]

The effort to teach *émigré* youth in France about Russia was intense, generous, high-principled – and short-lived. A review in 1938 by Arseny Stupnitsky for the Simpson study concluded on a deeply pessimistic note. "Almost nothing" existed of Russian secondary and post-secondary schools, save for a few of the former in the Baltic and Slavic lands of refuge. The reasons were depressingly familiar. Financial support had dried up; good teaching staff had been hard to replace as the old generation disappeared; those who remained could be paid little or nothing. No unity of direction existed to impose clarity and order. Problems abounded in matters of curriculum and instruction. There were, for example, passionate arguments between parents and teachers on the subject of the Soviet reform of Russian orthography. This was a perennial test of *émigré* loyalty. Did a teacher's instruction of the new spelling constitute a recognition of Bolshevism? And what of Russian history? Did it stop in 1917? The intensive effort, in France at least, had clearly run down. A minority of exile youth was still politically conscious and sought knowledge about Russia. But the large majority of those in France were not given to such reflection. Most young Russians, Stupnitsky felt, had the mentality of "the average European" of their age. They preferred lighter pastimes: radio, films, sports, escapist literature, and action. The extent to which they maintained their Russian quality depended on their families' vigour at resisting denationalization. But even these efforts were unlikely to avert gradual assimilation in a country which possessed as attractive a culture as France. Stupnitsky in fact concluded that assimilation was "the most practical solution" to the dilemma of the younger émigrés' future.[33]

If the terms denationalization and assimilation, so often employed by nervous Russian commentators, meant the abandonment of all Russian features, including religion and language, very few, if any, of those who arrived in France as adolescents or older would have been in danger. French and Russian observers noted the resistance of Russian refugees to assimilationist pressures, at least when compared with other national minorities in France.[34] Some Russian communities were better protected than others. Parts of the Paris colony, for example, might at times get along with only the most grudging acknowledgment that they were living in France. There even existed an émigré version of the old chestnut that "Paris would be a fine city if there were not so many French people in it."[35] The younger refugee, wholly or mostly raised in France, was undoubtedly vulnerable, but each case depended on its own particular circumstances.

Some idea of the complexities involved was provided in 1946 with the published results of an investigation carried out during the war by two French demographers into comparative rates of assimilation of Russian and Armenian refugees in France.[36] In looking at the former group, the investigators focused upon 420 persons of both sexes living in the Paris suburbs of Clamart and Petit-Clamart. Their ages were not given but the context suggests that most respondents came to France as adolescents or young children. The inquiry assessed the degree of the community's "psychological and social assimilation" on the basis of its knowledge of French, its education, social mobility, involvement in French culture, citizenship, and family life. On the language test, of those over forty who had arrived in France with their education completed, two-thirds spoke French well or very well, about fourteen percent badly or very badly. But the figures had to be seen in their context. If the Russian husband were a labourer, he was usually not present when the researcher called. His wife, often French, would answer the questions. On the other hand, if the Russian husband were a writer or journalist, he was probably present and spoke good French as befitted one from a background where that language had "a privileged place." Were the wife Russian, she might insist in flawless French that neither she nor her family was in any way assimilated.[37]

The research team found matters very different in the younger generation born in France. Their data confirmed the gloomy prognoses made before the war by Stupnitsky and other observers of the émigré scene. French tended to supplant Russian at every stage of the social ladder. Indeed, some writers, Russian-born but wholly or partly brought up in France, had gone over completely into the host culture. The investigators cited the names of Henri Troyat, Joseph Kessel, Elsa Triolet, and Romain Gary: all were now making important contributions to French literature, not to Russian.[38] The researchers found that French schools were powerful agents of denationalization. Russian institutions, notably the "Sunday-Thursday schools," where Russian subjects were taught in church basements to makeshift groups of children one or two evenings a week, could only slow the irreversible process.[39] The use of language was crucial. The investigators established that Russian children, unless closely supervised, lapsed into French in which they were clearly more at ease.[40] This finding could not have caused great surprise. Nine years before, H.W. Sams had reported to the Simpson study that Russian scout camps, where use of Russian was required, were encountering real linguistic problems by 1937. Of 379 children in their charge that year, five percent had no Russian at all, while ten percent spoke it badly and fifty percent not very well. Yet at the same time, Sams also discovered that children of Russian families on the land, in the Toulouse region, retained their Russian, speaking it far more fluently than French.[41] They had successfully resisted assimilation, at least on the language front. Still, as Stupnitsky recognized, the pressures on émigré youth to merge with the French life around them could not, indeed should not, be resisted for long. Sir John Simpson concurred in this judgment.[42]

One restless element in the younger generation attracted particular attention from its Russian seniors. Stupnitsky wrote of it as a politically conscious, experimenting minority that sought Russia in other than émigré sources.[43] This vocal fraction came under close examination in Vladimir Varshavsky's study of the "unnoticed" exile generation.[44] Its existence stimulated intense concern in Posledniia novosti, Vozrozhdenie, Sovremenniia zapiski, and other press organs, nervous at any evidence of youthful disloyalty toward established truths. Far too many younger Russians appeared to be taking an unseemly interest in temptations which, to editorial writers of the older generation, approached moral capitulation to Bolshevism. The lure came from the so-called postrevolutionary ideologies.

The term covered a variety of individuals and movements with certain beliefs in common. The most defiant postrevolutionary heresy suggested that the October Revolution was far from the alien, antinational coup that most senior émigrés insisted it was. On the contrary, it had important roots in Russian history and culture. From this flowed the equally subversive notion that the Soviet regime, while undoubtedly repressive, still possessed features of benefit to Russia. Underlying these convictions was another postrevolutionary belief that the pre-October regimes in Russia were either played out, as with traditional tsarism, or, as in the case of the liberal and democratic-socialist losers in 1917, had never had anything of value to offer Russia then or since.

From the emigration's beginnings the circumstances of defeat and exile had led a small minority of intellectuals to question initial *émigré* assumptions and in consequence to re-orient themselves to the changed facts of Russian life. The "Change of Landmarks" movement (*Smenovekhovstvo*) was the best known of these. Its notorious cry "To Canossa!", proclaimed by S.S. Chakhotin in July 1921, called for repentance and return.[45] The appeal fell on stone-deaf ears as far as the broad refugee mass was concerned; however, the belief that the new Russia was worth studying and serving remained thereafter present, if widely resisted, in exile life. The longer that exile persisted, the more difficult it became to insist that the Soviet reality was merely a brief, bloody aberration in Russia's proper historical evolution. Should there not be some movement toward the new reality from Russian exiles otherwise condemned to a sterile, alien existence of no benefit to anyone? Postrevolutionaries answered this question with a strong affirmative. One such school, the most dangerous of all in the eyes of conventional *émigré* opinion, was Eurasianism (*Evraziistvo*).

From the moment of its first appearance in 1921, with the publication by a handful of scholars in Sofia of *Iskhod k vostoku* (Exodus to the East), down to the end of the decade Eurasianism offered a series of intellectual propositions about Russia, rather than any coherent political programme. These have recently been analysed in a cogent article by Charles Halperin.[46] Russia was not European. She was Eurasian, and the emphasis since Peter the Great on forcing Russia into Europe had deformed the nation's proper identity. Russia had paid a heavy price for her unnatural involvement in European affairs: out of it had come such un-Russian ideas as liberalism, democracy, secularism, and capitalism. War and revolution were the most recent and terrible of Russia's infections from Europe. Atheistic Bolshevism, too, came from the West. Because of its origins and because it made war on Russian Orthodoxy, the nation's essence, Bolshevism could not guide Russia to her Eurasian future. This duty would fall to the Eurasianist intellectuals now in exile, who understood the laws of Russia's authentic historical nature.

Every article in the Eurasianist creed offended the instincts of older *émigrés*. It affronted the small democratic sector with its rejection of democracy and "bourgeois" civil liberties for the Russian masses, its slighting of the February Revolution and of that event's champions in the West. Simultaneously Eurasianism outraged the right with its repudiation of tsarism as it had become by the eve of its fall and as *Vozrozhdenie* continued to defend it. Both left and right were offended by Eurasianism's emphasis on Russia's Asiatic heritage, represented in the Mongol yoke, and its downplaying of the nation's cultural, historical links to Western Europe. Worst of all was the unpalatable fact that the movement succeeded in attracting the interest of younger *émigrés*. Several of these saw it as the source of new ideas which went beyond the old shibboleths and which were ready to consider Russia's future in terms radically different from those of both present and past. Current European trends, such as Italian fascism, also drew sympathetic attention from proponents of Eurasianism.[47] A small number of prominent *émigré* intellectuals embraced the new heresy or expressed an interest in it.[48] But it was Eurasianism's appeal to curious refugee youth that provoked the concern or vituperation so apparent in the *émigré* press. Eurasianists were not reluctant to take pride in this hatred.[49]

In spite of its occasionally attractive iconoclasm, Eurasianism proved as liable to the normal ills of exile as every other *émigré* doctrine and organization. To begin with, it rested on what Halperin justly describes as "fragile self-deceptions," eventually shattered by the stability of the Bolshevik regime.[50] Disputes and financial crises, inseparable from refugee politics, also exacted their heavy toll.[51] By the early 1930s the movement was in full decline. A Eurasianist congress in Brussels in 1930 attempted to paper over the cracks, but without success. Zinaida Shakhovskaia was a delegate at the meeting and she saw the hand of Soviet intelligence agents in the turmoil of denunciation and intrigue in the Belgian capital.[52] These characteristics never needed outsiders to import them into an *émigré* occasion, but she may well have been correct in this particular case.[53]

The waning of Eurasianism by no means signified the demise of postrevolutionary sentiment. There were still younger Russians in exile looking for some set of beliefs applicable to their lives, which could free them from former leaders and ideologies. In November 1933 they found a spokesman in S.N. Sirine, "a writer well known in the Russian circles of Paris." This was, it must be assumed, the thirty-four year old novelist Vladimir Nabokov, who sometimes wrote in Russian under the pseudonym Sirin. He contributed a commentary on Russian *émigré* youth to *Le Temps*, the last of several reports which that newspaper published on the mood of Europe's rising generation. Sirine saw *émigré* youth condemned to bear the consequences of the fateful gamble taken by their parents in leaving Russia. The young did not always share the responsibility for that decision, nor did they invariably comprehend why it had been made. In exile the older generation lived on two levels. One was their pre-October life as officer, politician, writer, industrialist, or banker. The other was their refugee life as labourer, taxi-driver, shopkeeper, or delivery man. Those under thirty, raised in exile, had been brought up according to the traditions of the first level. Then crisis struck. Unemployment, strikes, and general dislocation drew upon their strength and dissipated their hopes. Studies had to be abandoned; helpless families looked after; any kind of job acquired. Would they ever need the knowledge they had managed to gather? Perhaps on the day "when all will be changed" – their return home. But what remained for them until then? A few undoubtedly wished they were still in Russia. Others, a diminishing band, divided their loyalties among the old political parties, or what was left of them. Then there were the postrevolutionary groups. Sirine's sympathy was evident, though cautious. The roots of postrevolutionary thought were, to him, in nineteenth-century slavophilism, yet he could not deny the ideology's appeal to exiled Russian youth a century later. Post-revolutionary opinion had different currents, different nuances of emphasis. These would, Sirine wrote, become clearer in the near future.[54]

Sirine offered his analysis to French readers at a moment when one particular postrevolutionary group was making a determined bid for the support of *émigré* youth in France. Far noisier, more combative and intrusive than Eurasianism, the Young Russia movement (*Mladorussiia*) set out to give a Russian expression to that mood of European youth which the series in *Le Temps* had examined. In this it had some success. Varshavsky described Young Russia as "the first major ideological and political movement created entirely by *émigré* sons."[55] This independence from the older generation, indeed the movement's ostentatious defiance of its seniors' wisdom, certainly enhanced its appeal. It also combined a Russian patriotism with a limited acknowledgment of Soviet realities, together with a dexterity in profiting from the disillusionment apparent in European, including Russian refugee, youth.

Young Russia's origins lay in the emigration's turbulent early years. In February 1923 a twenty-one-year-old aristocratic refugee, Alexander Kazem-Bek, announced the existence of a "Union of Young Russia" at a founding congress in Munich. Its orientation was toward Russian youth at home and abroad, thus to Russia's future.[56] Groups and programmes declaring similar aims were common enough at the time and Kazem-Bek's bombast did not attract particular attention. A few years of inconspicuous existence followed; by 1928 Kazem-Bek was ready to make himself and his ideas more widely known. His most obvious debt was to Italian fascism, most evident in his movement's cult of himself as the charismatic *glava* (leader). Other than this, its basic principle was to be the vaguely defined, ungrammatical neologism of "Young Russianness" (*mladorosskost*). According to the *glava*'s manifesto of 1928 this concept would serve as the means of propelling Young Russia toward its major goal, a national revolution in Russia.[57] Unavoidably anti-Bolshevik, this national revolution must not be seen as mere counterrevolution. 1917 and its heroes were finished. This included Lenin, as well as all veterans of the imperial and provisional governments. Young Russia venerated Orthodoxy and Russian patriotism but its followers must have no illusions. The old regimes had gone for ever; they could not be revived. It remained for the revolution to be completed after the certain collapse of Russia's Marxist government. The Young Russia movement proposed itself as the instrument by which this would be achieved. Reawakening nationalism, reflecting Russia's collectivist traditions and not the selfish individualism of the West, would have a mighty role in this outcome.[58]

Other than Mussolini, Kazem-Bek's two chief inspirations seem to have been the Change of Landmarks school and Eurasianism. The *glava* was quite willing to admit the debt, though Eurasianists took no pleasure in the connection.[59] But one idea, his most notorious, was his own. It expressed Kazem-Bek's view of the appropriate form of Russia's government after the anticipated national revolution. This was to be nothing less than a political marriage between the legitimate Romanov heir, the Grand Duke Cyril Vladimirovich, then residing in Brittany, and certain basic Soviet institutions: a synthesis of old and new. Elaborating on this startling notion, the *glava* conceded that traditional monarchy had fallen for ever in Russia in March 1917. Yet the Lenin cult showed the people's hunger for leadership in personal terms. A monarchy might well be preceded by a dictatorship; in fact, this phase had already begun inside Russia. A new aristocracy existed and the transition to monarchy was surely inevitable. Of course, it would differ sharply from the pre-March 1917 model in Russia and from contemporary bourgeois monarchies in Western Europe. The post-Bolshevik Russian monarchy would preside above classes and maintain the tightest cohesion with the people through their soviets. A "spiritually defined" union between tsar and people, sealed by his blood, was the legacy of the tsar-martyr, Nicholas II.[60]

Not content with this monarcho-Soviet hybrid, Kazem-Bek outdid all other *émigré* politicians in his evaluation of Bolshevism. The Soviet regime, he noted in 1928, was in its tenth year. It did not hold power against the will of the nation, but with its now passive consent. Any reflection upon the years 1917 to 1921 must lead to the conclusion that the Russian people, "in the majority of its politically active strata, was on Bolshevism's side in its struggle against its countless enemies."[61] This observation declared war on the vast majority of refugees for whom Bolshevism remained the ultimate evil. But this did not unduly disturb Kazem-Bek, who was seeking the support, or at least interest, of a different constituency. Nor was he unsuccessful in finding it. By the mid-1930s his movement reached its zenith. A new weekly, *Bodrost* (Courage), circulated in France, attracting attention. It denounced with equal fervour the old *émigré* leaders and Joseph Stalin. All of them were of the past, *Bodrost* announced, only Young Russia faced the future.[62] Though hardly a proof of this claim, two Romanov grand dukes were enrolled among the *glava's* following, while even Cyril Vladimirovich, though not actually a member, allowed his sympathy for Young Russia to become known.[63] The highpoint of his appeal was reached in January 1935, when Kazem-Bek addressed a large gathering in Paris for two hours on his movement and its view of the moment. Crowds of blue-shirted youths whipped up ovations with gratifying chants of "*glava! glava!*"[64]

Neither the *mladorossy* nor, in their time, the still more aggressively fascist grouplets to their right were guided by any philosophy worthy of the name. More often than not, they had nothing but scorn for intellectuals and their concerns: had not these brought Russia and the refugees to their present state? The intellectual dimension to the postrevolutionary cause, lacking since Eurasianism's eclipse, reappeared in the early 1930s in the pages of two new journals, *Utverzhdeniia* (Affirmations) and *Novyi grad* (The New City). Iu.A. Shirinsky-Shikhmatov was the leading spirit behind the first of these. In it, this descendant of Genghis Khan, an ex-Eurasianist and Paris taxi-driver, attempted to revive themes from Eurasianist lecturers of the past decade. Nicholas Berdiaev collaborated in this. The influence of the man whom Sirine described as "the veritable apostle of the postrevolutionary movement,"[65] was heavily apparent in the three published volumes. In the first, Berdiaev addressed himself to the task of defining a position for postrevolutionary youth that was neither of the old, nor of the Fascist or Communist new. Certainly the West had nothing superior to offer Russia, whatever its defenders in the emigration might say. The October Revolution had finished off old Russia. Greater and more genuine than its February prelude, October had enabled new forms of life and social organization to emerge, based on Russia's collectivist tradition. Bolshevism remained pernicious, to be sure, but as a spiritual evil that denied God and man, not as politically wrong. It was painfully struggling, so far without success, to achieve social justice. No other political creed could claim to be superior. Conservative, monarchist, nationalist, liberal, bourgeois-capitalist, democratic, socialist – all, Berdiaev judged, had failed.[66]

Berdiaev's often cloudy postulations were not enough to win for the "affirmers" on *Utverzhdeniia* the respectful recognition of their more numerous "non-affirming" colleagues in the *émigré* intelligentsia. What exactly did the journal stand for in practical terms? Ekaterina Kuskova, prominent in liberal and moderate socialist circles, asked the question after perusing the first volume. She doubted that "a united postrevolutionary ideology" was an attainable objective; in any case the journal's discussion seemed quite unreal. Why the clouds of mysticism? And what of the refugees' primary concern? "Only we Russians," she wrote to the board, "walk through [other] peoples in a trance of universal missions, with the proud intention of saving the world, saving those sinful realists, for only we know the secret of salvation ..., we who were unable to save our own country." What was this universal mission? Just what could they "affirm?" And most important: what kind of struggle, based on such an ideology, was possible against Communism? From Kuskova's viewpoint, none at all.[67]

Utverzhdeniia lasted but three issues. Its mission was taken up by *Novyi grad*'s fourteen numbers, published at irregular intervals through the thirties. "To some degree also oriented toward [*émigré*] youth,"[68] *Novyi grad* was founded by Fedor Stepun and Ilia Fondaminsky, both also prominent in the pages of *Sovremenniia zapiski*. Their taste for questions of complex religious mysticism won them no significant younger readership, while the journal's willingness to denounce the defects of Western democracy distressed Fondaminsky's fellow-editors on *Sovremenníia zapiski*.[69]

Publications such as these, though aimed at younger readers, were written by figures from the older intelligentsia. It is impossible to know accurately how many of those raised in exile were attracted by the various postrevolutionary theories. Certainly the ideas in some form made an impact on many hundreds. What was also quite evident was that the left and right dogmas which so exercised the older generation of refugees exerted very few charms upon their children. Anton Kartashev, prominent in efforts during the early 1920s to organize moderate conservative opinion in the emigration, admitted as much in 1936. What he termed "fascist formations" and a certain degree of social radicalism were, he conceded, making the far right much more attractive to younger Russians abroad than the conservatism of his own generation.[70] Such tastes corresponded to a mood dominant in European youth of the time. The democratic left, for its part, had very few adherents. Alexander Kerensky marked the twentieth anniversary of his cherished February Revolution by devising a conversation between himself and "a spokesman for the postrevolutionary generation" which admitted this aversion. The encounter was, without a doubt, a literary distillation of several real collisions over the years. Kerensky's interlocutor made all the familiar charges. Postrevolutionary youth was alive. It stood for social justice over the sterile political liberty championed by the head of the unlamented Provisional Government. While Kerensky chattered on about freedom, Russian youth in his wonderful, democratic West enjoyed only the freedom of unbearable labour in conditions that degraded their human dignity. Kerensky continued to snivel *here*, but over *there* they were building a new world, a new humanity. Kerensky gave himself the last word – "We shall see!" – yet his young critic maintained his offensive to the end of their meeting.[71]

The appeal of postrevolutionary ideas, while limited to a minority, testified to a genuine hunger in the emigration's second generation for new thoughts about Russia and themselves. Lending urgency to the search were exile's unremitting pressures and their ultimate spectre of denationalization. If new answers were required a readiness to accept, even partially, Russia's altered circumstances since October 1917, several younger refugees and a handful of older intellectuals showed they were willing to consider this generally unthinkable proposition. Anti-Communist, anticapitalist, élitist, and nationalist, small wonder that the postrevolutionary responses often exhibited a distinct Fascist tinge. Eurasianism, Young Russia, and the "affirmers" also denounced the belief that the "best" or "real" Russia lay in emigration. This feature moved the historian and philosopher G.P. Fedotov to single out the postrevolutionaries for qualified approval in an otherwise gloomy assessment of the emigration's usefulness to Russia. He judged the postrevolutionaries as at least willing to study contemporary Russia, though not critically enough. He detected a certain utopianism in their conceptions, leading to "a worship of idols" unlikely to find devotees inside the USSR. Nevertheless, in spite of this rebuke – one surely merited – Fedotov judged postrevolutionaries at least closer than any other émigré groups to the new Soviet generations.[72] Four years later, on the eve of European conflict, Iu.K. Rapoport passed a not dissimilar verdict in his obituary of the Civil War emigration. Rapoport felt that pressure from postrevolutionary ideologies had induced the emigration to accept, "even against its will," the fact of change inside Russia. Young Russia had played a positive role in this. At its peak Young Russia had had a noticeable effect on minds which had been, so to speak, "hermetically sealed in immovable piety and hopefulness." Rapoport judged that Young Russia had bequeathed a simple, yet seditious idea: that the social processes underway inside Russia required attentive study.[73]

Rapoport's tribute, modest though it was, found no strong echo from émigré ranks. Kazem-Bek's disciples, like their postrevolutionary predecessors back to the Change of Landmarks, were written off by their fellow exiles as naive, treacherous, or, as in the case of the mladorossy, crude imitators of a European taste for fascism.[74] In practical terms the scoffers had a point. Even if it can be conceded that Kazem-Bek's vision of a Soviet monarch was not wholly unreal – though the actual ruler in fact was clearly not the one the glava had in mind – it must be admitted that the postrevolutionaries sought to square the circle by reconciling fundamentally incompatible components in their several models for Russia's post-Bolshevik order. They were moved to do so by the wish to get away from the endless recriminations of the irreconcilable émigré majority who, in Rapoport's words, "with loathing refuse to look at a Soviet film or eat a Soviet sprat," even as they recognized that their abstention "[would] not blow up the walls of the enemy fortress."[75] The postrevolutionaries were, of course, no more successful, though their more open attitude toward the Soviet regime enabled them to respond more easily to the earthquakes which struck them and Russia after 22 June 1941.

No member of the second émigré generation lived through the interwar decades without feeling the tug of competing loyalties. How each individual dealt with it depended on personal decision; the dilemma was equally vivid in fiction and fact. The former, for example, is well represented in Nadezhda Gorodetskaia's novel of generational confrontation, L'exil des enfants (1936). Her heroine, Nina, young and ardent, scorns the elder statesmen of the emigration with their eternal prattle of ancient times. Inexorably, seeing their lives in the West, she also loses respect for her fellow-émigrés and cannot feel at home in a society where Russians, in the author's sardonic words, "had been created to sew, drive taxis and entertain Americans."[76]

Russian exile youth wanted none of this. Sport and patriotic preoccupations dominate their preferences. Nina, their prototype, yearns to serve Russia and finds, with some reservations, that the postrevolutionary ideology expressed by Young Russia (here thinly disguised as "the New Russians") is personally the most satisfying. But what future can *émigré* Ninas have? Gorodetskaia's heroine tries to find happiness with a Soviet nonreturner, Malychev. Her hope is doomed, Malychev, suffering from tuberculosis and depression, kills himself and Nina is driven to apply to the Soviet consulate for a visa to return home. Her departure leaves her Russian friends in Paris perplexed and frustrated. The novel's dénouement seems pat, but Nina's quandary was real enough. It was shared in real life by many younger refugees unhappy with their elders, their prospects, and their condition in the West.

Zinaida Shakhovskaia was one who travelled part of Nina's road. Utterly weary of the old men and their nostrums, she and youthful friends amused themselves by letting off stink bombs at meetings addressed by political figures from the democratic part of *émigré* opinion.[77] More grown-up "propaganda of the deed" followed later when, as a Eurasianist, she organized the smuggling of the movement's pamphlets on board Soviet vessels calling at Antwerp.[78] Then, in Paris, she began what would develop into a distinguished literary career by joining the *émigré* Union of Young Poets and Writers. It met from time to time to discuss and declaim new works, either in a room on the rue Denfert-Rochereau, or in a decrepit café, La Bolée, in the heart of the Latin Quarter.[79] It was not an easy time. The French appeared quite indifferent, while her stateless condition continued to put her at the mercy of disdainful officials. To remedy at least this latter difficulty, Shakhovskaia took out Belgian citizenship, though she neither felt nor was regarded by her fellow-citizens as one of them.[80] In Europe and briefly in South America, she remained part of *émigré* Russia, immersed in its concerns. Even as she recognized the ghettolike nature of the refugee world and her need to escape from it, Shakhovskaia admitted that France and Western Europe were, in the years before the war, still exotic regions to her.[81]

Gorodetskaia's Nina returned home, Shakhovskaia stayed in the West but wrapped herself in Russian matters. Lev Tarasian, on the other hand, assimilated relatively easily into French life. Five years younger than Shakhovskaia, the young Tarasian was brought to France after evacuation from the Crimea. His parents, comfortably placed bourgeois in Moscow, adapted very badly to life in exile. They never lost hope in their eventual return and planned how they would remodel their Moscow house on that happy day. Meanwhile, the humiliations of refugee life accumulated. The family jewels were all sold; no one bought the hats his mother made; the bailiffs moved in and carried their furniture out. Through it all the boy, the adolescent, and the young man felt his French ties assert themselves at the expense of his Russian links. He at least had no language problem. Thanks to a Swiss governess in Russia, he had arrived in France with a good command of French. With this headstart the denationalization process accelerated, meeting no resistance from the young Tarasian. Experiences at his French school intensified his desire to be in the French "camp" rather than the Russian; fifty years later he recalled for a French interviewer the stages by which "they" became "we." Two events quickened his progress in that direction. The need to support his near destitute family impelled Tarasian, working on his first novel, to apply for a civil service job. This required French nationality. After endless form-filling and questioning, to the resigned regret of his parents, the deed was done. Then, when his novel was finished, his publisher told him that his foreign name would prove a liability in his quest for a French readership. Lev Tarasian duly made way for Henri Troyat, not without some understandable concern on his part as to what remained of his real identity. Over the next quarter century, his Russo-Armenian parents and the *émigré* community watched as their offspring became one of the most prolific and distinguished figures on the French literary scene. In 1938 he won the Prix Goncourt, France's principal literary award. Twenty-one years later, he was elected to the French Academy, the youngest of the Immortals and sole Russian so far to attain this pinnacle.[82] Russian themes dominate most of his writing, though they are drawn from a vanished era of Russian and *émigré* history. His major work, *Tant que la terre durera*, is his most autobiographical. In this family saga, he has drawn heavily upon his own childhood memories, with other authentic details supplied by ancient veterans and his own parents. Their deaths snapped Troyat's last personal links with old Russia.[83]

The refugee Russian, born in or brought still young to France, had no reason by the late 1930s to feel any faith in his or her future as a Russian. Usually alienated from the values of his seniors, knowing nothing directly of contemporary Russia, immune to communism, often embittered, always impoverished, conscious of his foreignness and uselessness – what future did he, or could he, have?

To this dilemma European war was to offer unexpected solutions.

CHAPTER FIVE

Ordeals and Triumphs

What did the French know of the Russians in their midst? The answers depend upon perspectives. On the level of individual contacts French impressions ranged from the relative friendliness encountered by Briunelli and others to the acerbic rudeness of a neighbour of Miliukov's, who dwelt in stiffly formal terms on the Russian's foreign status among those who had a far better right than he to live in France.[1] There were, of course, the standard, unavoidable images. In his 1982 novel of émigré life, *Le Montage*, Vladimir Volkoff sums these up succinctly. His protagonist, Dmitri Aleksandrovich Psar, in Russia a junior naval officer, in France a stablehand, arrived with hopes of finding a warm French gratitude for Russian services in the Great War. He was speedily disabused. "Your fine Russia," he was told by a French holder of tsarist bonds, "cost me my life savings." Following this, Psar had to endure reproaches from customers in a local bistro regarding Russia's desertion of France in the war. Dmitri Aleksandrovich protested these calumnies. They were not the fault of his Russia. She, in the person of her emperor, had remained true to the end. But Psar made as little impact as Briunelli. A final, dismissive French comment completed his discomforture: "All that [the Revolution] was because you were a boyar, but the people were badly off."[2]

But Russians also met with friendlier receptions. 1930 saw the publication of works by Ledré and Delage, both good friends of the Russian community. Seven years later, in the middle of the Spanish influx, another French journalist, André Beucler, called the Russians "the most important numerically, the healthiest in its composition, the most representative in its national elements and the most welcome from the start" of all the refugee waves into France.[3] Here and elsewhere there were tributes to the Russians' stoicism, to their dignity in adversity, and to their nobility of character.[4]

In assessing these several opinions, today's observer of the interwar Russian colony in France must bear in mind that the context within which these and most other judgments of the Russians were made was not one primarily defined by empirical observation. The attitude of the French writer, journalist, politician or "man in the street" toward the *émigrés* was more decisively shaped by his view of the Soviet Union and the French left. The Russians in France were, after all, victims of Bolshevism. All other European refugees in France fled from Fascism. In the polarized political world of the time that fact put Russian exiles on the right, even far right, of the political spectrum. This had both advantages and drawbacks. On the one hand, it conferred almost complete immunity from attack by the traditionally most xenophobic elements of the French press and political world. On the other hand, it isolated Russians from the other refugee minorities in France with whom they shared a common outcast status and, presumably, common problems of adjustment. Simpson's investigator into refugee groups in France heard of the Russians in 1937 that "they are no part of us" and that German refugee bodies refused to be represented on any international relief committee if the Russians were also to be present.[5] This slight did not unduly worry the Russians, very few of whom cared to have much to do with German, Italian, and Spanish refugees. One fact was, however, true for all exiles: their political origins largely determined their political friends and foes in France.

For the Russians, two lurid events in the early 1930s put the truth of this fact beyond challenge.

THE KUTEPOV AFFAIR

On 26 January 1930 General Alexander Kutepov, head of the principal *émigré* veterans organization, the Russian All-Military Union (ROVS), was kidnapped in the broad daylight of a busy Paris street. Bundled into an automobile by three unknown figures, he was thereafter not seen again by French or *émigré* eyes. Witnesses to the event spoke of a short struggle, while later that same afternoon chance observers on a Normandy beach noted the mysterious transfer of a bulky, oblong parcel to a motorboat, which then sped out to a steamship waiting offshore. The latter disappeared over the horizon. It subsequently proved to have been the Soviet freighter *Spartak*.[6]

The Russian All-Military Union, founded in 1923 by General Wrangel, commanded the loyalty of his former legions. Fiercely anti-Bolshevik, it had its headquarters in Paris and maintained branches in all important centres of Russian settlement abroad. Kutepov had shown himself an iron-willed commander during the Civil War and in the Gallipoli camps following the Crimean evacuation. President of the Association of Gallipoli Veterans, he had moved from that post to direct ROVS after Wrangel's death in 1928. The Union concerned itself primarily with the welfare of its several thousand members, in particular with finding them jobs, but Kutepov himself was also much involved in various murky schemes of "active" anti-Soviet agitation. None of the agents he dispatched into Soviet Russia on intelligence or destructive missions was ever heard from again.[7]

The *émigré* press did not have to look far to identify the perpetrators of Kutepov's seizure. All newspapers devoted vast attention to the incident. *Poslednia novosti* remained guarded in its evaluation of the situation. It had no real doubt about those responsible, but its editor could not muster any admiration for Kutepov or his strident defenders on the right wing.[8] *Vozrozhdenie* boiled over with rage. Hammering away at this latest Soviet affront, the paper expressed the hope that French justice would now act to rid the country of the Moscow-controlled conspirators plotting its subversion.[9] Second only to *Vozrozhdenie*'s obsession with Bolshevism's fall was its ambition to witness a diplomatic rupture between France and the Soviet regime. The Kutepov kidnapping furnished ample grounds for this, if only the incumbent Tardieu ministry would nerve itself to the deed. Meanwhile, Vladimir Burtsev got busy on the General's trail. Readers were regaled with the antics of a varied cast: Soviet secret police agents (the GPU), a "Liudmila in a beige coat," a mysterious red taxi-cab, and a confusing array of Russians Red and White.[10] While Burtsev's wide-ranging insinuations caused much indignation, not even the threat of a lawsuit could reduce "the Sherlock Holmes of the emigration" to silence.[11] As Burtsev laboured, the police investigator in charge of the case, improbably named Faux-Pas-Bidet, issued hopeful bulletins which did not appear justified on the basis of any of the revealed evidence.

The affair's sensational aspects reminded the French public more effectively than any sober study of the existence in their country of the Russian community. The press blossomed forth with articles about Kutepov and the Russian exiles. These accounts were fashioned more in accordance with political considerations than by a strict regard for the admittedly few indisputable facts in the case. *Le Temps* waited a week before it commented in measured tones on what seemed to the editor to be a political kidnapping. Who was responsible? Between the Bolsheviks or "certain Russian patriots, who disliked the General's moderation and caution," *Le Temps* refused editorially to commit itself. Four days later this reticence was visibly weakening. While still not actually naming the guilty party, *Le Temps* inveighed against the presence in France of agents of the GPU to whom it attributed much of the nation's social unrest. "It is intolerable that a band paid by the Third International or by the Soviet government can operate with impunity in our country, corrupt our workers [and] commit espionage and crimes." Nor did the editorial forget that "Russian *émigrés*, whatever their political beliefs, ... have the right ... to the same protection as French citizens." Men of good faith would find it impossible in the present case to simply pass on to next business, considering the kidnapping, perhaps even the murder, of General Kutepov as a minor news item.[12]

If the editor of *Le Temps* hesitated to make the categoric accusation, the shriller organs of the nationalist press leaped to make good his omission. The pack was led by *La Liberté*, a newspaper whose ferociously anti-Soviet views made it a source of comfort and support to *Vozrozhdenie*. *La Liberté* at once proclaimed that a new Bolshevik crime had been perpetrated by the GPU; Paris demanded justice against the criminals responsible. As the days passed without any solution, *La Liberté* published sensational details of proceedings at the Soviet embassy ("the Soviet lair in Paris"). Neighbours on the rue de Grenelle were, so the paper alleged, fed up with the drunken orgies and the sounds of mysterious digging in the garden at night. If the government would not act against the traitors of Brest-Litovsk, the people of Paris would take matters into their own hands.[13] This barrage kept up for several days and culminated in a protest meeting on 11 February of French and Russians who wished to express their outrage at "GPU crimes in France." There were passionate speeches by prominent figures on the political right, headed by Camille Aymard, *La Liberté*'s publisher. Others present included Pierre Taittinger, scion of the champagne family and founder in 1924 of the fascist Jeunesses Patriotes, and Jean Delage, who later translated his indignation into a book about the affair.[14] *La Liberté* pronounced the meeting a great success, though the more moderate press took little notice. Aymard no doubt thought his efforts worthwhile when Ambassador Dovgalevsky ("chief Soviet assassin") lodged a protest with the Quai d'Orsay at the anti-Soviet tone of the right-wing press.[15]

No newspaper on the right matched *La Liberté*'s invective. In the royalist *Action française* Léon Daudet attacked an incompetent police, a weak government, and a corrupt republic which permitted these excesses.[16] This was standard fare. The reaction from the opposite political camp was no less predictable. Newspapers on the left began by treating the affair lightly: "a fantastic tale, a rollicking adventure," probably engineered by forces inside the emigration, if not by Kutepov himself.[17] But when the matter refused to die away immediately, the Socialist tone grew more serious. The right-wing press and its deputies in the Chamber were using the affair to attack republican institutions and to demand a break with Moscow.[18] These efforts had to be resisted. On 11 February, the day of *La Liberté*'s anti-Soviet rally, Léon Blum demanded in *Le Populaire* that Kutepov must not serve as a pretext for a breach with the USSR. Blum warned that the reactionary campaign to whip up anti-Soviet hysteria was likely only to bring grief upon the *émigrés* if it succeeded. Moscow would then turn in insulted fury upon Soviet citizens who had links to the exiles in France. "Your own friends and relatives will curse you," he advised *Vozrozhdenie* in words which showed he had no illusions about Stalin's regime.[19] Herriot's *L'Ere nouvelle* also resisted demands for a break with Moscow. Calm and an end to polemics would help. *Émigrés* had a right to expect justice but Soviet diplomats were equally entitled to courtesy from the press.[20]

From the furthest left end of the spectrum, *L'Humanité* rose to the congenial challenge of matching *La Liberté's* rancour. For two weeks the Communist daily shrieked its defiance to the bourgeois press, the "counterrevolutionary jackels" of the government and the *émigré* world, aided and abetted by "Sir Deterding" and Pius XI. *L'Humanité* proclaimed the Kutepov affair nothing but an elaborate charade devised by the "White guard" emigration to poison Franco-Soviet relations, the harbinger of a vast anti-Soviet crusade.[21]

The campaign of charge and countercharge sputtered on until the end of February. It was not, however, in the nature of the Paris press to focus for too long on any one particular issue when many other more promising topics jostled for attention. The fall of the Tardieu ministry in the middle of the month diverted journalistic interest to the much more agreeable preoccupation with domestic political intrigue. Kutepov was irretrievably lost; Monsieur Faux-Pas-Bidet ceased his optimistic forecasts, and the Russian world in France could again be left to its own peculiar concerns.

Two years later, a second *cause célèbre* erupted between the Russian community and its French hosts. This one made a much deeper and more painful impression.

GORGULOV

On 6 May 1932 the president of the republic, Paul Doumer, was guest of honour at a Paris exhibition of books written by veterans of the Great War. As he moved among the crowd in the Hôtel Salomon de Rothschild, an unknown man stepped forward and fired a revolver point-blank at the president's head. Rushed to a nearby hospital, the victim lingered for a few hours, only to expire early the following morning. As he lay dying, an appalled Russian community learned, with the rest of France, that the president's assailant was one of their number, a Kuban Cossack, Paul Gorgulov.

The murdered president was hardly a nationally beloved figure, nor even especially well known.[22] All the same, his humble origins, irreproachable dignity and republican patriotism – four sons had fallen in the war – made his death particularly odious. Furthermore, as *émigré* leaders saw all too clearly, it was not hard to judge the attack upon Doumer as an assault on the republic itself from a quarter that had excellent reasons to be grateful to the French government and people. The worst months in the history of the Russian emigration now began.

In the torrent of French and Russian comment on the event of 6 May the figure of the assassin himself seemed at times almost incidental. His battered, bewildered face stared out from every newspaper in France, along with the wildest speculation as to who he was and why he had acted. Yet that act aside, Gorgulov was not untypical of the *émigré* mass from which he emerged so dramatically. After fleeing from Russia in the civil war, he first settled in Prague, where he studied medicine. He then eked out a difficult existence as a doctor ministering to fellow-refugees, few of whom could pay for his services. Eventually, like so many, he drifted to Paris, back to Prague, once again to Paris from which he was soon expelled for the illegal practice of his profession. His wanderings continued: Prague, Monaco, Paris again. Along the way he acquired two or three wives (the accounts differ), and wrote pamphlets announcing a "green" political programme. This was a mixture of pan-Russian populism and Mussolini-style fascism to which nobody paid any attention. His more serious literary efforts, read to Russian friends, including Vassily Yanovsky, were equally unappreciated.[23] In his loneliness, political obsessions, lack of papers, and rootless existence, Gorgulov was not unique. In his case, however, it appears that the frustrations of refugee life were enough to derange his mind.

As with Kutepov two years before, the right-wing press saw Gorgulov's deed through the prism of its primary concern. *Vozrozhdenie* stressed two aspects of the case. Gorgulov, "a semiliterate neurasthenic," had no links to anyone in the emigration, while his act put him "spiritually close to the Bolsheviks." *Vozrozhdenie* also declared, though its sources remain a mystery, that Gorgulov had ties to Kutepov's kidnappers and to a recently executed Korean bomb thrower in Shanghai.[24] On 9 May, "according to facts reported from Brussels," Gorgulov was described as a Bolshevik agent designated for propaganda work in the Congo. The next day the newspaper cast caution to the winds and announced that the assassin was a Soviet commissar.[25]

Posledniia novosti took a less apocalyptic view. Obviously Gorgulov was mentally unstable. His political loyalties, so far as these could be determined, were, by his own declarations to the police, to the far right rather than to the far left. But the overriding preoccupation of Miliukov's newspaper was to preserve the Russian colony from a hostile French backlash. French public opinion, Miliukov wrote on 7 May, was too chivalrous and sensible to blame all Russian *émigrés* for the act of a single madman.[26] The point was further underscored in formal letters of condolence sent to Premier André Tardieu, heading his third administration, and to Madame Doumer. The signatories comprised two dozen of the leading names in Russian France. When the widely-read, middle-of-the-road *Le Matin* asked that all politically active foreigners be expelled from France, *Posledniia novosti* reprinted the article without comment. On the following day, it gave over its editorial column to the journalist-novelist Pierre Mille. He had argued in *Excelsior* that to make all Russians suffer because of Gorgulov would be an error, almost an act of cowardice, which the French were too just to commit.[27] Ordinary Russians made their revulsion apparent. Hundreds signed sympathy messages to Madame Doumer and the press gave prominent coverage to a Russian waiter who flung himself from a sixth-floor window to his death in shame at the harm done to France by another Russian refugee.[28]

Emigré efforts to head off an unfriendly French reaction received strong backing from the government of the day. Doumer's murder came at a delicate moment in French political life, not least in the fortunes of Premier Tardieu. Six days earlier the first round of parliamentary elections had seen a surge in support for parties of the left; a second, decisive round, due on 8 May, promised to maintain this momentum. Conservatives thus stood on the defensive and were quite ready to brandish new evidence of the Red menace in one final attempt to avert electoral disaster. Using Gorgulov to that end did not seem particularly promising in the light of his statement, published in the press, that he was "president of the Russian Fascists, seeking to punish France for her aid to the Bolsheviks."[29] The interior ministry did its best, nonetheless, in its first communiqué on the case to create a contrary impression. The country read that Gorgulov was the founder in Prague of "a neo-Bolshevik pan-Russian peasant populist party." Literature found on him bore "the neo-Bolshevik insignia" of two scythes surmounted by a fir tree and two skulls. "Groups which use this emblem," the government explained, "are inspired by the Third International, which frequently employs them as agents provocateurs."[30] A confirmation came from Alexandre Millerand, who did what he could for the cause. Himself once president of the republic, forced out of office by the *Cartel des Gauches* in 1924, Millerand lost no chance to score off enemies. After presenting his condolences at the Elysée palace, he told waiting journalists of his ability to state categorically that Gorgulov was a member of "regular Bolshevik forces." Everyone must forget petty differences and unite before the major foe.[31]

The government's efforts went for nothing. The second round of elections resulted in an overall left majority in the new Chamber, rendering pointless any prolonged campaign around Gorgulov. Even the rightist French press was unenthusiastic. *La Liberté*, which two years before had strained every nerve to attack Moscow over Kutepov, noted briefly, probably via *Vozrozhdenie*, that "in Prague [Gorgulov was] considered a GPU agent." Four days later, still from the same source, the assassin "[was] said to be a People's Commissar."[32] Thereafter *La Liberté* downplayed this theme in favour of Gorgulov's probable insanity. Pierre Taittinger's ultraconservative weekly *Le National* was too absorbed in the need to prevent the left from returning to power, then too depressed when it did, to spare much attention for theories about Gorgulov's employers. In fact, *Le National* preferred to remind readers of a previous presidential assassination, that of Sadi-Carnot in 1894. On that occasion, the murderer, much more satisfactorily for *Le National*, had been an Italian anarchist.[33] In *La Victoire*, Gustave Hervé accepted that Gorgulov was deranged. But Hervé concluded he had been driven to that condition by shameful Western policies, especially French, toward the Soviets.[34] Unique as usual, *L'Action française* identified the assailant as "probably an agent of Moscow and Berlin." As in 1930, the royalist organ concentrated its fire upon domestic French targets: the police, the government, and the presidency.[35]

In the Kutepov case the right had pressed the offensive against the left and its real or imagined links to Moscow. Now the roles were reversed. The left, scenting victory, furiously resisted the government's attempts to alarm the public with mendacious reports about Gorgulov's patrons. In their counterattacks newspapers from *L'Ere nouvelle* leftward focused upon the community from which Gorgulov had sprung. The attention served to publicize convictions about Russians in France which, after Doumer's murder, might well carry greater weight.

L'Ere nouvelle approached the issue more in sorrow than anger. Reflecting the views of Herriot and his Radical Party, it had naturally welcomed recognition of Soviet Russia. At the same time the paper had been far from hostile to the refugees. Now there was a note of wariness. Both Red and White Russians had condemned Gorgulov; no doubt they were sincere. Neither side could deny, however, "that in their country elements of savagery exist even today which a too recent civilization has not been able to eradicate." It was unfortunately true, the paper added, that Doumer's assassination would encourage those who said, "not threateningly but firmly, there are already too many foreigners in France, above all too many Russians." French hospitality had been repaid with the blackest ingratitude.[36]

Le Populaire took a milder line. Léon Blum wrote that the murderer was obviously insane and had never belonged to any party in spite of the strange rumours about him. Socialists scorned to take advantage of a madman's ravings to arouse public opinion against White Russians in Paris whose military organizations were so curiously tolerated. Blum directed his sharpest criticisms at the government's manipulation of the crime. Efforts to pin a GPU label on Gorgulov were absurd. They were the work of the far right press, French and *émigré*, which hoped to engineer a break with Moscow. This hope would not succeed.[37] At that point *Le Populaire's* attention was diverted from the Russians in France by the fortuitous combination of Socialist electoral success; the death of a veteran party colleague, Albert Thomas; and the discovery in America of the Lindbergh baby's presumed corpse. Subsequent references to Gorgulov were sporadic, without further unsettling reflections on his refugee compatriots in France.

The preponderant share in the attack on the *émigrés* was enthusiastically borne by the Communist party, for whom the Gorgulov case seemed tailormade. An anti-Soviet Russian refugee, one of several thousand in France, a self-proclaimed Fascist, had murdered the highest official of the republic in the midst of crucial elections which the left was winning against a transparently deceitful, rightist cabinet. *L'Humanité* instantly sprang to the attack. On 7 May two pages of clamorous headlines announced that the Tardieu government had lied, the assassin was a White Russian. "Throw out the White Guards, Tardieu's agents! For peace, for defence of the USSR, tomorrow vote Communist!" Marcel Cachin then offered a four-column description of the *émigrés* that elaborated on these slogans.[38] The final election results brought no relaxation in the campaign, in fact the reverse. From the volume and scope of Communist attacks, it is apparent that they constituted a well orchestrated effort, in close collaboration with Moscow, to present the French right and the Russian exiles as the nucleus of a vast anti-Soviet warmongering conspiracy. For a month *L'Humanité's* front page bristled with epithets, which stood as mirror image to *Vozrozhdenie's* adjectives. Gorgulov was, at varying times, an imperialist agent, a member of a counterrevolutionary terrorist group, a police spy, an agent of Czechoslovakia, linked to *Vozrozhdenie* and – an improbable yoking – the Mensheviks. The *émigrés* were all Fascists, or the dupes of Fascists. Paris was their dunghill. Tardieu and Paris police prefect Jean Chiappe were their patrons and protectors, hence Doumer's real killers. And so on.[39]

Whether or not *L'Humanité's* virulence convinced large numbers of readers is impossible to judge. No doubt many French workers could see for themselves that not all Russians beside them on the assembly line were Fascist hyenas; moreover, *L'Humanité* did concede that refugee labourers might be won over from their "White Guard" officers.[40] A scattering of reports from departmental prefects indicated no general animus against Russians in the provinces in spite of occasional complaints at the ease with which foreigners could enter France.[41] In Alpes-Maritimes the police reported that Communists had plastered Nice with denunciatory posters. These proclaimed that "thousands of Russian refugees are in Nice and along the Côte d'Azur. They are nobles from the tsar's court, bourgeois exploiters of muzhiks, industrialists, financiers, and journalists – all who fled before the revolutionary wave!" The leaflets went on to complain that these same Russians were favoured by the police, who remained indifferent to their plots. In the meantime, far more deserving Italian refugees from Mussolini's tyranny were being subjected to brutal police repression.[42]

The outgoing Tardieu ministry paid no attention to these criticisms which, in *L'Humanité's* case, it ascribed to agents of the Comintern.[43] If this meant that the government believed Moscow dictated French Communist reaction to the Gorgulov affair, it underestimated the party's ability to express unprompted its longstanding line on questions relating to the Russian exiles in France. Party members knew their duty. Henri Barbusse, Stalin's most zealous devotee in France, contributed an inflammatory pamphlet which purported to name Doumer's real assassins, those who had guided Gorgulov's hand.[44] Two comrades, Henry Franklin-Marquet and Paul Vaillant-Couturier, gave similar accounts.[45] These took up all the familiar accusations in *L'Humanité* (not a difficult task since Vaillant-Couturier was the paper's editor), amplified them where possible, and added new ones. Undoubtedly aided by Moscow, they quoted extensively from *Chasovoi* (Sentinel), the belligerently interventionist organ of the chief émigré veterans group, the Russian All-Military Union (ROVS). Soviet sources also contributed "decisive details" from the USSR. Reporters had, it appeared, tracked down Gorgulov's mother in her Cossack village. She related that her son had been a notorious killer of revolutionaries before his flight from Russia.[46]

Gorgulov's four-day trial in late July probably confirmed French impressions, first gained during the Kutepov affair, that the Russians were a strange people. The defendant himself roared incoherently of moon rockets and peasant masses; however, the prosecution rejected defence claims that he was insane. He was Russian, his mentality was thus utterly un-French. This accounted for his misdeed. One had only to see the frequency of terrorist acts in Russian history to appreciate this truth. A Russian witness for the prosecution, who insisted that the bemused prisoner had been a bloodthirsty Cheka torturer in Rostov during the Revolution, known as "Comrade Mongol," no doubt reinforced the state's point. Certainly the jury accepted it without apparent difficulty. Gorgulov, duly convicted, was guillotined on 14 September.[47]

With his death the affair could at last fade from the French press. It had been a traumatic summer for Russians in France. Their political life, presence and national character had been subjected to a vast amount of publicity, almost all of it intensely disagreeable. A period of inconspicuous recovery was thus very welcome.

The Gorgulov ordeal, among its other effects, raised a question of vital interest to émigrés. No matter how fervent the Russian expressions of regret and dissociation were, recent events must have contributed to an unfortunate impression upon Frenchmen, one indeed suggested by *L'Ere nouvelle's* none too delicate reference to Russia's "too recent civilization," that Russians could scarcely be included among those fully civilized by contact with European culture. Gorgulov's trial did nothing to contradict this image. Accordingly, it was more than ever incumbent upon émigrés, particularly their "active" writing spokesmen, to affirm, in the midst of what Ivan Bunin called "our tragedy," the reality of Russian culture and its indissoluble ties to European civilization.[48] Two opportunities soon presented themselves.

The first of these took place two months after Gorgulov's execution. On 30 November the literary élite of Russian France gathered in Paris to honour the journal *Sovremenniia zapiski* on the occasion of the publication of its fiftieth volume. Telegrams of greeting from all centres of the Russian diaspora acknowledged the central role the journal had come to play in the twelve years since its birth. Though lacking the slightest degree of political cohesion, the emigration shared in V.V. Rudnev's pride at the extraordinary range of political loyalties represented at the festivities. This was, to Rudnev, unimaginable in any other émigré context. It was possible only on that occasion because they did not meet as proponents of any particular political faith, but as witnesses of an important event in Russian letters. Every message but two read out to the assembled guests underlined this by rejecting or ignoring the journal's commitment to the ideas of the February Revolution. That the two exceptions came from "the father and son" of that revolution merely emphasized the unanimity of the rejection. [49] But the journal's commitment to the free Russian word remained and made *Sovremenniia zapiski*, to a significant degree, the organ of the whole emigration. [50]

The banquet of 30 November was a private celebration by Russians of their greatest tangible asset in exile. A more public occasion for rejoicing over the same values came almost exactly one year later. On 10 November 1933, the world press announced that Ivan Bunin had been awarded that year's Nobel Prize for literature. Fourteen months after Gorgulov's head fell in payment for his crime, the worldwide Russian exile community experienced its proudest moment.

The Nobel award was providential on two counts. For Bunin personally the $47,300 came as a godsend. Living in ever more impoverished circumstances in a dilapidated house in Grasse, he had already been twice nominated for the prize and twice had seen it go to another. His disappointment was in part natural artistic pride – had not seven professors from various countries visited him and President Masaryk expressed his interest? – and partly a keen awareness of the difference the award would make to his material existence. [51] Galina Kuznetsova, who lived with the Bunins, witnessed his mingled joy, excitement, and bewilderment as congratulations and requests for interviews poured into Grasse. [52]

Bunin's prize resoundingly confirmed to the émigré intelligentsia the validity of its self-imposed mission. *Poslednaia novosti*, *Vozrozhdenie*, and *Sovremennia zapiski*, for one unique instant, could unite in unfeigned tribute to the same person. The award was "a great moral victory" for Russian literature and the emigration, "real Russia" rejoiced. [53] The three publications emphasized their closeness to Russia's new laureate. A gala evening on 26 November at the Théâtre des Champs-Elysées permitted the political and cultural leadership of old Russia, as well as less well known exiles, to join in united satisfaction at one of the very rare public occasions when political differences might be laid aside in honour of one of their own. Emile Haumant, "friend of Russia and Slavdom," with a few other French wellwishers, was present to hear Maklakov and other speakers salute Bunin and, through him, the living reality of Russian culture abroad. On behalf of his community Maklakov stressed this latest proof of the links between non-Bolshevik Russian values and European civilization.[54]

The award ceremony in Stockholm two weeks later was a still more significant occasion for pride. A Russian émigré was being honoured at the summit of the literary world. There he would speak for his compatriots and, if only for a moment, command a hearing from cultured Europe. Bunin was conscious of his responsibility and unique status. Unlike the other laureates, he had no ambassador to stand with him. Alexandra Kollontai, the Soviet minister, did not attend any of the proceedings, nor of course would Bunin have accepted her presence at his side. A search throughout Stockholm failed to produce a single pre-Bolshevik Russian tricolor, so, in deference to him, no flags were displayed except the Swedish.[55] At the dinner which closed the day's festivities Bunin reminded his audience that this was the first time the award had gone to a Russian and an exile. He pronounced the last word with defiant emphasis. They were, he told them, united by one truth, a complete freedom of thought and conscience to which they owed their civilization.[56]

His message, which included generous tributes to Sweden and France, met with a mixed reception. In Stockholm Swedish speakers praised Bunin as a great figure in the continuity of Russian classical literature. But he was wholly of the past. Professor Nordenson, of the Karolinska Institute, declared that Bunin had given the world "the most valuable picture of Russian society as it once was, and we well understand the feelings with which you have seen the destruction of the society with which you were so intimately connected." He extended the company's sympathies to comfort the new laureate "in the melancholy of exile."[57] In France the award and its attendant ceremonies made only a modest impression on a press which had had so much to say about the émigrés during the agony of the Gorgulov case. While some of Bunin's works had been translated,[58] his nationality and condition ensured that his prize would be judged, in part at least, on the basis of nonliterary criteria. Le Temps was friendly. It dwelt on Bunin's merits and noble character; it also gave details of the Stockholm ceremonies.[59] L'Ere nouvelle briefly noted the winner's major publications, insisting that his choice had no political significance.[60] L'Humanité sneered at the award to "a derelict of the old world swept away by the proletarian revolution." The bourgeoisie was crowning one of its own.[61]

As might have been expected, the most eloquent expression of the prize's meaning appeared in an editorial tribute in Sovremenniia zapiski. Bunin was an old friend. Many short stories, a novel (Mitina liubov'), and portions of a second (Zhizn' Arseneva) had already been published in twenty of the journal's fifty-three volumes. The Nobel Prize was a symbol of the world's recognition of Bunin's stature; it was also something more. "The solemn crowning of an *émigré* writer's work," the statement affirmed, "has confirmed before the whole world that we have something worth struggling for, in the name of which we shall not reconcile ourselves with those who are disfiguring Russia. This is a recognition of the value of free *émigré* expression." It gave meaning to their struggle, to their privations, endured for the sake of their ideals. Indeed, those hardships and the general tragedy of their exile could scarcely be justified otherwise. In spite of everything, Russian literature remained, for the editors, a single whole to which Soviet and *émigré* writers all contributed. Those writing outside Russia rejoiced when, despite the lack of freedom, outstanding works appeared *there*, in the USSR. "But we know that genuinely lofty creative work needs freedom, which we preserve *here*." Serving this freedom outside Russia required sacrifices. They had already renounced a numerous reading public, the protection of their own state, material rewards and honours. Other sacrifices were also demanded. "The more time has passed, the more often have our ordeals encountered the jeers of our enemies and the indifference of our European fellow-writers, the doubts of the weary, and the bitterness of those who have lost faith." Hence the joy in this dazzling success.[62]

The editors' pride was wholly legitimate. Yet it may be doubted whether many non-Russians endorsed, or were even aware of, the exiled intelligentsia's belief that Bunin's prize proved the value of its struggle in defence of Russian values abroad. There was no evidence to suggest, for example, that the *Stockholm* triumph did anything to erase French memories of the Kutepov and Gorgulov dramas. French men and women already disposed, for whatever reason, to resent the Russian presence in France were not to be won over to admiration either by Bunin's prize or his eloquence. Regrettably, the remaining years of European peace offered evidence which tended to reinforce the negative impressions, quite overshadowing the efforts of Russian intellectuals and their French friends on behalf of a more sympathetic image.

CHAPTER SIX

Russia and Europe

Along with the defence of their good name and of the legitimacy of their cause, the *émigré* intelligentsia had a third, related preoccupation, one which interested the newspaper-reading exile mass more than the two other concerns. In monographs, lectures, and countless columns of the press, *émigré* personalities of every political hue took it upon themselves to expose Soviet reality, as they saw it, to the scrutiny of exiled Russians and of anyone else who would listen. In the process, they became the world's first professional Sovietologists.

In the spring of 1924, following the British Labour government's recognition of the Soviet regime, the emigration's most prolific anti-Bolshevik commentator assessed in *Sovremenniia zapiski* what this act might mean for exiled Russians, who were united by nothing save their hatred for the men now ruling their country. Mark Vishniak felt that the moment was decisive. The floodgates now were open; the British deed would be widely imitated. It would probably have important economic, financial and juridical consequences. Yet truth and justice too had their own logic, which could not forever be ignored. Why, he asked, was no government prepared to make it a condition of recognition that the Soviet authorities acknowledge that their subjects too had rights?[1] Vishniak found particularly reprehensible the failure of those who ought to have known better to support the Russian popular cause with the same vigour as they did others. A recently concluded meeting in Luxembourg of the Executive Committee of the Labour and Socialist (Hamburg) International offered depressing evidence of this infirmity of will. Delegates had denounced the oppressive Horthy regime in Hungary and the European plutocracy which kept it financially afloat; they had sympathized with Armenians and Georgians whose countries were militarily occupied by the Soviets. The session had even justly "consider[ed] it the duty of all Socialist parties of all countries to support Russian Socialists in their struggle against the politically repressive regime" in the USSR. Yet why was nothing said specifically of the Russian people's right to freedom and justice? Why should not Russians enjoy the same right of full self-determination that the Socialist International demanded for Georgians and Armenians? The questions, Vishniak conceded, were rhetorical.[2]

Two aspects of Vishniak's evaluation remained painfully relevant to the *émigrés'* relationship to both Soviet Russia and the non-Russian world. Whatever the Russian exiles might insist, many foreign nations were ready, within half a dozen years of the Revolution, to see in Moscow a legitimate Russian government. No moral sanction might be involved, yet the parade of diplomats eastward demonstrated that the Soviet government was no longer a leper, except to its vanquished Russian foes abroad. This led to the second point. There was indeed a double standard where Russian democrats might least have expected it. The sins that could not be overlooked in Horthy, Mussolini, Salazar, and their ilk, the failures and follies of Western parliamentary regimes which would draw so much condemnation from enlightened, progressive opinion in the West, found little or no echo from that same source where the USSR was concerned. Refugee Russians who treasured democratic values for their own sake and for Russia's found themselves fighting with few foreign allies. In time this might bring its own vindication: at any rate Vishniak liked to think so. He consoled himself at difficult moments with a maxim he attributed to the historian Ernest Renan to the effect that "the way to be right in the future is at certain times to know how to submit to being out of fashion."[3] Awaiting history's judgment, passionately interested, yet powerless to affect the course of events, articulate Russian refugees exercised to the full their only rights in Soviet matters once the regime gained international respectability: to comment, denounce, warn, and prophesy.

The portrait of Soviet life which emerged from *émigré* sources in the years following recognition owed as much to its painters' certainties in Paris as it did to realities in Moscow. Sources of information, when used, such as the Soviet press, the occasional defector, the rare critical account from Western visitors, the even rarer details from correspondents still in the USSR, usually served to harden long-held convictions about the nature of the Soviet system. Common to all but the tiny Menshevik band – and even to it eventually – was the distinction that had to be made between the Russian people and the oppressive tyranny which weighed it down. To maintain and elaborate upon this eternal separation, to speak up for the persecuted majority and its interests, became a common, fundamental theme across the spectrum of the *émigré* press.

THE VIEW FROM THE RIGHT

The conservative and reactionary press invariably depicted the confrontation in terms of National Russia facing the dark, alien forces of the Communist International. At its extreme this press saw Russia as the victim of "messianistic Judaism [which] controls parliaments, Masons ... [and] the League of Nations."[4] Thus spoke N.E. Markov II, vociferous protagonist of a monarchical counterrevolution. *Vozrozhdenie*, at least under Struve, was more restrained. Struve sought to range his paper on the side of Russia's best liberal and conservative traditions. His loathing of Bolshevism and yearning for his country's pre-1917 past were, however, never in doubt. With Semenov at the helm, *Vozrozhdenie* sank into the most obsessive anti-Soviet vituperation. Nostalgia filled its columns. Every 16 July, for example, black-edged portraits of Nicholas II and his family reminded readers quite un-necessarily of Bolshevism's responsibility for the crime at Ekaterinburg. Frequent cartoons presented Soviet leaders as repulsive, alien bandits intent on the torture of the chained Russian bear. Every report of their ill health or, better, of their imminent political or physical demise was eagerly splashed across *Vozrozhdenie's* front page. With the present so unpromising, the unknowable future was invoked to aid in the struggle against Bolshevism. Hopeful scenarios appeared from time to time of a Russia cleared of its Soviet plague, old irritants removed, a more natural order in place.[5]

Vozrozhdenie's original mission and increasingly shrill style made it an early target for critics. The two main organs of liberal democratic opinion, *Posledniia novosti* and *Sovremenniia zapiski*, recognized an ideological op-ponent whose effort to give coherent form to reactionary political ideas had to be resisted. Miliukov, Vishniak and their several colleagues saw their task as all the more imperative given the unpopularity of Socialist, liberal, and democratic values inside the emigration, and the concomitant appeal of monarchical, conservative images. Within weeks of *Vozrozhdenie's* ap-pearance, Mark Vishniak was contesting Struve's belief that his views and following represented National Russia. "Who does not consider himself the defender of Russia's interests?"[6] How far and sad was Struve's fall! Even though Vishniak detected, throughout Struve's entire public career, his distrust of the people, he felt that the onetime Marxist had at least stayed within cer-tain limits and won respect for the acuity of his political commentary. But now, in joining ranks with the Grand Duke Nikolai Nikolaevich, Struve had gone beyond all limits and forfeited all respect. He had become to Vishniak nothing more than the editor of an official grand-ducal press organ, *"avocat des causes perdues."*[7]

When it came to lost causes, Vishniak was, if anything, more deserving of the title of their advocate than was Struve. *Vozrozhdenie's* zeal remained unflagging. Under Struve and Semenov obdurate hostility met all those seen or suspected of contemplating accommodation to Soviet realities. The postrevolutionaries were one such *bête-noire*, Miliukov emphatically another. Repeating a favourite assertion of the political right, *Vozrozhdenie* reminded the ex-foreign minister that in Russian matters there were only two sides, "those for us and those for them." No middle road was possible, though *Posledniia novosti's* editor seemed to think he had found one.[8] Semenov's anti-Bolshevik mania and the polemical hatred with which he pursued suspected waverers won *Vozrozhdenie* no flock of new readers. Rather the reverse proved the case. These features may also have cost *émigrés* the sympathies of the centre and moderate left sectors of French public opinion.[9] On one occasion the newspaper's unthinking anti-Soviet reflex exposed it to a journalistic hoax perpetrated by Mikhail Koltsov, *Pravda* correspondent in France, gleefully applauded by the French left-wing press.[10] Semenov remained defiant. Successive waves of Stalinist terror against peasants, urban middle class, and Communist party were seen in the editorial office as the regime's desperate twisting as to whether the Bolsheviks were paper had no patience with speculation as to whether the Bolsheviks were in their Thermidorean or Bonapartist stage. It was a dissolving tyranny, and the arrest in 1937 of Marshals Tukhachevsky and Gamarnik announced that the end had come. Reports circulated in Paris, duly displayed on page one, that Stalin had been arrested and power was now firmly in Voroshilov's hands.[11] When the new "dictator" unaccountably refused to use his authority in the desired direction, Semenov judged him to be in decline and no fighter. Perhaps Mekhlis would do better?[12]

To read *Vozrozhdenie's* account of Soviet events is to encounter in full force the impotent fury of the dispossessed, forced to watch from afar as others drove Russia along a hated new road. No effort was made to analyze or assess. The Soviet repudiation of the tsarist past, its attacks on the old intelligentsia and war on religion proved to Semenov and his colleagues that their country was in the grip of an international conspiracy which had somehow selected Russia as its first victim. Why this should have been so, and just how it was that the Communist conspirators managed to hold on to power in spite of endless crises and limitless popular hatred were never satisfactorily explained. The editors were not, in any case, looking for rational explanations. It seemed enough to portray Russia as in the grip of alien demons.

Occasionally, bizarrely, the two worlds came together. Lev Liubimov, *Vozrozhdenie's* senior reporter and as vituperative as Semenov towards their critics,[13] wrote in the summer of 1937 of his encounters with Soviet visitors to Paris. The meetings did not lack a certain piquancy. On the one side stood Liubimov, a refugee from the highest reaches of tsarist society now much reduced in station. Facing him were Stakhanovite workers and others of the new Soviet élite. Their meeting took place in *Vozrozhdenie's* bookshop. As the tourists gazed upon photographs of the late imperial family, they exchanged views with their guide on the events then raging in Russia. They appeared to find him interesting; they urged him to return, protesting his assertion that he would be shot if he did so. Liubimov found his guests simple, friendly and sincere, even if only "semi-intellectual. But what can be expected," he wondered, "from people who know nothing except that which from childhood they have been obliged to accept, without ever suspecting that they could learn something else?"[14] If Liubimov sensed the larger relevance of his query, he showed no sign of it.

The most insistently sounded chord in *Vozrozhdenie's* anti-Soviet refrain was its conviction that regime and people remained fixed in deadly opposition. It therefore followed that National Russia, the cause of the Russian people, must be aided by all means inside and outside their tortured homeland. Any leader, party or cause in the world which inscribed anti-Communism on its banners won *Vozrozhdenie's* sympathetic attention. Under Struve, the paper displayed a guardedly positive attitude toward Mussolini, who had indeed a wide range of foreign admirers.[15] The rise of German National Socialism was of greater moment. At first perturbed by "demagogic demands of an almost Socialist character," Semenov and his colleagues soon cast their reticence to one side: Hitler's anti-Bolshevism exerted an irresistible attraction.[16] By the summer of 1931, P.M. Muratov was reminding readers, in "Quo vadis, Germania?", that Germany undoubtedly had grievances. Her inability to unite with German-speaking Austria and her "fantastically drawn Eastern borders" gave legitimate offence. These, of course, were problems for which National Russia bore no responsibility, inasmuch as she had not been represented at either Versailles or Locarno. Muratov assured *émigrés* that they might react "most calmly" to so extreme and harsh a political movement as National Socialism despite the occasionally regrettable practices of Hitler's followers. But Germany emphatically had a responsibility for the Bolshevik Revolution, ruinous to Russia and mortally dangerous to Germany. A total breach with the USSR was the only way Germany might avoid a civil war fomented by Moscow.[17] Eighteen months later, with Hitler newly installed as chancellor, Semenov doubted whether he would have a free hand. Germany's new leader had made too many concessions and a rupture with Moscow did not seem likely.[18]

The comparatively restrained note, as if the editors could not quite believe their good fortune, dissipated as the German chancellor's anti-Communist credentials took on brighter lustre. Comparing the respective political scenes in France and Germany a week after Hitler's inauguration, Semenov noted the approaching end of instability and chaos on the far side of the Rhine. "France still seeks, Germany has already found."[19] Editorial satisfaction with Germany's anti-Communist paladin – "his battle is ours too!" – easily digested his antidemocratic methods.[20] The newspaper recorded American protests at the new regime's first antisemitic measures.[21] But when Vishniak wrote in *Sovremenniia zapiski* that Hitler and Stalin were both pernicious and to choose between them was to demand a preference between cholera and the plague, N.S. Timashev replied in a sharp rebuff that, in the abnormal conditions of contemporary Germany, democratic rules were simply not adequate to solve the nation's problems.[22] Stalin was incomparably worse. *Vozrozhdenie's* position in the several crises which convulsed Europe during the later 1930s remained consistent to the end. Along with editorial approval of Fascist repression of the Third International in Spain and Austria – for so the paper saw matters – went pessimism over the deepening decay of French political institutions.[23] The Franco-Soviet pact of May 1935 was another bitter pill, though hardly "the Valmy of the Russian emigration" seen by a post-World War II observer.[24] *Vozrozhdenie* consoled itself with the views on the pact of Jacques Doriot. This former Communist champion had undergone a conversion which *Vozrozhdenie* readers might justifiably have compared to that of Saul on the road to Damascus. As recently as May 1933 he had led the Communist party's offensive in the Chamber of Deputies on behalf of the Franco-Soviet non-aggression treaty signed the previous November. During the debate he had paid tribute to the Soviet Union's peace policy and in harsh terms had demanded the dissolution of "White guard organizations" in France.[25] A year later, after well publicized differences with his leader Maurice Thorez, Doriot was expelled from the party. Thereafter he moved rapidly rightward toward a nationalist, populist, and ultimately Fascist position. While on this journey, he levelled a vitriolic attack on the 1935 pact as nothing but "a manoeuvre of the Third International."[26] As this coincided exactly with *Vozrozhdenie's* opinion, Doriot's judgment clearly deserved the widest support. He was, after all, "a specialist on Comintern and Soviet affairs," unlike others, such as Herriot, who spoke up in favour of the new alliance.[27]

If the Soviet Union were useless, even harmful, as an ally, was she worth defending in the event she were attacked by Japanese or German Fascists? This question assumed an overriding importance inside the emigration, as the diplomatic scene in Europe darkened. How should patriotic, anti-Soviet Russians abroad react if their country fell victim to an aggressor? Would Russians at home rally behind a government that had tormented them for so long? Or would an attack not be followed by the collapse of the regime, hence a victory for the people? To ask these questions was, for *Vozrozhdenie* and the openly Fascist press, to answer them. The suggestion that the martyred Russian people could fight in defence of Soviet power was insultingly ludicrous. Put arms in the people's hands and they would be turned against Stalin and his fellow-bandits. To plead that Russia be defended at home by the people and abroad by the *émigrés* played into the hands of the Comintern. *Vozrozhdenie* foresaw the possibility of an assault on the USSR without anxiety and awaited the outcome with confidence. Any other diplomatic preoccupation distracted energies from the primary confrontation. Semenov thus felt none of the anguish of the *Poslednüa novosti* or *Sovremennüa zapiski* editors over the resolution of the Czech crisis in

September 1938. President Beneš got what he deserved. He had turned his country into a Bolshevik outpost, forced France into her alliance with the Soviets, and advocated Soviet entry into the League of Nations. "A quarrel between Nuremberg and Prague is one between good sense and Marxism. Good sense must triumph."[28] A sad, ungrateful epitaph on a government which had been particularly generous to the Russian refugees, Semenov's verdict on Munich illumined the extremity that might be reached by conservative nationalists rigidly fixed in blinkered anti-Soviet loathing.

Another voice from the right spoke in somewhat different accents. The Young Russian *Bodrost* exulted at what it saw as the growth of healthy nationalist forces inside Soviet Russia. The old internationalist leaders were, it noted, being swept aside: "We greet the Communist party purge. It strikes at Communism and the old Bolsheviks!"[29] A nationalist dictatorship was in the wings but Stalin was not the man to lead it. He had shed too much blood, made too many mistakes, and was too old. An army figure would be much more appropriate. Everything now depended on the longed-for outcome, "the fall of Caesar Joseph. All power to the army! All power to the young Bolsheviks! All power to the nationalists!"[30] Six months later, when Stalin rounded on the army leadership, Kazem-Bek's scenario lay in ruins and he himself was reduced to proclaiming the Soviet dictator Russia's main defeatist. The country's defence required a change of regime.[31]

The *glava's* effusions contained much that invited, and received, derision. Moreover, though he professed a confidence in the imminent triumph of Russian nationalist forces inside the USSR and even hailed his own Young Russian disciples there,[32] he had no means to advance that happy day by even a second. He could only search the Soviet horizon longingly for some as yet unperceived Bonaparte, who might emerge at the head of his troops to purge the Kremlin of its current unworthy occupants.

On the war and peace issue, however, Kazem-Bek decisively parted company with Semenov and other irreconcilables. A threat hung over Russia from Nazi Germany; *émigrés* must recognize the danger and mobilize to meet it. The *glava's* warning did not come from any instinctive repugnance to German Fascism. On the contrary, he admitted to an early admiration for Hitler's internal policies.[33] The German leader's promise of national regeneration, coupled with a strong anticommunism, was not dissimilar to Kazem-Bek's programme for his own country. But Hitler's anti-Slav and, most particularly, his anti-Russian obsessions were impossible to ignore. They directly threatened the Russian people, and those in the emigration who overlooked this were guilty of defeatism. Extracts from *Mein Kampf*, published in *Bodrost*, reminded the ignorant and forgetful of the Führer's plans for Russia.[34] If only Stalin could somehow be replaced by a patriotic Russian general! The Young Russian dilemma was acute. Nevertheless, forced to choose between a Russia governed by Stalin and German invaders bent upon the enslavement of the Russian people, Kazem-Bek could hardly waver.

RUSSIA FROM THE LEFT

In 1928, on the occasion of an international press exhibition in Cologne, Miliukov summed up what his newspaper represented to Europe and the emigration. His evaluation was characteristically didactic and immodest. He distinguished two important missions for *Posledniia novosti*. It defended the interests of the Russian emigration before European public opinion. This meant acquainting Europe with *émigré* realities and educating public opinion to see contemporary Russia realistically, rather than as it now did, where the left was taken in by Moscow's revolutionary language and the right saw the Russian people and the Soviet regime as one, condemning both. A second duty that devolved upon the newspaper was to serve as a loudspeaker for Russian opinion silenced at home. "To seek out in Russia elements struggling in some way against the Bolsheviks" – this was how the paper's editor expressed it. *Posledniia novosti* wished to discuss with these elements, once they were identified, "tactical questions of the near future, to familiarize them with ideas of organization and science which they lack."[35]

Other than defending *émigré* interests, a charge whose precise nature depended on the definer, these ambitions went unrealized. Anti-Bolshevik elements inside Russia remained elusive; nor did European public opinion, such as it was, pay any noticeable attention to editorial lessons from the rue de Turbigo. Yet the image of Russia which emerged over the years from Miliukov's paper has more of value to offer the reader then and now than was contained in *Vozrozhdenie's* howls of hatred.

Miliukov's espousal of his notorious "new tactic" in 1921 exposed him to repeated charges thereafter that he had made his peace with Bolshevism. These accusations were unjust. He was, however, vulnerable to the lesser charge of a passive wait-and-see attitude in Soviet matters. A few months after the Cologne exhibition, where he had rejected this reproach, *Posledniia novosti* reprinted an editorial from *Le Temps*. Offered without comment from the Russian side, the *Le Temps* article reiterated the newspaper's revulsion at Bolshevism. The unfortunate impression was, nonetheless, being created, declared the Third Republic's most authoritative press organ, that the Russian people was now so exhausted by twelve years of Communist tyranny that it could no longer find in itself the strength to overthrow the dictatorship. The West therefore had to await the fall of the regime as a result of its own errors and decay. This could not be far off. When it happened, there could be no return to the past. "Revolutions, however cruel and foolish they may be, always create new ideals, new feelings, which inevitably are expressed in a new structure built upon the ruins of the old."[36] Miliukov himself could not have put matters more succinctly; this was how he saw the future in the USSR. Until then Russians abroad, like everyone else, would have to wait upon events, though not in silence.

Posledniia novosti watched Soviet affairs with two predominant editorial concerns in mind. Its interest in what was going on in Russia impelled the newspaper to chronicle Stalin's successive victories over party rivals, the legacy of Lenin, and the peasantry to the point where, in 1930, an editorial proclaimed that the coronation of the Revolution's Bonapartist autocrat was at hand.[37] Thereafter, while Stalin's tyranny and catastrophic economic policies were all too evident, he was seen to be just as subject to evolutionary pressures as were all other forces in nature. These must and would bring change. A lecture that Miliukov read to a packed public meeting in January 1936 elaborated on this theme. Speaking against a barrage of heckling from young Fascists in his audience, the seventy seven year old politician and historian painted a broad canvas in his topic of "Europe, Russia and the emigration." On the second subject of this trio he declared that his listeners were witnessing the gradual end of the dictatorship. Life evolved, the regime was obliged to do likewise. An aristocracy was emerging of bemedalled heroes (*ordenonostsy*), Stakhanovites, and other privileged persons. Ideology was dead. What remained was a bureaucratic machine trying to prop up a giant on feet of clay.[38] Kazem-Bek would not substantially have disagreed.

Within a few months of these hopeful observations, Stalin launched his ferocious assault on party, army, and nation. *Posledniia novosti* watched the unfolding of the terror against Lenin's old comrades without *Vozrozhdenie's* gloating joy or *Bodrost's* congratulations. It attributed the bloodletting to internal party rivalries and to Stalin's determination to create a new order. To speculate further on what lay behind the absurd indictments or to blame it all on the dictator's insanity was an unproductive exercise.[39] But by the time Bukharin disappeared, bewilderment had given way to urgent alarm on the rue de Turbigo. The slaughter in Moscow was having adverse effects upon the Soviet Union's international credibility, lessening its potential in the anti-Fascist cause.[40]

The need to resist Fascism, especially its anti-Slav German variety, was the second of Miliukov's overriding preoccupations as editor. Along with its moral imperatives, this issue, as Miliukov never wearied of pointing out, posed an urgent question to Russian anti-Bolsheviks abroad. What was their attitude toward German Fascism's designs on Russia? Were they ready to defend their homeland, Communist-ruled though it was, from aggressive racism? Miliukov ranged himself and his newspaper on the side of those who answered this question with an unhesitating affirmative. Nothing else could have been expected. Forebodings about the new German government prompted him editorially to warn Edouard Daladier, whose Radical-Socialist cabinet took office one day after Hitler, against German revanchist ambitions.[41] Then came doubts about the official version of the Reichstag fire.[42] By April, with the first officially inspired boycott of Jewish businesses in Germany, Europe's best known champion of Russian liberal values saw Germany reduced to the same state of moral collapse as Bolshevik Russia.[43] A year later the Nazi Blood Purge confirmed for Miliukov that Germany was governed by racist thugs utterly alien to European civilization.[44]

As a humanist and rationalist, profoundly imbued with a sense of the unity of European culture, Miliukov could hardly have reacted otherwise to the new regime in Berlin. Repeated anti-Nazi diatribes conveyed his outrage at the betrayal of European values within a country that had given so much to world culture. But his indignation was immeasurably reinforced by his awareness, as historian, diplomat, and patriot, of what Germany under her new masters might mean for Russia. That it threatened the Soviet government was eagerly applauded on the émigré right wing in the loudly professed conviction that what was bad for Stalin was good for Russia. Miliukov could not agree. He warned others, particularly Vozrozhdenie, that anti-Bolshevik refugees, who hoped that foreign Fascists would achieve what had been beyond the power of Russian nationalists, were doomed to disappointment.[45] The year before, for example, some rightists had placed their hopes in Japan's anti-Soviet potential. A stormy public meeting in Paris in March 1932 argued over this prospect against the background of criticisms made in Posledniia novosti and Dni of exiles who looked hopefully to the Japanese army in Manchuria. A Count Olsufev raised the possibility that Japanese arms might even wrest a piece of Russian territory from the Soviet grip. Exile youth might then be moved there and thus "continue" Russia. Perhaps the Far East could become a land of émigré settlement, a Russian Canada! When a recent Soviet defector, Grigory Besedovsky, rose to object that Russian peasants would resist a Japanese attack, he was denounced from the floor for his "provocation." Miliukov and Kerensky, the latter present on the platform, came under abuse for their "defensist" position.[46]

Supplementing his warnings of the peril facing Russia, Miliukov also instructed anyone willing to listen on the means by which Russia was being led back to traditional paths in her foreign policy. A lengthy study of this subject, published in 1934,[47] explained that the Bolsheviks remained committed to world revolution. But survival was an even greater imperative. The Soviets' desire to maintain their hold on Russia obliged the regime to favour European peace and promote national unity in the face of external disintegrative forces. This corresponded to the objective interests of the Russian people. The force of circumstances, rather than Stalin's will, made Russia an ally of the Western powers. "May this united front with the doctrinaires of universal war be blessed if it serves the cause of peace," the author concluded in half-sardonic, wholly sincere benediction.[48] Given this logic, the writer welcomed the Franco-Soviet pact, greeting it with a series of approving propositions. It was a positive step, corresponding to genuine needs. The Bolsheviks remained harshly oppressive and Russian democrats must continue to oppose and criticize their excesses. Yet they were evolving, most of all in foreign policy. Voluntarily or not, Russia's present rulers defended Russia's national interests. The nation had not disappeared, still less did it live in exile. It was where it should be, nobody's prisoner, even though governed by a lawless regime. The pact with France served the interests of the nation and European peace.[49]

To no one's surprise, conservative nationalist opinion, led by *Vozrozhdenie*, angrily rejected the suggestion that the Soviet government might defend their country's honour and interests.[50] But one very prominent *émigré*, whom *Vozrozhdenie* might reasonably have supposed to be firmly in its camp, proved unreliable. General Anton Denikin spoke out ringingly on the Fascist danger. Invited by Miliukov to expand on his warnings, the White military veteran delivered a detailed exposé, in three issues of *Posledniia novosti*, dedicated to "the international situation, Russia and the emigration." Denikin took a position somewhere between that of the two warring newspapers. He approached *Vozrozhdenie* in his insistence that, in view of the nature of Bolshevism and the low capacities of the Red army, the USSR could never be a significant factor for peace in Europe. Yet he was as alive as Miliukov to the threat of Hitler's racial theories. If the German Führer held to his Eastern programme, "he will be the most evil enemy of Russia and the Russian people." If war came, *émigrés* could not possibly co-operate with foreign aggressors trying to seize Russian territory. On the other hand, "it is impossible for us to co-operate directly in defending Russia with the army now calling itself Red." What remained for exiled Russian patriots? Denikin reached toward that favourite *émigré* mirage, a military coup. If the Red Army turned on the regime, exiles might then join hands with people and army to resist the foreign invader.[51] This optimistic hypothesis, accompanied by a stout defence of the emigration's usefulness in such a situation, received short shift from *Posledniia novosti's* editor.[52] Nevertheless, Denikin's wish to distance himself from the *Vozrozhdenie* "school" suggested it was possible to be of the conservative nationalist camp – and Denikin's credentials could not be doubted – yet still avoid the defeatist obsessions of the far right.

Miliukov rarely lost an opportunity to draw readers' attention to evidence of Soviet evolution. But he too had evolved, as Nikolai Ustrialov observed. Where would Miliukov end up? The pro-Soviet Change of Landmarks veteran wondered in 1934 if perhaps in another fourteen years *Posledniia novosti's* present editor might not be willing to admit "the great historic truth of the Soviet Revolution."[53] While it is, indeed, not easy to follow every nuance of Miliukov's shifting view of Soviet Russia's masters, his assessment of international events and of Russia's proper place in them presents fewer complexities. The final years in Europe's plunge toward war were unhappy ones for him and his cherished causes. In Russia, Stalin's orgy of bloodshed engulfed the army high command and the foreign affairs commissariat. This seemed to threaten Russia's international standing and her attractiveness as an ally against Fascism. Was not the Nazi press openly exulting over these senseless events? The only certainty on the Soviet scene was that anything might be expected.[54] Far worse, because so unexpected, were the crushing disappointments the aged editor suffered at the hands of the Western democracies. Spain and Austria in turn abandoned to Fascism, "a more shameful result for Europe could not be imagined."[55] A much more poignant personal grief came in the lingering dismemberment of Czechoslovakia. Presidents Masaryk and Beneš were close personal friends; they were also patrons of the Russian democratic cause in exile. Ideologically, spiritually, politically, their small republic embodied Miliukov's deepest convictions. Masaryk's death in September 1937 was a blow, mitigated only by Miliukov's confidence that the founder of Czech democracy had left a solid structure behind him. The Munich pacts demolished everything, including years of public and private argument. Nowhere had the democracies made a stand in defence of their professed beliefs; on the contrary, they had hastened to contribute to the triumph of reaction. And what could be in store for absent Russia in Europe's new order?[56]

The most despairing portrait of Soviet realities through two decades of exile appeared in the successive volumes of *Sovremennia zapiski*. Initially this derived naturally enough from the editorial commitment of 1920 to the February Revolution as Russia's moment of genuine liberation, vastly superior to the antipopular "October coup." But editorial aversion to the Soviet intruder was enormously enhanced as the four men watched in appalled helplessness while the regime tightened its grip, destroying the achievements which had made Russia a part of European culture. Mark Vishniak was heart and soul of the journal's anti-Bolshevik crusade. Without indulging in the crude, ranting stereotypes of *Vozrozhdenie*, the former secretary of the Constituent Assembly was no less implacable in his assault on the Assembly's supplanters. No compromise was possible in Russian democracy's defence. The Bolsheviks remained evil throughout, their breach with Russian history and the Russian people was unbridgeable.

Sovremennia zapiski's analysis of Soviet events makes depressing reading. The editors presented their subject matter in the most sombre shades, as befitted the grim truth they tried to tell. Nothing the regime did, short of suicide, could serve the interests of the people; its increasingly frenzied actions only harmed the national welfare. And yet it could not endure. Editorial faith in the liberty-loving Russian people permitted no other conclusion but that Bolshevism was an ugly aberration of history, a brief interruption in Russia's march toward freedom. Invoking another of the historical maxims he so favoured, Vishniak pledged himself to defend this certainty. Like William the Silent, "I need not hope in order to undertake, nor succeed in order to persevere."[57] The words attest to the presence in the journal's pages of Russian democratic ideals, unyieldingly hostile to "the spirit of the age" in Russia and the West.

The editors fought their battles on a wide front, one which began in their own journal. Contributors whose accounts of Soviet conditions appeared either too sanguine or whose too view of the Russian people's prospects seemed too gloomy were called to order, gently or not as the case required. The former professor of medieval history at the University of Petrograd, G.P. Fedotov, several times incurred editorial displeasure;[58] so too did letters "from an old friend over there." These gave too optimistic an impression of Soviet evolution, thus provoking Rudnev's understanding, but firm corrective.[59] Political comrades outside the journal also provided cause for concern. A major source of alarm was to be found in the reception given by Russian and European Socialists to Stalin's collectivization of the peasantry. Too many comrades failed to appreciate the frightful tragedy unfolding in the Russian countryside. While it was possible, wrote Vishniak, to excuse most foreign commentators on the grounds of their ignorance of Russia, immense pain was still caused by reactions such as that of the Vienna *Arbeiterzeitung*. This mouthpiece of the Austrian working class declared in an editorial that collectivization was an experiment of unheard-of boldness, which deserved the deepest interest and study of European Socialists. Worse yet, an unnamed "important Socialist veteran of the People's Will" had wondered aloud whether, in spite of all the errors and excesses, something profitable to genuine collectivism might not emerge from all the suffering.[60] This hint that the bloody means might conceivably find some justification in a better end could not be allowed to pass unchallenged under any colours, least of all Socialist ones.

Quick to reprove any sign of compromise on the part of fellow SRS, *Sovremenniia zapiski* editors also followed the polemics within the tiny Menshevik band on the nature of Stalin's dictatorship and the presumed direction of the Soviet Union under him. The smallest, most penurious of all exile factions, forced to flee Berlin in 1933 for even worse material misery in Paris,[61] the Mensheviks spent the remaining years of the decade in growing dispute about the correct line to follow in Soviet matters. Their general attitude toward the October Revolution and Soviet power was, it need hardly be stressed, far more positive than that of any other exile group. Until the late 1930s, they appeared more as a long-suffering but basically loyal opposition to the Stalin regime, maintaining contact with Soviet personalities.[62] At no time did they regard themselves as just another part of the *émigré* political kaleidoscope. Fedor Dan, the most willing to see positive features in Stalinist Russia whenever possible, earned thereby *Sovremenniia zapiski's* particular censure.[63]

Without a doubt, the most vigorous reproaches that the Right SR editors had to make against the Menshevik leaders had to do with the so-called "Kazan telegram." This footnote to the history of international Socialism between the wars came in the midst of intense discussions inside Socialist ranks on the merits of an alliance with Communists in order to block the further advance of Fascism. This preliminary to the Popular Front involved also exiled Russian Socialists, though in their case the question was theoretical, rather than immediately practical. Dan demanded such a union. He was certain that Socialist reservations about Stalin ought to pale into insignificance when set against the anti-Fascist potential of the proposed alignment. Other Mensheviks were not so certain and the respective view-points were fought out in the party and its newspaper *Sotsialisticheskii vestnik.*[64] Suddenly, on 12 August 1934, *Le Populaire* published a telegram it had received from three Mensheviks still in the USSR, who had not been heard from in twelve years. They hailed the pact for common action agreed upon a month earlier by the French Socialist and Communist parties. They expressed the hope that the French example would be followed by the inter-national working class movement. In an effusive accompanying editorial, Léon Blum thanked his Russian comrades for their "precious encourage-ment." It was, he enthused, all the more valuable in that it had been offered without the prior condition that European Socialists first demand conces-sions from the Soviet government on behalf of Mensheviks imprisoned in the Soviet Union.[65] Rafael Abramovich agreed exultingly. He proclaimed in *Sotsialisticheskii vestnik* that the telegram from Kazan was "the most im-portant event of our party life in recent times." His comrades' language was noble, they had not abandoned their internationalist faith. Even allowing for the NKVD's obvious collaboration, Abramovich felt that the message's publication could have significant results. He joined Blum in congratulating the senders on not having demanded the release of imprisoned colleagues as the price of their co-operation. Stalin's sincerity toward European Socialists seemed genuine; he had accepted the Menshevik position.[66]

Abramovich's jubilation appalled the *Sovremenniia zapiski* board. Hav-ing no great enthusiasm for the Popular Front idea to begin with, the editors judged that European democracy had reached a parlous condition indeed if it now sought added strength in a union with its bitterest enemy. The Right Menshevik S.I. Portugeis, writing as St. Ivanovich, was unsparing in his criticism. The Kazan telegram represented capitulation, not triumph. Rus-sian Socialists refrained from telling the truth, while Communists for the moment agreed to renounce lies. Of course, it would have made no practical difference if the Menshevik prisoners in the NKVD had tried to drive a bargain with the NKVD. But their comrades in the Western democracies need not rush so eagerly to surrender their principles. "From the Russian viewpoint," Ivanovich concluded, "the united front must be regarded as direct international support of the Soviet dictatorship."[67]

The unrelenting outrage felt by Vishniak and his colleagues at the brutality of Stalin's rule closed their eyes to any perception of the Soviet evolution so insistently announced by Miliukov. In fact the editors parted company with their occasional and respected contributor on that point. They also disagreed with his contention that the USSR could be a valuable ally in the struggle against fascism. In every domain – political, moral, military – Stalin, they believed, was leading the country to its ruin.[68] Was there a way out? In the spring of 1936 Ivanovich conceded pessimistically that one did not seem apparent. Certainly no serious internal danger menaced Stalin, But the appetite of the Russian people for material and moral sustenance would undoubtedly grow, presenting the regime with an increasingly difficult challenge.[69] This was a very long-range prospect. The legion of arrests in the Soviet Communist party shortly after Ivanovich's article appeared then raised another possibility. Might the dictator one day finish by sharing Robespierre's fate? P. Berlin thought it conceivable. "The Moscow trials," he wrote, "taken in their chronological sequence, have established an instructive and ominous tendency for the Stalin regime. The fires of discontent which have spread from the lowest to the highest levels of the social pyramid ... have seized elements touching ever more closely upon the Bolshevik nucleus."[70] But this too was a weak reed.

The foreign scene was equally unpromising. Hitler was clearly impossible, worse than Stalin, if that were imaginable. To make a choice between them struck Vishniak as asking whether he preferred to jump out of a window on the sixth floor or the fifth.[71] The *Sovremenniia zapiski* democrats confronted an insoluble dilemma. Ought they to choose the defensist cause, endorsed in varying ways by Miliukov, the postrevolutionaries, and the extreme left? Or should they opt instead for the vision of a Soviet defeat which so enticed the right? The editors, Vishniak in particular, struggled to avoid a choice between cholera and the plague, between a sixth floor window and a fifth. In spite of ghastly convulsions at home and foreign complications of every sort, the Stalinist regime continued to do as it wished with the Russian people. To close their eyes to the horrors and call for support to Stalin as the present ruler of their endangered country meant the renunciation of beliefs to which the editors had dedicated their lives. And yet to hope for the Russian people's liberation at the hands of German Fascist armies was plainly out of the question for the journal's Jewish, Socialist, democratic editors. In consequence, the Russian emigration's most important cultural organ could not come down on either side of the most contentious issue of *émigré* public life during the later 1930s. Its contributors could only evoke hopeful images, such as an army coup, and stress, despite wide *émigré* disagreement, the inseparability of political democracy and the Russian national cause. Not until the final international crisis, with the board in disarray, would one of the editors grasp the nettle more firmly.

For the man who shows some concern for his fellow-man, a journey to Russia is, before everything else, an exceptional chance to meditate profitably on social experiments [and] to develop an opinion on the behaviour and future of the species.[72]

George Duhamel, *Le voyage de Moscou*

THE STRUGGLE AGAINST
WESTERN PILGRIMS

Criticism of Russian Socialist backsliders represented the smaller part of *Sovremenniia zapiski*'s campaign against those in the West seduced by Bolshevism. A wider, parallel struggle also went on against the alluring visions of Soviet life depicted by influential Western visitors to the USSR. Nothing caused *émigré* writers or the *émigré* mass greater distress than the willingness of European and American intellectuals, living in political democracies of whose shortcomings they were often scathingly critical, to write approvingly of Soviet conditions, ignoring or denying the grim realities. "Why is the world silent?" asked a group of Mennonite peasants imprisoned in Siberia.[73] Rudnev took up the question. "Why does world public opinion," he asked, "so hotly outraged by a Fascist and Hitlerite regime, remain indifferent when confronted with the unheard-of, unprecedented crimes of the Soviet government? Why do public circles of the left in Europe and America, parading their devotion to the ideas of freedom and justice, remain so blind and deaf to the sufferings of the Russian people, even as often they ingratiate themselves with its executioners?" Socialists were guilty with the rest. Rudnev noted bitterly that a section of the Second International, in a recent manifesto, had condemned the state of affairs in Italy, Austria, and Germany. But no word of protest was uttered against "the super-terroristic regime of the Bolsheviks," nor did the Menshevik delegates present do anything to rectify the omission.[74]

Rudnev's questions went to the heart of Western intellectual life between the World Wars. The phenomenon of what Paul Hollander has called "the political pilgrim" derived from a variety of causes which he has recently subjected to detailed scrutiny.[75] Impelled by motives that ranged from anti-Fascism to an infatuation with the idea of a new and better world, prominent writers and public figures journeyed to the USSR and all too often willingly deceived themselves about the society they had briefly witnessed there,

On their return home most wrote glowing accounts of their impressions. Faced by this, émigré critics could only alert their exiled compatriots to the successive hymns of praise which these visitors sang and compose passionate refutations of their arguments. Unfortunately, even when these refutations became known to non-Russian readers, they had no greater success in reversing the prevailing fashion than did the occasional negative account of Soviet conditions by Western tourists.[76] The two themes which appeared most frequently in laudatory foreign descriptions of Soviet life provoked the strongest émigré responses. One suggested that Soviet Russia was a gigantic laboratory where, in an interesting experiment, the Russian people was being remoulded into a juster, nobler society. The other, taking some notice of the more visible defects, explained them (after a one- or two-week trip to the Soviet Union) with glib references to popular backwardness, an inherited autocratic tradition, or to some variant on the infinitely suffering Russian soul. Together or singly, these characteristics were deemed to make Russia different, her people unsuited for Western "bourgeois" liberties.

Examples of this thinking can be found at any point during the emigration's existence. When George Bernard Shaw declared that there was going on in the USSR "the most interesting experiment in the world," and, some years later, that he felt "Stalin [had] delivered the goods to an extent that seemed impossible ten years ago and I take my hat off to him accordingly,"[77] he spoke for those foreign intellectuals who admired, usually at a distance, the brave new world being built in the east. Then there was the novelist Georges Duhamel, who asserted in his very popular Le Voyage de Moscou (1928) that "Russians are used to dangerous pastimes. Prison, outrages, executions, reprisals: one scarcely finds anything else throughout their entire history."[78] Vishniak protested the libels, as he denounced yet again "the myth of October." But his insistence on the October Revolution's complete failure – "it's blindingly obvious!" – went unheeded.[79] How could the unknown Vishniak compete with Shaw and such lions of the Paris literary world as Duhamel and Romain Rolland?[80] Even André Gide's celebrated "return" in 1936 failed to provide the émigrés with unqualified cause for jubilation. Recognizing a major occasion, Kerensky and Adamovich devoted long reviews to the work on behalf, respectively, of Sovremenniia zapiski and Posledniia novosti. They pointed out Gide's continued faith in the promise of October, even as he deplored those Soviet deformities which stemmed from that event. Both reviewers expressed surprise that the French writer should have been repelled by the philistinism, arrogance, and political repression he encountered in the USSR. It was, they noted, well known in France that Soviet Russia possessed these features in abundance. Kerensky insisted that the truth about the Soviet Union was fully available to any member of the European intelligentsia. Could one really agree with the publisher's boast of his author's admirable intellectual honesty? Adamovich conceded this quality to the book itself, but he doubted whether Gide's view of the USSR before his journey merited such praise.[81]

If Gide, who eventually saw the light, still showed signs of error, how much more culpable in *émigré* eyes were the democratic politicians of Western Europe who, for some illusory short-term gain, rushed to offer Moscow their friendship. True, some might occasionally admit one or two negative features in life "over there." But all too frequently the reservations faded away when set against the surging faith that European democrats inexplicably continued to express whenever they looked toward Soviet Russia. Through the two interwar decades, this school's outstanding French exemplar was Edouard Herriot.

From the start of their exile the Russian refugees in France had reason for both gratitude and indignation toward the leader of the Radical party and mayor of Lyons. On the one hand, Herriot gave valuable aid to destitute Russian intellectuals when they arrived in France in the early 1920s.[82] This was certainly to his credit. So too was the goodwill he regularly displayed toward Russians in his own city. Yet the debit side of the ledger contained many more entries, at least as far as the Paris-based intelligentsia was concerned. Herriot's early insistence that France establish commercial and diplomatic relations with the Soviets had been combatted with what few weapons were at hand; recognition came as a heavy, though not unexpected psychological blow. Most *émigrés* admitted that recognition, however bad in principle, was a matter for the French to decide for themselves. Herriot's far greater offence to Russian sensitivities lay in his repeated willingness to render judgments on Russia that were based, not on his knowledge of the country or its people, but on evidence supplied by his Soviet hosts. His opinions thus appeared to serve the propaganda interests of the Bolshevik regime. He first exhibited this propensity after his 1922 trip to the young Soviet republic. Speeches, articles, and a first book bore witness to his belief in a new Russia, much superior to the old. His message found a ready audience.

In the years that followed the Herriot cabinet's recognition of the USSR, the course of Franco-Soviet relations ran unevenly. A change in the French political climate contributed first to a deepening chill between the two countries. A year after ambassador Krasin moved into the rue de Grenelle, Aristide Briand's eighth ministry inaugurated a series of short-lived, increasingly right-wing governments, none of which had any affection for the link to Moscow. In September 1927, after accusations of Comintern interference in French domestic affairs, Premier Poincaré, heading his fourth cabinet, demanded the recall of Krasin's successor Christian Rakovsky. Then followed the re-opening by the Quai d'Orsay of the war debts issue, accompanied by complaints of Soviet commercial dumping and by plans for strong French countermeasures.[83] A nadir in relations was reached in 1930; in June of that year Stalin pronounced France "the most aggressive and militaristic of all the aggressive and militaristic countries of the world."[84] At the year's end, to lend substance to his displeasure, the dictator included a broad range of French politicians in the indictments handed down in the "Industrialist Party" show trial. Poincaré, Briand, and the leaders of the Socialist Party stood in the dock as unseen accused behind Professor Ramzin and his codefendants. There they were joined by a motley émigré representation: Kerensky, Miliukov, the *Vozrozhdenie* editors, and a few former industrialists living and dead.[85] It was all too much for Herriot. He wrote an article for the Paris *Le Capital* which denounced the judicial farce in Moscow and Stalin's ludicrous attempts to whip up popular rage against France. *Izvestiia* returned a sneering reply that dwelt upon the French politician's services to a newspaper bearing the name of Karl Marx's immortal work. This one, however, only served the interests of the French petty bourgeoisie.[86]

A warming trend soon set in on both the personal and international levels. The parliamentary elections of May 1932, briefly threatened by Gorgulov's crime, returned the left to power; in June Herriot took office for the third time.[87] Before long, the revival of German nationalism pushed his government and that of the USSR to conclude a non-aggression pact, the first step in a process of *rapprochement* which would culminate in the alliance of May 1935. Stalin now evidently impressed Herriot as a man of good sense – one aware, like the French premier, of Europe's geostrategic realities. At home too, Stalin was acting as a statesman; twenty years later Herriot was still willing to commend the Soviet dictator's "intelligent liberalism" in calling off the persecution of the bourgeois specialists.[88] Clearly, Stalin's Russia merited inspection. The fall of Herriot's cabinet in mid-December 1932 freed him from the cares of office. He might now see for himself the changes brought about in the USSR since his first visit.

Herriot journeyed to the Soviet Union for the second time in August–September 1933. He went ostensibly as a private citizen to inform himself on what was happening inside Russia, particularly in the light of reports then current of widespread famine in the Ukraine. From the moment of his arrival in Odessa, the visitor was treated as a privileged, highly honoured guest. The French ambassador followed in his wake, while a train of attendant journalists recorded his least utterance. There were several of these.

At a time when the most terrible famine was gripping the Ukraine, Herriot's bland assurances of the abundance he saw on every side made painful reading for those who knew, or suspected, otherwise. Dr Ewald Ammende was one of that number. A Baltic German by birth, he had been active in Russian relief work in the 1920s. In 1933 he was appointed honorary secretary of an interdenominational committee set up by the

Archbishop of Vienna, Cardinal Innitzer, to provide aid for the starving in Russia. In the face of Moscow's refusal to co-operate, or even to admit the need, the committee's chief task became "to enlighten world public opinion on the real position in the Russian famine areas and the necessity of joint action."[89] To that end Dr Ammende published in 1936 his account of the unprecedented tragedy. His book was, and is, an indictment of a Soviet policy of genocide and of foreigners who, knowingly or not, allowed themselves to be used to screen the truth. Herriot proved so outstanding an example of this latter phenomenon that Ammende devoted an entire chapter of his book to the Frenchman's 1933 visit.

The mayor of Lyons arrived in the Soviet Union with the self-admonition, as he later recorded, that "it is essential to exercise a critical faculty" throughout his travels. Equally, "we must know and understand before we can pass judgment."[90] Yet the tone of his reporting from Russia and of his remarks when back in France was, if anything, even less critical and more euphoric than it had been in 1922. Some of his exchanges with his hosts deserve honourable mention in any chronicle of Soviet cynicism toward Western visitors eager to hear and see the best of Soviet Russia. Two examples should suffice. Visiting a collective farm in the Ukraine, Herriot concluded that the peasants were obviously prospering. The government was ensuring this state of affairs; indeed, it allowed every agricultural worker to have his own cow and freely to leave the collective if he wished. On this last point the French visitor received the assurance that any attempts to restrict this liberty were severely punished. "All who use compulsion with the peasants are expelled from the party," Herriot heard and reported.[91] A few weeks later, when he was being welcomed home, Herriot admitted to his fellow-guests in Lyons that he had observed a shortage of milk in Ukrainian towns. Upon inquiry, he had been informed by Mikhail Kalinin, titular head of the Soviet state, that milk production had, in fact, enormously increased. But so too had the government's social services to the people. This had led to a temporary situation where, according to Kalinin, "milk consumption tends to exceed production with the result that regulations had to be made with regard to distribution."[92] On the famine issue Herriot was categoric. Though the story "[was] being brandished around like a scarecrow, [it was] nothing but the dubious product of Hitlerian propaganda."[93]

Once back in France, Herriot embarked on the familiar routine of lectures, articles, and another book elaborating upon his Russian impressions. As in 1922, Russian *émigrés* watched from the sidelines, largely powerless to combat the author's more bizarre judgements. *Vozrozhdenie* did what it could. The newspaper's attacks stung the mayor of Lyons into making pointed references to its partiality toward German and Japanese Fascism, particularly if these might dispose of Bolshevism. He spoke more approvingly of Kazem-Bek's Young Russians, who opposed all such notions.[94] A

Vozrozhdenie contributor, K.I. Zaitsev, a well known *émigré* writer, produced a brochure in French listing Herriot's more egregious fatuities, but it is unlikely that the work convinced, or even reached, large numbers of French readers.[95] It had, after all, to compete with Herriot's own account. All the same, it is just possible that the visitor to the USSR came to regret some of his effusions. His memoirs, published in 1952, five years before his death, devote a scant twenty-five lines to his 1933 trip and over half this passage records his impression of a ballet he saw on the theme of the French Revolution. Readers curious to learn more are directed to his book *Orient*. In contrast, his 1922 expedition, also the subject of a book, is described in over five pages of detailed narrative.[96]

Herriot's willingness to propagate the official Soviet thesis on the famine – that it did not exist – adversely affected the efforts of those like Dr Ammende who were struggling to convey a more accurate picture to the world. Unfortunately the circumstances of the day were what they were. A former premier, a cultured man of letters, a statesman of international stature and impeccably democratic reputation told enlightened, anti-Fascist Europe what it wanted to hear. Ten Ammendes would have made no difference. But even figures with far less impressive credentials than Herriot seemed able to command the same audience with a similar message. Tatiana Chernavina, a *Sovremenniia zapiski* reviewer of books on the USSR, singled out two works, both published in 1935, which represented to her the very worst in superficial foreign judgments of Russia. These were Walter Duranty's *I Write As I Please* and Anna Louise Strong's *I Change Worlds*. Duranty, the mendacious Pulitzer Prize-winning correspondent of the *New York Times* in Moscow, wrote glibly of the Russian capacity for suffering, popular passivity, the iron necessity of Progress and the grandeur of Stalin's rule. Strong, a humourless zealot of the new order, also saw virtues in the Soviet regime. She justified the terror as needed in the creation of a mighty state. Chernavina confessed to feeling genuine pain in making her way through the two books, whose authors, she reflected bitterly, passed for Russian experts. She herself had spoken out against their books in the United States but to little effect.[97]

In fairness to Duranty's profession at least, it ought to be recorded that Chernavina had been happy, a short time before, to acknowledge another journalist's very different portrait of life in Stalin's Russia. Malcolm Muggeridge had served as the *Manchester Guardian's* Moscow correspondent. His early enthusiasm for the Soviet experiment – nurtured in England – quickly waned once inside the USSR. On his return to Britain he published a novel expanding on his disillusion with the dictatorship of the proletariat and what he termed "its imbecilic foreign admirers." *Winter In Moscow* (1934) won Chernavina's unstinting praise. It gave a "merciless" description of Soviet conditions, together with devastating impressions of credulous Westerners explaining away the more awkward evidence of terror and collectivization. She felt the book deserved the widest readership.[98]

Chernavina's opinions were not widely shared in the non-Russian community where she and her editors would have liked to make converts. Duranty's memoir received a generally warm reception, while Muggeridge drew down upon himself the opprobrium of the intellectual left.[99] At the dawn of the Popular Front era the time was out of joint for anti-Stalinist democrats, whether Russian or foreign.

The democratic sector of *émigré* opinion did not fight its battle alone. The much more numerous conservatively inclined intelligentsia also did what it could, though with no greater success. There was, for example, the celebrated case of the British Trades Union Congress delegation to Soviet Russia late in 1924. Following upon British and French recognition of the Soviet government, the visit made a painful impact upon the dispirited exile community in the West. Worse was to come. A few months after its return, the delegation issued an official report of its impressions, "so as to do all in its power to put the British electorate in possession of the real facts in Russia."[100] Both visit and report were a foretaste of things in store for the Russian emigration.

To a reader today, the TUC delegation can serve as the prototype of Hollander's "political pilgrim" to Russia, who seeks a better world and is willing to take the word for the deed and the promise for its fulfillment. The spell began at the frontier. Delegates were welcomed by a children's choir singing revolutionary songs. "We seemed to be called back through centuries of persecution and ... we could hear the wailing cry of a people long oppressed brought into contact with a glimpse of freedom and hope for a better future."[101] Then came visits to Soviet officials and institutions. Delegates had heard of the Solovetsky monastery prison and asked to inspect it. On being told it was the wrong season they settled for the Butyrki prison in Moscow. There they spoke with some of the Socialist Revolutionaries who had been condemned in 1922. Their only complaint to the British group was that they were obliged to read the foreign bourgeois press instead of the "Labour" papers they preferred: the visitors got this injustice put right. They saw nothing in their month of strenuous travel which suggested that the regime was unduly repressive – had not the Cheka been abolished? In fact, "the Soviet system of representation and its scheme of constitutional and civil rights [have] given in many respects to the individual a more real and reasonable opportunity of participation in public affairs than does parliamentary and party government." In other respects it was true that such participation was still severely restricted and that the system remained under the close control of its creators. However, this "permanence in power [was] the result of past circumstances, not of the present constitution." That document provided possibilities certainly as great, and possibly greater, than other constitutions did in respect of popular government, political peace, and social progress. Vast strides had been made in all areas of public and private life. Sexual mores furnished one good example, contrary to lurid stories in the West of the nationalization of women. While noting primly that "from the British point of view, Russia was never a particularly moral country," the report's authors rejoiced that the onetime blights of prostitution and "immorality among children" were being eradicated.[102]

The political and cultural leadership of old Russia found the TUC claims unendurable. They might also prove dangerous, if allowed to pass unchallenged amongst foreigners who knew nothing of Russia. Accordingly, a dozen of the surviving "names" of pre-October days merged their individual expertise to produce what was intended as the authoritative response from knowledgeable Russians to the naive statements made by representatives of the British working class. The volume they produced represents also the greatest single effort of the emigration's senior members to neutralize pro-Soviet propaganda in a foreign country.[103]

Like almost every Russian refugee body, the collective that formulated the émigré answer to the TUC report overwhelmingly reflected a common ideological viewpoint. Those involved in the work came, with one or two exceptions, from the conservative nationalist camp. Some were from the right wing of the former Kadet Party sundered at Miliukov's insistence a few years earlier. Others had served tsarism. The volume's editor was M.M. Fedorov. He was assisted by the two successive editors of Vozrozhdenie, Struve and Semenov. Other collaborators included two former ministers of finance, several prominent members of the commercial, financial, and industrial world of pre-October Russia, and specialists in questions of law, religion, the press, and education.[104] One contributor was clearly of the left. S.P. Melgunov, once of the Popular Socialists, wrote as an authority on matters relating to the Cheka and the terror. An English edition of his major work on this subject appeared just too late for the TUC authors, assuming they would have paid it any attention.[105]

Drawing upon published Soviet sources but also from their own bitter certainties, Fedorov's collective set out to demolish the TUC document. Its authors, they maintained, knew nothing of Russia. Her history, language, and culture were all quite unknown to them. Every page of the report seemed, to its émigré critics, to bear witness to British credulity. The authors' defence of Soviet democracy, their belief that the majority of the population supported the regime, their blindness to the menace of the Comintern, and their confidence in the real improvement in the national economy and welfare proved the report's utter worthlessness. Writing in the tone common to all the contributors, E.P. Kovalevsky could not contain his indignation when he came to the TUC claims on behalf of the improved condition of Russian youth under the Soviets. Soviet schools were bestial institutions of corruption: "schoolchildren smoke, have a disorderly sexual life and many already use cocaine."[106] Overall, the reality was that there ruled in Moscow a despotic, oligarchic government and that Soviet citizens, ruled by terror, were deprived of the most elementary human rights. The TUC delegation's refusal to admit this and other truths pointed up the criminal frivolity of its evaluation of Soviet life.[107]

The 600 pages of passionate rebuttal, replete with charts and footnotes, presented a picture familiar to any reader of the rightist press. Gloom, despair, and ruin were Russia's lot in the ninth year of her martyrdom. Nothing grew, nor could grow. The nation remained in the grip of an alien conspiracy; famine stalked the land. The portrait failed to convince as much by its monochromatic hopelessness as by the identity of its painters. The latter point was, as ever, a fatal liability. Progressive Europe was not to be persuaded by the expertise and statistical tables of former servants of tsarism, nor of tsarism's enemies if, like Melgunov, they joined in an anti-Soviet chorus with Fedorov, Struve, and the others. The 2,200 published copies of their diatribe sank without attracting much non-Russian attention. And yet, while the apocalyptic theme even today seems excessive, and the refusal to admit anything positive in Soviet Russia under NEP was no doubt obtuse, it is difficult to withhold sympathy from the authors. André Gide was later to write in his most notorious work that too often the truth about the USSR was written with hate, the lie with love.[108] Fedorov's collective unquestionably wrote with a visceral hatred of the Soviet regime: every line of their study showed this. Yet not everything they said can be dismissed as the ravings of dispossessed reactionaries. Their evaluation of Soviet political realities was generally closer to the truth than the TUC tributes. Melgunov certainly saw Soviet penal conditions, here and elsewhere, in terms that Alexander Solzhenitsyn would confirm. Of course, none of this made a difference in the two interwar decades. In 1936 Gide was scorned by much of the left. The Communist press denounced him with particular vigour in the venomous terms long familiar to émigré critics of the USSR.[109] Ten years earlier, in the midst of the NEP "Thermidor," these same critics might much more plausibly be brushed aside, not just by Communists, as defeated anti-Bolsheviks with very visible axes to grind.[110]

This burden continued to hamper all émigré commentators on the USSR, including those who tried to distance themselves from the bleak panoramas of most older writers. One such example from the 1930s was a detailed academic study by a former diplomat, Nicholas Bazili. Published first in Russian, then in French and English editions, *Russia under Soviet Rule. Twenty Years of Bolshevik Experiment* (1938), was based on a careful analysis of the Soviet press and by no means wholly condemned the Soviet years of Russian history. However, Bazili mourned the rupture he perceived in his country's past since March 1917. The upheaval of that month came as the consequence of European war, the personal defects of the imperial couple, and the vast, unbridged gulf within Russian society. These combined calamities deflected Russia from the path of peaceful evolution along which, in spite of reversals and setbacks, she had been proceeding. The Provisional Government had been helpless to overcome the liabilities it inherited at a moment of intense popular expectations and complete political inexperience. The November "epilogue" came as the final denial of Russian intellectual traditions evident since Radishchev and the Decembrists. It drew rather upon the popular tradition of revolt, "from the ferocious enmity of the disinherited for all that surpasses him."[111]

Bazili was an ardent Westerner, evidently much influenced by Miliukov. Like his mentor, he tried to avoid the stereotyped *émigré* image of Russia since November 1917. Bazili admitted Lenin's intellectual gifts, although he stressed also the Soviet leader's fanaticism, intolerance, and lack of pity. He was willing to acknowledge that industrial progress had definitely taken place in the USSR since the inauguration of the first five-year plan, though the human cost had been appalling.[112] But otherwise the picture was bleak. Bazili judged that the system rested upon a senseless political terror, a Byzantine glorification of Stalin, a new party ruling élite, and a ruthlessly exploited peasantry and proletariat. In sum, he saw the features which Western historiographical consensus would later suggest did characterize the Soviet Union as the Great Terror reached its climax.

To be sure, Bazili had his eccentricities. He detected, for instance, a cult of Alexander Pushkin developing among Soviet youth. This interest, in the centennial year of the poet's death, "is penetrating deeper and deeper into the popular masses [and] is a very grave portent for the central power: it forebodes the reawakening of the individual principle." The new, emerging Soviet élite would capitalize on this and the liberation struggle would get underway. The popular masses would join in and the Soviet regime "will at last be driven to an irremediable collapse."[113]

Bazili's work had a modest reception. V.V. Rudnev reviewed the original Russian version warmly enough in *Sovremenniia zapiski*, not failing to express reservations about Miliukov's influence on the author's ideas.[114] In London a brief notice in the *Times Literary Supplement* summarized the book's major points and admitted that the writer's indictment of Soviet policies rang true. But Bazili's optimistic view of Russia's evolution toward democracy during tsarism's final years "unfortunately runs counter to high authority." The anonymous reviewer felt that this deficiency brought the work into question.[115] Underlying his remarks seemed to lurk a doubt that a tsarist diplomat could have anything to say about the Soviet Union that could be useful to contemporary readers. Five years later, a major bibliographical review in England spoke much more enthusiastically of Bazili's study.[116] But 1943 was an unpropitious year to promote a work in

Britain and the United States which focused heavily on the imperfections of their heroic Soviet ally.

The problem of his credentials thus weighed upon every Russian in the West who tried to reach a foreign audience with his views on Soviet Russia. Whether directly, in books and articles, or indirectly, as commentary on another's work, *émigré* analyses were perceived first and foremost as coming from people, in Basile Kerblay's tactful words, "too preoccupied with events to take a sufficiently detached view of developments in the Soviet Union."[117] Their opinions thus made little impression upon foreigners, unless already persuaded of the justice of the cause.

Tatiana Chernavina's own experience offers an instructive example of this reality. University educated by the time of the Civil War, she remained in Russia working in various archival and cultural posts. In 1931 she and her husband were arrested, victims of Stalin's assault on the prerevolutionary intelligentsia. Miraculously she managed to engineer their escape from a prison camp with their young son into Finland; she then wrote an account of their adventures.[118] The book, translated into English, was widely reviewed on both sides of the Atlantic. A restrained, though approving note in the *Times Literary Supplement* declared the book's appearance opportune "at a moment when the outside world, in the contemplation of other Continental sufferings, may be inclined to forget the misery of educated people in Russia."[119] In the *New York Times* J. Donald Adams reacted with complete admiration. Chernavina's memoir and Muggeridge's *Winter In Moscow* were "the two most remarkable books about Soviet Russia which have yet appeared in this country." *Escape From The Soviets* had "extraordinary merit" and it was Adams's "earnest conviction" that the book would still be read "when the present Kremlin dictatorship is an episode in history."[120] Journals and commentators further to the left generally admitted the dramatic power of Chernavina's tale but reproved her evident distaste for the regime which had imprisoned her. Thus, Ella Winter declared in the *New Republic* that, "if Chernavina had forgotten she was writing a propaganda book, and had not stopped her little story of one family to drag in stupid and ignorant remarks about the Soviets in general, her book would have been better literature." As it was, her book bore the stamp of truth "except when she is talking of the Soviet Union."[121] Lewis Gannett of the *New York Herald-Tribune*, via the *Nation* and the *Manchester Guardian*, quite unfairly dismissed the book as "obviously a semi-hysterical, subjective picture of doubtful objective validity."[122] London's leading journal of the left was more subtle. T.H. Marshall, writing in the *New Statesman and Nation*, found Chernavina's story "unforgettable and ... probably accurate. But nobody will imagine that it is a picture of Russia. Her view is not merely personal, but is seen through the eyes of a class, or rather of a dying civilisation."[123] To critics such as these, Chernavina and, by implication, her fellow writers in exile were either vulgar liars or else they stood blindly in the path of history's chariot. Those Europeans and Americans who considered themselves progressive (a category which, as a matter of course, included anyone interested in the Soviet Union), discounted negative comment from those whom Ella Winter dismissed as "pupp[ies] yapping at the heels of history."124

It may be concluded from their experience in making their case known that Russian émigrés of all political shades might justifiably have joined Mark Vishniak in invoking consoling maxims on the need for patient perseverance until better days. Certainly the audience which they most wished to impress with their case: the writers, journalists and politicians who shaped public opinion and fashionable ideas, remained, with too few exceptions, far out of reach.

CHAPTER SEVEN

Human Dust?

As the second decade of European peace moved to its end, the Russian exile community was made increasingly aware of its own deepening twilight. Whatever purpose they might collectively have served in the past, émigrés found it impossible to be optimistic about their future. There had been so many disappointments, none keener than on the central issue. "We gave them two weeks, then two months, then two years" a *Posledniia novosti* editorial recalled on the twentieth anniversary of the October Revolution: every prediction proved wrong.[1] And now, after a decade of slaughter and upheaval unmatched in Russia's entire history, the regime sat more solidly entrenched than ever, while its Russian critics abroad were left to ask themselves yet again just why they were in exile and what, if anything, they had achieved outside Russia. In 1935, G.P. Fedotov contributed a major essay on these questions to *Sovremenniia zapiski*. "Why are we here?" began by reviewing, and dismissing, the political doctrines put forward through the years by spokesmen of left and right. With a qualified exception in the case of the postrevolutionaries (drawing the automatic disapproving note from the editorial board), Fedotov judged that no political message derived to survive. The historian of revolutionary Russia could ignore this political page; the emigration's service to Russia lay not here, but in the defence of Russia's cultural charge. The nation's pressing instruction to the émigrés had been to carry and protect Russia's cultural inheritance. This remained their duty still. Literary culture abroad lived in a vacuum; Russian writers lacked publishers, critics and readers. But they still wrote, hearkening to their inner voice, "for Russia, for the world, for eternity."[2]

Fedotov's assessment may well have comforted the dwindling band of exiled writers pledged to that defence of Russian cultural values espoused by *Sovremenniia zapiski* fifteen long years before. But by then surviving members of the Paris-based intelligentsia probably felt little optimism that this mission could be sustained for much longer. The frustrations of their existence, the passage of time, Stalin's apparent invincibility all took their toll. Poverty remained an ever-present reality. Roman Gul, who arrived in Paris in September 1933 from Nazi-ruled Germany, experienced some hard times in the French capital, as he attempted to make a living with his pen. Home for him and his wife was a small fifth-floor room at 158, rue de la Convention. A cupboard, a rickety table where he wrote, a tiny gas stove, and a mattress purchased at the flea market, then deloused in kerosine, provided their furniture. Often they could not afford the price of a tram ticket. Barring a stroke of good fortune – one such did come the Guls' way – this was the sort of life that most refugees knew best.[3] Defections and deaths – Kuprin, Tsvetaeva, Pavlova, Chaliapin – thinned the ranks of Russia Abroad's best known figures. Looking back thirty years later, Nina Berberova described the pervasive exile depression of the late 1930s. They all seemed "universal Akaky Akakieviches," filled with guilt for Europe's problems, for Stalin, for Hitler's rise, for Gugulov's crime.[4] Yet they were as helpless as Gogol's protagonist to do anything about these calamities. Local misfortunes continued to add their share to the *émigré* malaise.

THE MILLER AFFAIR

On 24 September 1937 *Posledniia novosti*, the sole surviving daily of Russian Paris, announced the astounding news that General E.K. Miller, head of the Russian All-Military Union (ROVS), had vanished. His disappearance was followed within a few hours by that of his aide, the head of the ROVS counter-intelligence section, or "Inner Line," General N.V. Skoblin. Quite unnecessarily the paper reminded its readers of the kidnapping seven years earlier, under similar circumstances, of Miller's predecessor, General Kutepov. The sinister parallels between the two events became still more striking with *Posledniia novosti*'s details of a grey truck which had arrived at Le Havre at 4 A.M. with three passengers and had left with two. Later that morning, the Soviet vessel *Maria Ulianova*, berthed at Le Havre, left port unexpectedly early.[5]

Whatever had been the *émigré* certainties in 1930, Kutepov's disappearance remained, officially at least, an unsolved mystery. Its sequel, thanks to its victim, was less of an enigma. It transpired that Miller, a normally cautious man who never forgot his predecessor's fate, had written a note prior to his last appointment informing his staff that he was leaving for a meeting with General Skoblin and two officials of the German embassy. Skoblin, who had not known of the note's existence, vanished after being apprised of its contents by Miller's distraught deputy Kedrov. The matter was then handed over to the French police. Their first action in the case was to arrest Skoblin's wife Nadezhda Plevitskaia, a well known singer, as an accomplice in her husband's evident treachery.[6]

These successive thunderbolts left the Russian community in a state of utter bewilderment. *Posledniia novosti* reflected this. Kutepov's abduction had obviously been the work of the GPU, the newspaper felt. But who could want or profit from Miller's seizure? And why should the NKVD, the GPU's successor, if it were responsible, be still interested in the White veterans when Trotskyists were the regime's main enemies? Skoblin was clearly involved, but for whom was he working? The paper advised calm so as to allow the known facts to be pursued.[7]

As in the Kutepov case, no one was willing to act on this advice. As soon as he could, Semenov weighed in with a furious editorial in *Vozrozhdenie* reminding readers that this was the second time that an ROVS president had been kidnapped by the Soviets in the French capital. The perpetrators of the first coup had gone unpunished; naturally they had tried again. Would the government have sufficient firmness to deal with this new affront? Semenov hoped that it would, for all of Miller's reputation as a reactionary in some quarters. *Emigrés* must close ranks, resolve differences, pay forgotten dues, rejoin if departed. The war went on.[8] Other voices, usually disregarded, also chimed in. Vladimir Burtsev loudly proclaimed his conviction from the start that Skoblin and Plevitskaia were the instruments of Miller's disappearance. "The aged revolutionary Pinkerton"[9] knew more, but chose not to reveal it for the time being.[10] The Nazi-oriented National Labour Alliance of the New Generation[11] announced a public lecture on the subject of Soviet intelligence work within ROVS and the Miller case. When the day arrived, speakers harangued the crowded hall less about Miller than about their own organization; they also had much to say about *provocateurs* throughout the emigration. Protesting cries greeted the several names offered; threats of legal action followed.[12]

French reactions on press and official levels were more languid than in 1930. Even in Kutepov's case, one of the most right-wing cabinets in France's interwar history, seconded by *Le Temps* and every newspaper to its right, had confined its reprisals to loud anti-Soviet invective. Seven years later, with the international and domestic scenes drastically altered, not even that much could be expected, as Semenov probably recognized. The Popular Front ministry of the day, with Blum as vice-premier, faced a genuine threat from Fascist gangs in the streets of Paris. The same menace loomed across the nation's Italian, German, and now Spanish frontiers. Too vigorous an inquiry into the fate of an obscure, reactionary Russian general might ruffle important ideological, perhaps even diplomatic alliances. This reality became clear to all as the investigation proceeded.

On the extreme right, the Fascist *Je suis partout* and the royalist *Action française* made their ritualistic denunciations of "the 2,000 GPU agents in France" and general police incompetence.[13] Reflecting on this latter aspect, Léon Daudet suggested that the dilatory investigation reflected official policy.[14] Closer to the centre, *Le Temps* reported the whole affair in a subdued tone, noting major developments on its inside or back pages without comment.[15]

The left saw the event as one concerning only Fascists. *Le Populaire*, possibly after some prompting from *émigré* friends, informed readers that Miller had been criticized on the exile far right for a lack of enthusiasm in urging young Russians to fight in Spain for Franco. "Hitlerites" who swarmed in the White part of the emigration were doubtless responsible.[16] Within a week, the Socialist organ decided that Skoblin had been paid by foreign Fascists to get rid of Miller, "a known Francophile."[17] The left-centre *L'Oeuvre* was more accusingly direct. "What exactly is the political activity of the White Russians in France?", the paper asked. Its reporter, Robert Danger, conducted an investigation which came to some disquieting conclusions. If the Fascists rose up in France, as in Spain, to challenge the republic, Danger saw "tens of thousands" of Russian *émigrés* trained in war supporting the insurrection. "Thus they would thank the republic for its generosity toward them."[18] Danger's tendentious analysis left unclear whether he regarded the vast majority of the emigration as a threat – his figure of "tens of thousands" suggests as much – or, like *Le Populaire*, suspected only the more easily identified military chiefs and monarchofascist elements on the far right edge of refugee politics. In either case Danger ludicrously exaggerated the emigration's potential and desire for antirepublican activity. *L'Oeuvre* followed up Danger's cry of alarm with an article under the ominous title "France for the French!" Its author, Senator Joseph Paul-Boncour, was a former premier and foreign minister. For too long, Paul-Boncour wrote, this slogan had belonged to the right, which had used it to cover its attacks on Jews. But this "ignoble past" should not prevent republican democrats from employing the slogan today if the target were appropriate. He did not have penniless refugees in mind, though they had often been its victims. The search must aim higher, at the authors of international terrorism secure in their embassies.[19] Nothing in Paul-Boncour's observations singled out Russians for specific censure. However, the article's appearance in the days after Miller disappeared, along with *L'Oeuvre's* continued criticisms of "White Russians" in France, were not reassuring.[20] *L'Humanité's* version of events contained the fewest surprises. It ascribed the whole Miller episode to a Fascist plot involving Franco, the Gestapo, and the Japanese. Skoblin was a Nazi agent who had got rid of Miller as Miller had got rid of Kutepov.[21]

These domestic repercussions to Miller's kidnapping needlessly reaffirmed that the French far right and far left still viewed the Russians in France through the prism of ideological conviction. While French conservatives published approving articles on the *émigré* far right, holding up the vision of "a nation preparing its resurrection,"[22] Communists snarled hatred of

"White guard spies" working for the Third Reich in France.[23] But Paul-Boncour's editorial was more significant. It suggested, or rather it confirmed, that moderate opinion was losing patience, not so much with Russians, as with all foreign refugees in France. The problem was that they were too numerous, too noisy, and too noticeable. In 1937 the nation's alien population stood in excess of 3 million, or between 7 and 8 percent of the total. Statistics further indicated that foreigners committed 21 percent of all murders and 18 percent of the aggravated thefts; they also constituted 27 percent of the prison population and 15 percent of those in insane asylums. With unemployment in their ranks very high, large sums had to be spent on their relief – 80 million francs in Paris alone.[24] Every day brought a new influx from Spain of those whom middle-class opinion was quite prepared to believe were anarchists; then came Miller's disappearance and the ensuing murky revelations from the Russian exile world. It was all too much. The centrist *Le Matin* exploded: "France is not a no man's land. She belongs to the French. If there are foreigners who have scores to settle between them or quarrels to fight out, let them do it in their own country, not in ours. We are as little interested in the shade of their opinions as we are in the shade of their emblems. What does interest us is our tranquillity." Its anger boiling over, *Le Matin* raged that "not only do we not clean our own doormat, but we even hold it out to the muddy of the whole world so that they might come and wipe their feet on it."[25]

It has been noted that Communists, while quick to champion the cause of refugees from Fascism, felt no such obligation in the case of Bolshevism's Russian victims in France. And yet, in spite of the party's regular onslaughts upon "White guard spies" in the Miller affair, the far left was not averse to wooing the shrinking, proletarianized mass of Miller's onetime legions. If the blow sustained by ROVS in the loss of its president could be followed up by the defection of large numbers of veterans to the cause of working-class solidarity, the White cause would suffer fatal damage. Accordingly, through its Russian section,[26] the Communist-led Confédération générale du travail (CGT) urged the Russian worker to separate himself from "the adventurism, venality and complete moral collapse of the leaders of these military groups.[27] Miliukov welcomed the CGT campaign. He saw French opinion painting the whole emigration in the same reactionary colours, with the result that all *émigrés* were being compromised by the military organizations.[28] Labour spokesmen addressed Russians in Paris and the provinces on the need to put class ahead of nationality. *Vozrozhdenie*, a hostile witness, described one such session in the capital's fifteenth *arrondissement*. From a district of dense Russian settlement, only eighty to eighty-five people could be cajoled into attending. Lenin's portrait hung on the wall, and the presiding committee, consisting of two French Communists and two Russians, harangued those present on their duty to abandon the old military chiefs. The appropriate resolution received majority approval only out of fear of reprisals, according to *Vozrozhdenie's* reporter.[29]

Vozrozhdenie to the contrary, the CGT campaign appeared to make inroads into the *émigré* labouring mass. *Russkii shofer*, defending democratic views within the ranks of Russian taxi-drivers, claimed in the summer of 1937 that 2,000 drivers were now members of the Union of Russian Drivers (*Union des chauffeurs russes*), compared to 600 a year earlier.[30] Some may have succumbed to intimidation, but it is more likely that this large increase in so short a time was part of the general explosive growth of union membership that occurred throughout France following the Popular Front's victory. While the class struggle was not, in itself, an idea likely to win many adherents among Civil War veterans, even if proletarianized, the fact was nonetheless undeniable that a government of the left had done a great deal to improve material conditions for workers in France. Even Vishniak, no admirer of the Popular Front, wrote of knowing old regime generals and officers who blessed the name of Léon Blum.[31] Thanks to this Jewish Socialist, a real improvement was underway in the grim conditions of the *émigré* worker. No conservative, anti-Communist administration had done as much to ease his life in France. Yet this was far from meaning that large numbers of Russian refugees were now ready to embrace leftist causes. For one thing, no Russian in France could fail to know that the persons trying most energetically to sever *émigré* loyalties to old leaders identified their own political faith with that of Soviet Russia, or that they at least looked sympathetically in Moscow's direction. Why should the Cossack taxi-driver or Russian miner not benefit from union membership and the advantages offered by a Socialist government, and at the same time remain a staunchly anti-Soviet Russian patriot faithful to his old associations? Whatever the left might say, Russian *émigrés* did not need to view these two options as incompatible.

In December 1938 Plevitskaia came to trial. Her weeklong hearing was the last occasion when Russian *émigré* matters engaged a measure of French public attention. The experience, though less traumatic than Gorgulov's judgement, offered Russians no reasons for self-congratulation. Questioned by Plevitskaia's defender Filonenko (one of the few practising Russian members of the French bar), police officials revealed that their pursuit of the Soviet trail had either seemed unproductive or, when suggested, had been discouraged by superiors on the grounds that it threatened to disrupt the good relations then existing between France and the USSR.[32] Efforts to substantiate this point by issuing a subpoena to Marx-Dormoy, the Socialist minister of the interior in September 1937, failed when he invoked ministerial privilege to avoid an appearance. The state's chief police witness, introduced as one who knew Russian circles in Paris well, spoke so disparagingly of them that the presiding judge was moved to gentle protest. It was unlikely, he remarked, that everyone in the Russian community lied, cheated, and betrayed: otherwise why credit any Russian witness?[33] *Le Populaire*, which followed the trial closely, drew attention to the peculiar world of *émigré* politics. Its reporter, "Rivarol," saw the peasant-born defendant as the victim of other people's machinations: her husband, French officials and, most of all, Russian reactionaries in Paris.[34] Others have not been so kind to "the Kursk nightingale."[35] Nevertheless, "Rivarol"'s indignation at the guilty verdict and sentence of twenty years hard labour for the unfortunate singer seems justified. Who were the real targets in this harsh penalty? "Rivarol" had no doubts. The twelve jurors selected from the middle and petty bourgeoisie struck at Plevitskaia to punish an impudent foreign woman, to vent their hatred of unattainable enemies such as the Soviets, the Reds, the left, and finally to thumb their noses at the French Revolution.[36]

In spite of its obscurities, the Miller case can only have been the work of Soviet intelligence organs. For them the risk was minimal. Skoblin seems to have been their man for at least ten years, during which time he had transformed the "Inner Line" into a Soviet spy network inside ROVS[37] Kutepov's removal must have suggested to the Soviets that, if a conservative French government limited its reaction to verbal abuse at Moscow, a Socialist administration, sorely beset from the right, would not go even that far on behalf of a White general. Had Miller not left his incriminating note, Skoblin might well have inherited the ROVS presidency and delivered the Civil War veterans wholly into Moscow's hands.

It might well be wondered, as *Posledniia novosti* did, why the Soviets felt it necessary to pursue long-vanquished foes in the West. While the answer to that question cannot be conclusively known until Soviet archives yield their secrets, such zealousness was not incompatible with Stalinist paranoia against all enemies real or imagined. In Miller's case, the dictator may even have had a better reason than usual. Two years after the general's abduction the defecting head of Soviet military intelligence in Western Europe reported that Miller had been eliminated because of his involvement in Stalin's fabricated case against Marshal Tukhachevsky and other victims in the Red Army's high command.[38] But *émigrés* had already witnessed several examples of Moscow's unforgiving vendetta against them. Indeed, Soviet intelligence seems to have taken the emigration's anti-Soviet potential far more seriously than anyone else. There was, of course, the Kutepov precedent, and even before this it was no secret that Soviet agents had been devoting much effort to penetrating *émigré* organizations, especially those on the far right. The notorious "Trust," set up by the GPU in the early 1920s to achieve this goal, brought off its most spectacular coup in 1926 when it stage-managed the "secret" return trip to the USSR of the prominent antisemitic monarchist V.V. Shulgin. On his return to France, Shulgin published an account of his excursion, which created a sensation.[39] He had travelled widely inside the Soviet Union and concluded at the end that everything in Russia was as before, "only a little worse." The nation was so thoroughly permeated with secret monarchist cells that a restoration was surely imminent. He quit Russia certain that he had found his country again. "Trust" thereupon revealed that the visitor's entire journey had been an elaborate hoax. From the moment Shulgin had stepped over the frontier, all his monarchist contacts had been GPU agents. This dénouement, which spelled the end of "Trust," left Shulgin looking exceedingly foolish, all the more when he reflected that he had dispatched the proofs of his book to his supposed monarchist hosts to make sure that there was no detail therein which betrayed them to the Soviet authorities.[40]

The seizure of the two White generals, though different from the Shulgin operation in the details, was fully in the same audacious spirit. Together they had a devastating impact on the confidence and credibility of the émigré far right.[41]

The Miller case focused attention upon a particular segment of the emigration at a time when tens of thousands of ordinary Russians were eking out far less conspicuous lives. In the closing months of 1937, this mass came under scrutiny from Sir John Simpson's investigation of refugee conditions throughout the world. One of his agents, H.W.H. Sams, examined the several national groups which had found refuge in France; when he came to the Russians he sounded some familiar themes. He noted, for instance, the multiplicity of émigré charitable organizations, all trying, with meagre individual resources, to succour fellow-refugees. This diffusion of effort was, to Sams, regrettable, though he detected a hopeful sign in the recent formation in Paris of a coordinating committee on which thirty-three Russian bodies would henceforth co-operate in making sure that Russian refugees benefited from all available welfare support.[42]

Through Sams's description the nation's second city offered a microcosm of the Russian emigration in France. The Russian colony in Lyons lived a hard life in spite of the popularity of Mayor Herriot, who gave a Christmas tree each year to the Russian community in his city. According to Sams, only 1 percent of Russians felt they were leading a normal life. 80 percent declared themselves barely able to keep going, while about 100 Russians in Lyons were reduced to living as vagrants under the Rhône bridges. Popular attitudes to the refugees were good in the city itself, but in the eastern working-class sections of Villeurbanne and Vaulx-en-Vélin Communist party influence made for some hostility. Four Orthodox parishes were split in allegiance between Metropolitan Evlogy and the Sremske Karlovtsy synod. Twenty seven local Russian bodies were represented on a central émigré committee, which had few funds. A Cossack section had 270 members, while a Ukrainian group proclaimed its separatist loyalties and would have nothing to do with the *émigré* committee.[43]

Elsewhere on the provincial scene Sams found as little cause for rejoicing. Marseilles had fourteen different organizations, which had just got together in a refugee committee; there was little co-operation so far. 8,000 Russians still lived on the Riviera between St-Raphaël and the Italian frontier; half of these were in Nice. They were an elderly population, which had entered the unskilled labour market already middle-aged. Their lives were very exhausting. Bordeaux had about 300 Russians in a tightly self-contained group; while the mines of northeastern France still employed good Russian workers. Drunkenness was, it appeared, rife in this band, but "[this is] a common failing among the Russians, unfortunately."[44] As far as relations with the host country were concerned, Sams observed some improvement since 1935. In that year, following the assassination of King Alexander of Yugoslavia and French foreign minister Barthou by an alien terrorist, French xenophobia reached its pitch. This had produced a sharp increase in expulsions and restrictions on foreigners in France. The advent of the Popular Front had led to a modification of the worst of these measures. But Sams saw the Russians as still unprotected. If another xenophobic wave broke over France, their position could be as bad as in 1935.[45] His judgment, soon tested, proved accurate.

What could lie ahead for the Russians? One possibility noted by Sams and others was assimilation. If this imprecise term meant the complete abandonment of what Sams called "Russian qualities and features," the denationalization so dreaded by the older generation for its young, Sams saw the Russians as very slow to assimilate. Language was the great barrier to all but a highly educated few of the older *émigrés*; many still hoped to return to Russia. As for the young, it was impossible to generalize. Sams did observe the inroads made by the French language, and he admired the struggle waged by Russian parents against their children's absorption into French culture.[46] Legal definition scarcely solved the problem. New regulations in August 1927, for example, decreed that children born in France of a French parent were French; they also widened the categories eligible for naturalization.[47] As far as the first measure went, while Russians were slower than West European immigrants to marry French wives or husbands, and only a minority of Russians marrying did so, as many as forty-four per cent of Russian males who married between 1927 and 1931 took a French bride.[48] In the long run, this fact, particularly if sustained, was a far more powerful impulse to denationalization/assimilation than any law. As Robert Gessain and Madeleine Doré observed in their 1946 survey, a French mother made for French children, not just legally but, more importantly, mentally (*de pensée*) as well.[49] Naturalization statistics indicate that between 1920 and 1940 about 18,000 Russians acquired French citizenship.[50] In itself this total does not mean that a corresponding loss took place in the number of those who considered themselves Russian. It is likely, though unprovable, that many applicants for naturalization were moved by the same consideration that prompted Zinaida Shakhovskaia to obtain Belgian citizenship. The new citizenship (*natsionalnost*) ended many vexations, yet "Russian qualities and features" (*narodnost*) remained. Russians found the distinction crucial.[51]

One alternative to assimilation, its reverse in fact, was a return to the Soviet Union. As has been seen, this was a path taken by a thin trickle of intellectuals from the Change of Landmarks group to the Eurasianists (though certainly not all of these); they were joined by a scattering of cultural figures. Advocates of this way out of exile's frustrations were few. A.V. Peshekhonov, from the left end of the Popular Socialists, was one of them. His book, written after his expulsion from Soviet Russia, adopted the Change of Landmarks position. Attacking basic *émigré* assumptions, he called on the exiles to return to Russia even without guarantees of freedom or employment.[52]

A mass repatriation was an idea briefly pursued in the early 1920s by Dr Nansen's office for the Russian refugees. About 3,000 Cossacks from the Don, Kuban, and Terek regions, swept up in the exodus from Russia, returned under Nansen's auspices in 1922. The high commissioner's representatives visited them in their villages and reported cautiously that the returners' personal liberty did not appear less than that of the rest of the population "except in full freedom of movement."[53]

Of the handful of prominent returners one in particular angered conservative opinion by his defection. Count Aleksei Ignatiev was serving as Russian military attaché in Paris at the time of the February Revolution. He grew steadily more disenchanted with the Provisional Government and after October opposed the Allied intervention in and blockade of the young Soviet republic. Like General Brusilov and some other senior tsarist officers, Ignatiev found his patriotic instincts stimulated by Russia's struggles to the point that in 1923 he appeared at the Soviet mission in Berlin to request a Soviet passport. This "treason" to the emigration from one of his name brought whatever retribution could be mobilized. He was attacked in the rightist press and, so he later maintained, his mother was banned from the Alexander Nevsky cathedral in Paris until she and her family had broken with the renegade.[54] In the Soviet Union he became the second "Soviet count" to serve Stalin, A.N. Tolstoi being the first; among other duties he taught table manners to officers in the Red Army. Back in France briefly in the 1930s as a Soviet diplomat, Ignatiev finally returned to Moscow in the inauspicious year 1937. However, he survived it and Stalin to write his memoirs. As Ignatiev left Paris, an unforgiving Semenov railed at "the unworthy reject of the family of the counts Ignatiev, which owes everything to the Romanovs."[55]

Ignatiev proved susceptible to the patriotic appeal at a time when Russia was assailed from all sides. His country might be Bolshevik-ruled but he saw her as Russia still: great, powerful and his homeland. In due course other refugees would feel the same stirrings. It was a message insistently proclaimed in Paris by an organization set up after recognition and clearly supervised from Moscow. This was the Union of Return to the Motherland (*Soiuz vozvrashcheniia na rodinu vo Frantsii*). The Union's "informational-literary bulletin" *Nash soiuz* (Our Union) tirelessly propagandized the achievements of Soviet construction, contrasting them with the dismal reality of the *emigrantshchina*: poverty, unemployment, denationalization, and rude treatment by landladies. The Union's strident insistence that a return to the USSR was the only proper course for *émigrés* made its premises on the rue de Buci the logical target of a police raid in the days following Miller's disappearance. Nothing incriminating was unearthed.[56]

From the start of its existence, the Union of Return faced a natural, profound distrust among refugees in France. A frontpage appeal in *Nash soiuz* in December 1933 complained of this suspicion. It was a legal organization; its purpose was evident and nonconspiratorial. Yet the most absurd rumours persisted of its clandestine activities. Addressing ordinary *émigrés* over the heads of "the Miliukovs, Kerenskys and Millers," *Nash soiuz* claimed "more than 7,000 former readers of *Poslednii novosti* and *Vozrozhdenie*" had seen the light and were now Soviet citizens, "giving their strength and knowledge to the people, to their country and to Soviet construction."[57] The figure quoted seems high. If it is accurate, it suggests that neither the Union nor the USSR was quite the pariah that conventional *émigré* wisdom dictated. A change of name in 1937 to Union of Friends of the Soviet Motherland (*Soiuz druzei sovetskoi rodiny*) emphasized the club's basic propaganda function. The convulsions of Stalin's domestic policies during the later 1930s made the editor's task a daunting one.[58] His paper continued nonetheless to attack all aspects of *émigré* life, pausing only to acknowledge one or two positive features in the Young Russia movement.[59] General respectability still eluded the organization, though perhaps some improvement occurred in the years following the 1933 complaint. In November 1937 the Union apparently had 300 members in Paris and, so Sams reported, 1,200 *émigrés* attended its 7 November ball that year.[60] But it took a major war to move greater numbers of Russian refugees any further in demonstrating their interest in living in a Soviet environment.[61]

On 12 April 1938 the Radical Socialist Edouard Daladier formed his third ministry. In doing so, he effectively ended the Popular Front.[62] Anxious to accelerate the lethargic pace of the nation's rearming, the new premier moved with gathering momentum toward a confrontation with rebellious unions and their supporters among his late political colleagues. Daladier's imposition in November of his notorious decree-laws, modifying the forty-hour week and other important gains of the Popular Front era, brought matters to an angry climax. Government and employers collaborated vigorously to suppress the avalanche of strikes and factory occupations which rolled across the country at the month's end. Their successful counteroffensive to recover ground recently lost to the left exacerbated still further the yawning divisions within French society on the eve of renewed European war.

Russians closely watched these events, which affected them directly. They had already seen the perils in store for foreign workers during times of French labour agitation. Refusal to join in work stoppages could bring retaliation from French workmates; while to join in invited dismissal with no prospect of reinstatement. Renault discharged 28,000 strikers in November 1938 alone and, though few Russians may have been involved in that particular purge, the uncompromising mood on both sides left foreign workers dangerously exposed. [63] The storm signals were flying. In May 1938, *Vozrozhdenie* solicited *émigré* aid for 300 Russians who had fallen foul of recently tightened regulations governing the employment, movement and residence of foreigners in France. [64] In this instance it seemed likely that the government had in mind Spanish and Italian refugees, rather than Russian. [65] Marius Moutet, a minister in Blum's first government, remained a loyal, helpful friend to the Russians; even so, they could feel no security [66]

Apart from news of such hardships, *Vozrozhdenie's* columns remained dedicated to traditional themes. Anti-Soviet hatred and monarchical nostalgia predominated as usual. In November 1938, as working-class France flamed around them, the newspaper devoted much attention to the 950th anniversary of Russia's conversion to Christianity and to the coincident celebration by the Society of Friends of National Russia in honour of Anna Iaroslavna, eleventh century Kievan princess and queen of France. [67] News items of that sort made more congenial reading than did details of strikes and lockouts.

Vozrozhdenie spoke for and to a vanishing constituency. On the eve of the war aging *émigrés* nostalgic for the old times were forced to endure a strident new voice, one not directed at them, but rather at impatient younger exiles with no attachments to pre-October Russia. This was, pre-eminently, Young Russia's domain. But Kazem-Bek had a rival, one much more willing than he to hitch its star to the fortunes of German National Socialism. The National Labour Alliance of the New Generation – Solidarists (*Natsionalno-trudovoi soiuz novogo pokoleniia – solidaristy*), to employ one of the several variations of nomenclature the movement used, [68] became the noisiest and most combative of all exile groups during the closing years of the decade. Its members seemed to be everywhere. Whether rising to denounce Miliukov, joining in the Anna Iaroslavna celebrations, or "explaining" Miller's disappearance, they had a talent for provocative self-advertisement. Detested by other émigrés, the young, aggressive "solidarists" earned an attention far in excess of their numbers or importance.

The movement was founded in Belgrade in the early 1930s by an athletic Cossack veteran of Wrangel's army, V.M. Baidalakov. Unlike Kazem-Bek, Baidalakov reacted with enthusiasm to a Nazi-ruled Germany. He appears to have shared none of the glava's reservations about Hitler's anti-Slav obsessions; he certainly shared Nazism's antisemitism. His National Labour Alliance (NTSNP) endorsed a defeatist line should the Soviets become involved in war and it sponsored "direct action" against domestic Soviet targets by "solidarist" infiltrators. None was ever heard from again. Less perilous objectives were available inside the emigration. In accordance with the image of youthful activism the group like to project, young "solidarists" were taught "how to break up speeches, debates and meetings" of the emigration's senior statesmen.[70] This they did with enthusiasm. All these symptoms pointed toward a Fascist orientation, and in fact "the Fascist nature of prewar solidarism was not in doubt to anyone in the emigration," according to the historian of the younger, "unnoticed" generation, Vladimir Varshavsky.[71]

At the sixth "congress" of the NTSNP's French section in November 1938, its leader, V.D. Poremsky, spoke favourably of the party's prospects, though with the warning that political upheaval in Russia must come from internal sources, not from foreign intervention.[72] His point was perhaps less convincing than his party's known predilection for the Nazis. Furthermore, Poremsky's optimism about their prospects did not disguise the fact that the "solidarists" had only their rhetoric and energy to attract recruits. As others had found before them, these provided thin sustenance for the unending, sterile trek across the exile desert. After all, the pressure on younger émigrés to surrender to the culture around them was harder to resist in 1938 than ten or fifteen years earlier. A Poremsky lieutenant, I.Ia. Savich, admitted this reality a short time later. He repeated a cautionary tale doing the rounds concerning a certain Andrei Vorobiev, who gave up the unequal struggle and turned himself into André Demoineau. "We all know other sad examples," Savich declared, as he went on to contrast Russian apolitical apathy with the firmness of political purpose displayed by Spanish youth in their country's civil war.[73]

Other than its highly developed capacity to enrage older émigrés, the NTSNP offered nothing particularly enticing to refugees in France. The movement promised nothing particularly enticing to refugees in France. The movement promised action on Russia's behalf but was vulnerable to the accusation that its devotion to Russia could hardly be reconciled with its loudly professed admiration for Adolf Hitler. This latter was, in any case, a quite onesided affection. The German section of the movement was obliged to dissolve itself in August 1938 under pressure from the authorities who, it may be presumed, objected to foreign refugees offering unsolicited advice on sensitive issues.[74] Then came the Nazi-Soviet pact, a cruel blow, which induced some long overdue reservations among "solidarists" about those governing Germany.[75] However, the Nazi aggression against the USSR saw many "solidarists" in the van of the German armies. The opportunity for patriotic, anti-Stalinist action inside Russia was too good to miss and several of Baidalakov's followers ran afoul of the Gestapo as a result.[76] Some survived all the ordeals and were able to resume their anti-Soviet crusade in Europe after World War II.

Deepening European crisis did not bring the emigration's warring factions any closer. Semenov, in *Vozrozhdenie*, rejoiced at Munich and at the resignation, a week later, of President Beneš, a major *bête-noire*. Satisfaction remained strong until the dissolution of the rump Czechoslovak state in March 1939. This provoked a nervous tremor. S. Oldenburg felt Russian nationalists could not be happy at this latest development. German strength could not be augmented by the absorption of a Slav state. Where was Europe heading?[77] Not to a Soviet-Anglo-French accord, if Semenov could prevent it. Through the summer his editorial drumbeats sounded the alarm. As ever, his refrain warned of Moscow's duplicity and of its nefarious plans for those who sought its friendship. The Nazi-Soviet pact thus drew a response that amounted to a song of triumph over a dazzling vindication. "They have sold and betrayed": had not *Vozrozhdenie* always said they would? Semenov turned on his critics. All those who for twenty years had put their trust in Soviet evolution: the Miliukovs, Lloyd Georges, Benes's, Briands, and Roosevelts, with their credits and recognition, might now see what it had all achieved.[78] Four days later, with war imminent, Ivan Tkhorzhevsky tried to put some distance between the paper and France's impending enemy. Given the record, his was not an easy assignment. Anti-Bolshevism justified any alignment, "but we are with those who are against Bolshevism only while they are against Bolshevism." Addressing "secret former Hitlerites in our midst," Tkhorzhevsky advised them that they had erred. "You have forgotten that the orientation of Russians can only be Russian." His editor promised, in an editorial in French, that Russians in France would do their duty "come what may," but Semenov's conviction that the Allies were fighting the wrong enemy blazed forth from every line.[79]

Bodrost spoke out more honestly. The end of Czechoslovakia dispelled Kazem-Bek's guarded hopes for European peace. Unlike *Vozrozhdenie*, *Bodrost* rejoiced at the sight of Western envoys soliciting Soviet support. A Russian Great Power stood once more, though Stalin was not the man to maintain it. On 20 August Prince S. Obolensky greeted the alliance now forming, as he saw it, between East and West: the Third Reich had been warned.[80] The next issue, forced to come to terms with the astounding news from Moscow, manfully insisted that the Nazi-Soviet pact could have advantages if viewed from a strictly Russian standpoint.[81] The declarations of war sharpened the paper's animus against Stalin. His defection for a dubious short-term advantage deprived their countrymen of the chance to join the Western powers against Russia's historic secular adversary,[82] Messages to Daladier placed the Young Russia movement unreservedly at French disposal, while anti-Nazi and anti-Stalin exhortations filled *Bodrosr*'s columns in the opening weeks of the war.[83]

Kazem-Bek's satisfaction at the growing international weight of the USSR was shared by several of Stalin's critics in the democratic sector of *émigré* opinion. Vishniak, the severest of all, was not among them. In May 1938, after months of editorial differences over the tone of their journal,[84] he quit the *Sovremenniia zapiski* board for the more congenial atmosphere of a new periodical, *Russkiia zapiski*.[85] Even though this latter appeared "with the closest participation" of three of Vishniak's old colleagues, his departure was not imitated by any one of them. In fact, Nikolai Avksentiev, whom Vishniak had particularly expected would follow him out,[86] remained as editor to publish in the summer of 1939 a detailed analysis of contemporary diplomatic complexities. He examined point by point the various issues which had excited so much polemical debate inside the emigration. Few may have taken his instruction to heart – there was no evidence that *Sovremenniia zapiski*'s political judgment was any more popular in its final year than in any other – but Avksentiev's article remains a cogently argued assessment of existing realities, in which the author made a clear, unambiguous statement of his own preference. It can withstand scrutiny better than any other *émigré* analysis of the subject from right or left.

"The Peace Front' and Russia" begins with an expression of pride. "Regardless of our hostile attitude toward Soviet power," Avksentiev wrote, "we cannot help but feel a sense of national satisfaction when the world importance of Russia is being re-established in Europe's eyes, and we agree with most of the counterproposals made by the Soviet government to the British." Those he termed "the patriots of woe" had been wrong to delight in Russia's exclusion from Munich as a *quantité négligeable*. It was obvious that there could be no stable European or world balance without the USSR. If only Russian democrats could be certain of Soviet sincerity, their approval of Moscow's recent diplomacy would be wholehearted.[87] In effect addressing Kerensky, Vishniak, and other obdurate critics on the left, Avksentiev declared that it was short-sighted to insist that the Soviet government in no way and under no circumstances could ever act in Russia's interests. The force of objective necessity sometimes obliged it to do so in the interests of its own preservation, even though detested by the people. Miliukov himself might have been writing.

Avksentiev recognized that many in the emigration found the prospect of an alliance between Stalin and the Western democracies extremely painful. He did not count the ultra-right edge of the political spectrum, "those ready to submit to anyone from whom they might achieve restitution or those who, for mercenary or non-mercenary reasons, shout hosannahs to Hitler ... until they are hoarse, [seeing him as] an idealist struggling to save Russia and the world from the 'diabolical' power of the Bolsheviks." He was addressing émigrés who accepted that Russia's liberation must come internally, at the hands of domestic "national forces." It was morally important that they decide on which side of the rival blocs now forming they wished to see Russia, even though they themselves had no power whatever to influence events. They must resolve the question without illusions, not taking the desirable and expected for the real. The Russia they preferred did not exist, and no one knew when it might. But a real Russia did exist and lay under a deadly threat. "We do not understand how people can set against this real Russia – even though in Bolshevik clutches – some imagined 'national' [Russia] whose interests are alien to 'combinations'."[88]

Several favourite émigré notions came under Avksentiev's critical gaze. To those who insisted that Soviet Russia could add nothing to an Anglo-French alliance, that she was economically chaotic and that her army was badly equipped, led and demoralized thanks to the recent repressions, the editor replied in words that were as frank as they were rarely heard. "We must in fact admit that we really know nothing about the military potential of the Red Army; we have no clear idea of its combat capabilities, as opposed to those who insist on their own diagnoses based on 'irrefutable facts.' None of us has irrefutable facts; we have information and stories of various kinds, often differing widely from each other." And if the USSR were indeed helpless, why were Great Britain, France, and Germany so interested in an alliance with her? The writer dealt equally firmly with two other recurrent objections to his plea for a measure of realism. The regime's ideological cast did not prevent it from collaborating with the democracies in defence of peace; necessity knew no doctrinal barriers. As to the fear of subversion, Avksentiev agreed that the Soviet record inspired distrust. The example of republican Spain was instructive in this regard. However, Great Britain and France were not civil-war Spain. NKVD agents might attempt something underhand, but that was a potential danger. Fascist aggression was a genuine, undeniable menace of the moment.[89]

One final question remained. It was, Avksentiev admitted, the hardest objection to meet for it sprang from the most deeply held of all émigré certainties about the USSR: that the Russian people regarded its tyrannical oppressor with unquenchable hatred. War offered that people the means to get rid of its oppressor, whereas an alliance between Stalin and the Western powers would reinforce the chains of slavery. Cautiously Avksentiev agreed that information out of Russia indicated that defeatist attitudes might exist there. But the evidence could be wrong. "Here too we must recognize our ignorance of the real mood of Russia's population. But even if [assertions of widespread defeatism] were true, we could not, in the name of Russia and her interests, think other than we do." Certainly Avksentiev and those who thought like him wanted peace. But war threatened. If it came to Russia, they did not wish to see her defeated. Therefore, to the critical question whether Russia's victory "[might] not temporarily strengthen Soviet power, postpone still further the hour of its fall and thus increase popular suffering," Avksentiev could only answer that he did not think so. A victorious people was better able to fight for its rights than one demoralized by defeat. Of course even this might be wrong. "We must admit," Avksentiev wrote, "that the first hypothesis [of a Soviet regime reinforced by victory] is possible. But even in that hypothesis we cannot answer otherwise. ... No one will venture the least reproach to those whose sufferings, not experienced by us, have led them to a hopeless, defeatist condition ... But the victory of [the Fascist powers] will bring a still more bitter slavery, for they will act in Russia as they are now acting in Czechoslovakia." Russia's true path lay in alliance with the democratic states in defence of peace.[90]

Alexander Kerensky, the emigration's most voluble and peripatetic Socialist, also had much to say on these matters. No less than Avksentiev could he deny stirrings of the deepest national satisfaction at Anglo-French courting of Russia. Yet a genuine, constructive role in Europe for his country was unattainable under present conditions. With Stalin at the helm, world revolution remained the regime's primary objective. This would not change, even with the Soviet dictator on the verge of his greatest triumph, a pact on equal terms with the Western powers.[91] A contributor to Kerensky's journal, Elena Izvolskaia, also admitted to mixed feelings. The daughter of one of tsarism's most distinguished diplomats shared her editor's doubts that Stalin's Russia would prove itself a fully worthwhile ally. Terror against peasantry and army had reduced the country to catastrophic conditions. Both writers decisively rejected assertions in the Young Russian *Bodrost* that a Russian Great Power stood once again. Before that could happen, the Russian people needed the fresh air and sun of freedom.[92]

All thoughts, whether hopeful, resentful or resigned, of a Soviet partnership with the Western democracies were swept aside by the news and pictures from Moscow on 23 August 1939. The Nazi-Soviet pact caught Russian democrats, as others, totally by surprise.[93] They had foreseen only two alternatives open to Stalin: neutrality in isolation or alliance with the democracies. A third option in the form of an alignment with Hitler was out of the question: "psychologically unthinkable even for Stalin" according to S. Soloveichik in Kerensky's *Novaia Rossiia*; "an imaginary danger," N. Bassekhes assured readers of *Posledniia novosti* five days before the pact's signing.[94] Stalin's handshake with Ribbentrop proved this confidence was misplaced. *Posledniia novosti* reacted calmly at first, taking its cue from official British and French responses.[95] But indignation boiled over a few days later. European war was now imminent. The dictator Stalin's criminal, amoral act had helped to make it so and must evoke horror from Russians at home and abroad. They could not be held to account for Soviet misdeeds against public morality and world democratic solidarity. Russians in France would loyally support the country that had given them refuge.[96] On this point at least, *Posledniia novosti*, *Vozrozhdenie*, and *Bodrost* were for once in agreement.

WAR IN THE WEST

The six years of European and World War fell into two unequal parts for Russian exiles everywhere. The first ran to 22 June 1941, the second followed. No matter what their individual opinions were, no *émigré* could remain indifferent to the German invasion of the USSR and still consider himself Russian. Yet their experiences during the eighteen months preceding the attack on Russia rubbed home to the refugees as nothing before the liabilities of their nationality, or rather their lack of one, as well as their vulnerably dependent status.

Russians in France felt themselves, not without cause, to be among the first victims of the Hitler-Stalin pact. On 1 September *Vozrozhdenie* reported that Russians in Paris were bearing the brunt of popular resentment. Taunts of "dirty Russians" and other unpleasantnesses were being encountered more frequently since 23 August.[97] Worse followed the Anglo-French declarations of war and the Soviet attack on Poland. With the Western front still quiescent, Vasily Maklakov noted that his Russians were being treated as if they were the enemy. Taxis with Russian drivers would not be hired, Russian shop assistants were dismissed, others denied work permits.[98] This hostility was dismaying, but Russians were not the sole target. They shared in a general animus against all foreigners in France.[99] The Hungarian-born Arthur Koestler, himself a victim of it, observed "the tide of xenophobia [which] swept over France with morbid rapidity" in the first weeks of the war. Interned for a week in the Roland Garros stadium, Koestler was able to form, and later to pass on, a personal impression of Russian *émigré* complexities. Almost half of his fellow internees were Russian. Koestler divided them into two camps, the "White-Whites" and the "Red-Whites." Neither was on speaking terms with the other. The first group, identified by Koestler as "former tsarist officers and NCOs who had fought under Kolchak and Denikin," was implacably hostile to Bolshevism. The "Red-Whites," less numerous and less well-to-do, accepted the Revolution as an accomplished fact and wanted to return to Russia. He detected splits in the "Red-Whites" between the conditionally loyal and those who submitted to Moscow to the improbable point of seeking admission to the Soviet Communist party. Each side accused the other of playing the enemy's game, though they occasionally collaborated in a mixed choir, giving "first class recitals of Russian songs."[100]

The next ordeal for the émigrés came with the Soviet attack on Finland at the end of November. Articulate opinion overwhelmingly condemned Moscow's aggression. S. Oldenburg, in *Vozrozhdenie*, saw the Finns fighting for the same cause as National Russia; while his editor, in a statement from which the military censor removed several paragraphs, proclaimed that the Comintern's destruction was now more imperative than ever.[101] Over the next few months Semenov drew great satisfaction from the USSR's expulsion from the League, the enforced return to Moscow of the Soviet envoy in Paris, Iakov Surits, the proscription of Communist deputies in the Chamber, and the seemingly brutalized nature of Soviet soldiers captured by the Finns. What else was to be expected after twenty years of Bolshevik rule?[102]

The left was appalled by the Nazi-Soviet pact and the Finnish war. Right SRs denounced Soviet perfidy with a vehemence that equalled that of *Vozrozhdenie*.[103] Kerensky, who spent the winter of 1939–40 in the United States, affected to find the coup of 23 August unexceptional. He lectured to the annual congress of the American Federation of Labor on the pact's inevitability; only those ignorant of Bolshevism were surprised at it.[104] The Menshevik remnant in Paris felt the most betrayed. Of all Russian refugee politicals, they had tried the hardest to understand their fellow Marxist-internationalists and to defend Soviet achievements. But a Soviet alliance with Hitler and Soviet troops attacking Poland obliged Mensheviks to conclude that Stalinist despotism now appeared in its true colours: a nationalist-imperialist clique no better than Hitler.[105] It was a judgment reached after much heart-searching; it was followed by an anguished effort to avoid drawing the logical conclusions as to the appropriate tactics which should now be adopted in Soviet matters. Dan in particular held back; a break with his colleagues came the following spring.[106]

One very prominent émigré voice did not join fully in the chorus of condemnation. Miliukov never recovered from his shocked grief over the Anglo-French abandonment of Czechoslovakia. Ill and depressed, he was persuaded by his wife and doctor to leave Paris on the outbreak of war, first for Fontainebleau, then for Vichy. In Fontainebleau the former embodiment of Russian liberalism lived without heat, light, or fuel, often on a diet of potatoes. He continued to write, but the daily supervision of his newspaper had to be confided to other hands. His own reaction and that of *Posledniia novosti* to the attack on Finland were all that critics could have wished. An editorial by I.P. Demidov, who had taken over the newspaper's direction, expressed sympathy and support for the small victim of Stalin's "second criminally mad act." A week later, Miliukov endorsed Demidov's stance.[107]

Soon reservations were voiced. Complaints from members of his Republican-Democratic association that Demidov was insufficiently "patriotic" in his coverage of the Finnish war and that to support the Finns was to take a defeatist line toward Russia struck a responsive chord in the eighty year old refugee. Was not the war proof of his thesis that, objectively, Stalin's foreign policy initiatives served historic Russian interests? Finland had, after all, once formed part of the Russian empire, giving valuable protection to Peter's capital. Hence derived Miliukov's cold conclusion: "I feel sorry for the Finns but I want Vyborg province."[108] When that prize was duly wrested from Finland, Miliukov's approval was evident. A series of articles in *Posledniia novosti*, transmitted from Vichy in the spring of 1940, analyzed the course of European diplomacy since September 1939. Miliukov's assessment of Stalin's role was on the whole positive. He decided that the dictator had not signed his agreement with Hitler in the interests of the Comintern or of world revolution, but rather to win German agreement to the return to Russia of territories lost after the Great War.[109]

Miliukov's volte-face on Finland, the latest of several abrupt turns in his career, imparted a distinct ambivalence to *Posledniia novosti's* last months of life. It also put him in unusual company. The Young Russians' *Bodrost* took a cautious line on Finland. It basically disapproved, accepting still the necessary distinction to be made between regime and people. But editorials reminded readers that Russian interests must be paramount when judging Soviet acts. In spite of everything, a national reform process was underway which made another revolution unnecessary.[110] This evolutionary line at such a moment drew Miliukov's qualified approval. He could agree with almost all of it, he told visitors from Paris. He admired, too, *Bodrost's* willingness to write without regard for the censor.[111] The first page of the 24 September issue, for example, appeared entirely blank under the masthead, although what the authorities objected to remains a mystery. At any rate, Miliukov's tribute was unexpected in the light of the relations up to then between the two antagonists. In its way it was an early example of the dissolving effect that a Russia at war could have on longstanding *émigré* certainties.

Social democratic circles remained impervious to this appeal. Still on his American lecture tour, Kerensky told the Overseas Press Club that the Russian people had nothing to do with the Finnish war or the pact with Hitler. He informed his audience, which included former President Hoover, that Russians continued to be inspired with the same faith and strength that had animated the Mayflower settlers.[112] When back in France, he opened an offensive against the Miliukov line. The cause of Russian freedom was not in his view best served by seeing Stalin as a new unifier of Russian lands, doing a clean job with dirty hands. [113] Mark Aldanov gave literary support in a conversation he devised between *émigré* "A", arguing a strictly patriotic position in Miliukov's style, and *émigré* "B", who defended a principled stand on Finland and Russia. Aldanov's sympathies and, he was certain, those of the large exile majority, lay with "B". [114]

The polemic between the two former ministerial colleagues raged on to the end. On 10 May 1940, as the lull on the Western front abruptly ended, Kerensky accused Miliukov and his friends of being "imperial-style Russian patriots," prepared to condemn Stalin's means, but happy to accept his foreign policy ends as historically justified. [115] A month later, with German armies swarming across the Somme, Miliukov accepted the epithet. [116] He could not in good conscience have done otherwise.

The time was not far off when larger number of exiles would have to consider these questions. In the meantime they were exposed to the mounting French exasperation with foreigners noted by Koestler and Maklakov. The Finnish tragedy made even Frenchmen who should have known better forgetful of the all-important difference between National and Soviet Russias. Charles Maurras, for instance, delivered himself of some strongly critical opinions on Russia while praising Finland in *Je suis partout*. The most vitriolic pen on the French right dismissed Russia as "a monstrous territorial conglomeration, the shame of the globe ... mere administrations are not a state, steppes added to steppes do not make a nation." [117] This was anti-Russian, not merely anti-Soviet. It moved Lev Liubimov to publish an open letter to Maurras reminding him of Russian services to France in 1914. [118] Denikin too protested the calumnies he and other veterans were forced to endure about their country's military record. [119]

French bureaucracy made its own contribution to *émigré* burdens. One, probably inevitable but regretted all the same, was the elimination of the *de facto* exemption from military obligations enjoyed by most male refugees. Technically liable since 1928 to some form of military service, stateless males had not in fact been conscripted in significant numbers. To Russians the issue was sensitive. If they, in their various countries of refuge, were incorporated into national armies, they might well end up fighting each other or Russia in the name of one or more foreign nations. Maklakov pressed this consideration upon French officials, and when his approaches were combined with some administrative confusion about precisely which stateless ought to be called to what units, they sufficed to keep most *émigrés* out of the army down to the late 1930s. [120] Yet at a time when the alien presence in France was coming under intense criticism, it was impossible to sustain the notion that Russians need not actually share in the defence of the country which had given them shelter. In July 1937 new regulations ordered that stateless males in France born after 1 June 1915 should be liable, with some exceptions, to service in the regular army; in 1939–40 subsequent decrees amplified these provisions.[121] Other requirements laid down new registration procedures for stateless residents, including finger-printing and permission from still more officials before employment might be accepted.[122]

All things considered, it was a depressing time to be an exile in France, especially a patriotic anti-Soviet Russian. Nina Berberova wrote to friends that their "shabby, unhappy, provincial emigration" was ending: "my generation will be killed at war, the old will die off in quick order."[123]

The débâcle of May–June 1940 dealt the Russian community, along with the Third Republic itself, a mortal blow. The first émigré casualty was cohe-sion: the Paris head lost contact with the rest of the body. In the capital the surviving Russian press collapsed. Vozrozhdenie's last issue concentrated its attention, not upon the clash on its doorstep, but on what to Semenov was a far grimmer apparition of Soviet jackals lurking in the wings. His principal reporter warned that Europe was face to face with the Russian question. Until its solution there could be no peace.[124] As the Germans closed in on the city, the paper's owner, Gukasov, fled in his Rolls Royce, if we can believe a later, unfriendly Liubimov.[125] Posledniia novosti strug-gled on until 11 June when Demidov set out on a five-day bicycle journey to join Miliukov in Vichy.[126] Others in the democratic camp decided to try for a more distant asylum. Jewish and Socialist contributors to Sovremen-niia zapiski could harbour no illusions about their probable fate in a German-ruled France. Marshal Pétain's mournful tones, announcing on 17 June that the struggle must cease, persuaded Vishniak and his associates that their life in France was over. It should resume in America if they could only get there.[127]

It is impossible not to admire the stubborn persistence of the handful of Russian Socialists, none of them young, determined to carry their cause to safety across the Atlantic. The obstacles were overwhelming. For the second time in twenty years their world lay in ruins about them; they possessed negligible material means, and they needed permission from at least three governments to realize their dream. Yet realize it they did. The journalist Andrei Sedykh, one of their number, wrote a vivid account of their travails. These included the struggle to get from Paris to the unoc-cupied zone, their siege of the Spanish, Portuguese, and United States con-sulates in Marseilles, the contemptuous arrogance of Vichy officials and bureaucratic tribulations of every sort.[128] Vladimir Nabokov's ironic pen caught the frustrations of those desperate days when frenzied refugees "were trying to get from reluctant authorities certain papers which in their turn would make it lawful to apply for a third kind which would serve as a step-ping stone toward a permit enabling the holder to apply for yet other papers which might or might not give him the means of discovering how and why it had all happened."129 When "the usa serum," the vital American visas, came through, Sedykh witnessed the resulting emotions: one apparently healthy applicant succumbed to a fatal heart attack when handed his papers.130 Deflected from Spain by a capriciously closed border, the refugees were redirected to Casablanca. There they underwent their final harassments prior to embarkation for the New World. A Russian Socialist nucleus eventually arrived in New York to resume its defence of Russian democratic values. There, as in Berlin and Paris, disputes both ancient and modern continued to enliven their existence.

A bleaker prospect awaited Russians left in France. To begin with, there were the 10,000 or so Russians in the French army.131 Whether, like the Francophile and utterly unmilitary Adamovich, they had joined up to fight Fascism, or to hasten their naturalization,132 or whether they had been compulsorily enrolled, Russian recruits met obstruction and contempt in the aftermath of the armistice. On 1 October regulations were announced subjecting stateless males between 18 and 55 in the unoccupied zone to unpaid, obligatory labour, if it was decided that they were surplus to needs in their area and were unable to return to their country of origin.133 Others found themselves interned without papers or any prospect of civilian employment. One such internment camp was at Septfonds, near Montauban, originally used for Spanish refugees. Russian witnesses testified to the defeatist cynicism apparent in the French officers they encountered there.134

These difficulties moved Vasily Maklakov to attempt an intervention. He had remained in Paris after the German entry and complaints from Russians continued to be sent to his office. The ex-ambassador lived in anomalous conditions. On 28 August the German authorities dissolved all foreign organizations throughout the occupied zone; this included approximately 800 Russian cultural, educational, and charitable bodies.135 His own office, though not at first affected, was more or less ignored. He had not yet been repudiated by Vichy, so that his representative function still remained intact in the unoccupied zone. At any rate he was the only intermediary the Russians had. On 11 December he submitted their case to Pétain. His letter was characteristic. Respectful, apologetic, legalistic, organized with an eye to the recipient, it laid before the marshal an exposé of Russian émigré griefs. Maklakov expressed his belief that recent restrictive decrees were aimed at harmful foreign involvement in French life. This could not include the Russians. They presented no threat of "gradual invasion," their numbers were in fact declining. They were martyrs to their national ideal; their Russia had fought beside France in the Great War. Pétain's fellow-marshals Foch and Joffre had testified that the Russian aid so unstintingly given had been vital in helping to save France. Could not Pétain's administration reconsider its policies?136 The plea, if ever read by its intended recipient, had no discernible effect.

Several Russian survivors of the war in France wrote later of their lives during those hard years. The most detailed accounts come from the postvictory returners to the USSR and bear ample evidence of their new loyalty. They are not without interest all the same. Lev Liubimov's 1957 memoir in *Novyi mir* contrasted the patriotic instincts of the Paris proletariat (for whom he had never displayed any noticeable concern) with the cowardly collaborationism he witnessed among the bourgeoisie and the denizens of the Jockey Club.[137] Viktor Sukhomlin contributed his impressions to the same journal a few years later. He had been a Left SR; his father, a veteran of the People's Will, had perished in Stalin's terror. Prewar Paris, he told Soviet readers, had been a holy city to him; he had completely identified with French culture. The 1940 collapse had seemed to herald the end of France, the death of her civilization. Some of Sukhomlin's fellow exiles gloated over France's ordeal – "let us see how they will like it!" – but Georgy Fedotov, his mind fixed on Russia, apparently blamed Gogol for his country's misfortunes.[138] Fedotov then departed for the United States. Fondaminsky-Bunakov, though also in possession of an American visa, decided to stay in France and share the common fate. He perished in Auschwitz.

Among those who joined the exodus from Paris was General Denikin and his family. Their flight in a taxi driven by a faithful Cossack ended in Mimizan, a village on the Atlantic coast halfway between Bordeaux and Bayonne. There, as they endured the next five years, Ksenia Denikina kept a diary, eventually published by her daughter, that is a unique portrait of *émigré* fortunes at their lowest ebb. Madame Denikina, too, heard complaints about foreigners, though her peasant neighbours in Mimizan were hospitable. Extremes of heat and cold, material privations, moments of danger and fear, alternating with anguish for Russia, these were the concerns of her wartime life, shared with all her compatriots.[139] It was impossible, early in 1941, to see any light on their horizon. With Stalin still Hitler's partner, America neutral, France prostrate, and Britain expelled from Europe, it would have taken a rash *émigré* to predict openly the victory of the democracies or, on a lesser scale, any great improvement in their own lives.

A more practical consideration also dictated prudence. The occupation authorities were becoming impatient with the flood of requests and complaints pouring in from Russians in France; at the same time the first open calls for collaboration were being heard within *émigré* ranks. A Prince Gorchakov, grandson of Alexander II's chancellor, emerged from obscurity to suggest to Maklakov that they divide representational functions between them. Gorchakov would handle all dealings with the Germans, Maklakov would attend to everything else.[140] The "most serene prince" was the leader of an insignificant monarchist clique and his initiative was probably his own idea. Boris Aleksandrovsky gave Soviet readers in 1969 a malicious portrait of the emigration's first would-be führer. He was glimpsed seated at his desk under portraits of Nicholas II and Hitler, concocting odd schemes to induce Russians to support the German war effort.[141] Though he was certainly hostile to Jews and Freemasons, Gorchakov was too eccentric to serve as a reliable Nazi tool.[142] In April 1941 the authorities in Paris selected a Colonel V.K. Modrakh to organize a "Mutual Aid Committee for Russian Refugees in France." The basis for his selection, other than his evident Fascist proclivities, remains unclear. According to the unfriendly Aleksandrovsky, Modrakh and his wife had supervised a showroom of artistic lampshades before the war and, when that failed, a restaurant.[143]

On this shadowy figure was now conferred the responsibility for Russians in the occupied zone. He gathered around him a committee of assistants as right-wing and obscure as himself and from an office on the rue Blomet set about his campaign on behalf of France's conquerors. He was to be their agent within the Russian colony, their conduit for instructions and their shield against refugee importunings. It was a dismal outlook for the already profoundly demoralized Russian community in France.

Into this and all other fragmented remnants of Russia Abroad fell like a lightning bolt the news of the German assault on the Soviet Union.

CHAPTER EIGHT

Dissolution

On 22 June 1941 a second, decisive phase opened in the history of the surviving Russian emigration throughout the world. Ksenia Denikina summed up a common reaction of conservative *émigrés* in her recorded response to the events of that day: "O Russia, the cup has not passed you by! The two Antichrists have come to blows. Of course this means the end of communism in Russia, but what a cruel ordeal for our country!"[1] Democratic opinion dispensed with the religious motif but equally anticipated a ruinous sequel to Stalin's misrule. "The gigantic experiment has ended in gigantic catastrophe": so Miliukov judged matters as news spread of the first great Soviet disasters.[2] Once again in the United States, Alexander Kerensky began by telling Americans that, while the time was not right for settling accounts with Stalin, the dictator must at once dismantle his repressive tyranny so that the Russian people might feel it was fighting for a new, free life.[3] Half a year later, with German armies poised to seize Moscow, the head of a previous war government of Russia ventured another of his prophecies. One thing he saw as certain: Stalin had been politically destroyed by the war. The totalitarian Bolshevik dictatorship was already in the past; a "programme of restoration," in which *émigrés* had their part, would build a new Russia.[4] N.D. Avksentiev was less convinced of the regime's impending or completed fall. But he hoped that the repulse of German armies before Moscow, even as he wrote, might help the Russian people win recognition of its rights from the embattled dictatorship.[5]

In France one immediate repercussion of the Nazi attack on the USSR was the arrest throughout both zones of large numbers of Russians between the ages of fourteen and sixty-five.[6] In most cases nothing especially unpleasant occurred, but the episode suggested that the authorities now saw all Russians in France as actual or potential fifth columnists. They were wrong in this, but not entirely so. The Soviet-German war was still young, as many refugees began to see that their basic assumptions about their great enemy stood in need, if not of complete revision, then at least of re-examination. The result was a spectrum that stretched from collaborators to repentant petitioners for Moscow's forgiveness.

Emigré collaborators were few in number and, as even Soviet spokesmen came to admit, not typical of the emigration as a whole. Their political allegiance unsurprisingly tended toward the ultraright, restorationist wing of exile opinion which had always been stronger in Germany, the Balkans, and the Far East than in France. The Führer's anti-Bolshevik campaign brought out these recruits. The German civil and military government in France received congratulatory messages from the Union of Guards Regimental Officers and from a group around Modrakh.[7] This last included such right worthies as General Nikolai Golovin, the Hetman of the Don Cossacks, Count Grabbé, the Sremske Karlovtsy metropolitan in France, Serafim, and Modrakh's deputy, one Zherebkov, soon to be a name of sinister omen to Russians in France. The new war, they hopefully proclaimed, was not against Russia or her people, but was one to destroy the Jewish-Bolshevik system. The signatories offered their full support and co-operation in this endeavour.[8] Serafim himself appealed to all "faithful sons of Russia" to aid the German effort to purge the earth of "the masonic star and the hammer and sickle."[9] Simultaneously a manifesto in the name of the Harbin-based All-Russian Fascist party circulated through Russian Paris. It exulted at the international Fascist crusade now underway and polyglottally hailed its heroes: "Heil Hitler! Viva Mussolini! Banzai Mikado! Hurrah Rodzaevsky!"[10]

These messages to the occupying power represented the opinion of a small handful of individuals to whom the anti-Communist aspect of the war outweighed all other considerations. Apart from the personalities noted, the idea of a German crusade did not, with two exceptions, attract prominent figures from the cultural or political leadership. The symbolist poets Dmitry Merezhkovsky and Zinaida Hippius possessed so despairing a view of Russia's moral corruption under the Soviets that any means to hasten the end of "the Devil Number One" was to be preferred.[11] Other conservatives, utterly anti-Soviet, could not stifle their love of Russia or their fears for her future at German hands. To ensure their full compliance nonetheless, the Gestapo now imposed its own candidate on the Russian community, who dispossessed all others. The new supervisor, or *Leiter* (Leader) as he was officially termed, was Modrakh's deputy, Iury Zherebkov, grandson of one of Nicholas II's adjutants, a naturalized German and, if testimony from two notorious returners is to be believed, a professional dancer in emigration.[12] His major asset was probably his friendship with Hitler's theoretician on race questions, Alfred Rosenberg.[13] He lost no time in making known his views to his new charges. On 25 July some 250 prominent Russians were summoned to hear, "without expressing approval or disapproval," just what the future held in store for them. Zherebkov told them that all *émigrés*, ominously excepting Jews, were to come under his jurisdiction; he was even to operate in the unoccupied zone through Vichy's minister de Brinon. The *Leiter* insisted on his knowledge of the Germans. The future belonged to them; they would determine Russia's fate. The White movement had tried and failed to overthrow Bolshevism. It had no further role to play in or for Russia. Only Adolf Hitler knew what had to be done.[14]

Zherebkov was a Russian quisling, the conquerors' grovelling agent eager to chain his people to the juggernaut of the Third Reich. He demanded not so much co-operation as submission and the abandonment of patriotic instincts, even from those Russians firm in their hatred of Stalin. Five months into the war he told a gathering in the Salle Rochefoucauld in Paris that they must not fear the word conquest when contemplating the German campaign in Russia. By its resistance, by its evident willingness to fight for Stalin, the Russian people was showing how much it had been corrupted by Soviet rule. Only National Socialist Germany could re-awaken Russia.[15]

This sort of language evoked contempt from its audience and beyond,[16] but it was dangerous to display open hostility. Zherebkov's committee was invested by the Gestapo with administrative powers over the refugees which it was quick to employ. All Russians were required to register with Zherebkov's agents, even Maklakov, whose omission of the two necessary guarantors brought veiled threats of sanctions.[17] Since many saw registration as a preliminary to compulsory labour in Germany, compliance was far from universal.[18] This defiance took courage. The *Leiter* announced in his newssheet that anyone who did not register by 3 September 1942 would be considered the equivalent of a Soviet citizen and subject to administrative measures; it took no imagination to foresee what these might be.[19] Meanwhile the harassments continued. Appeals poured in to Maklakov; he could do nothing.[20] In January 1942 Vichy officials terminated his remaining representational function, by then meaningless. Maklakov had seen the blow coming and, while concerned about the fate of his Russians without him, was also anxious not to be bundled out of his office at the last minute, as from his embassy in 1924.[21] Shortly thereafter, the Germans made good Zherebkov's threat by confining the aged ambassador in La Santé prison for two months in the early summer of 1942. He emerged unscathed, but without files, standing, or influence with France's masters of the moment.[22]

By the time of Maklakov's release, the condition of his recent charges was truly abysmal. Whether in Billancourt under RAF bombs or in the provinces, scratching for every ounce of food and scrap of news, refugees lived on the edge of survival, perhaps finding that their common penury linked them more tightly than hitherto to their French neighbours.

In circumstances such as these, Russians in France watched the spectacle of their country at war. Reading between the lines of the collaborationist press, straining to catch some neutral station through the buzz of jamming on their ancient radios, Russian refugees were confronted by the fact that the central assumption of so many of their calculations was turning out to be false. The Russian people was defending itself heroically and therewith, willy-nilly, the government which directed its efforts. This realization compelled not a few to think again about Russia and themselves.

Those *émigrés* who later chose to identify with the Soviet victor have had a great deal to say on this point. None of it is surprising. Yet it would be unjust to write off their accounts as mere hypocritical time-serving, the necessary price of their re-admission to Russia. No doubt this element was to some degree present in the several volumes of reminiscence. But the common theme of rediscovery of a powerful homeland was neither artificial nor unprecedented: Alexei Ignatiev had shown the way. There was, for example, Lev Liubimov. His war record between June 1940 and the autumn of 1943 was, to say the least, equivocal. The novelist Don Aminado later dismissed him outright as a German hireling; Liubimov himself was discreetly uninformative about his activities during this period in his otherwise richly detailed memoir. He did confess to Soviet readers that, when the German-Soviet war opened, he shared the common *émigré* assumption that Stalin's regime must collapse. How could a corrupt tyranny withstand the twin assaults of German might and Russian popular fury? His patriotism, he admitted, took time to develop. Before long he saw that the Russian people fought for itself and for Russia under the banner of Communism. All his old convictions crumbled away under these impressions and he was filled with a desire to identify with the new Russia.[23]

For a few refugees the Soviet choice was immediate. They came in the main from the far left end of the *émigré* political world. In New York Dan raised the call of the fatherland in danger. He urged unconditional support to the USSR in the conviction that a more democratic Russia must emerge in victory.[24] In France, where there was no independent Russian press, the choice was up to the individual. From the depth of the countryside, the writer Mikhail Osorgin (Ilin), a Left SR in other days, demanded in August 1941 that refugees everywhere recognize their duty to support the Soviet Union. Bombs upon the Kremlin, he wrote to the New York *Novoe russkoe slovo* (The New Russian Word), were not exploding over Stalin, but over Russia's very heart. Like Dan, he was sure that war and eventual victory would bring vast changes for the better. Previous errors and crimes would be compensated and corrected.[25]

Though the *émigré* majority was not yet ready to share his optimism, the evidence of popular resistance, impossible to deny, became a powerful solvent of old inflexibilities. Meeting Soviet prisoners of war enrolled in the Wehrmacht was another moving experience, perhaps most of all in the Denikin household. The Soviet boys gazed upon the general, "Enemy of the People Number One," long presumed hanged for his sins, while Ksenia Vasilievna saw all of her Russian motherland pass through her cottage.[26] Vladimir Varshavsky recalled his reaction to a similar encounter: was it to save him from such as these that his parents had dragged him to the West? They were like him! He too consoled himself with the hope that victory might reconcile government and people.[27]

The Russian community contributed handsomely to the active anti-Nazi cause. The Resistance chronology begins with the names of two Russians, naturalized French, Anatoly Levitsky and Boris Vilde. Both were ethnologists at the Musée de l'Homme in Paris; both became involved in one of the first Resistance cells in France. The Germans uncovered their activities and sent the two men to a firing squad at Mont Valérien on 23 February 1942. General de Gaulle awarded them posthumously the Medal of the Resistance; today a large plaque in the entrance hall of the museum records their names and service to France. Then there was the symbolist poet Elizaveta Skobtsova, friend of Blok and Belyi. She entered religion as Mother Maria, sheltered Jews and escaped Soviet prisoners of war, and died in the gas chamber. Her life in exile, one of extreme material hardship and blazing moral courage, has inspired legitimate pride in Russians everywhere.[28] Princess Vera Obolenskaia also enrolled in the Resistance. When arrested, she was offered her life in exchange for her co-operation; she refused and was executed. She received the Legion of Honour, the Croix de Guerre and the Medal of the Resistance for her exploits.[29] Another aristocrat, Tamara Volkonskaia, "the red princess" to her Resistance comrades, specialized in promoting the defection to the *Maquis* of Vlasovite recruits in the Wehrmacht; her record was eighty-five in one day.[30] For refugees caught between Russia and the West, unsure of their nationality and future, the Resistance offered a way to combat the common enemy of France and Russia. It enabled many to feel for the first time that their lives had a useful, worthwhile purpose.[31]

Of the prewar political leadership still in France, it was Miliukov who first declared himself. Living in near destitution in Aix-les-Bains, frail and unrecognizably thin to his rare visitors, the eighty-three year old fighter polemicized to the end against opponents who failed to see the new realities. The Soviet struggle had become his struggle. Don Aminado visited Miliukov in his last months. On the wall of his dingy room in the Hotel International hung a map of the Russian front; incessantly Miliukov referred to "our front, our army, our troops."[32] Hearing that Vishniak, from the safety of New York, was still publicly insisting on the truth of anti-Bolshevism, even as he criticized Russians in France for their jingoistic support of Stalin's leadership,[33] Miliukov composed a reply whose very title was an act of apostasy. "The Truth of Bolshevism" ended sixty years of political commitment. Proudly the author admitted himself a jingoist. "I do not and cannot belong to the neutrals." "There were moments – this was one – when a choice had to be made. Between Hitler and Stalin he, Miliukov, had chosen. Certainly his old attitude had been different. But "when one sees the end, one understands better the importance of the means to that end." The Jesuitical flavour could not be helped; to think otherwise meant one must mercilessly condemn the behaviour of "our Peter the Great." As for the October Revolution, though it had been enormously destructive, out of it had come creative forces. Far from being a grievous, ephemeral episode, as Vishniak maintained, the Revolution and Soviet power were now an organic part of Russian history. Furthermore, the Soviet triumph on the Volga moved Miliukov to challenge Vishniak directly on the fundamental article of his faith. In spite of Vishniak's protests to the contrary, the people and Stalin were united.34 Miliukov thus seemed, on the eve of his death, to have come to the point Ustrialov had speculated in 1934 he might one day reach, of recognizing "the great historical truth of the Soviet revolution." If so, it was the spectacle of Russian armies victorious over Germany which brought him there.

Miliukov's diatribe circulated underground in mimeographed copies and was widely regarded as the first signal for *émigré* reconciliation with Moscow.35 Apart from the handful of men committed to the Zherebkov line, political figures responded with varying degrees of enthusiasm. A few of the old irreconcilables suspended their most hostile attacks on the Soviet regime but remained unconvinced that its wartime exertions would induce Stalin's government substantially to modify its structure or philosophy. Most of those on the defeated left fell into this category. In France it included S.P. Melgunov and the Georgian Menshevik Irakly Tseretelli; in America their recent SR collaborators Kerensky, Vishniak, and the rest. They had suffered too much at the hands of their erstwhile fellow Socialists in revolution to believe that these had now changed their ways. The heroism of the Russian people must and would be honoured, but the glory was the people's, not the government's. A new *émigré* periodical, *Novyi zhurnal* (New Periodical), appeared in New York early in 1942 with this among its intentions. The journal placed itself squarely in the *Sovremenniia zapiski* tradition, sharing several of its contributors and editors.36 Unlike its exemplar, however, *Novyi zhurnal* made political questions, rather than cultural matters, the focus of its attention; the times demanded it. Invoking Clemenceau, the editors insisted that they would ardently support Russia's war effort, but they could not remain silent about the crimes and errors of the Soviet regime of yesterday and today.37 This duality was common. In France, the onetime Eurasianist Zinaida Shakhovskaia, though hating the Communist regime, very much desired a Russian victory.38 Ksenia Denikina, absorbed in "our soldiers" and the Stalingrad drama, rejoiced at Russian victories even as she admitted to a depression at the thought of what those victories meant for Russian popular freedom.[39] General Denikin himself resisted German attempts to draft his name for the anti-Soviet cause, while entertaining the hope, assuredly not alone, that a Soviet Bonaparte might emerge from victory to rid Russia of her Communist deformities.[40]

For a few months in 1943 it seemed to many Russians in France that the saviour so anxiously sought for so long might at last be at hand in the person of General Andrei Vlasov. In this Soviet officer turned anti-Stalinist patriot, conservative nationalist émigrés saw a cause they might justly support, a way out of their dilemma. Was he not a Russian general at the head of his own troops holding out the promise of Russia's liberation at Russian hands? Zherebkov realized Vlasov's potential here; through the summer his newssheet appealed to refugees to enroll in or support Vlasov's mission.[41] At the risk of annoying the occupation authorities, the *Leiter* brought Vlasov's deputy, Malyshkin, to Paris. On 24 July the visitor addressed an overflow audience of several thousand in the Salle Wagram. He had a warm reception. His remarks contained an evident antisemitic theme, yet far more striking was the Russian national motif with its perceptible, if unspoken, anti-Nazi implications. This was going too far. Malyshkin was quickly returned to Germany and Zherebkov had his knuckles rapped for his impudent, even dangerous initiative.[42] The euphoria of the Salle Wagram meeting rapidly ebbed, as it became obvious to Russian Paris that Vlasov was nothing but a Nazi pawn, ill used at that. His was not a path that many émigrés chose to follow, though Nina Gourfinkel saw units of Russians, mostly Cossacks, leaving Lyons for service with the German armies in the east.[43]

Stalingrad and, if they managed to read it, Miliukov's manifesto on "the truth of Bolshevism" gave a strong push to exiles like Liubimov who were undergoing a process of personal reappraisal. In November 1943 he and some twenty others gathered in a Paris apartment to organize the clandestine Union of Russian Patriots. This band dedicated itself to the task of promoting reconciliation between an infinitely glorious, magnanimous motherland and her errant, remorseful children abroad.[44] An underground newssheet, *Russkii patriot*, appeared irregularly. *Emigrés* from backgrounds other than Liubimov's "conscience-stricken gentry" co-operated in the venture. *Russkii patriot's* editor, Dmitry Odinets, a historian and lawyer in emigration, had been a member of the Popular Socialists and in the Union of Regeneration, a brief alliance of Kadets and Socialist Revolutionaries in the Civil War.

Between anti-Stalinist émigrés and the minority now courting Moscow's favour lay a middle ground, occupied eventually by Vasily Maklakov and likeminded sympathizers. The drama in the east involved the former ambassador no less than other patriotic Russian exiles. Though he was too wedded to legality and constitutionalism to overlook Stalinist arbitrariness, he could not ignore the leadership qualities of the Soviet government nor the degree of popular support given it. He concluded that, as patriot and longtime doyen of the emigration in France, he should give guidance to the surviving Russian community, bewildered by the vistas opening up in the wake of the retreating German armies. The result of his reflections and consultations was the formation of a "Russian Emigré Action Group" that in June 1944 drew up and circulated a report to the emigration on the prospects ahead.[45]

The Action Group document, certainly more Maklakov's work than anyone else's, invited *émigrés* in France and America to rethink basic axioms: the refrain of "the emigration must recognize" and "the emigration has understood" echoed through the document's eight sections. What it must recognize was clearly spelled out. Great Russia had not succumbed in twenty-six years of Bolshevik rule, as it would have under the Germans; neither had patriotism, nor the nation's healthy forces. Soviet power had nurtured these and together they had saved Russia from foreign conquest. The necessary conclusion inexorably followed: "After all that has happened, the Russian emigration cannot fail to recognize the Soviet government as a Russian government."

As for the October Revolution, Maklakov's group saw it not as an isolated local episode, but as the start of a world process, one which unavoidably produced a sharp clash between old and new. But this was a temporary phenomenon, and in Russia was now over. Evolutionary processes, moving Russia away from revolution, had begun well before 1941; one need only compare the constitutions of 1918 and 1936. The national war for the motherland's salvation could only intensify and deepen this healthy evolutionary trend. Those in exile need not be ashamed of their past. They had not opposed Soviet power for personal or party reasons; they did not defend obsolete privileges, nor were they against the foundation of a new social structure. They had opposed rather the methods and tempo employed in effecting changes. These had seemed to trample upon eternal values: legality, respect for the individual, and the right of the population to be governed according to its wishes. *Emigrés* may have made mistakes in defending these ideas, but the cause itself was just.[46]

Maklakov's exculpatory analysis scarcely applied to all sectors of *émigré* opinion. There can be no doubt – Lev Liubimov's pre-1941 career furnishes one good example – that "personal and party reasons," to say nothing of restorationist dreams, certainly played their part in shaping some *émigré* attitudes toward Soviet Russia. Nevertheless, in the final section of his report, Maklakov addressed an issue of new, urgent relevance to many *émigrés*: the possibility of a return to Russia. This, he recognized, depended on Stalin. Each refugee would have to make up his own mind, deciding for himself how genuinely Stalin's Russia had moved away from "the revolutionary fury," of earlier days. The younger stateless generation ought in particular to reflect upon this matter. It was Russian by family, yet its received culture was often alien and its knowledge of that "land of wonders," Russia, nonexistent. Now, with victory in sight, they could take legitimate pride in their unknown country. For all *émigrés* there now seemed to be a possibility of a sincere reconciliation between them and Soviet power. Should this develop, it would be a symbol of the end of Russia's revolutionary epoch and of the restoration of internal peace inside their homeland.[47]

Common to the Maklakov, Miliukov, and Liubimov views of their suffering country was a readiness to identify a victorious USSR with the best of the purely Russian past. The reconciliation of Orthodox church and Bolshevik state and Stalin's invocation of ancient tsarist heroes thrilled exiles in the West eager to find in a triumphant Soviet Union their Russia under new guise. The man at the head of the Soviet state and its armies benefitted from this urgency. After Stalingrad, the Georgian-born revolutionary came to embody Russian glory to those in France who had constituted themselves the chief defenders of Russia's honour. Miliukov and, after his death, the Union of Russian Patriots were ready to acknowledge in Stalin the heir of Peter the Great. But which exile spokesman, if any, would get the generalissimo's nod?

The question occupied several minds. The Union of Russian Patriots evidently felt that its unconditional devotion and censure of less enthusiastic *émigrés* placed it in the forefront of those seeking Moscow's favour.[48] After the liberation of Paris, Zherebkov slipped away from his headquarters on the rue Galliéra, the Union moved in, and set about perfecting its credentials as Stalin's most faithful disciples within the Russian diaspora. Their day seemed to have arrived. The reopening of communications throughout France unleashed within exile ranks, as inside the country generally, strong pressures on all to prove their devotion to the winning side. In New York Andrei Sedykh later commented feelingly on the many Russians who, for insurance purposes after a compromising war record, chose immediate membership in the Union of Russian Patriots or analogous bodies as the best evidence of their patriotism.[49] Committees sprang up in areas of Russian settlement, established or strengthened links with the Resistance, and demanded news from Maklakov on the most important *émigré* organizations, their relationship to "our" embassy and the general line now to be followed.[50] The first openly published issues of *Russkii patriot* took up these several points.

An editorial by Odinets, "The Road Home," set the tone. The air in the West, he wrote, often created unhealthy conditions for a Russian life. *Émigrés* had been forced to accept this, but they need do so no longer. The road home lay open. Nikolai Roshchin, another ex-*Vozrozhdenie* staffer, announced the end of emigration. Refugees now belonged to a powerful country and did not have to rely any longer on committees, politicians, and the steering-wheels of taxis. Lev Liubimov's more elaborate *mea culpa* took up most of two pages. His old editor, Semenov, had begged him to hold back – "America has not yet spoken!" – but the new Soviet enthusiast would not be silenced. He admitted his anti-Bolshevik past; however, the war cancelled out old hatreds. Soviet Russia was National Russia reborn, stronger, more beautiful, more united than ever under tsarism. How and at what price that unity had been achieved need not concern them now. It was enough that it existed. All, Red and White, were Russians.[51]

Succeeding issues elaborated on these themes. More contrite articles appeared from former anti-Soviet zealots, along with hymns to "our flag," "our national anthem," "our 7 November holiday" and "Lenin as Russian patriot."[52] Material such as this suggested by the end of 1944 that the newspaper board and its associates must be far ahead of any rival in the quest for Soviet approval. Yet to the stupefaction of Russian exiles everywhere, it was Maklakov, at the head of a representational delegation, who was formally received at the Soviet embassy on 12 February 1945. There he exchanged toasts with Ambassador Bogomolov and, in so doing, apparently received Moscow's blessing as its favoured element within the emigration in France.

The February reception at 79, rue de Grenelle was the biggest sensation in *émigré* ranks since June 1941, even perhaps since their exile began. In stepping over the threshold of the building he had once ruled, Maklakov knew he was committing an act which many would find incomprehensible, if not actually treacherous. Much of his time in subsequent months was taken up in explaining his reasons for the visit, probably the most decisive act of his political career. In New York the wildest rumours circulated as to what had transpired; it was there that Maklakov sent off his own account of the historic confrontation. On 21 June he wrote to Kerensky that exiles in the United States must understand the ordeal of *émigré* life in wartime France. The utter penury and isolation of their existence, the strong pressures from Zherebkov's agents, which had seduced not a few, and the effect of Soviet popular resistance obliged remaining *émigré* spokesmen to consider the future of their dwindling community. The thought that some might return home provoked excited discussion, and Maklakov, whose Action Group had first raised the possibility, was besieged with queries about the chances of such a development. At that point the Soviet embassy suggested via a sympathetic member of his group that Maklakov request an interview with Bogomolov. Maklakov ignored the hint; it was repeated. He then contemplated acceptance, telling Kerensky that he foresaw a confrontation no less dramatic than his encounter with Stolypin forty years before. Bogomolov's sudden departure for Moscow in the company of General de Gaulle seemed to end the matter. In the meantime, various "patriotic" groups had made overtures, possibly on behalf of the embassy. On Bogomolov's return a third invitation went off, naming 12 February as the day. After the usual heated arguments inseparable from any émigré political occasion, Maklakov and his colleagues decided to accept. They would go as a delegation representing only a part of the emigration, "not as ancient prophets to enlighten kings," but in search of reconciliation and compromise, bearing a flag of truce.[53]

Although in a few months Maklakov's reasoning would seem wishful thinking even to himself, at the time it was understandable. Strong incentives of the kind he described certainly existed. Moreover, his Action Group's statement of the previous June had spoken of the need to reconcile old and new Russia. A visit to the embassy would demonstrate spectacularly his willingness to contribute to that end, though it signalled also a momentary abandonment of his extreme caution in political questions affecting the emigration. It was also his recognition that, whatever his private reservations, he owed some response to the émigrés who looked to him for an initiative at that moment in their lives.

From the Soviet viewpoint Maklakov's presence as the delegation's head made good sense. He was certainly a far more suitable intermediary than the editorial board of Russkii patriot, even if that journal had purged itself of those with particularly embarrassing prewar records.[54] Maklakov had standing in the émigré community and had, too, the respect of de Gaulle's provisional government, which had reinstated him in his old liaison position. Unquestionably, Bogomolov realized that Maklakov's presence at the embassy and the reconciliation it suggested served as a useful counterthrust to the efforts of Soviet wartime defectors to the West to establish a common front with the previous generation of refugees from the USSR.[55] In a wider context his presence also emphasized the continued Soviet interest in promoting unity between pro-Moscow forces and nationalist anti-Fascist elements. These several motives combined to create a powerful case in favour of a meeting between the representatives of National and Soviet Russias. Rumours in New York suggested that de Gaulle forced Maklakov to see Bogomolov, threatening to end émigré residence rights in France if he did not. This is very unlikely and was, in any case, unnecessary. The Russian reasons were enough.[56]

Eight men accompanied Maklakov on 12 February. They represented the major part of the prewar political spectrum, ranging from Right Kadets to Right SRs and Popular Socialists. The visitors included the last Provisional Government minister still in France, Verderevsky, and his fellow admiral, Kedrov, the head of the Russian All-Military Union. He had managed to escape the fate of his predecessors Kutepov and Miller.[57] Judging from Maklakov's record, the meeting passed off amicably enough, considering who was involved and where they were. Maklakov opened the proceedings, the ambassador returned a few remarks. Each delegate then gave a short address, Bogomolov a longer one. Among other points, he brought some clarification to the issue of Russian patriotism old style and new. The Soviet people, he declared, had certain reservations about the *émigrés* and remained to be convinced of their sincerity. He did admit their positive acts since June 1941 and agreed with their contention that there was much to treasure in Russia's past. The Soviet government and people thought so too; they admired the reforms of Peter the Great and had instituted the orders of Suvorov, Kutuzov, and Alexander Nevsky. Church and state had effected an improvement in their relations. But none of this implied a backsliding to pre-October 1917 days. Russian patriotism alone was insufficient; Soviet patriotism was higher and nobler. There was, Bogomolov insisted, no hope at all of maintaining their nationality outside Russia. The fate of denationalization awaited *émigrés* who continued to languish in the West.[58] This touched a nerve in some of his hearers, who denied *émigré* susceptibility to foreign pressures. Generally, however, the ambassador's guests displayed a willingness to accept the lecture read to them by the former state security policeman turned diplomat. He brought the proceedings to a close by inviting all present to lift their glasses with him to the Soviet people, its armies, and its great leader. Different versions exist as to the unanimity of the response.[59]

In speeding his guests on their way, Bogomolov passed on one final admonition: there should be no conflicts between those represented at their meeting and the *Russkii patriot* group. Foreigners should not be able to profit from *émigré* division.[60] This concern for their unity may well have struck his guests as ironic in the light of their past relationship. The ambassador quickly found out how elusive *émigré* cohesion in fact was. His strongest supporters in the Union of Russian Patriots were chagrined that they had not been included in his guest list of 12 February, whereas others had been. Complaints flowed into the embassy. Why should a second pro-Soviet newspaper, *Russkie novosti* (Russian News), be allowed? Could not Bogomolov have it suppressed? And why did he permit his letters of thanks to go to other than bona fide Union members? Bogomolov answered briefly, repeating his advice on unity. All in vain. The same intolerant vindictiveness which for two decades had plagued mutual relations inside the anti-Soviet camp was now to be seen in its rival successor. A "congress" of various Moscow-oriented groups, meeting in Paris on 10 March, was symptomatic. The agenda was rigorously controlled, as the Union's chairman, Matiazh, excluded a broad range of subjects which some delegates wished to raise. When protesters called for complete democracy throughout the proceedings so as to attract a greater degree of *émigré* support, they were howled down by a group of noisy Communist interlopers shouting "Down with Maklakov! Down with Miliukov! [dead two years] Down with the White generals!" The situation in the south of France was the same. At one meeting in Nice of the Friends of the Soviet Motherland, "a Khlestakov in a skirt," Comrade Tamara (Volkonskaia?) appeared. She declared herself a Soviet citizen and set about purging the local organization. "Ignorant and illiterate" French Communists took the place of those driven out, and they at once imposed "the dictatorship of the proletariat" on the Nice branch. No one could be expected to follow bodies such as these.[61]

Factional wrangling among Russians in France was matched in intensity of feeling at least by the reaction of the exile handful in New York to the first partial reports of Bogomolov's reception. The news hit the SR group, in the words of one of them, "like an exploding bomb."[62] The lack of details added to the torture. How much had been conceded? Who had said what? *Novyi zhurnal* opened an inquiry, inviting comment on the visit from several contributors, recent arrivals from Paris. Vishniak and Melgunov remained defiant. They would not grovel; they could not forget; they would not forgive; they yielded nothing. Others were prepared to see how matters developed. Nikolai Vakar welcomed the visit to the Soviet embassy, as his mentor Miliukov would have done. Vakar saw the handshakes at 79, rue de Grenelle as ending a state of civil war, one more psychological than real. It was the end of an illusion. In any case, he argued, no Russian living safely in New York for the past few years could condemn those left to face the perils of wartime France. The onetime Left Kadet A.I. Konovalov also sympathized with the refugees in France. In his view, Maklakov had taken a decisive step in the history of the emigration. The editorial board was not so sure. Nothing significant had been conceded from the Soviet side; a host of questions remained.[63]

Dan and his Menshevik band welcomed the embassy visit unreservedly. Dan saw the possibility of a spiritual, if not physical return home for the *émigrés*. Like some others, he still insisted on the inevitability of greater democratization in Soviet Russia. He did not doubt that, thanks to her socio-economic system and war experiences, the Soviet Union would before long become the freest country in Europe. Dan condemned the unremitting hostility of most exiled Russian Socialists toward their native land. It had saved the West, rather than the reverse.[64] Social democratic obstinacy, embodied in Kerensky and Vishniak, signalled that the headquarters of the anti-Soviet portion of the older *émigré* generation was now firmly in the New World. Another symbol of this same transfer was General Denikin's decision in the spring of 1945 to mark his displeasure over the pilgrimage to "the Soviet Canossa" by moving his family to New York.[65]

Vasily Maklakov was caught uncomfortably in the middle of these currents. His representative function, resumed without enthusiasm,[66] can never have seemed more onerous than in the final months of war and the first of peace. He was seventy-six, increasingly deaf, and confronted with heavy new demands upon his energies. Thousands of appeals poured into his office from Russian victims of the wave of reprisals against suspected collaborators in France. In this orgy, "White Russians" were a convenient target for French Communists or anyone else who wished to establish healthy anti-Nazi credentials. Nina Berberova, for instance, was briefly tied up and threatened with hanging by a zealous Communist neighbour;[67] other Russians suffered a grimmer fate merely because they found themselves in the wrong place, with the wrong nationality, at the wrong time.[68] The task of intervening on the émigrés' behalf fell upon Maklakov. His office sent out over 2,000 letters of intercession between April and December 1945 and another 2,200 in the following ten months.[69] Cautious as always, he discouraged efforts by other émigré bodies to achieve the same result.[70] It was better to do the work himself than to scatter precious resources in a proliferation of effort. In fact, as Sofia Zernova discovered, the best émigré asset with French officialdom was Maklakov's name.[71]

In addition to these new ordeals, Russians also encountered some familiar vexations. Again came reports of bureaucratic harassments, again the old stories of difficulties with labour and residence permits.[72] It was not surprising, under the circumstances, that some refugees found attractive the idea of a new country, or even of their old one. Maklakov himself was carried along for a few weeks by the momentum of his visit to the embassy and the hopes that it had engendered. In late March 1945 his Action Group turned itself into an "Association of the Russian Emigration for Reconciliation with Soviet Russia." This body had as its stated purpose "the objective study of Soviet Russia and [the consideration of] any kind of activity which will contribute to the rapprochement of émigrés and motherland."[73] This cautiously optimistic mood lasted about two months. On 16 April Maklakov wrote to a Kadet party colleague, Ariadne Tyrkova-Williams, that he was "at the stage of hope"; five weeks later his article in Russkie novosti, entitled "Soviet Power and the Emigration," analyzed what to him were the essential features of the émigré-Soviet relationship. These included a respect for Soviet achievements in peace and war, a recognition of the need for reconciliation between all Russians, an insistence that the emigration had fulfilled a worthwhile purpose, and a belief in the need for greater individual freedom in the USSR. None of this was new, but public qualification of Soviet perfection was unacceptable to Russkie novosti's editors, Stupnitsky and Adamovich, former collaborators of Miliukov's on Poslednia novosti. Their introduction to Maklakov's article pointed out that the ex-ambassador's stress on liberalism and individualism reflected nineteenth century values. The reality of the twentieth century was the defence of group interests: this was what the Soviet regime was trying to accomplish. Nor could the editors agree that the emigration had served a useful purpose. Moreover, it had been blind to changes inside the Soviet Union such as the growth in the nation's military power and patriotism.[74]

It did not take long before Maklakov, and others who cared to see, could observe that overwhelming Soviet victory had brought in its wake a return to the old intransigence. In June his letter to Kerensky admitted that the rumours "from over there" were not good; two weeks later the first postwar Soviet amnesty excepted "counterrevolutionary crimes, banditry, and murder" from its provisions: these were the usual epithets for *émigrés*.[75] Far from welcoming the motherland's errant children home, embassy personnel in Paris were reminding *émigrés* who inquired where they might live that Siberia was in the USSR, as well as Moscow.[76] As for life in France, the surviving Russian colony had no reason to feel sanguine about its prospects, particularly if *émigrés* were not yet ready to sing praises to Stalin's genius. *Russkie novosti* gave enthusiastic voice to the new cult. The irony that Stupnitsky and Adamovich, lately pillars of *Posledniia novosti*, should now rhapsodize about a system that was the antithesis of that newspaper's liberal democratic values was not lost on less enchanted readers.[77] However, other than a move to the United States, alternatives to vegetating in France did not seem to exist. Articles in *Novoe russkoe slovo* drew a gloomy picture of the remaining Russian community. Several collaborators went on public trial. Among them was N. Piatnitsky, editor of the pro-Nazi *Parizhskii vestnik*, who appeared sleek, prosperous and quite unchastened, dressed in an expensive fur coat. He drew ten years imprisonment.[78] Then there were periodic scandals in the Union of Soviet [formerly Russian] Patriots over the membership of some of Piatnitsky's erstwhile followers. Details of the Russians' great material want and frequent obituaries of exiles prominent in earlier times completed the portrait of a community in full dissolution.[79]

At that point Stalin provided another alternative. Since the closing stages of the war, Russians in the West, and West Europeans generally, had been making the acquaintance of a new generation of Russian refugees. This was "the second emigration" from Soviet Russia: Vlasovites and other "nonreturners" (*nevozvrashchentsy*), who resisted repatriation, trumpeting to the world an image of the USSR diametrically opposed to that presented in *Russkie novosti*. They had a harsher reception than their predecessors in flight from Russia. British, American and, to a lesser degree, French authorities, to their shame, forcibly returned many thousands to the NKVD's tender mercies.[80] Meanwhile, those who succeeded in remaining in the West were often taken aback to meet *émigrés* excited at the possibility of their own return to Russia and boastfully proud of Soviet achievements.[81] The exiles in America remained utterly defiant, ready to carry their message to a new audience.[82] A desire to neutralize some of these negative impressions and prevent any cohesion between the first and second emigrations were probably the major reasons behind the Soviet government's gesture toward the senior *émigré* remnants. On 14 June 1946 the Presidium of the Supreme Soviet issued an amnesty decree aimed at subjects of the former Russian empire in France and at Soviet citizens there who had lost their nationality.

Both groups and their families were given five months to register at the Soviet embassy and receive, if they wished it, Soviet citizenship.[83]

Moscow's gesture was not unexpected. Previous edicts had already been issued for the benefit of Russians in Manchuria (10 November 1945, 22 January 1946), and in parts of China (20 January 1946).[84] The decision whether or not to accept the invitation was the last issue collectively to confront the first emigration. Maklakov refused to give a lead. His Reconciliation Association was finding it impossible to square its patriotic inclinations with what its members saw as brutal Soviet highhandedness in Eastern Europe and Stalin's continuing domestic repression.[85] On the other side, L'iubimov and his fellow enthusiasts in the Union of Soviet Patriots boiled with a righteous joy. No longer need they be stateless and endure the taunt of "dirty foreigners!"; now they could enjoy the respectful attentions of French officialdom and declaim Maiakovsky's lines on the beauty of a Soviet passport.[86] According to Boris Aleksandrovsky, the first of these crimson booklets to be distributed, bearing a symbolic "1", was destined for the Orthodox metropolitan in France, Evlogy, as he lay near death.[87] If true, the gift represented a logical sequel to Evlogy's decision of the previous summer when, with much public display of cordiality between himself and Ambassador Bogomolov, the aged metropolitan had resubmitted to Moscow's ecclesiastical jurisdiction.[88] His transformation and, even more, that of his ultra-monarchist, pro-Nazi rival, Metropolitan Serafim, were perhaps the most spectacular examples of Soviet victory's impact upon the defeated side in the Russian Civil War.

The pros and cons of acceptance provoked intense debate inside the surviving Russian colony. Crucial questions remained to be answered. Did citizenship mean obligatory return to the USSR? Or could the émigrés stay on in France as Soviet citizens? If they ignored this opportunity, would it ever be repeated? And what would happen to those who did ignore the offer? Naturally, the Union of Soviet Patriots urged the duty of citizenship and return upon all refugees. It offered twenty of its members to the embassy to handle the expected deluge of applicants.[89] *Novoe russkoe slovo* reported that most of the Union's "6,500 members in fifty branches throughout France" would take out citizenship, which seemed logical.[90] How many others followed their example is impossible to say. Kovalevsky later wrote that some 6,000 *émigrés* went back to the USSR as citizens after the amnesty.[91] No major figure from the cultural or political emigration took up Moscow's offer, though Nikolai Berdiaev told an inquiring *Russkie novosti* reporter that he felt it was the duty of all *émigrés*, with a few honourable exceptions, to assume Soviet citizenship.[92] Though invited to do so by Soviet authorities, he himself did not apply for a crimson booklet bearing the hammer and sickle insignia.[93] Neither did Ivan Bunin, whose return to the fold was also much desired on the rue de Grenelle. He lived on in Grasse and Paris, unwell, the Nobel windfall long gone. He contributed to *Russkie novosti* and visited the Soviet embassy in 1946, but he did not come close to accepting Moscow's overtures.[94] Friends in New York sent off food parcels and money to the impoverished handful of writers still in Paris, encouraging them to move to the United States.[95] In Bunin's case this was not to be.

Those who finally did decide to accept the Soviet invitation did so for reasons that were hardly complex. The chance to die in Russia for the old, an opportunity to make something useful of their lives among their own people for younger refugees; for both, the wish to identify with a powerful, apparently forgiving motherland and thus end their drab existence under alien skies – all these motives played a part in the decision.[96] They were the members of the Russian diaspora who, in a certain sense, "came in from the cold," though in another, more literal sense the metaphor is inexact since many ended up in Siberian prison camps, along with the forced repatriates from Eastern Europe and the Soviet contingent of returned Vlasovites, prisoners of war, and deportees. Zinaida Shakhovskaia's cousin, Mikhail Volkonsky, was one of the unfortunates. A first secretary at the Yugoslav legation in Paris, Volkonsky succumbed to Soviet offers of research facilities at home for a book he longed to write on the Decembrists. The conversion of someone with his name may have stimulated a special effort; once inside the USSR Volkonsky vanished into a camp.[97] In the *Gulag* the former *émigrés* struck Alexander Solzhenitsyn as the resurrection of buried history.[98]

A few others found a middle road in taking out Soviet citizenship but staying on for a time in the West. P.A. Obolensky, one of several representatives in France of that illustrious family, made his way to the rue de Grenelle with the others. For some reason his papers were delayed, so he remained in Paris driving a bus for the American Express travel agency. A Soviet ex-prince was a figure some of his acquaintances found dismaying; however, he held on until his return in 1955.[99] Another Obolensky had a different tale to tell. S.S. Obolensky had been one of Kazem-Bek's Young Russians, a contributor to *Bodrost*. He welcomed Soviet patriotism as revealed by the war, and hoped it might herald the rebirth of "national, religious Russia." Employed by *Russkie novosti*, he naturally was one of those who took out Soviet citizenship, then worked for a short time for *Sovinformburo*. There, surrounded by Soviet colleagues, he saw he could never be a part of their Russia. French Communists were more "ours" to the embassy and to his employers than he could ever be. Arrogance, intolerance, and dogmatic Communism reigned supreme to the point where Obolensky could stand it no longer. Like a handful of others not yet irretrievably committed by their return, he was able to re-emigrate back to French life.[100] His old party chief Kazem-Bek waited until 1956 before he too returned to Russia.[101] As for Lev Liubimov, he stayed on in Paris, continuing his efforts on behalf of *Sovetskii patriot*. In November 1947 the French government finally wearied of Soviet political activities in the capital and expelled Liubimov with eighteen colleagues from France. This enabled him at last to savour for himself the joys of Soviet life which he had been extolling for the past few years.[102] It is unlikely that anyone regretted his departure.

The number of those left in France continued inexorably to decline: 66,000 in 1939, 55,000 in 1946, 35,000 in 1951.[103] It was left to the survivors to reflect upon their vanished world. Maklakov settled into a gentle resignation, admitted the futility of his embassy visit, and hoped his biographer would ignore his life in emigration.[104] In any case, as he could see, the exiles' responsibility for defending anti-Stalinist Russian interests was ceasing to be uniquely theirs. The "nonreturners" of the second emigration were now much more in evidence; but co-operation between the two refugee waves from Russia, logical in theory, proved far from easy in practice. No "psychological wall" may have divided them as Russians,[105] and they certainly had their hatred of Stalinist despotism in common. Yet the Soviet "displaced persons" in Western Europe had undergone a political and cultural formation at home very different, indeed alien, to that experienced by the Civil War *émigrés* and their children. This was jarring.[106] Then, too, the refugee centre of gravity had shifted: by the early 1950s New York had replaced Paris as the political, then cultural capital of the anti-Stalinist Russian diaspora. The first emigration, centred in Paris, with strong roots in pre-October Russia and no direct experience of Stalinism, belonged to history.

Epilogue

"Profligate Russia has cast to us her most splendid talents, squeezing them out from Russian soil ... Profligate Russia! But fortunate America. Fortunate world, to possess the riches of Nabokov and the others."[1] Thus did Harrison Salisbury, a longtime, knowledgeable observer of the Soviet scene, characterize one of the striking phenomena of our century: the departure from Russia, generation after generation, of so many of her most gifted sons and daughters. They left or chose not to return, either because they could not endure to live and work under the dominant political system, or because that system decided it would no longer endure their presence in Russia. Salisbury had in mind the cultural élite: the writers, poets, painters, artists, musicians, and dancers who have given so much to the world since Lenin's Bolsheviks seized power in their country. Hundreds of thousands of quite ordinary Russians without particular artistic gifts have joined in this exodus for a variety of reasons, political and other. They have added their own contributions to Western life. No other nation can match the quality, range and duration of this outpouring.

The Civil War refugees established the pattern and have left behind tangible memorials of their presence. In Paris one may still find the YMCA Press, bookstores, a handful of restaurants, the Alexander Nevsky cathedral and lesser churches, the Russian corner of the rue Pierre-le-Grand, perhaps one or two rare survivors of the great days of Russian taxi-drivers. Above all there are the cemeteries. Today's wanderer through the peaceful necropolises at Sainte-Geneviève-des-Bois or Caucade in Nice, to name the two largest in France, finds traces of a Russia that existed for centuries before October 1917. The headstones evoke a very distant age: Bezobrazov, Tatishchev, Obolensky, Golitsyn, Suvorov, Iusupov, Apraxin, Romanov, "ladies-in-waiting to Her Imperial Majesty," state councillors, ministers, even "the founder of Russian scouting." Beside them lie the writers, poets, and artists, among them Bunin, Merezhkovsky, Remizov, with a host of lesser known compatriots.

Libraries contain the lion's share of Vladimir Nabokov's "bird-signs and moon-signs." They begin with the seventy volumes of *Sovremenniia zapiski*, in themselves an imposing monument to cultural vitality in material adversity; they go on to incorporate the innumerable newspapers and journals of the Russian diaspora, and finally books from several thousand *émigré* pens. Was the effort worthwhile? The literary intelligentsia insisted that it was. Georgy Fedotov's stated conviction in 1935 that Russian culture deserved every sacrifice found no dissent from his peers, who may well have disputed every other opinion he advanced. Their duty as intellectuals required nothing less of them. "In my paintings there is not one centimeter that is free of nostalgia for my native land," wrote Marc Chagall in a sentence that all artists and writers who arrived in the West could echo.[2] But the audience they most longed to reach has remained largely ignorant of what lies beneath the desert dust. Alexander Solzhenitsyn wrote in 1973 of his own encounter in the *Gulag* with this portion of Russia's buried past. Long conversations with cellmates who landed up outside of Russia, then returned, voluntarily or not, revealed to him that "the outflow from Russia of a significant part of her spiritual forces, which occurred in the Civil War, had deprived us of a great and important stream of Russian culture." He dreams of living to the day when the domestic stream and its "tributary abroad" will join in cultural wholeness.[3]

On 5 August 1951 Nikolai Ulianov, a literary historian from the second emigration, addressed the Russian colony in Casablanca on the subject of "culture and the emigration." His tone was valedictory. With the memory still keen of the immediate postwar Zhdanov years and their assault on "kowtowing to the rotten West," Ulianov began his speech, made on the day set aside to celebrate the triumphs of Russian culture, with a reaffirmation of Russia's European nature. She was inseparably connected to European civilization: had not Catherine the Great proclaimed her a European power? Woe to the Russian who ever forgot that fact. *Émigré* intellectuals, artists, musicians, and dancers had added enormously to the stock of European culture; Ulianov paid tribute to a few of the great names. But generally their day was done. The war had accelerated their end, to be sure, yet that end was inevitable, being implicit in their condition. The intelligentsia of the first emigration had lived, Ulianov suggested, as *rentiers* on intellectual capital they had brought with them out of Russia. In exile they had achieved great things but had generated no new funds. When their capital was exhausted, they passed from the scene. This had already happened in many areas of creativity, and the day could not be far off when in all areas White Russia must give way to Red.[4]

Ulianov's assessment drew a vigorous riposte from the historian M.M. Karpovich. Among other objections, Karpovich directed attention to

Ulianov's failure to consider the major figures who grew up and started careers in emigration, notably Vladimir Nabokov.[5] That particular omission was, indeed, a startling one, though Ulianov had noted other members of the younger intelligentsia. Still, Ulianov's pessimism was understandable, given the gloomy prospects for Russian culture in 1951. At home Stalinist misrule crushed every effort at creative originality, abroad the great figures of the older exile generation were rapidly disappearing. Who was going to replace them? To the survivors and to those who treasured Russian cultural values Ulianov could hold out little hope of relief. He offered a glorious memory, exhortations to continued struggle, and the prayer once raised by desperate Muscovite princes that one day "God will change the Horde."[6]

The political dimension of the *émigrés'* life in France seems on the surface the least compelling part of their historical legacy. All political alternatives to Russia's Soviet reality advanced by expatriate Russians "from Markov to Martov" lie more thickly covered by desert dust than any other artefact of exile life. When looking back on his own career, Mark Vishniak confessed that his generation "was too often obliged to put itself forward as the advocate of lost causes."[7] Those lost causes certainly included his cherished February Revolution, but the Mensheviks, the monarchy and the postrevolutionaries seem no less vigorously repudiated.

Yet there is more that must be said on this point. In defending the political emigration from Ulianov's faint praise, Karpovich asserted that it at least "made attempts to help the Western world correctly evaluate the significance of the events going on in Russia and to understand the nature of the Soviet regime."[8] The claim is just. The commentators who filled the columns of the *émigré* press or who lectured foreign audiences on Soviet affairs were pioneers in the new, arcane science of Sovietology. The level of their judgments was far from uniform. As these pages have shown, an intense loathing of the Bolshevik interlopers strongly coloured most assessments of Soviet life. The passionate, instinctive hostility from all but a few Mensheviks undermined the efforts of *émigré* Sovietologists to impress unpersuaded Europe with their views of Soviet reality. In several cases – Semenov's *Vozrozhdenie* and the ultra-right press come to mind – this non-Russian disdain was usually merited. But there still remained some remarkably acute observers, particularly in the pages of the democratic press. Their portrait of Soviet life and conditions compares favourably today with the very different impressions conveyed by so many earlier admirers of the "heroic experiment" going on in the USSR. Half a century after the accounts by Herriot, Duranty, and their ilk, members of the third emigration from Soviet Russia have discovered this truth for themselves. They have shown themselves ready to recommend *Sovremenniia zapiski* and other critical works from the interwar years to any in the West still drawn toward Moscow.[9]

Today criticisms made of Soviet conditions by Russian expatriates can command an attention from the non-Russian world that was unattainable sixty years ago. The Civil War exiles in their time spoke out loudly, but their voices usually fell on deaf ears. Several reasons accounted for this. Yet *émigré* fractiousness, so often deplored by their spokesmen, was not a major cause of their political ineffectiveness. Few emigrations in history have been able to unite for long, or at all, and nothing in the Russians' own prevolutionary experience suggested that solidarity would be easy to achieve. To expect that the misfortunes of exile should impose their own unity, as Vladimir Burtsev and others appeared to believe, flew in the face of history and human nature. In any case, even if the Russians had somehow miraculously achieved the tightest cohesion, it is improbable that they would have been able materially to weaken Soviet power.

Much more damaging to *émigré* credibility than their divisiveness was the fact that collectively and individually they represented defeated causes and, so it seemed to many, outworn political values. When Mark Aldanov, commenting on a Kerensky version of the events of 1917, remarked that the fashion in 1935 among "extremely influential circles" was in no way concerned with the ideals of Kerensky's revolution, but that, on the contrary, "Mickey Mouse is all the rage among aesthetes,"[10] he was giving ironic expression to a truth evident to any refugee who cared to consider the matter. From right to left they were out of fashion. Democratic socialism, liberalism, constitutional monarchy, the rights of man and his property were slogans from the nineteenth century. The twentieth century, at least from Aldanov's vantage point, seemed overwhelmingly to favour collectivist models of social and political organization. Even some Russian exiles were seduced.

The refugees' apparent irrelevance to the dominant spirit of the age was powerfully reinforced by their perceived qualities as Russians. Were they not all generals and princes? The French press seemed to suggest as much, whenever "White Russian" affairs attracted general notice; exile politics and one or two eccentrics contributed to an impression that the Russian national mentality differed profoundly and peculiarly from the French. Robert Williams has noted the circumstance that a Russian elite, which in Russia regarded itself as Western, "found itself viewed as something exotic and 'Eastern' when living as refugees in the West."[11] This stimulated French imaginations; the Russians had many opportunities to witness the results. As late as September 1941 Mikhail Osorgin commented to *Novoe russkoe slovo* on the fantastic illusions about Russian ways still prevalent among the French. He himself had just read a French novel *à la russe* whose three heroines were named Annushka (Annie), Babushka (granny) and Petrushka (little Peter). Then there was "the famous sentence" from the French textbook which described "the Russian tsar Ivan [the Terrible] who, for his cruelty, was nicknamed Vasilievich."[12]

In spite of these unpropitious circumstances, it did not follow that the Civil War exiles lived useless lives out of Russia. Kovalevsky's several volumes, reinforced by Roman Gul's memoir, spell out the details of a contrary truth. There was scarcely a field of human inquiry or endeavour where exiled Russians did not have a contribution to make. The great names of émigré culture have been noted and are familiar; it is primarily they who win for their community the title bestowed by Marc Raeff of the Great Russian Emigration. But the historian of their life in France cannot fail to acknowledge the tens of thousands of unsung Russians who laboured in mine, farm, taxi garage, and automobile factory, many finally to offer themselves in the nation's defence in war. French literature has been enriched by the talents of Henri Troyat. Zoë Oldenbourg, Elsa Triolet, Romain Gary, and Zinaïda Schakovskoy, all born in the Russian empire, who grew up or began careers in French exile. In all this there is surely to be found a Russian proof of Paul Tabori's contention "that exiles have made an important and lasting contribution to whatever country was willing to receive them; that in the long run, whatever the cost to their hosts, they have repaid it many times over."[13]

In the Russians' case, one part of this repayment deserves particular acknowledgement. When Karpovich wrote in 1952 of the emigration's efforts to help the West correctly evaluate what was going on in Russia, he evidently did not only have in mind the political commentators whose lectures to Europe and the world had been so little heeded between the World Wars. There were also those who had been working over the years to teach a new, younger public about Russia of past and present. Their efforts naturally took time to produce results. Two prominent, though not unique, examples are to be found in Karpovich himself and his fellow historian George Vernadsky. In 1927 both men embarked in the United States upon lengthy careers of teaching and scholarship at Harvard and Yale respectively. There they inspired hundreds of American students with their love of Russian history and culture. Their influence was profound. Ralph Fisher's tribute to Vernadsky: "the ill wind that drove him from his country brought good fortune to our own," gracefully admitted the debt.[14] In the aftermath of World War II this promising beginning swelled to vaster proportions. The shifting American perception of the nation's recent Soviet ally meant that Stalin's earliest and most knowledgeable critics found themselves and their ideas in fashion. Sovietology entered upon its days of glory. Mark Vishniak was hired by Time magazine as a specialist on Soviet affairs, while Russian studies blossomed on US university campuses. Émigré scholars continued to play a key role in this discovery of Russia. In 1966 the diplomat and historian George Kennan paid tribute to one of the most zealous of émigré teachers, the Menshevik politician-scholar, Boris Nikolaevsky, who had died shortly before. "If today," Kennan wrote, "the interest in Russia, and the study of Russia, in this country, and particularly among our youth, are in-comparably deeper and more serious than was the case thirty years ago, we owe this in no small measure to Boris Ivanovich, to his inexhaustible in-terest in everything that was taking place in his homeland [and] to his long and sustained literary endeavor."[15] Here perhaps is to be found at last a vin-dication of Vishniak's favourite aphorism during the lean exile years in France: "the way to be right in the future is at certain times to know how to submit to being out of fashion."

In the mid-1980s memories of the Russian France of fifty years ago are preserved in the novels of Henri Troyat;[16] recently they are also to be en-countered in the reminiscences of Vassily Yanovsky, looking back on the "Elysian fields" of his younger years in Russian Montparnasse. But the echoes grow fainter and fewer. *Vozrozhdenie* reappeared in Paris in 1949 as a monthly publication, edited by Melgunov, still invoking the principles which had guided it before the war. One of its most cherished features was, however, eventually abandoned. In January 1970, "for technical reasons and so that a matter of secondary significance does not get in the way of genuinely important issues," *Vozrozhdenie* finally went over to the "new" spelling.[17] In Paris today the weekly *Russkaia mysl* (Russian Thought) naturally devotes itself to contemporary questions, though with an occa-sional glance at matters which passionately interested exiled Russians half a century ago.[18] In Saint-Briac, meanwhile, the current Romanov pretender, Vladimir Kirillovich, unobtrusively maintains his rights. It must be said, however, that he seems to interest French royalists more than Russian, assuming any of the latter still exist.[19]

In the Soviet Union too there have been echoes from Russia Abroad. Those refugees who returned to the USSR after the war, voluntarily or other-wise, and who managed to survive Stalin, often became objects of intense, friendly interest to their Soviet compatriots. A spate of memoirs, in-augurated by Lev Liubimov, appeared in the 1960s. All recorded this curi-osity. The several accounts share the common theme of an alien exploitive exile ended by return to the magnanimous motherland. At the same time – and this, no doubt, interested the reader most – they provided a feast of details about a different, distant Russia and of life in the alluring West. The near-centenarian Vasily Shulgin, forcibly repatriated and imprisoned, after his release wrote articles, a book, and even appeared in a sympathetic film about his life, *Before the Court of History*. More recently, in October 1984, the remains of Fedor Chaliapin, brought from Paris, were solemnly reburied in Moscow's Novodevichy cemetery. An attendant crowd of Soviet dignitaries, presided over by the sempiternal first secretary of the composers union Tikhon Khrennikov, saluted the great singer's return to his motherland after six decades of exile.[20]

Two waves of emigration from the USSR separate us today from the Civil War exodus. These later arrivals differ from their predecessors in several important ways. To begin with, they are Soviet refugees; they have had no Russian experience other than that furnished by Stalin and his heirs. The old political dimension is thus absent. Europe and America no longer witness waiters and taxi drivers putting on faded uniforms after work, addressing one another as "Excellency" and "Highness" as they plan the future of post-Soviet Russia. Those who compose the second and, in particular, the third emigrations left the USSR with no expectation that the regime's days were numbered, nor, *pace* Solzhenitsyn, is there any widespread belief in a substitute political system for their former country. The third emigration is far less politically active than the first. This has caused occasional unease among refugees,[21] but it remains apparent that the battles which raged between *Vozrozhdenie* and *Posledniia novosti* or the anguish once provoked by accepting spelling changes have no parallels among Soviet emigrants today.

Yet powerful themes of continuity survive. From the approximately 130,000-strong Soviet *émigré* community in the United States come some familiar views of their old and new countries. A recent survey has found, for example, that most *émigrés* are "vehemently anti-Soviet," quick to criticize US government officials for laxity when negotiating with Moscow. There are also fears for the denationalization of *émigré* youth, dismay at the grimmer aspects of American urban life, and, from a few, regret at ever having left their homeland. Problems of adjustment, even the suspected presence of Soviet agents in their midst, are also causing concern.[22]

The role of Russian culture remains crucial. The influx into the United States has been one rich in cultural talent, containing, according to one observer, "the highest proportion of artists and intellectuals since the exodus from Hitler's Germany in the years before World War II."[23] They have found themselves surrounded by an immensely seductive and intrusive culture, though it is one which many arriving Soviets reach out to embrace, unlike their predecessors in France sixty years ago. Margarita Tupitsyn, curator of the Contemporary Russian Art Center of America, in New York, herself a Soviet *émigré*, told an inquiring researcher in 1982 that Soviet artists and writers begin in America "by denying all connection with anything Russian. They want only the new, never the old. Gradually, though, their attitudes moderate. As they come to accept the fact that they really are someplace else, they come back to thinking of themselves as Russian artists, they want to have a part in the continuation of Russian culture."[24] In so doing, they are encountering many of the difficulties of alienation and poverty known to previous exile generations. Then there is "the paradoxical situation" outlined by the exiled Soviet writer Sergei Dovlatov: "one wants to be read by the Russian public, but one also wants to reach the American public, to make one's living as a writer."25 Freely to serve Russia and her culture, while surviving in a new, alien environment – the challenge to *émigrés* is a familiar one. Recently, some cryptic hints from the new leadership in the Kremlin have provoked discussion in the West, among *émigrés* and others, that a more tolerant Soviet policy in cultural matters might be at hand. Nevertheless, it is still far too early to proclaim as imminent, or even in sight, the union of Russian culture's parent stream and its "tributary abroad."

While it may be inappropriate to suggest that Brooklyn's Brighton Beach is the "new Mecca" of today's Soviet *émigrés*, sufficient evidence does exist to suggest that the most recent exodus from Russia contains within it a range as diverse as its predecessors, with no less talent, even genius. And there is again Harrison Salisbury's reminder. Three emigrations in sixty years testify to an enduring reality of Soviet life, one not yet overcome by the forces of *glasnost*: that the free Russian word and the free Russian spirit have for too long found little place in the USSR. In consequence, they have sought shelter abroad.

Abbreviations

AFK	Aleksandr F. Kerenskii
AN	Archives nationales, Paris
CGT	Confédération générale du travail
DPF	*Dictionnaire des parlementaires français*
CHEKA / GPU /	
NKVD / KGB	Soviet security police
NEP	Lenin's "New Economic Policy" (1921–8)
NR	*Novaia Rossiia*
NRS	*Novoe russkoe slovo*
NTSNP	National Labour Alliance of the New Generation
NYT	*New York Times*
NZH	*Novyi zhurnal*
PN	*Posledniia novosti*
PNM	Pavel N. Miliukov
ROVS	Russian All-Military Union
RP	*Russkii patriot*
RSKHD	Russian Student Christian Movement
SR	Socialist Revolutionary party
SV	*Sotsialisticheskii vestnik*
SZ	*Sovremenniia zapiski*
TLS	*Times Literary Supplement*
TUC	Trades Union Congress
VAM	Vasilii A. Maklakov
VMZ	Vladimir M. Zenzinov
VZ	*Vozrozhdenie*

Notes

INTRODUCTION

1 Delage, *La Russie en exil*, 28.
2 Ledré, *Les émigrés russes en France*, 7.
3 Simpson, *The Refugee Problem*, 3.
4 Yanovsky, *Elysian Fields*, x.
5 Nabokov, *The Gift*, 8; *Le Don*, 8.
6 Struve, *Russkaia literatura v izgnanii*; Brown, *Russian Literature since the Revolution*.
7 Marrus, *The Unwanted*, 10.
8 Tabori, *Anatomy of Exile*, 37.

CHAPTER ONE: EXODUS

1 *Russkaia armiia v izgnanii*, 1; *The Times, Le Temps*, 15–17 Nov.1920; Luckett, *The White Generals*, 364–84, for Wrangel's "last stand." For a representative portrait of family division on leaving Russia, see Schakovskoy, "Lumières et ombres," 361.
2 Stoupnitzky, "Les origines de l'émigration russe," 1–11. Marrus, *The Unwanted*, 53–61, 88–9.
3 Nikitine, "L'émigration russe," 191.
4 "Nashe priamoe delo," Bunakov & Hippius, *Chto delat'*, 11.
5 Gul', *Ia unes Rossiiu*.
6 Daudet, *Histoire de l'émigration*, 1:5.
7 Hessen, *Gody skitanii*, 2:52.
8 The main *Zemgor* relief body was the Russian *Zemstva* and Towns Aid Committee for Russian Citizens Abroad. It was founded in January 1921 under the chairmanship of Prince G.E. Lvov. The committee professed humanitarian aims only, not political, and concentrated its energies on

helping *émigré* youth. Half its funds came from foreign governments, the Nansen Office, and private relief foundations; the other half came from various *émigré* sources. Between 1921 and 1937 it spent slightly over 71 million francs: [Ross, *zemgor komitet*], *Mémorandum*, 2–4. The Russian Red Cross also began its relief work in 1921. Its emphasis was largely on medical aid. It organized a hospital in Villejuif and several clinics elsewhere. This was an *émigré* cause favoured by aristocratic ladies: the Grand Duchess Maria Pavlovna, Princess Obolenskaia, Countess Shuvalova, and others. Financial stringencies severely curtailed their ability to meet the community's ever growing health care needs. [Krasnyi krest], *Pomoshch' bezhentsam*, 1–7.

9 Simpson, *Refugee Problem*, 68, 82.

10 Ibid, 68.

11 *Russkaia armiia v izgnanii*, 6–7. On 2 April 1921 Philippe Berthelot, secretary-general at the foreign ministry, informed Prince Lvov that his government would immediately end and all aid to the refugees in Constantinople. The continued existence of Wrangel's military units on foreign territory "[was] inadmissible from an international point of view." If disbanded, Wrangel's men "would probably look for work, go back home or emigrate to Brazil. Thus in four months they would have found the means to cease being a public charge." Miliukov Papers, Box 6, Arranged Correspondence (copy).

12 League of Nations, Report of the High Commissioner, 15 March 1922, 3–11. Hereafter as *Nansen Reports*.

13 Conférence des organisations russes, *Mémorandum*; Nansen Reports, 24 June 1924, 2. The repatriation issue is more fully examined in Chapter Seven.

14 Kadet Party Archive, 2:162, with dismissive comment about Nansen as "a naive old man."

15 Rimscha, *Der russische Bürgerkrieg* (1924); *Russland jenseits der Grenzen* (1927).

16 *Der russische Bürgerkrieg*, 51.

17 *Simpson*, 109.

18 Ibid, 82, 112, 559.

19 See below fn. 59.

20 *Marrus*, 61.

21 Tributes appeared in volumes 42:385–412 on Masaryk's 80th birthday; 58:336–43 on his 85th birthday, and in 65:282–7 on his death.

22 *SZ*, 63:431–3; Postnikov, *Russkie v Prage*, 41–9.

23 Fischer, "The Russian Archive in Prague," 289–95; Grimsted, *Archives and Repositories*, 127.

24 Volkmann, *Die russische Emigration*, 9–10; Williams, *Culture in Exile*, 143–6 on the generally tolerant attitude of the German authorities toward their uninvited Russian guests.

25 *Simpson*, 559; *Volkmann*, 5. The 1937 figure for Germany was a Nansen Office estimate.

26 Nabokov, *Speak Memory*, 283.

27 De Giers Papers, Box 19, file 48, Zemgor Reports, I[nformatsionnyi] L[istok] – 14, 7 May 1923; IL–24, 22 Sept. 1923, with comment on the sharp increase in the number of Russians arriving in France from Germany and the Balkans.

28 Belov, *Beloe pokhmel'e*, 48.

29 Romanov, *Always a Grand Duke*, 17–30.

30 Ellis, *La colonie russe*, 2–5, 281; *La cathédrale orthodoxe russe*, 18.

31 Malia, *Herzen and the Birth of Russian Socialism*, 358–9.

32 Herzen, *My Past and Thoughts*, 2:264.

33 For a lively account of the artist–*cité* of *La Ruche*, see Wiser, *The Crazy Years*, 95–100.

34 Quoted in Laffitte, *Chekhov, 1860–1904*, 151.

35 Lesure, "Les réfugiés révolutionnaires russes," 421.

36 Ibid, 427–9.

37 Ehrenburg, *People and Life*, 62–70, 94–100.

38 Corbet, *L'opinion française*, 426.

39 In his first volume of memoirs Ehrenburg related some of the mutual misconceptions. On the French side he traced much of "the journalistic nonsense" he read about Russia to the mythical "spreading cranberry tree" (*razvesistaia kliukva*) described by Alexandre Duman *père* after a trip to Russia: *Ehrenburg*, 117–19. For an acerbic discussion of this point, see Nicolas Nabokov's essay "Under the Cranberry Tree," 35–6.

40 Hemmings, *The Russian Novel in France*, 3.

41 *Le roman russe* also included a sixth article published outside the *Revue des deux mondes*.

42 *Hemmings*, 21.

43 *Corbet*, 420.

44 Relevant major works are Vandal's *Louis XV et Elisabeth de Russie, étude sur les relations de la France et de la Russie au 18e siècle* (1882) and *Napoléon et Alexandre 1, l'alliance russe sous le Premier Empire* (1897); Rambaud's *Histoire de Russie* (1878), *La Russie épique* (1876), and *Français et Russes, Moscou et Sébastopol* (1877); by Leroy-Beaulieu, *L'empire des tsars et les Russes* (1881–2), and *La France, La Russie et l'Europe* (1888); by Leger, *Russes et Slaves* (1890), *La littérature russe* (1892), *Histoire de Russie* (1907), *La Russie intellectuelle* (1914).

45 *La culture française en Russie, 1700–1900*. The work was first published in 1910, then republished in 1913 "couronné par l'Académie des sciences morales et politiques."

46 Ibid. (1913 ed.), 527–9.

47 Vishniak, *Gody emigratsii*, 9.

48 Ibid, 9,10.

49 Yousoupoff, *En exil*, 37.

50 Mauco, *Les étrangers en France*, 78–81, 123–5.

51 Ibid, 134,141. Mauco cites an average of 515 immigrants into France per 100,000 French inhabitants.

52 The 1919 papers of Ambassadors de Giers and Maklakov contain numerous petitions, draft proclamations, and political-diplomatic exposés addressed to the Great Power delegations at Versailles from a wide variety of Russian anti-Bolshevik sources. See John Thompson's *Russia, Bolshevism and the Versailles Peace* for a thorough discussion of related issues.

53 De Giers Papers, IL–24.

54 *Delage*, 7.

55 Yanovsky, *Elysian Fields*, 91.

56 Kessel, *Nuits de princes*, 15.

57 See *Simpson*, 115–16 for a discussion of the Ukrainian dimension of this question. The issue of minority separatism worried *émigré* defenders of Russian unity. Spokesmen within the democratic sector of exile opinion several times pointed out that Stalin had utterly crushed particularism inside the USSR, yet it seemed to survive in pockets of the emigration. See Postnikov, "Literatura emigrantskogo separatizma," 450–7; and Odinets, "Iz istorii ukrainskogo separatizma," 369–87.

58 See chapter three.

59 *Nansen Reports*, 24 June 1924; 2; *Rapport du secrétaire-général*, 30 August 1930, 12.

60 *Ledré*, 28; *Mauco*, 104; de Bryas, *Les peuples en marche*, 76. In 1937 Mauco revised his 400,000 estimate sharply downward, telling an international symposium in Paris that in 1931 there were 71,000 Russians in France. His new figure presumably reflected data from the 1936 census.

61 *Belov*, 44; Shkarenkov, "Belaia emigratsiia," 103.

62 *Simpson*, 109.

63 Ibid., 561.

64 Kovalevskii, *Zarubezhnaia Rossiia*, 31.

65 Gessain & Doré, "Facteurs comparés d'assimilation," 100.

66 [France], *Mouvements migratoires*, 108.

67 *Kovalevskii*, 31.

68 *Simpson*, 303, n. 2.

69 *VZ*, 20 May 1938, citing the Paris Prefect of Police.

70 *Delage*, 19.

71 Mauco, *Etrangers en France*, 169.

72 Aleksandrovskii, *Iz perezhitogo v chuzhikh kraiakh*, 86.

73 Beucler, "Russes de France," 868.

74 Ibid, 869–71.

75 Arseny Stupnitsky, for example, reported to Sir John Simpson that there were six distinct elements in the emigration. First came the "purely political." It comprised persons from the tsarist and Provisional governments, together with all anti-Bolshevik political formations, individuals from the worlds of commerce, industry and finance, intellectuals, scientists, and members of the liberal professions. The remaining categories were the military; the purely civil emigration; "civil and military bureaucrats" from areas of the former empire that were now independent states or parts of such; Russians [presumably nonbureaucrats] from newly annexed or independent territories; and Jews: Stoupnitzky, "Composition de l'émigration russe," 2; *Simpson*, 83.

76 *Ehrenburg*, 72.

77 *Yousoupoff*, 55; Couratier, *Les rues de Boulogne–Billancourt*, 113.

78 Crespelle, *La vie quotidienne à Montparnasse*, 65. The test appears to have been their respective knowledge of French language and literature.

79 Ehrenburg, "Neobychainye pokhozhdeniia Khulio Khurenito," 11.

80 *Crespelle*, 67.

81 *Elysian Fields*, 32; *Wiser*, 38.

82 Shakhovskaia, *Otrazheniia*, 10.

83 Ellis, 319, 323–4, where he gives 156 Russians living in the Alpes-Maritimes *département* in 1918; 1,982 in 1919; in 1924 3,000; in 1930 5,312; in 1939 3,699. Simpson cited a higher figure of between 7–8,000 Russians on the Riviera between St-Raphaël and Menton in 1938: *Refugee Problem*, 308.

84 *PN*, 10 March 1921, 25 Oct. 1932. The fleet was eventually broken up and sold.

85 *Simpson*, 304–10 passim.

86 "Ot redaktsii," *SZ*, 1:i.

87 Dostoevsky, *Diary of a Writer*, 2:1048. The *émigré* literary critic and historian Vladimir Veidle (Weidlé) cited the passage with slightly different wording in *Russia Absent and Present*, 62.

88 Preserving the Russian equivalent of the letters USSR, Gul's version was *Soiuz sukinykh synov revoliutsii: Ia unes Rossiiu*, 2:72.

89 Beyssac, *La vie culturelle de l'émigration russe en France.*

90 *Yousoupoff*, 32.

CHAPTER TWO: ELUSIVE UNITY

1 Liubimov, "Na chuzhbine." He seems to have begun the parade of memoirs by former *émigrés* back in the USSR published in the late 1950s and through the 1960s.

2 Yakobson, "Twenty Years of Russian Emigration," 10.

3 His own version of these years is contained in the volumes of memoirs he

published in exile: *Pervaia gosudarstvennaia duma; Vtoraia gosudarstven-naia duma*; and *Vlast' i obshchestvennost' na zakate staroi Rossii.*

4 Adamovich, *Vasilii Alekseevich Maklakov*, 53–5.

5 Rosenberg, *Liberals in the Russian Revolution*, 34, 119, 216; Karpovich, "Two Types of Russian Liberalism," 129–43.

6 *Ledré*, 69.

7 *Thompson*, 66–79, on the Russian Political Conference.

8 Rimscha, *Der russische Bürgerkrieg*, 53–4; Tongour, *Diplomacy in Exile*, 114–246, passim, on the propaganda effort waged by the Russian Political Conference and on the background of intra-*émigré* bickering.

9 Papers of the Russian Embassy in Paris, Box 5, packet 3, file XIII, April 1919.

10 Ibid., Box 7, packet 4, file XXIII, 3 March 1919.

11 *Ledré*, 70.

12 *Rimscha*, 109.

13 Cited by Vakar, "P.N. Miliukov v izgnanii," 369.

14 *Tongour*, 87–99, with details of this and of Miliukov's disastrous visit to Paris in December 1918 which he was obliged to cut short because of French disapproval of his presence in the country.

15 Kadet Archive, 2:26–139, with the record of the debates.

16 Ibid., 2:247–50. Twelve members heard a report in this sense and on Lenin's weariness with power from a "Mrs N.," who left Russia in November 1921.

17 Miliukov, *Poslednia novosti/Dernières nouvelles*, 13. In this brochure, prepared for an international press exhibition in Cologne in 1928, Miliukov boasted that the importance of his political group "[was] grow-ing daily."

18 Miliukov, *Respublika ili monarkhiia?*, 23.

19 Miliukov, "The Russian Emigration, Origin and Development," 23. Ac-cording to a map he provided in his brochure for the Cologne exhibition, only New Zealand appears to have had no subscribers.

20 Williams, *Culture in Exile*, 208–9.

21 Pipes, *Struve, Liberal on the Right*, 338–9.

22 Nazhivin, *Glupost' ili izmena?*, 5. Further attacks in the same vein came in his *Sredi potuvshikh maiakov* and *Neglubokouvazhaemye.*

23 *Ledré*, 168.

24 Cited in *Rimscha*, 111.

25 Felix Iusupov, for example, sneeringly referred to Kerensky, "alias Aaron Kirbis," in his 1953 memoir *En exil*, 133.

26 Interview with Vladimir Weidlé, 21 January 1976.

27 Kadet Archive, 2:79, 139–51.

28 Kerenskii, "Fevral' i oktiabr'," where the author responds sharply to criticisms of the Paris SRS by the party chairman in Berlin Viktor Chernov.

29 Miliukov, *Emigratsiia na pereput'i*, 6.

30 *Pipes*, 390–3 for Struve's bitter parting from *Vozrozhdenie* and his reactions. On *émigré* fascism, see Stephan, *The Russian Fascists*.

31 *PN*, 6–23 Jan. 1921; *Rimscha*, 115; Koons, *Histoire des doctrines politiques*, 220.

32 *Pipes*, 341–4. It produced a National Committee of 77 members, later 111, that gave voice to moderate conservative opinion. For 15 years it issued periodic reports, progressively gloomier, on the state of its cause: Kartashev, *Sbornik russkogo natsional'nogo komiteta*.

33 Rimscha, *Jenseits der Grenzen*, 68–79; Baschmakoff, *Mémoires* for a loyal view of the "court" at St-Briac; and Snessarev, *Kirill pervyi imperator ... koburgskii* for a disenchanted account by a onetime adherent.

34 "K russkim liudiam," 1 Feb. 1926, De Giers Papers, box 19, file 47.

35 *Posledniia novosti* kept up a steady critical barrage through late March and early April 1926. The Soviet press picked up the tone, describing the *émigré* scene around the Congress as "Gogolesque": Shkarenkov, *Agoniia beloi emigratsii*, 100.

36 *Pipes*, 383.

37 *VZ*, 4–10 April 1926.

38 St. Ivanovich, "Tashkentsy zagranitsei," 401.

39 Schakovskoy, "Lumières et ombres," 361; Wiser, *The Crazy Years*, 83–94.

40 See Chapter Four.

41 For a more or less complete list of *émigré* newspapers, see *Bibliografiia emigrantskoi periodiki 1919–1952*.

42 Struve, *Russkaia literatura v izgnanii*, 21; Rimscha, *Der russische Bürgerkrieg*, 56. A typical example is furnished by *Za kazachestvo*, "an illustrated journal of independent Cossack life," published in Nice by one Sergei Makeev. In its first year, 1934, seventeen issues appeared; in 1935 ten; in 1936 two; in 1937 and 1938 one each; then collapse: *Bibliografiia*, 31.

43 *PN*, 27 April 1920.

44 Ibid., 1 March 1921.

45 Aminado, *Poezd na tret'em puti*, 265.

46 *VZ*, 3 June 1925.

47 These included important figures from the literary world: Bunin, Zaitsev, Kuprin, Merezhkovsky; from politics: Gurko, Nolde, Tyrkova-Williams, Shulgin; the historian Vernadsky, General Golovin, and others.

48 *Pipes*, 390–1. Some dozen of *Vozrozhdenie*'s contributors and staff (not including Liubimov) withdrew in protest.

49 Rimscha, *Der russische Bürgerkrieg*, 88, 98.

50 Ledré, 172; Graham, *Russia in Division*, 225–6 for further uncomplimentary remarks about Burtsev.

51 *Dni*, 4 May 1930.

52 Liebich, *Les mencheviks en exil*, 8.

53 Berberova, *The Italics Are Mine*, 216, where she relates her reaction on visiting the paper's "crowded and dirty" office in 1924: "one already felt the soundness of this originally unstable enterprise."

54 Miliukov, "The Russian Emigration," 23.

55 *Ledré*, 226.

56 Aleksandrovskii, *Iz perezhitogo v chuzhikh kraiakh*, 141.

57 *Don Aminado*, 317.

58 *Struve*, 24.

59 Text of the decree in *Notes et matériaux sur l'histoire de l'église russe en Europe occidentale*, 29–30.

60 Ibid., 2; Stoupnitzky, "L'église russe à l'étranger," 5. In May 1922 Evlogy was raised to the rank of Metropolitan of the Russian Orthodox Church in Western Europe. For Evlogy's career, see Pospielovsky, *The Russian Church under the Soviet Regime*, 1:133–42.

61 *Notes et matériaux*, 3.

62 *The Times*, 17 March 1930.

63 *Stoupnitzky*, 20–30; texts in *Notes et matériaux*, 32–5, 47–52, 56–9, 61–6.

64 Ibid., 66–73, with texts of the letters between Sergei and the Ecumenical Patriarch Fotius on the developments in the church.

65 *PN*, 27 June 1930.

66 Ibid., 5 Jan. 1929.

67 *Ledré*, 235.

68 Georges Maklakov, *Les dissensions de l'église russe des émigrés*, 18.

69 *Berberova*, 307.

70 *PN*, 5 Jan. 1929.

71 "Une manière de vivre," 113.

72 Kovalevskii, *Zarubezhnaia Rossiia*, 87–8.

73 Sams, "Report on Russian … Refugees," 43.

74 Iswolsky, *Light Before Dusk*. This memoir has much to say on the religious dimension of émigré life. The daughter of Alexander Izvolsky became a Uniate at 25; thereafter she frequented Orthodox and Catholic circles in France.

75 Maklakov, "Russkaia kul'tura i A.S. Pushkin."

76 Miliukov, *Emigratsiia na pereput'i*.

77 Veidle, "Granitsy Evropy," where this idea is staunchly defended.

78 Cited in Rimscha, *Der russische Bürgerkrieg*, 125.

79 Foster, *Bibliography of Russian Émigré Literature, 1918–1968*.

80 Poltoratskii, *Russkaia literatura v emigratsii*, 353, where Vishniak cites the opinion in this sense of the writer B.K. Zaitsev.

81 Vishniak, *Vospominaniia redaktora*, 90–98, for details of the journal's planning and birth. Portions of this section were previously published in *Canadian Slavonic Papers* and are reprinted with permission.

82 Ibid., 90.

83 *Don Aminado*, 303.

84 *Berberova*, 304.

85 Vishniak, *Vospominaniia redaktora*, 9, on the always menacing financial position.

86 "Ot redaktsii," *SZ*, 1:11.

87 The *versta* measured slightly more than one kilometre.

88 *Yanovsky*, 20, 62–83; Field, *Nabokov*, 214–15.

89 *Struve*, 57.

90 Ibid, 246; *Poltoratskii*, 107–20.

91 Adamovich, "O literature v emigratsii."

92 Brown, *Russian Literature*, 348.

93 Peter Obolensky, prince turned taxi-driver, noted how French was invading the daily conversation of his compatriot workmates. "Voitiura" and "aksidan" were two commonly used gallicisms: Obolenskii, "Na chuzhoi storone," 8:215.

94 Troyat, *Un si long chemin*, 81–4.

95 Tolstoi, *Rukopis' naidennaia sredi musora pod krovat'iu.*

96 N. Tolstoy, *The Tolstoys*, 298–300; *Brown*, 204.

97 *Struve*, 154, 267–8; Aldanov, "Pamiati A.I. Kuprina."

98 Ehrenburg, *Memoirs, 1921–1941*, 25.

99 *Brown*, 293.

100 *PN*, 9 March 1933.

101 Beyssac, *La vie culturelle de l'émigration russe*. She lists about two dozen such groups active during part or all of the decade. "The Green Lamp," "The Nomad Camp" (*Kochev'e*), "Orsiusk," and the Turgenev Artistic Society met the most frequently.

102 *Russkii narodnyi universitet*, 3, 8, 10.

103 *Beyssac*, 68, 93.

104 Ibid, 70–304 passim. She lists 111 lectures given under the Academy's aegis during the decade.

105 Kovalevsky, *La dispersion russe*, 34. Helen Iswolsky recorded Berdiaev's regret that *émigré* youth did not appear to have much interest in his ideas: *Light Before Dusk*, 96. But the postrevolutionary school was influenced to some degree by his theories. See below, Chapter Four.

106 Anderson, "Notes on the Development of YMCA Work," 1–8.

107 In addition to the works noted above, Kovalevsky published *Nashi dostizheniia*, as well as articles. Roman Gul also compiled lists of Russians prominent in cultural and political matters in exile: *Ia unes Rossiiu*, 2:72–138.

108 They were M.I. Rostovtsev, the economist A.M. Mikhelson, biologist S.N. Vinogradsky, sociologist K.N. Davidov, and mathematician-physicist D.P. Riabushinsky.

109 Chaliapin, *Man and Mask*, 304–5.

110 Ibid, 308, 315, 318–19.
111 Vertinskii, "Chetvert' veka bez rodiny," 5:217.
112 *PN,* 13 April 1938.
113 Lifar, "Russkii balet v Rossii, na zapade, i v zarubezh'i," 75.
114 Nestyev, *Prokofiev,* 240–5.
115 "Chetvert' veka bez rodiny," 5:210, 211, 216. Pavlova's Anglo-Russian biographer presents a rather different impression of her life in England: Oleg Kerensky, *Anna Pavlova.*
116 "Chetvert' veka bez rodiny," 4:215.
117 *VZ,* 6 Jan. 1939.
118 Shakhovskaia, *Otrazheniia,* 10.

CHAPTER THREE :
LIFE IN FRANCE

1 Vladislavlev, *Iz zapisnoi knizhki bezhentsa,* 10–21, 41–2.
2 Kadet Party Archive, 2:26.
3 Ibid, 27.
4 Rimscha, *Der russische Bürgerkrieg,* 113–18.
5 *PN,* 16 March 1921.
6 Mourin, *Les relations franco-soviétiques,* 129–30.
7 *Tongour,* 311–99 passim.
8 On the involvement of Soviet Russia in the Genoa Conference, see White, *Origins of Detente.*
9 De Giers Papers, "Genoa Conference"; *PN,* 10 Jan.1922, for Miliukov's disapproving view.
10 *Mourin,* 136.
11 "Genoa Conference," with press clippings.
12 De Giers Papers, "Soviet Russia. Insurrections against Bolsheviks," 9 May 1922.
13 De Giers Papers, "Conference at the Hague," 5 July 1922.
14 "Genoa Conference," 26 April; "Conference at the Hague," 23 July 1922.
15 *Mourin,* 143.
16 Maklakov Papers, "Miscellaneous Correspondence," VAM to secretary-general of presidency, 7 June 1923.
17 Soulié, *La vie politique d'Edouard Herriot,* 89, 99.
18 Herriot, *La Russie nouvelle,* 118.
19 Herriot, *L'état actuel de la Russie,* 3–21.
20 Ibid, 26–49.
21 Ibid, 60–5.
22 *Russie nouvelle,* 178.
23 Ibid, 296–7.
24 This failure is considered at fuller length in Chapter Six.

25 *Mourin*, 151.

26 De Monzie, "Du droit pour un Français de penser à la Russie," 6. De Monzie's subsequent trivial work on the new Russia maintained this animus against "the makers of February." Citing Michel de Montaigne, he wrote that "they set the torch to the state and were the first to be consumed in its collapse." *Petit manuel*, 331.

27 *PN*, 5 Jan. 1924.

28 *Mourin*, 152.

29 In a continuing rubric through the spring and summer "Frantsiia i sovetskaia Rossiia."

30 So de Monzie remarked to a Russian reporter: *PN*, 3 June 1924.

31 Ibid., 7 June.

32 Ibid., 13 June.

33 Ibid., 3 July, 11 Oct.; *Tongour*, 378–80.

34 *PN*, 30 Oct.

35 Ibid., 31 Oct., 1 Nov. Prince Dolgorukov's suggestion regarding the embassy silver was duly passed on to the French police, along with other gossip, by a Russian informant, Gregor Alexinsky, AN, "Notes russes," A–3838, 14 October 1924.

36 *PN*, 2 Nov.

37 "Miscellaneous Correspondence," Noulens to VAM, 4 Nov.

38 Kovalevskii, *Zarubezhnaia Rossiia*, 22–4 on the steps up to this point.

39 Ibid., 24–5.

40 *Tongour*, 377–8, 503 n. 242.

41 Champcommunal, *La condition des Russes à l'étranger*, 8–9.

42 The issue was further clouded by a Russian denunciation of certain of the 1874 provisions on the eve of the Bolshevik coup. The French denounced other sections in May 1922: ibid., 5–6. One contentious problem was divorce. The French finally came to insist that Russian petitioners must submit to French civil law procedures and not merely obtain a religious dissolution from the Orthodox church authorities in France. VV. Shulgin experienced difficulties on this point: Maklakov Papers, "Personal Correspondence," Shulgin file.

43 *PN*, 19 Dec. 1924.

44 Pétchorine, *Questions concernant la condition des Russes*, 21–22.

45 Ibid., 40.

46 Stoupnitzky, "Statut juridique des réfugiés," 4. The former Russian consulates in Nice, Marseilles and Lyons became regional branches of Maklakov's Office.

47 *DPF*, 5:1795.

48 Ibid., 6:2230–1; *VZ*, 27 May 1938 has an account of the society's first meeting.

49 *VZ*, 21 March 1935.

50 Ibid., 19 June 1925.

51 Ibid., 16 Oct. 1934 in an obituary tribute.

52 Ibid., 13 May 1928.

53 *Mourin*, 183.

54 *Le Temps*, 31 Jan.: *Dni*, 19 Jan. 1930.

55 *DPF*, 7:2535–7; *PN*, 22, 23 Nov., 1 Dec. 1934, 9 March 1935.

56 *PN*, 6, 17, 30 Jan. 1935.

57 Ibid., 5 July; *VZ*, 16 July 1935.

58 *PN*, 19 July.

59 Ibid., 1 Dec. 1935.

60 *VZ*, 3 Dec. 1935.

61 *PN*, 8 Feb. 1934.

62 *VZ*, 8 Feb. 1934.

63 *Emigré* views of the Popular Front governments of the mid-1930s are examined in Chapters Six and Seven.

64 "Notes russes," Jan. – Nov. 1924.

65 AN, "Étrangers en France," 26 Feb. 1925. Very incomplete replies indicated no significant mention of Russians other than their resistance to assimilation.

66 Fragmentary reports in the archives indicate that information on the Russians was still coming in at the end of the 1920s, much of it from Gregor Alexinsky. Though marked by him "extremely important," his details are the same mixture of rumour and gossip familiar to the police for years. It is hard to imagine that the material could have attracted much attention. AN, "Russie," (1929). On Alexinsky, a well known informer, see Aleksandrovskii, *Iz perezhitogo*, 148–50.

67 The Russian Academic Group, the Franco-Slavic Society, the Franco-Russian Association of the University of Paris, the Russian Historical-Philological Department of the University all sponsored such lectures: Beyssac, *Vie culturelle*, 5–306 passim.

68 A general suspicion of Freemasonry existed in most sectors of the emigration. Its faults seemed patent: alien in origin, secular, secretive, and with international loyalties often assumed to supersede national patriotic duty. Several leading members of the Provisional Government had been Masons, one more reason to suspect the worst of both: Berberova, *Italics*, 311. The second editor of *Vozrozhdenie*, Semenov, was a particularly acid critic, though Liubimov, his chief reporter, was a longtime Mason: "Na chuzhbine," 3:184–5.

69 Beyssac, 231, 249, 253, 303, 305.

70 "They teach the country of Descartes that it must look at the world without vain presumption, without false modesty": Ledré, 268.

71 *Cahiers de la Quinzaine*, 5 March 1930, 30–55; Beyssac, 265.

72 *Russkaia gazeta*, 3 Dec. 1923. The film in question was probably *Peter der*

Grosse, directed by Dimitri Buchowietzky, which starred Emil Jannings in the title role.

73 *VZ*, 21 Dec. 1929. The author himself thought that his play was less successful than others he had written: Rostand, *Confession*, 278.

74 *VZ*, 8 July 1938.

75 *PN*, 30 Oct. 1938.

76 It found work for 60,000 Russian and Armenian refugees. Vernant, *Refugees in the Post-War World*, 44.

77 AN, Fonds Albert Thomas, No. 391, "Lettres de B. Maklakoff." Depending on circumstances, the fee might be reduced or even waived.

78 Lapierre, *Les cent visages du cinéma*, 180.

79 Kuznetsova, *Grasskii dnevnik*, 275, 290, 298.

80 Pécoud, *L'étude et l'exercise de la médecine*, 40–2; Farçat & Morin, *Code pratique*, 219–28.

81 *Aleksandrovskii*, 262.

82 *PN*, 7 July 1936.

83 *Aleksandrovskii*, 268.

84 In a preface to the volume by Marcel Livian, *Le régime juridique des étrangers en France*, v–vii.

85 *VZ*, 27, 28 Oct. 1936

86 Farçat & Morin, 11–12; Zeeler, *Spravochnik*, 33. Depending on the type granted, the identity card also served as a labour permit.

87 Zeeler, 33. The Nansen passport did not, of itself, permit reentry into the issuing country.

88 Farçat & Morin, 25.

89 *Aleksandrovskii*, 197–8.

90 Sams, "Report on Russian ... Refugees," 36.

91 Sedykh, *Liudi za bortom*, 7–55.

92 Obolenskii, "Na chuzhoi storone," 8:211.

93 *PN*, 5 Nov. 1924.

94 *Russkii shofer*, 3 (May 1929).

95 Ibid., 4 (October 1929); *Za rulem*, 6 (October 1933). This latter had a more prosperous, substantial look than its democratic rival.

96 *Le Populaire*, 6, 26 February 1934.

97 Kin, "Stranitsy proshlogo," 6:200.

98 Flanner, *Paris Was Yesterday*, 45.

99 Yousoupoff, *En exil*, 35.

100 *Wiser*, 77.

101 Mauco, *Etrangers en France*, 79–81, 124–5; E.K. Miller Papers, Box 8, file 28, with letters to and from Miller on this subject as it involved army veterans.

102 *Mauco*, 196. According to his further figures, commerce claimed 5,000 Russians, the liberal professions 3,800, tailoring and dressmaking 3,000,

transport [taxis] 2,400, agriculture 1,600, construction 1,800. 1,000 Russians were living on income or had no declared profession. Ibid., 200.

103 *Parizhskie zavody*, 3.

104 *Mauco*, 270.

105 Ibid., 271, citing A. Pairault, *L'immigration organisée* (1926).

106 His name appears in a list of those attending a meeting of Miliukov's Republican-Democratic Association, very much a minority loyalty. *PN*, 8 March 1924.

107 Briunelli, *V fabrichnom kotle*. He does not say, but the film was probably Carl Theodor Dreyer's masterpiece *La Passion de Jeanne d'Arc*, filmed in Paris in 1927–8.

108 Ibid., 1:44–6, 2:12–14, 3:19–20.

109 Markov, *Kak russkie ustraivaiutsia na frantsuzskoi zemle*, 11–12. A rare success story seems to have been the experience of a General Lomnovsky. Having learned the business during his first exile years in Bulgaria, he operated a profitable yoghurt dairy in Nice. Ellis, *La colonie russe*, 322.

110 *Mauco*, 376; *PN*, 25 Jan. 1921, describing Count Ignatiev's long working day on a suburban farm.

111 Markov, 40; [Ross.zemgor. komitet], *Otchet po soveshchaniiu russkikh ispol'shchikov*, 1–7.

112 Ibid., 9–13; *Markov*, 13.

113 *Markov*, 13, 26, 39; *Otchet*, 22.

114 *Otchet*, 27–8. About 1,500 Russian settlers were represented at the Toulouse meeting. They were a mixture of independent farmers, sharecroppers, and agricultural labourers: *Mauco*, 440.

115 *Sedykh*, 82.

116 Markov, 6; *Biulleten' ross. zemgor komiteta*, No. 9–10 (15 Dec. 1922).

117 *PN*, 11 Feb. 1935. For a further unflattering description of the General Beliaev *stanitsa*, see Shostakovskii, *Put' k pravde*, 210–15.

118 *Markov*, 7.

119 Ibid., 8.

120 *Chto delat russkoi emigratsii?*, 36.

121 Orwell, *Down and Out in Paris and London*, 40.

122 Schaufuss, "The White Russian Refugees," 53.

123 Ledré, 142–3.

CHAPTER FOUR:
FATHERS AND SONS IN EXILE

1 Delage, *La Russie en exil*; Ledré, *Les émigrés russes.*

2 Delage, 12.

3 *Chto delat' russkoi emigratsii?*, 5–8, 16.

4 Delage, 118.

5 Ibid., 167.

6 "Rossiia i zapad," 280. He argued the same point in his *Russia Absent and Present*, 139–45.

7 Cited in Aleksinskaia, "Emigratsiia i ee molodoe pokolenie," 27.

8 Kovalevskii, *Zarubezhnaia Rossiia*, 111. Aged 64 in 1922, Fedorov had behind him a considerable public career. He had served under Witte as head of the ministry of trade and industry; during the Great War he had directed a major *Zemgor* supply committee for the army. In emigration he helped Burtsev to organize the 1921 National Congress and became vice-chairman of its resultant national committee.

9 Tsentral'nyi komitet, *Russkaia molodezh' v vysshei shkole*, 3–4.

10 Ibid., 5.

11 An "Academic Group," formed in 1920 in Paris by Russian and French academics, constituted the major professional organization for exiled Russian university personnel. It played the chief role in creating the Russian Popular University. In 1922 Miliukov, fresh from disrupting his party, decided that the Academic Group was too right-wing. He seceded, with a few colleagues, to form an "Academic Union" (*soiuz*). Both were represented on Fedorov's committee.

12 *Russkaia molodezh'*, 5.

13 Ibid., 40. On this occasion the committee despairingly reproached "the entire world's mad policy of artificial support to the lying criminal power of the communist international."

14 Ibid., 27.

15 Ibid.

16 Aleksinskaia, 25.

17 Ibid., 26.

18 Ibid. Cyril's gesture provoked the derisive comment that it was fortunate the couple had no son, as Russian history already had its Donskoi. Liubimov, "Na chuzhbine," 3:160.

19 *Russkii narodnyi universitet*, 4.

20 *Kovalevskii*, 22.

21 *Russkii narodnyi universitet*, 7–10.

22 Ibid., 25–6.

23 *Refugee Problem*, 104

24 Zemgor, *Zarubezhnaia russkaia shkola*, 128.

25 Ibid., 131.

26 Ibid., 278.

27 *RSKhD za rubezhom*, 8.

28 Stoupnitzky, "Rôle des états," 24–5. Full statistics in *Russkaia molodezh'*, 29.

29 Ibid., 39.

30 Zernov, *Za rubezhom*, 142–7.

31 Ibid., 152–7.

32 Writing of difficulties in the Boys Section between those who had memories of Russia and those who had left as infants or had been born in France, Anderson observed that "the chief difficulty arose because the leader of work among boys exhibited certain traits of character which were not considered compatible with the Movement spirit." Anderson, "Notes on the Development of YMCA work," 25.

33 "Rôle des états," 26–40.

34 AN, "Étrangers en France," where departmental prefects replied to a ministerial request of 26 Feb. 1925 for information on concentrations of foreign populations in France. Russian clannishness and resistance to assimilation were mentioned in three of the few surviving replies. Russian commentators on this include Kovalevsky in *Zarubezhnaia Rossiia*, 37–7; and Nina Gourfinkel's autobiography of her interwar years in France. She observed that even after thirty years residence many Russians in France remained on the margin of French life, unassimilated and unassimilable: *Aux prises avec mon temps*, 2:77.

35 *Zernov*, 123.

36 Gessain & Doré, "Facteurs comparés d'assimilation chez des russes et des arméniens."

37 Ibid., 101–2.

38 Ibid., 102. Troyat (Tarasian), Triolet (Kagan) and Gary (Katsev) were all born in Russia. Kessel was born in Argentina of Russian parents.

39 Ibid., 103.

40 Ibid.

41 Sams, "Report on Russian … Refugees," 49–53.

42 *Refugee Problem*, 317–18.

43 "Rôle des états," 38–9.

44 *Nezamechennoe pokolenie*.

45 "V Kanossu!", *Smena vekh*, 1:150–66.

46 "Russia and the Steppe: George Vernadsky and Eurasianism."

47 "Reforma vlasti v Italii," *Evraziia*, 29 Dec. 1928.

48 Berdiaev expressed his sympathy in a letter to a highly critical *Sovremenniia zapiski* editorial board: "V zashchitu khristianskoi svobody (pis'mo v redaktsiiu)." George Vernadsky, the historian, was also attracted to Eurasianism: *Halperin*, passim.

49 "Pis'mo iz Parizha," *Evraziiskaia khronika*, No.3 (1926), with hostile conservative reaction. Petr Savitsky, a Eurasianist lecturer, collected several of the most critical attacks in his volume *V bor'be za evraziistvo*. For a vitriolic assessment from the democratic sector, see Bitsilli, "Dva lika evrazistva," where Arakcheev and Lenin are invoked as the movement's spiritual forebears.

50 *Halperin*, 97.

51 The movement's dislocation can be followed in the correspondence between

the *Smena vekh* veteran Nikolai Ustrialov, in Harbin, and Eurasianists in Paris. Ustrialov Papers, file 4, "Moia perepiska s porevoliutsionerami," and file 6, "Moia perepiska s P.P. Suvchinskim."

52 Schakovskoy, "Une manière de vivre," 201–7.

53 R. Vraga, "Trest," 127, where this former Polish intelligence officer describes Soviet penetration of Eurasianist circles in the West.

54 "La jeunesse de l'émigration russe."

55 *Nezamechennoe pokolenie,* 52.

56 Hayes, "Kazem-Bek and the Young Russians' Revolution," 258.

57 Kazem-Bek, *K molodoi Rossii,* 8.

58 Ibid., 8–20.

59 Ibid., 43–6; *Hayes,* 263.

60 *Kazem-Bek,* 82–91, 96.

61 Ibid., 95

62 *Bodrost',* No. 1. This scorn did not fulfill the *glavo* from private overtures toward Miliukov. "Your opinion and authoritative criticism would be extremely valuable and real to me ... As an old fighter for freedom, you cannot be indifferent to the efforts at liberation of members of other generations fighting the same struggle with different methods." Miliukov Papers, Box 6, "Arranged Correspondence," 23 Jan. 1933.

63 *Bodrost',* No. 35. *Vozrozhdenie* much disliked this relationship. Liubimov solicited a statement from Cyril Vladimirovich which emphasized his position above all classes and parties in the emigration: *VZ,* 18 July 1935. But *Bodrost'* was not discouraged.

64 *Varshavskii,* 59–60.

65 "La jeunesse de l'émigration russe."

66 *Utverzhdeniia,* 1·9–15.

67 "Chto imenno utverzhdaetsiia?", 127.

68 Struve, *Russkaia literatura v izgnanii,* 226.

69 *Varshavskii,* 277; Rudnev, "Politicheskie zametki (eshche o 'Novom grade')"; Vishniak, *Vospominaniia redaktora,* 309–18.

70 Kartashev, *Sbornik russkogo natsional'nogo komiteta,* 1.

71 "Razgovor o fevrale," 320–30.

72 "Zachem my zdes'?", 439.

73 "Konets zarubezhia," 373–81.

74 Kuznetsova, *Grasskii dnevnik,* 293, reporting Bunin's view. Miliukov agreed: *PN,* 31 Jan. 1936.

75 "Konets zarubezhia," 376.

76 *L'exil des enfants,* 37–8, 140.

77 "Une manière de vivre," 119; *Otrazheniia,* 11–12.

78 "Une manière de vivre," 201.

79 Ibid., 227–8.

80 Ibid., 258.

CHAPTER FIVE:
ORDEALS AND TRIUMPHS

1 Miliukov Papers, Box 6, letter from H. Thouvenet, his neighbour in an adjoining apartment on the blvd. du Montparnasse, 7 April 1936.
2 *Le Montage*, 14–15.
3 "Russes de France," 866.
4 Such as those in *Le Messin* (Metz) of 29 Jan., 9, 10, 18 Feb, 1928, cited in Bonnet, *L'Homme du fer*, 252–3. Russian miners were "men of strong character who triumph, in spite of the modesty of their job, because they are strong through the exercise of their will." They endured their hard life "with an admirable resignation."
5 Sams, "Report on Russian ... Refugees," 57.
6 The Kutepov kidnapping attracted much journalistic and literary attention at the time and since. Major accounts are to be found in Bailey, *The Conspirators*, 89–117; Grey, *Le général meurt à minuit*, and an anniversary article by Sedykh, "25 let so dnia pokhishcheniia generala A.P. Kutepova." Contemporary accounts came from a Soviet defector, Bazhanov, *L'enlèvement du général Koutépov*, and Delage, *Koutépoff, la carrière militaire*.
7 Grey, 24–5.
8 *PN*, 27 Jan. – 4 Feb. 1930.
9 *VZ*, 28–30 Jan.
10 Grey, ch. 12; *PN*, 1 Feb. – 1 March.
11 As he made clear in his later pamphlet *Borites's GPU!*, filled with veiled and open accusations of *émigré* involvement in the Kutepov abduction. "Sherlock Holmes" in Rimscha, *Der russische Bürgerkrieg*, 146.
12 *Le Temps*, 4, 9 Feb.
13 *La Liberté*, 28 Jan. – 2 Feb.
14 *Ibid.*, 4, 13 Feb.
15 *Ibid.*, 10 Feb.; *PN*, 1 Feb.
16 Editorials from 1–5 Feb.
17 *L'Ere nouvelle*, 2 Feb.; *Le Populaire*, 31 Jan.–2 Feb.; *Le Peuple*, 2 Feb.
18 *L'Ere nouvelle*, 5 Feb.; *VZ*, 5 Feb.
19 *Le Populaire*, 11 Feb.
20 *L'Ere nouvelle*, 5 Feb.
21 *L'Humanité*, 30 Jan. – 11 Feb.
22 Flanner, *Paris Was Yesterday*, 82–3.

81 *Otrazheniia*, 12.
82 Biographical details from Troyat's conversations with Maurice Chavardès in *Un si long chemin*.
83 Ibid., 92–104, 230.

23 His life was outlined in *Le Temps*, 8 May, and in *VZ* and *PN* on 7 May. Yanovsky's association in *Elysian Fields*, 16–17, 175.

24 *VZ*, 7 May.

25 Ibid., 9, 10 May.

26 *PN*, 7 May.

27 Ibid., 14, 15 May.

28 *PN*, *VZ*, 9 May.

29 *PN*, *Le Populaire*, 7 May; *Le Temps*, 8 May.

30 *Le Temps*, 8 May.

31 Cited in a reassuring editorial in French, written by Jean Delage, in *VZ*, 8 May.

32 *La Liberté*, 9, 13 May.

33 *Le National*, 8, 15 May.

34 *La Victoire*, 7 May.

35 *Action française*, 7, 8 May.

36 *L'Ere nouvelle*, 8 May.

37 *Le Populaire*, 7, 8 May.

38 *L'Humanité*, 7, 8 May.

39 Ibid., 10–30 May.

40 Ibid., 3 June.

41 AN, F7–13964, "Menaces d'attentat," May 1932.

42 Ibid., police report to interior ministry, 8 May.

43 Ibid., 19 May. The interior ministry forwarded this report to the ministry of justice.

44 Barbusse, *J'accuse!*

45 Franklin-Marquet, *Ceux qui ont tué Doumer*. Vaillant-Couturier wrote an enthusiastic introduction.

46 Ibid., x–xi, 22–40.

47 Details of the trial in *Le Temps*, 26–29 July.

48 *Kuznetsova*, 272.

49 Rudnev, "K iubileiu 'Sovremennykh zapisok'," 443.

50 Ibid., 439.

51 *Kuznetsova*, 231, 275.

52 Ibid., 298.

53 "Moral victory" in *PN*, 10 Nov.; "real Russia" in *VZ*, 10 Nov.

54 *PN*, 27 Nov.

55 *NYT*, 11 Dec.

56 Frenz, *Nobel Lectures: Literature*, 314.

57 Ibid., 315.

58 Some short stories, including his most famous *A Gentleman from San Francisco*, and his 1924 novel, *Mitina liubov'*, had appeared in French editions.

59 *Le Temps*, 11 Nov., 12 Dec.

60 *L'Ere nouvelle*, 12 Nov.

61 *L'Humanité*, 10 Nov.

62 "Ot redaktsii," *SZ*, 54:195–6. Original emphasis.

CHAPTER SIX:
RUSSIA AND EUROPE

1 Vishniak, "Priznanie," 334–5.

2 Ibid., 348–50.

3 Ibid., 335. He repeated the aphorism at least twice in later articles.

4 *Dvuglavyi orel*, 2/15 April 1927.

5 One such vision, half-hopeful, half-satirical, appeared on the paper's first birthday. It depicted their country ten years in the future. Russia in 1936 would long have been cleansed on the Bolsheviks, whose leaders were all in Paris working at humble jobs. A military dictatorship governed in Moscow. Kerensky had returned, ruled for a hundred days "without authority," then fled. Miliukov briefly joined the Bolsheviks, then the SRS, and finally became "a liberal conservative of the far right," *VZ*, 6 June 1926.

6 Vishniak, "Vozrozhdenie," 396.

7 Ibid, 415.

8 *VZ*, 9 July 1925, for a Struve editorial in this sense. On 2 Feb. 1936 Semenov wrote an editorial harshly critical of "the Miliukov group" in *Posledniia novosti*. He accused it of inciting the French authorities against *Vozrozhdenie*. There may have been some truth to the charge: see the following note.

9 Two major examples, already noted, were Edouard Herriot and Marius Moutet. Both singled out *Vozrozhdenie* for censure. They were presumably kept informed of the paper's views by their contacts within the democratic sector of *émigré* political opinion.

10 In the issue of 29 Nov. 1933, as Russian exiles celebrated Bunin's Nobel Prize, *Vozrozhdenie* published a letter from a certain "Liza," inside the USSR, forwarded to it by a member of the Gallipoli Veterans Association, one Krestovsky. Her letter described the horrors of Soviet life in the standard *Vozrozhdenie* terms: famine, revolts, degradation. Semenov cited this letter in his polemic with Herriot over the latter's failure to acknowledge the truth about the USSR during his 1933 trip there (see below). Semenov, on the other hand, claimed to base his accounts on genuine sources, such as "Liza"'s letter. Koltsov thereupon revealed that he and his wife were the letter's real authors. Krestovsky did not exist, as Semenov could easily have found out by checking with the Gallipoli Association. So much for the paper's zeal for accuracy. As a final, authenticating shot, Koltsov also

announced that the first letter of the fifth word in each sentence stood for "Our white bandit journal publishes all slanders on the USSR." *L'Ere nouvelle*, 10 Dec, *L'Humanité*, 11 Nov. 1933.

11 *VZ*, 13 Feb, 10 April 1937.

12 Ibid., 7 Jan. 1938.

13 He had been suspended by the Union of [Russian *Emigre*] Writers and Journalists for a vitriolic piece on Miliukov.

14 *VZ*, 24 Sep. 1937.

15 Pipes, *Struve, Liberal on the Right*, 413.

16 Ibid., 413–14 for Struve and Nazism; *VZ*, 3 Sep. 1930 for Semenov editorial on Hitler's "demagogic demands."

17 Ibid., 13 July 1931.

18 Ibid., 31 Jan. 1933.

19 Ibid., 6 Feb.

20 Ibid., 2 March.

21 Ibid., 27 March – 6 April 1933.

22 Ibid., 25 May.

23 Editorials of 24 Jan. 1931, 6 Feb. 1933 and 13 Jan. 1934.

24 Ennesch, *Emigrations politiques d'hier*, 121. At Valmy, on 20 Sept. 1792, French revolutionary armies decisively defeated Prussian troops under the Duke of Brunswick. The French Republic was thenceforth a reality which monarchical Europe was obliged to accept.

25 *Le Temps*, 18 May 1933.

26 Bonnefous, *Histoire politique*, 5:378.

27 *VZ*, 21 Feb. 1936.

28 Ibid., 9 Sep. 1938.

29 *Bodrost'*, No. 12.

30 Ibid., No. 118.

31 Ibid., No. 135.

32 Ibid., No. 148. His journal reproduced a note from *Komsomol'skaia Pravda* announcing the arrest in Leningrad of a certain Kirsanov, charged with propagating Young Russian teachings acquired while studying in the West.

33 Ibid., No. 178.

34 Ibid., No. 224.

35 *Posledniia novosti/Dernières nouvelles*, 14–16.

36 *PN, Le Temps*, 6 April 1929.

37 *PN*, 30 May 1930.

38 Ibid., 31 Jan. 1936.

39 Ibid., 20–5 Aug. 1936.

40 Ibid., 15 June 1937, 2, 6 March 1938.

41 Ibid., 2 Feb. 1933.

42 Ibid., 1 March.

43 Ibid., 1 April.

44 Ibid, 1 July 1934.

45 Ibid., 9 Dec. 1933.

46 *VZ*, 25 March 1932. The term "defensist" (in Russian *oboronicheskii*) described those *émigrés* who supported the cause of defending the USSR, if it were attacked by fascism.

47 *La politique extérieure des soviets.*

48 Ibid, 4, 476.

49 *PN*, 3 May 1935.

50 *VZ*, 5 May.

51 *PN*, 23–5 Jan. 1934.

52 Ibid., 28, 29 Jan.

53 Ustrialov, "Sdvigi P.N. Miliukova."

54 *PN*, 15 June 1937.

55 Ibid, 12 March 1938.

56 Editorials between 26 Sep. and 8 Oct. 1938.

57 "Protiv techenii," 389.

58 Three examples will illustrate the range of Fedotov's heresies. In "Problemy budushchei Rossii: politicheskaia problema diktatury," he announced that the very idea of freedom had been extirpated in Russia, "politically we have gone to conditions of the 17th century." "Pravda pobezhdennykh" focused on the overwhelming and irresistible nature of the Bolsheviks' victory over their enemies; while "Novyi idol" proclaimed the end of world revolution as an integral part of Bolshevism. It had been replaced by a Soviet nationalism. All three articles drew vigorous editorial dissent. On Fedotov as a contributor, see Vishniak, *Vospominaniia redaktora*, 243–57.

59 "X", "Ottuda. Pis'ma starogo druga."

60 Vishniak, "Geroi nashego vremeni," 448.

61 Liebich, *Les mencheviks en exil*, 42, citing Rafael Abramovich.

62 This was most dramatically demonstrated when Nikolai Bukharin visited Paris in 1936. While there, he had a long, revealingly frank conversation with Fedor Dan concerning the contemporary Soviet political scene. This encounter formed the basis for Boris Nikolaevsky's *Letter of an Old Bolshevik*. Dan's widow also contributed her memoir of the occasion: Tsederbaum-Dan, "Bukharin o Staline."

63 "Geroi nashego vremeni," 448. Also P. Brutskus' review in *SZ*, 48:501.

64 *Liebich*, 51–4.

65 *Le Populaire*, 12 Aug. 1934.

66 Nos. 15–16 (324–5).

67 "Edinyi front i krizis demokratii," 334–40.

68 Rudnev, "Kommunizm i natsionalizm," 412–18; Vishniak, "Narodnyi front," 338–53.

69 "Puty svobody Rossii," 398–402.

70 "Uroki moskovskikh protsessov," 402–3.

71 "Protiv techenii," 402.

72 Duhamel, *Voyage de Moscou*, 9.

73 Walpole, *Out of the Deep. Letters from Soviet Timber Camps*.

74 *SZ*, 55:448–9.

75 Hollander, *Political Pilgrims. Travels of Western Pilgrims to the Soviet Union, China and Cuba, 1928–1978* (1981).

76 Two critical postrecognition accounts were by Charles Sarolea, *Impressions of Soviet Russia* (1924) and Henri Béraud, *Ce que j'ai vu à Moscou* (1925). Sarolea, professor of French literature at the University of Edinburgh, claimed to be the first to approach Soviet Russia dispassionately. His book of impressions was a diatribe against "the band of madmen, thieves and murderers" governing in Moscow. The French translation was highly praised in the *émigré* press. Béraud trumpeted his proletarian origins and love of French revolutionary traditions. He was repelled by Moscow in the grip of NEP, seeing much in common between the Soviet regime and Italian Fascism. However, the regime in Moscow "is an Israelite Fascism." *Béraud*, 52–3.

77 "Interesting experiment" cited in Vishniak, "Mif oktiabria." 382; "I take off my hat" in the *New Statesman and Nation*, 8 Dec. 1934.

78 *Duhamel*, 210.

79 "Mif oktiabria," 365.

80 Rolland, a prolific novelist, dramatist, and biographer, possessed, according to Larousse, "a generous, ardent soul exalted by noble causes." One of these was Soviet Russia. He had a major international reputation, perhaps greater than the fame he enjoyed at home. He won the Nobel Prize for literature in 1915.

81 *PN*, 19, 26 Nov. 1936; *SZ*, 62:454–7. Lev Liubimov reviewed the book in *Vozrozhdenie*. He hailed it without reservation. Gide "saw, understood, wrote." His volume was a much more powerful blow than one from declared enemies of the USSR. It was a sign of the times. *VZ*, 21 Nov. 1936.

82 Herriot, *Jadis*, 2:97–8.

83 *Mourin*, 159–67.

84 Ibid, 167.

85 *Le Temps*, 29 Nov., 4, 6 Dec., *Le Populaire*, 1 Dec. 1930.

86 Herriot, *Les procès politiques en URSS*, 7–12.

87 His second ministry, in July 1926, lasted one day.

88 *Jadis*, 2:272, 532.

89 Ammende, *Human Life in Russia*, 20.

90 *Eastward from Paris*, 12.

91 Ibid, 129.

92 *Le Temps*, 16 Sep. 1933.

93 *Le Journal des débats*, cited *Ammende*, 254–5.

94 *Eastward from Paris*, 310.

95 Zaitseff, *Herriot en Russie.*

96 *Jadis*, 2:102–08, 368.

97 *SZ*, 65:462–5.

98 Ibid., 56:442–5.

99 Muggeridge, *Chronicles of Wasted Time*, 2:17. His friend and fellow-novelist Anthony Powell later commented feelingly on "the force of Muggeridge's virtually one-man onslaught" on the USSR in the 1930s: *To Keep the Ball Rolling*, 3:84.

100 *T.U.C. Official Report*, 1.

101 Ibid., xiii.

102 Ibid., 16, 17, 104.

103 Fedoroff, *La Russie sous le régime communiste* (1926).

104 These other participants included Count V.N. Kokovtsev, M.V. Bernatsky, B.I. Sokolov, S.N. Tretiakov, V.F. Sologub, A.A. Pilenko, N.S. Timashev, A.V. Kartashev, A.V. Izgoev, E.P. Kovalevsky.

105 Melgounov, *The Red Terror in Russia* (1925).

106 *Fedoroff*, 165.

107 Ibid., 565, 569.

108 *Retour de l'URSS*, 14.

109 Caute, *The Fellow-Travellers*, 98–9.

110 International socialism also reacted critically to the TUC report. Friedrich Adler, secretary of the executive of the Labour and Socialist International, edited that body's official response in *The Anglo-Russian Report. A Criticism of the Report from the Point of View of International Socialism.* (1925). Adler, like Fedorov, pointed out the British reliance on materials supplied by the Soviet hosts and accepted uncritically by the visitors.

111 *Russia under Soviet Rule*, 42–91 passim.

112 Ibid., 204–5, 257–68.

113 Ibid., 477–8.

114 *SZ*, 65:465–8.

115 *TLS*, 22 Oct. 1938.

116 "The most thorough survey of Soviet history and achievements yet made by an *émigré*, despite the author's hostility to the regime and the fact that he has not visited the USSR, it is a most valuable book." Grierson, *Books on Soviet Russia*, 72.

117 "Soviet Studies in Western Europe: France," 59.

118 Tchernavin, *Escape from the Soviets* (1934).

119 *TLS*, 26 October 1933.

120 *NYT*, 20 May 1934, Section 5.

121 *New Republic*, 25 July 1934.

122 *New York Herald-Tribune*, 16 May 1934.

123 *New Statesman and Nation*, 25 Nov. 1933.

124 *New Republic*, 25 July 1934. Miss Winter was married to the American journalist Joseph Lincoln Steffens, himself very friendly to the Soviet Union and author of perhaps the most notoriously positive (and mis-quoted) verdict on that country: "I have been over into the future, and it works."

CHAPTER SEVEN: HUMAN DUST?

1 *PN*, 7 Nov. 1937.
2 "Zachem my zdes'?", 438–40.
3 *Ia unes Rossiiu*, 2:272–3. On a friend's recommendation, Gul secured a job as technical adviser to the film director Alexander Korda for his film *Knight without Armour*. With the £900 proceeds, Gul bought a small farm in Cagoony.
4 *Berberova*, 358.
5 *PN*, 24 Sept. 1937.
6 Ibid., 26 Sept.; Lehovich, *White against Red*, 442–5.
7 *PN*, 26 Sept.
8 *VZ*, 26 Sept.
9 Meier, "*Vozrozhdenie* i belaia ideia," 12.
10 *PN*, 5 Oct.
11 This noisy group is more fully examined below.
12 *PN*, 11 Oct.
13 *Je suis partout*, 1 Oct.'; *Action française*, 30 Sept.
14 *Action française*, 1 Oct.
15 *Le Temps*, 24, 25, 29 Sept.
16 *Le Populaire*, 24 Sept.
17 Ibid., 29 Sept.
18 *L'Oeuvre*, 27 Sept.
19 Ibid., 28 Sept.
20 Ibid., 29 Sept. – 3 Oct.
21 *L'Humanité*, 24–29 Sept. This included a vituperative attack on *Vozrozhdenie* as the headquarters of Russian fascism.
22 *Le National*, 11, 20 Nov., 4 Dec; Gulevich, "Rôle et espoirs de l'émigration russe."
23 Lambert, *La Société des Nations et les émigrés*, 16.
24 Statistics cited in Bonnefous, *Histoire politique*, 6:201.
25 Ibid., 202.
26 This was attached to the CGT as one of several foreign sections representing immigrant labourers in France. The Russian section's leader was a certain Rossel, identified by Sams as a pre-1914 *émigré* "of distinctly left tenden-cies." While his section professed nonpolitical aims, its appeals to Russian

workers were couched in standard Communist party jargon. See *General'naia konfederatsiia truda i sovremennye sobytiia.*

27 Ibid., 14–15.

28 *PN*, 30 Oct. 1937.

29 *VZ*, 26 Nov. 1937.

30 *Russkii shofer*, Nos. 17–18. Sams reported that at the end of 1937 there were about 2,500 Russian taxi drivers in the Paris region: "Report," 31. Union recruitment drives still did encounter "less firm" Russians, who refused to sign up. The Russian section judged these as psychologically still *émigrés*, not yet a part of the working class. They had to be won over from the influence of "dark, reactionary, Fascist elements" in the emigration. *General'naia konfederatsiia truda*, 10.

31 "Opyt Bliuma," 355.

32 *Le Temps*, 8 Dec.

33 Ibid, 8, 11 Dec.

34 *Le Populaire*, 10 Dec.

35 *Lehovich*, 447–8; Grey, *Le général meurt à minuit*, 125–49. In 1943 Vladimir Nabokov wrote a sardonic, thinly disguised account of the affair and of Plevitskaia's role in it in his short story *The Assistant Producer*, reproduced in *Nabokov's Dozen*, 75–93.

36 *Le Populaire*, 15 Dec.

37 *Lehovich*, 445; Bailey, *The Conspirators*, 121–31, on Skoblin's background and activities in the emigration up to 1937.

38 Krivitsky, *In Stalin's Secret Service*, 237–40. Krivitsky wrote that the Gestapo had fed the doctored evidence to the OGPU via ROVS. Bailey also has details of this, 259–66.

39 *La résurrection de la Russie. Mon voyage secret en Russie soviétique.* The original Russian version was *Tri stolitsy.*

40 Vraga, "Trest," 114–35. The episode was described to Soviet readers in a lightly ironical article by Lev Nikulin, "Istoriia odnogo voiazha." Shulgin survived until almost 100. He lived in Yugoslavia during World War II until his capture by the Soviets in October 1944. He spent the following 12 years in a camp. He lasted through it all and, under Khrushchev, published appeals for peace and detente addressed to Russian *émigrés* throughout the world.

41 *Vraga*, 135. Showing no favouritism, the NKVD in August 1936 raided the premises of the Paris section of the Amsterdam-based Institute of Social History. The Menshevik Boris Nikolaevsky was its director. Some forty packages of papers from the Trotsky archive, deposited by Leon Trotsky's son, were stolen.

42 Sams, "Report on Russian ... Refugees," 5–6. His report is largely reproduced in *Simpson*, 304–13.

43 *Sams*, 11, 25.

44 Ibid., 11, 23, 28.

45 Ibid., 36.

46 Ibid., 46.

47 *Les naturalisations en France*, 18–19.

48 Ibid., 63.

49 "Facteurs comparés d'assimilation," 108.

50 *Les naturalisations en France*, 29, 52.

51 "Facteurs comparés," 108.

52 *Pochemu ia ne emigriroval?*, 28–9.

53 *Rapport sur les travaux du Haut-Commissariat*, 4 Sep. 1923, 17–20.

54 Ignat'ev, *Piat'desiat let v stroiu*, 2:377–449 passim.

55 *VZ*, 6 Aug. 1937. Just before his departure Ignatiev met the Young Russian leader Kazem-Bek. The *glava's* enthusiastic reaction to Ignatiev earned him much *émigré* abuse. *Bodrost'*, No. 141, transmitted Kazem-Bek's thanks to those who had stood by him in the uproar.

56 *PN*, 24 Oct. 1937.

57 *Nash soiuz*, No. 49.

58 Ibid., Nos. 3–4 (87–88); *PN*, 9 July 1937.

59 Voronin, "O mladorossakh," and "Eshche o mladorossakh i o natsional'noi revoliutsii."

60 *Sams*, 54–5.

61 A second Soviet-oriented organization, The Russian Defensist Movement (*Rossiiskoe oboronicheskoe dvizhenie*), existed in Paris from 1936 to 1938. Through its publication *Oboronicheskoe dvizhenie*, renamed in March 1938 *Golos otechestva* (Voice of the Fatherland), it argued the case for defending the USSR unconditionally. Miliukov and the Young Russians earned a measure of cautious interest.

62 Prost, "L'éclatement du Front populaire," 43.

63 Prost, "Le climat social," 106.

64 *VZ*, 20 May 1938.

65 The May 1938 regulations included a provision that alien refugees in France for ten years or more would have priority in obtaining work permits. This would have included most Russians.

66 *Gul'*, 2:273–4. Moutet assisted him to bring his family to France from destitution in Germany.

67 *VZ*, 11, 25 Nov. Anna Iaroslavna was the wife of Henri I, the third king of the Capetian dynasty.

68 Other versions at varying times before and after World War II were the National Alliance of Russian Youth, the National Alliance of the New Generation, National Labour Alliance, and National Labour Alliance – Russian Solidarists.

69 Dvinov, *Politics of the Russian Emigration*, 115–22.

70 Ibid., 130–46.

71 *Nezamechennoe pokolenie*, 77.

72 *VZ*, 18 Nov. 1938.

73 NTSNP, *Molodezh' v bor'be za Rossiiu*, 16, 19. Savich's anecdote, taken from the press, turned on the common root meaning of the two names – Sparrow.

74 [US Government], *NTS: The Russian Solidarist Movement*, 1–2.

75 *Dvinov*, 121.

76 Steenberg, *Vlasov*, 42–4, 126–7.

77 *VZ*, 7 Oct. 1938, 17 March 1939.

78 Ibid., 28 Aug. 1939.

79 Ibid., 1 Sept.

80 *Bodrost'*, No. 239.

81 Ibid., No. 240.

82 Ibid., Nos. 241, 242.

83 Ibid., No. 243.

84 Vishniak detected a growing partiality on the part of his colleagues for religious and philosophical essays in their journal; there were also differences on technical matters. All this led to a situation that he later described as "objectively pernicious and subjectively insulting." *Vospominaniia redaktora*, 327.

85 *Russkiia zapiski* was organized as a "socio-political and literary journal" to defend Russian democratic principles. It thus closely duplicated the mission assumed by *Sovremenniia zapiski* in 1920. *Emigrés* from Far Eastern centres of settlement gave financial support. Miliukov eventually assumed the editorship.

86 *Vospominaniia redaktora*, 328–9.

87 "Front mira' i Rossiia," 318–20.

88 Ibid., 321–2.

89 Ibid., 324–7.

90 Ibid., 328.

91 "Rossiia i Evropa," 1–2.

92 "Velikoderzhavniki ili oprichniki?", 11–12.

93 One left-wing Franco-Russian observer who did foresee the probability of such an alliance was Stalin's biographer Boris Souvarine. Writing in *Le Figaro* (7 May 1939), he dismissed ideology as "merely literature" and stressed the overwhelming pressures on Stalin to come to an agreement with the most powerful, most dangerous and nearest of his capitalist adversaries, Nazi Germany.

94 "Mezhdunarodnyi krizis i sssr.,", *PN*, 18 Aug.

95 *PN*, 23–25 Aug.

96 Ibid., 28 Aug.

97 "Russkie v Parizhe," *VZ*, 1 Sep.

98 Maklakov Papers, "Miscellaneous Correspondence with French Statesmen," 13 Oct. 1939, VAM to Pierre Mille.

99   Varshavsky, *Sem' let*, 11–12.

100   Koestler, *Scum of the Earth*, 49, 87–9.

101   *VZ*, 8 Dec.

102   Ibid, 15 Dec, 9 Feb. 1940.

103   *NR*, Nos. 71, with reactions to the Nazi-Soviet pact, and 74–75 on the Finnish war.

104   Ibid, No. 72.

105   *SV*, No. 17 (445); *Liebich*, 55. The Menshevik Foreign Delegation's statement condemning the Nazi-Soviet pact and dissociating the Soviet people from it was published in *Le Populaire*, 26 Aug.

106   "Nashi raznoglasiia," *SV*, No. 8 (460).

107   Vakar, "P.N. Miliukov v izgnanii," 374; *PN*, 1, 7 Dec.

108   *Vakar*, 375.

109   "Kto zachinshchik?".

110   *Bodrost'*, Nos. 254, 255.

111   *Vakar*, 376–7.

112   *NR*, No. 78–79. The *New York Times* reported Kerensky's major addresses in the US: *NYT*, 21 Sept., 13 Nov., 4 Dec. 1939, 3 Feb. 1940.

113   "Rossiia i voina."

114   Ibid.

115   "O voine, o Kremle, o patriotizme."

116   "Prodolzhenie emigrantskikh razgovorov."

117   *Je suis partout*, 9 Feb.

118   *VZ*, 16 Feb.

119   Maklakov Papers, "War and German Occupation," copy of Denikin letter to the French press.

120   Stoupnitzky, "Service militaire des réfugiés russes en France."

121   Ibid.; PN, 19 Jan. 1940 with summaries of the relevant decrees.

122   *VZ*, 8 Sept. 1939, 15 March 1940.

123   *Berberova*, 389.

124   *VZ*, 7 May.

125   "Na chuzhbine," 4:154.

126   *Vakar*, 377.

127   Vishniak, *Gody emigratsii*, 120.

128   *Doroga cherez okean* (1942).

129   "That In Aleppo Once," *Nabokov's Dozen*, 148.

130   *Sedykh*, 9; "USA serum": *Nabokov*, 150. They owed their visas to the intervention of a Jewish Labor Committee in New York and to an appeal to President Roosevelt from William Green, president of the A.F. of L.

131   This was the figure cited by Maklakov in his letter to Pétain. See below.

132   Adamovich, *L'autre patrie*, 50.

133   Desmarest, *La politique de la main d'oeuvre en France*, 132–3. Spanish refugees were the main target of the new rules.

134   *Adamovich*, 55–6; Ratz, *La France que je cherchais*, 72–8; Soyfer,

135 "War and German Occupation."

136 Ibid., 11 Dec. 1940, VAM to Pétain.

137 "Na chuzhbine," 4:157.

138 "Gitlerovtsy v Parizhe," 11:120–1, 135. He had Fedotov blaming Gogol for Russia's current state because of the writer's "malicious libel" (presumably *Dead Souls*) on Russian aristocrats, who had preserved cultural oases in a dark, barbaric land. Madame Fedotova was, according to Sukhomlin, even harsher in her condemnation of Russia.

139 Grey, *Mimizan-sur-guerre*, 20–114 passim.

140 Sedykh, "Zagadka V.A. Maklakova."

141 *Aleksandrovskii*, 333.

142 Gorchakov briefly ran a small publishing house in Paris, "Doloi zlo" (Down with evil). It ground out tracts against Jews, Masons, and Anglo-Saxon capitalists, who tried, via "Methodist money," to undermine the emigration's religious unity.

143 *Aleksandrovskii*, 333–4. Maklakov received an unsigned warning from the prefecture of police that Modrakh's committee was seeking registration. The application had been rejected. The Germans evidently overruled the prefecture, though Modrakh does not seem to have been recognized by Vichy: "War and German Occupation," prefecture to VAM, 26 Feb. 1941; VAM to Admiral Darlan, 30 May 1941.

CHAPTER EIGHT: DISSOLUTION

Parts of this chapter were previously published in *The Russian Review* and are republished with permission.

1 Grey, *Mimizan-sur-guerre*, 118; Liubimov, "Na chuzhbine," 4:161, with his father's similar reaction.

2 Vakar, "P.N. Miliukov v izgnanii," 377.

3 *NYT*, 23 June 1941.

4 "Peredyshka," 200.

5 "Rossiia v voine," 212–13.

6 *Grey*, 118–20; *Berberova*, 408.

7 Maklakov Papers, "War and German Occupation," Gulevich to von Stulpnagel, 29 June; "Fremde Volksgruppen in Frankreich," Golovin et al. to Abetz, 26 June.

8 "Fremde Volksgruppen."

9 *Vernye syny Rossii*. On 29 October 1940, French officials told Maklakov that the occupation authorities recognized only Serafim's administration. Metropolitan Evlogy was specifically not recognized: "War & German Occupation."

10 Cited in *Kto my?*, a collection of Fascist materials published immediately upon the German invasion by a "Young Volunteer of the All-Russian

Fascist Party." Konstantin Rodzaevsky was the party president and would-be *Duce* of all exiled Russian Fascists. See Stephan, *The Russian Fascists*, 51–4.

11 Pachmuss, *Zinaida Hippius*, 280–1.

12 Sedykh, "Zagadka Maklakova"; Liubimov, "Na chuzhbine," 4:169; *Aleksandrovskii*, 336.

13 "Zagadka Maklakova."

14 "War & German Occupation."

15 Ibid., 22 Nov.

16 "May the devil carry him off!" was Ksenia Denikina's judgment on the *Leiter*: Grey, 136–7.

17 "War & German Occupation," *Komitet vzaimopomoshchi russkim emigrantam* to VAM, 9 March 1942.

18 Reportedly less than half of the 60,000 holders of Nansen stateless papers in France presented themselves for registration: "Zagadka Maklakova."

19 *Parizhskii vestnik*, No. 8. The Germans also changed the name of Zherebkov's "mutual aid committee" to the more accurate "Directorate of Russian Emigré Affairs in France."

20 "War & German Occupation," July 1941, with letters to VAM from Russians interned in Compiègne; Kovalevskii, *Zarubezhnaia Rossiia*, 232.

21 "Zagadka Maklakova"; "War & German Occupation," VAM to de Brinon, 1 Aug. 1941; VAM to Darlan, 29 Dec. 1941.

22 "War & German Occupation," VAM to Bérard, 28 Sep. 1942, with an account of his ordeal.

23 "Na chuzhbine," 4:163–4; Aminado, *Poezd na tret'em puti*, 325.

24 "Otechestvo v opasnosti!", 81–3.

25 *Pis'ma o neznachitel'nom*, 234–6.

26 Grey, 316.

27 *Sem' let*, 166, 170.

28 These heroic figures are presented in most accounts of wartime Russian France. The fullest description of *émigré* activity in the Resistance is to be found in the article by Krivoshein, "Russkie uchastniki soprotivleniia vo Frantsii," and in *Vestnik russkikh dobrovol'tsev*. English language monographs on the two major individuals are by Blumenson, *The Vildé Affair*, and by Stratton-Smith, *The Rebel Nun*. A Soviet film *Mat' Maria* (Mother Maria) was released in the early 1980s.

29 Varshavskii, *Nezamechennoe pokolenie*, 363.

30 Krivoshein, 99–101; *Vestnik russkikh dobrovol'tsev*, 49–50.

31 *Nezamechennoe pokolenie*, 309–10.

32 Aminado, 320.

33 Vishniak, "Pravda anti-bol'shevizma," 206–23.

34 "Pravda bol'shevizma." Vishniak did not read it until 1945: *Gody emigratsii*, 192.

35 "Zagadka," "Na chuzhbine," 4:166.

36 The two founding editors, both frequent contributors to *Sovremenniia zapiski*, were M.A. Aldanov and M.O. Tsetlin. The historian Mikhail Kar-povich assisted them and soon took over the editorial duties.

37 *NZh*, 1:5.

38 "La folle Clio," 162.

39 *Grey*, 271.

40 *Lehovich*, 463–6.

41 *Parizhskii vestnik*, Nos. 40–58.

42 Ibid., No. 59. The incident is fully described in *Steenbergs*, 111–12.

43 "L'autre patrie," 77.

44 "Na chuzhbine," 4:173.

45 "War & German Occupation," June 1944. Memorandum on the organiza-tion of a "Groupe d'action des *émigrés* russes."

46 Text in "Zagadka."

47 Ibid.

48 Liubimov later described how alienated he was by Maklakov's "naive and childish incomprehension" of the USSR when they met in August 1944: "Na chuzhbine," 4:178.

49 "Zagadka."

50 Maklakov Papers, "Posle osvobozhdeniia," letter to VAM from a "Union des patriotes russes au sud de la France," 30 Oct. 1944.

51 *RP*, No. 1 (14): "Na chuzhbine," 4:179.

52 *RP*, Nos. 2 (15)–13 (26).

53 Zenzinov Papers, Arranged Correspondence, VAM to AFK, 21 June 1945 (copy).

54 In his "Zagadka V.A. Maklakova" Sedykh related that the two ex-*Vozrozhdenie* writers, Liubimov and Roshchin, were requested in January 1945 to leave the paper. In Liubimov's case at least, some sort of link clearly persisted.

55 "Posle osvobozhdeniia" contains several appeals from Soviet "non-returners" to the *émigrés* to join together against Stalinism.

56 Abraham, *Alexander Kerensky*, 251.

57 Other than the two admirals, Maklakov gave as present himself and A.F. Stupnitsky (both ex-Kadets), A.S. Alperin and A.A. Titov (both Popular Socialists), E.F. Rogovsky and M.M. Ter-Pogosian (both Right SRs), and V.E. Tatarinov, a conservative journalist.

58 Maklakov Papers, "Ob'edinenie russkoi emigratsii dlia sblizheniia s sovet-skoi Rossiei," 12 Feb. 1945, typed protocol of meeting. This was published in "Emigranty u Bogomolova."

59 One of the several rumours in New York had it that none of the guests save Kedrov had responded to the toast and he did so with the added salute "za khoziaina!" (to the boss); Zenzinov Papers, VMZ to VV. Nabokov, 11 June 1945.

60 "Emigranty u Bogomolova," 279.

61 "Posle osvobozhdeniia," copies to VAM of pro-Soviet resolutions and accounts of meetings from émigré bodies in southern France, March–April 1945.

62 "Ob'edinenie russkoi emigratsii," VMZ to Ter-Pogosian, 12 April 1945.

63 "Emigratsiia i sovetskaia vlast'."

64 "Vozvrashchenie domoî" & "Besslavnyi konets."

65 Lehovich, 480–2.

66 So he told Kerensky in his letter of 21 June 1945. His beloved sister was dying and he himself living in very difficult material conditions: Zenzinov Papers, VAM to VMZ, 15 Jan. 1945.

67 Berberova, 431–2. Posters appeared in Paris after the Liberation bearing the warning "Frenchmen! Do not forget that your enemies are Germans, White Russians and collaborators!" NRS, 20 March 1945.

68 "Zagadka" on the murder of a Russian engineer Kosovich.

69 Note sur l'activité de l'Office central, 2–3.

70 Zernov, Za rubezhom, 323.

71 Ibid., 319.

72 "Posle osvobozhdeniia," Dec. 1944 – Aug. 1945, letters to VAM from Russians in difficulties. Edouard Kowalski describes some of the administrative hardships endured by immigrants after the Liberation in his Les immigrés au service de la France.

73 "Ob'edinenie russkoi emigratsii," protocol of organizational meeting, 24 March 1945. Maklakov became honorary chairman but took no active part in the discussions.

74 Maklakov Papers, Correspondence; "Sovetskaia vlast' i emigratsiia."

75 Pravda, 8 July 1945.

76 NRS, 31 Oct. 1945.

77 Zenzinov Papers, AFK to VAM, 7 July 1945; Russkie novosti, No. 20.

78 NRS, 10 Feb. 1946.

79 Ibid., 4, 9, 26 Jan., 4, 10 Feb., 23 March 1946. Zenzinov's correspondence also contains several letters from friends in Paris with details of their difficult life in France.

80 As documented in Nikolai Tolstoy's fine study Victims of Yalta (1977). Tolstoy records the forcible return to the USSR of several thousand Nansen passport holders, including some who had lived in France, whom the Soviet authorities had neither demanded nor expected: ibid., 249–77.

81 Koriakoff, Je me mets hors la loi, 206.

82 Vishniak, for example, became "writer–analyst" for Time magazine on its newly created Russian affairs desk.

83 Russkie novosti, No. 58 bis.

84 Ginsburgs, Soviet Citizenship Law, 114. Other decrees of 14 June covered émigrés in Yugoslavia and Bulgaria, 26 September those in Japan, 5 Oc-

tober those in Czechoslovakia, 28 May 1947 in Belgium.

85 "Ob'edinenie russkoi emigratsii," protocol of meeting of 15 March 1946.
86 "Na chuzhbine," 4:184.
87 Iz perezhitogo, 207; NRS, 9 July 1946. Evlogy died on 8 August 1946.
88 Russkie novosti, No. 17,
89 NRS, 27 June 1946.
90 Ibid, 30 June.
91 Zarubezhnaia Rossiia, 235.
92 No. 59.
93 Marcadé, Colloque Berdiaev, 19.
94 Bethea, "Ivan Bunin and the Time of Troubles," 10–13.
95 Zenzinov Papers, "Posylki vo Frantsiiu." Zenzinov, Aldanov, and Nikolaevsky organized this effort, which eventually helped to feed over 600 Russian intellectuals in France. Also NRS, 26 Jan. 1946.
96 The Soviet "non-returner" Koriakov met an old émigré colonel thrilled by Soviet victories. The colonel's son-in-law, a window cleaner on the Champs-Elysées, had fifteen such jobs behind him. Both looked longingly at life in the USSR: Koriakoff, 185–7.
97 "La drôle de paix," 40–1.
98 Gulag Archipelago, 1:262.
99 Obolenskii, "Na chuzhoi storone," 8:220–1.
100 Varshavskii, Nezamechennoe pokolenie, 365–9.
101 Hayes, "Kazem-Bek and the Young Russians' Revolution," 268.
102 Sovetskii patriot, 28 Nov., 5 Dec. 1947; "Na chuzhbine," 4:190–2.
103 Vernant, The Refugee in the Post-War World, 257.
104 Adamovich, Vasilii Alekseevich Maklakov, 207, 223.
105 Novikov, "Vstrechi s sovetskimi poddannymi," 207.
106 The theatrical producer N.N. Evreinov, a pillar of the interwar émigré cultural scene, recorded his sense of cultural alienation from the Soviet "displaced persons" he encountered in Paris after the war: Pamiatnik mimoletnomu, 13.

EPILOGUE

1 "The Russian Writer As World Conscience," 20.
2 Cited by Russell in "Farewell to Chagall," 31.
3 Gulag Archipelago, 1:269.
4 "Kul'tura i emigratsiia," 261–9.
5 "Kommentarii. 1. Emigratsiia i kul'tura," 276.
6 "Kul'tura i emigratsiia," 272.
7 Vospominaniia redaktora, 330.
8 "Kommentarii. 2. Emigratsiia i politika," 281.
9 Korzhavin, "Psikhologiia sovremennogo entuziazma," 170.

10 *SZ*, 57:477.

11 *Culture in Exile*, 372.

12 *Pis'ma o neznachitel'nom*, 249.

13 *Anatomy of Exile*, 12.

14 *Slavic Review*, 33, No. 1, 208.

15 Ibid., 25, No. 2, 377.

16 *Le bruit solitaire du coeur* (1985).

17 *VZ*, 216:6.

18 The issue of 2 August 1985, for instance, devoted its page of historical recollection to an examination of Trotsky's role in the assassination of the imperial family. A portrait of the family accompanied the article.

19 *Point de Vue – Images du Monde* (Paris), 9 July 1976.

20 Shulgin, *The Years*, xiv; *Literaturnaia gazeta*, 31 Oct. 1984.

21 Mushkov, "Budushchee emigratsii."

22 Cullen et al., "Émigrés Born in the USSR," 62.

23 Shames, "For Many Soviet Artists in Exile, These Are Lean Times," 1.

24 Ibid., 22.

25 Cited by Schoen, "The Russians Are Coming!", 20.

Glossary of Foreign Terms

Arrondissement. Administrative subdivision of Paris, presided over by a mayor.

Département. Administrative subdivision of France, presided over by a prefect.

Glava. Chief, leader. Title assumed by A.L. Kazem-Bek in his Young Russia movement.

Kadets. Constitutional Democratic party. Sharply opposed "left" and "right" tendencies within the party.

Kolkhoz. Soviet collective farm.

Left SR. Left wing of the Socialist Revolutionary party. After the October Revolution, a separate party. Briefly allied with Lenin's Bolsheviks until March 1918.

Mensheviks. Political party, consisting loosely of that portion of the Russian Social Democratic Labour party opposed to Lenin's Bolsheviks.

Mladorossy. Followers of Kazem-Bek's Young Russia movement.

Muzhik. Peasant.

Right SR. Main body of Socialist Revolutionary party. Strongly hostile to Lenin's seizure of power.

Smena vekh. Change of Landmarks movement in the emigration.

Stanitsa. Cossack village.

Zemgor. Union of *Zemstva* and Towns. The principal relief and supply organization in World War I Russia. It continued its welfare work in exile.

Zemstva. Institutions of local self-government in Russia (1864–1917).

Bibliography

UNPUBLISHED SOURCES

Anderson, Paul. "Notes on the Development of YMCA Work for Russians outside of Russia, 1918–1939." Box 6, "Russian Work," Paul B. Anderson Papers, University of Illinois Archives, University Library, Urbana, IL.

Archives Nationales, Paris.

Fonds Albert Thomas, 94 A.P. Correspondance B.I.T. (1ère série), Nos. 381 (Lettres de Kerensky), 391 (Lettres de B. Maklakoff).

Ministère de l'Intérieur. F7–13493, "Notes russes" (1924); F7–13500, "Russie" (1929); F7–13502, "Notes russes manuscrites" (1930); F7–13518, "Étrangers en France, Main d'oeuvre étrangère," (1925–33); F7–13964, "Menaces d'attentat. Notes et rapports sur l'attentat contre le Président de la République, mai 1932."

Briunelli, P.A., V fabrichnom kotle. Zapiski russkogo emigranta, 1920–1932 gg. 3 vols. in 2. Typescript deposited in the Bibliothèque de Documentation Internationale Contemporaine (BDIC), Université de Paris-X, Nanterre.

Constitutional Democratic Party Archive. Papers of the Paris group of party members in emigration. 2 vols. Hoover Institution Archive, Stanford University.

Ellis, LeRoy. "La colonie russe dans les Alpes-Maritimes des origines à 1939." Doctoral thesis, Université d'Aix-Marseille, 1955. Copy deposited in the Archives Municipales, Nice.

Giers (Girs), Mikhail N. de Papers. Hoover Institution Archive, Stanford University. The following materials:

Box 19, file 47, "Papers of the Conference held beyond the Frontier (Zarubezhnyi s'ezd)," 8 September 1925–12 May 1926; Box 19, file 48, "Zemgor Reports (I.L. series)," 3 January 1923–22 December 1926; Box 23, file 60, "Conference at the Hague," 31 May–23 July 1922; Box 23, file 61, "Genoa Conference," 3 January 1921–5 April 1922; Box 36, file 88, "Soviet

Russia. Insurrections against Bolsheviks," 16 March 1921–8 February 1924.

Gessen, Iosif V. Gody skitanii. 2 vols., Typescript. Hoover Institution Archive, Stanford University.

Koons, T.B. Histoire des doctrines politiques de l'émigration russe, 1919–1939. Doctoral thesis, Université de Paris, 1952. Copy deposited in the BDIC.

Maklakov, Vasilii A. Archive of the Russian Embassy in Paris, 1918–1923. Hoover Institution Archive, Stanford University.

——. Personal Papers. Hoover Institution Archive, Stanford University. The following materials: Box 6, "Miscellaneous correspondence with French statesmen and authors"; Boxes 7 and 16, Correspondence with A.V. Tyrkova-Williams and V.V. Shul'gin; Box 22 (World War 2), "War and German Occupation," "Posle osvobozhdeniia," "Ob'edinenie russkoi emigratsii dlia sblizheniia s sovetskoi Rossiei."

Miliukov, Pavel N. Papers. Bakhmeteff Archive, Rare Book and Manuscript Library, Columbia University. Boxes 1, 2 and 6 of his Correspondence. Box 2 contains a copy of N.V. Ustrialov's paper Sdvigi P.N. Miliukova (1934).

Miller, General Evgenyi K. Papers. Hoover Institution Archive, Stanford University. Files of correspondence.

Miliukov, P.N. "The Russian Emigration: Origin and Development," Vol. 2, No. x.

Sams, H.W.H. "Report on Russian, Armenian, Spanish, Italian, Saar and German Refugees, October–December 1937," Vol. 7, No. 1.

Stoupnitzky, A. "Les origines de l'émigration russe. Note sommaire." Vol. 1, No. 1.

——. "Statut juridique des réfugiés russes en France en rapport avec les conventions de Genève," Vol. 1, No. v.

——. "Service militaire des réfugiés russes en France," Vol. 1, No. vii.

——. "Rôle des états, des organisations internationales et des organisations privées des réfugiés dans l'organisation de l'aide aux enfants des réfugiés," Vol. 2, No. iv.iii.

——. "L'église russe à l'étranger," Vol. 2, No. v.

Yakobson, S. "Twenty Years of Russian Emigration," (December 1937), Vol. 2, No. xii.

Refugee Survey. 7 vols. of manuscript submissions later edited, abridged, and published in one volume by Sir John Hope Simpson as The Refugee Problem. Report of a Survey (1938) Library of the Royal Institute of International Affairs, Chatham House, London. The following original reports were consulted:

Tongour, N. "Diplomacy in Exile, Russian Emigrés in Paris, 1918–1925." Ph.D. diss., Stanford University, 1979.

United States National Archives, German Foreign Office Records, Microfilm series T–120, roll 2398, "Fremde Volksgruppen in Frankreich," (June 1940–December 1942).

Ustrialov, Nikolai V. Papers. Hoover Institution Archive, Stanford University. The following materials from his Correspondence:

File 4, "Moia perepiska s porevoliutsionerami."

File 6, "Moia perepiska s P.P. Suvchinskim."

Weidlé, Wladimir. Interview with author. Paris, 21 January 1976.

Zenzinov, Vladimir M. Papers. Bakhmeteff Archive, Rare Book and Manuscript Library, Columbia University. Materials from Box 5 of his Correspondence and Box 32, "Posylki vo Frantsiiu."

BOOKS

Abraham, Richard. *Alexander Kerensky. The First Love of the Revolution.* New York: Columbia University Press 1987.

Adamovich, Georgii. *Vasilii Alekseevich Maklakov: politik, iurist, chelovek.* Paris: Druz'ia V.A.M. 1959.

——. *L'Autre patrie.* Paris: Egloff 1947.

Adler, Friedrich. *The Anglo-Russian Report. A Criticism of the Report of the British Trades Union Delegation to Russia from the Point of View of International Socialism.* London: P.S. King & Son 1925.

Aleksandrovskii, Boris. *Iz perezhitogo v chuzhikh kraiakh.* Moscow: Mysl' 1969.

Ammende, Ewald. *Human Life in Russia.* 1936. Reprint. Cleveland: Zubal 1984.

Bailey, Geoffrey. *The Conspirators.* New York: Harper 1960.

Barbusse, Henri. *J'accuse! Pourquoi n'arrête-t-on pas les véritables assassins de Doumer?* Paris: Dangon 1932.

Baschmakoff, Marie de. *Mémoires. Quatre-vingts ans d'épreuves et d'observations.* Paris: Besson et Chantemerle 1958.

Basily, Nicolas de. *Diplomat of Imperial Russia, 1903–1917. Memoirs.* Stanford: Hoover Institution Press 1973.

——. *Russia Under Soviet Rule. Twenty Years of Bolshevik Experiment.* London: George Allen & Unwin 1938.

Bazhanov, Boris. *L'enlèvement du général Koutépov.* Paris, 1930.

Below, V. *Beloe pokhmel'e. Russkaia emigratsiia na rasput'i.* Moscow, 1923.

Béraud, Henri. *Ce que j'ai vu à Moscou.* Paris: Editions de France 1925.

Berberova, Nina. *The Italics Are Mine.* Translated by Philippe Radley. New York: Harcourt, Brace & World 1969.

Beyssac, Michèle, comp. *La vie culturelle de l'émigration russe en France. Chronique (1920–1930).* Paris: Presses universitaires de France 1971.

Blumenson, Martin. *The Vildé Affair. Beginnings of the French Resistance.* Boston: Houghton Mifflin, 1977.

Bonnefous, Edouard. *Histoire politique de la Troisième République.* 7 vols. Paris: Presses universitaires de France 1956–67.

Bonnet, Serge, ed. *L'homme du fer. Mineurs de fer et ouvriers sidérurgiques lorrains, 1889–1930.* Nancy, 1975.

Braunthal, Julius. *History of the International.* Translated by John Clark. 2 vols. New York and Washington: Praeger 1967.

Brown, Edward. *Russian Literature Since The Revolution.* Cambridge, MA: Harvard University Press 1982.

Bryas, Madeleine de. *Les peuples en marche. Les migrations politiques et économiques en Europe depuis la Guerre Mondiale.* Paris: Pédone 1926.

Burtsev, Vladimir. *Bortsev's GPU!* Paris, 1932.

——. *Prestuplenie i nakazanie bol'shevikov.* Paris, 1938.

Caute, David. *The Fellow Travellers. A Postscript to the Enlightenment.* London: Weidenfeld & Nicolson 1973.

Chaliapin, Fedor. *Man and Mask. Forty Years in the Life of a Singer.* Translated by Phyllis Mégroz. 1932. Reprint. Westport, CT: Greenwood Press 1970.

Champcommunal, J. *La condition des Russes à l'étranger et spécialement en France.* Paris: Sirey 1925.

Chernavin, Ivan. *Russkaia zarubezhnaia tserkov' i moskovskaia patriarkhiia.* New York, 1945.

Conférence des organisations russes. *Mémorandum sur la question des réfugiés russes présenté au Conseil de la Société des Nations.* Paris, 1921.

Corbet, Charles. *L'opinion française face à l'inconnue russe (1799–1894).* Paris: Didier, 1967.

Couratier, E. *Les rues de Boulogne-Billancourt.* Paris, 1962. Mimeograph.

Crespelle, Jean-Paul. *La vie quotidienne à Montparnasse à la Grande Epoque, 1905–1930.* Paris: Hachette 1976.

Daudet, Ernest. *Histoire de l'émigration pendant la Révolution française.* Vol. 1, *De la prise de la Bastille au dix-huit fructidor.* 2nd. ed. Paris: Hachette 1905.

Delage, Jean. *La Russie en exil.* Paris: Delagrave 1930.

——. *Koutépoff: la carrière militaire, l'exil, l'enlèvement.* Paris: Delagrave 1930.

Desmarest, Jacques. *La politique de la main d'oeuvre en France.* Paris: Presses universitaires de France, 1946.

Don Aminado [A.P. Shpolianskii]. *Poezd na tret'em puti.* New York: Chekhov 1954.

Dostoevskii, Fedor. *The Diary of A Writer.* Translated & annotated by Boris Brasol. 2 vols. London: Cassell 1949.

Duhamel, Georges. *Le voyage de Moscou.* 32nd ed. Paris: Mercure de France 1928.

Dvinov, B.L. *Politics of the Russian Emigration.* Santa Monica, CA: Rand Corporation 1955.

Ehrenburg, Ilya. *People and Life, 1891–1921.* Translated by Anna Bostock & Yvonne Kapp. New York: Knopf 1962.

———. *Memoirs, 1921–1941*. Translated by Tatiana Shebunina & Yvonne Kapp. Cleveland & New York: World Publishing 1964.

Ennesch, Carmen. *Emigrations politiques d'hier et d'aujourd'-hui*. Paris: Editions I.P.C., 1946.

Eudin, Xenia and Fisher, Harold. *Soviet Russia and the West, 1920–1927. A Documentary Survey*. Stanford: Stanford University Press 1957.

Evreinov, N. *Pamiatnik mimoletnomu. Iz istorii emigrantskogo teatra v Parizhe*. Paris, 1953.

Exarchat du Patriarche de Moscou en Europe Occidentale, *Notes et matériaux sur l'histoire de l'église russe en Europe occidentale*. Paris, 1972.

Farçat, R. and Morin, J. *Code pratique des étrangers*. Paris: Sirey 1939.

Fedoroff, Michel, ed. *La Russie sous le régime communiste. Réponse au rapport de la délégation des trades-unions britanniques, basée sur la documentation officielle soviétique*. Paris: Nouvelle librairie nationale 1926.

Field, Andrew. *Nabokov, His Life in Part*. New York: Penguin 1978.

Flanner, Janet. *Paris Was Yesterday, 1925–1939*. Edited by Irving Drutman. Toronto: Popular Library 1972.

Foster, Liudmila, comp. *Bibliography of Russian Emigré Literature, 1918–1968*. 2 vols. Boston: G.K. Hall & Co. 1970.

France. Ministère des Finances. Service national des statistiques: Direction de la statistique générale. *Les naturalisations en France (1870–1940)*. Paris: Imprimerie Nationale 1942.

———. *Mouvements migratoires entre la France et l'étranger*. Paris: Imprimerie Nationale 1943.

Franklin-Marquet, Henry. *Ceux qui ont tué Doumer. La vérité sur l'affaire Gorgoulov*. Paris: Bureau d'édition 1932.

Frenz, Horst, ed. *Nobel Lectures. Literature, 1901–1967*. London & Amsterdam: Elsevier 1969.

Gide, André. *Retour de l'URSS*. 19th ed. Paris: Gallimard 1936.

———. *Retouches à mon retour de l'URSS*. Paris: Gallimard 1937.

Ginsburgs, G. *Soviet Citizenship Law*, Leyden: A.W. Sijthoff 1968.

Gorodetsky, Gabriel. *The Precarious Truce. Anglo-Soviet Relations 1924–1927*. Cambridge & London, Cambridge University Press 1977.

Gorodetzky, Nadejda. *Lexil des enfants*. Paris & Bruges: Desclée De Brouwer 1936.

Gourfinkel, Nina. *Aux prises avec mon temps*. 2 vols. Paris: Editions du Seuil 1953.

Graham, Stephen. *Russia in Division*. London: Macmillan 1925.

Grey, Marina, ed., *Mimizan-sur-guerre. Le journal de ma mère sous l'Occupation*. Paris: Stock 1976.

———. *Le général meurt à minuit. L'enlèvement des généraux Koutiépov 1930 et Miller 1937*. Paris: Plon 1981.

Grierson, Philip, comp. *Books on Soviet Russia, 1917–1942*. 1943. Reprint.

London: Methuen 1969.

Grimsted, Patricia, ed. *Archives and Manuscript Repositories in the USSR.* Princeton: Princeton University Press 1972.

Gul', Roman. *"Ia unes Rossiiu." Apologiia emigratsii.* 2 vols. New York: Most 1984.

Haumant, Emile. *La culture française en Russie (1700–1900).* 2nd ed. Paris: Hachette 1913.

Hemmings, F.W.J. *The Russian Novel in France, 1884–1914.* London: Oxford University Press 1950.

Herriot, Edouard. *L'état actuel de la Russie.* Boulogne-sur-Seine 1922.

——. *La Russie nouvelle.* Paris: Ferenczi 1923.

——. *Eastward From Paris.* Translated by Phyllis Mégroz. London: V. Gollancz 1934.

——. *Les procès politiques en URSS.* Paris: Librairie du Travail 1937.

——. *Jadis.* 2 vols. Paris: Flammarion 1948–52.

Herzen, Alexander. *My Past and Thoughts. The Memoirs of Alexander Herzen.* Translated by Constance Garnett, revised by Humphrey Higgens. 4 vols. London: Chatto & Windus 1968.

Hippius, Z.N. and Bunakov I.I. eds., *Chto delat' russkoi emigratsii?* Paris: Rodnik 1930.

Hollander, Paul. *Political Pilgrims. Travels of Western Pilgrims to the Soviet Union, China and Cuba, 1928–1978.* New York and Oxford: Oxford University Press 1981.

Huntington W.C. *The Homesick Million. Russia-out-of-Russia.* Boston: The Stratford Co. 1933.

Ignat'ev, Aleksei. *Piat'desiat let v stroiu.* 2 vols. Novosibirsk 1959.

Institut po izucheniiu istorii i kul'tury sssr. *Bibliografiia emigrantskoi periodiki, 1919–1952 gg.* Issledovaniia i materialy. VI. Munich, 1953. Microfiche.

Iswolsky, Helen. *Light Before Dusk. Recollections of a Russian Catholic in France.* Toronto: Longmans, Green 1942.

Iu[nyi] D[obrovolets] V[serossiiskii] F[ashistskii] S[oiuz]. *Kto my?.* Paris, 1941.

Jolly, Jean, dir. ed., *Dictionnaire des parlementaires français 1889–1940.* 8 vols. Paris: Presses universitaires de France 1960–77.

Karpovich, Michael. "Two Types of Russian Liberalism: Maklakov and Miliukov." In *Continuity and Change in Russian and Soviet Thought,* edited by Ernest J. Simmons. Cambridge, MA: Harvard University Press 1955.

Kartashev, A.V. ed., *Zadachi, kharakter i programma russkogo natsional'nogo ob'edineniia.* Paris 1921.

——. *Sbornik russkogo natsional'nogo komiteta.* Paris 1936.

Kazem-Bek, A.L. *K molodoi Rossii. Sbornik mladorossov.* Paris 1928.

——. *Rossiia, mladorossy i emigratsiia.* Paris, 1936?

Kerblay, Basile. "Soviet Studies in Western Europe: France." In *The State of*

Soviet Studies, edited by Walter Z. Laqueur & Leopold Labedz. Cambridge, MA: The M.I.T. Press 1965.

Kerensky, Oleg. *Anna Pavlova*. New York: Dutton 1973.

Kessel, Joseph. *Nuits de princes*. Paris: Julliard 1928.

Koestler, Arthur. *Scum of the Earth*. New York: Macmillan 1941.

Koriakoff, M. *Je me mets hors la loi. Pourquoi je ne rentre pas en Russie soviétique*. Paris: Monde nouveau 1946.

Kovalevskii, P.E. *Istoricheskii put' Rossii. Sintez russkoi istorii po noveishim dannym nauki*. Paris, 1946.

_____. *La dispersion russe à travers le monde et son rôle culturel*. Chauny, 1951.

_____. *Nashi dostizheniia. Rol' russkoi emigratsii v mirovoi nauke*. Munich, 1960.

_____. *Zarubezhnaia Rossiia. Istoriia i kul'turno – prosvetitel'naia rabota russkogo zarubezh'ia za polveka (1920–1970gg)*. Paris: Cinq Continents 1971.

Kowalski, E. *Les immigrés au service de la France. Rapport présenté au Congrès national des immigrés*. Paris, 1945.

Krasnyi krest. *Pomoshch' bezhentsam vo Frantsii komitetov russkogo krasnogo kresta (staroi organizatsii)*. Paris, 1925?

Krivitsky, Walter. *In Stalin's Secret Service*. 2nd ed. New York: Harper 1939.

Kuznetsova, Galina. *Grasskii dnevnik. Sem' let v dome Bunina*. Washington: Victor Kamkin 1967.

La cathédrale orthodoxe russe Saint-Nicolas, Nice. Son histoire, sa description. Nice? n.d.

Laffitte, Sophie. *Chekhov, 1860–1904*. Translated by Moura Budberg & Gordon Latta. London: Angus & Robertson 1974.

Lambert, Léo. *La Société des Nations et les émigrés politiques: gardes-blancs, espions et terroristes autour de l'Office Nansen*. Paris: Editions universelles 1938.

Lapierre, Marcel. *Les cent visages du cinéma*. Paris: Grasset 1948.

Ledré, Charles. *Les émigrés russes en France: ce qu'ils sont, ce qu'ils font, ce qu'ils pensent*. Paris: Editions Spes 1930.

Lehovich, D.V. *White Against Red. The Life of General Anton Denikin*. New York: Norton 1974.

Liebich, André. *Les mencheviks en exil face à l'Union soviétique*. Montréal: Interuniversity Centre for European Studies 1982.

Livian, Marcel. *Le régime juridique des étrangers en France*. Paris: Librairie générale de droit et de jurisprudence 1936.

Luckett, Richard. *The White Generals*. New York: The Viking Press 1971.

Makarov, A.F. *Kak naturalizovat'sia vo Frantsii?*. Paris, 1926.

Maklakov, Georges. *Les dissensions de l'église russe des émigrés*. Paris: Presses universitaires de France 1930.

Maklakov, Vasilii. *Pervaia gosudarstvennaia duma (vospominaniia sovremennika)*. Paris, 1939.

———. *Vtoraia gosudarstvennaia duma (vospominaniia sovremennika)*. Paris, 1947.

Malevsky-Malevitch, P. *A New Party in Russia*. London: G. Routledge & Sons 1928.

———. *Russia-USSR. A Complete Handbook*. New York: W.F. Payson 1933.

Malia, Martin. *Alexander Herzen and the Birth of Russian Socialism, 1812–1855*. 1961. Reprint. Universal Library, New York: Grosset & Dunlop 1965.

Marcadé, Jean-Claude, comp. *Colloque Berdiaev*. Bibliothèque Russe de l'Institut d'Etudes Slaves, vol. 46. Paris: Institut d'Etudes Slaves 1978.

Markov, L.L. *Kak russkie ustraivaiutsia na frantsuzskoi zemle*. Paris, n.d.

Marrus, Michael. *The Unwanted. European Refugees in the Twentieth Century.* New York & Oxford: Oxford University Press 1985.

Mauco, Georges. *Les étrangers en France: leur rôle dans l'activité économique.* Paris: Colin 1932.

———. *Mémoire sur l'assimilation des étrangers en France*. Paris: Institut international de coopération intellectuelle 1937.

Meisner, Dmitrii. *Mirazhy i deistvitel'nost'. Zapiski emigranta*. Moscow: Novosti 1966.

Melgounov, S.P. *The Red Terror in Russia*. London: Dent 1925.

Miliukov, Pavel. *Tri platformy respublikansko-demokraticheskikh ob'edinenii.* Paris, 1925.

———. *Emigratsiia na pereput'i*. Paris, 1926.

———. *Posledniia novosti/Dernières nouvelles*. Exposition internationale de presse à Cologne. Paris, 1928.

———. *La politique extérieure des soviets*. 2nd. ed. Paris: Giard 1936.

Millet, R. *Trois millions d'étrangers en France: les indésirables, les bienvenus.* Paris: Médicis 1938.

Mirsky [Mirkin-Getsevich], Boris. *V izgnanii*. Paris, 1922.

Monzie, Anatole de. "Du droit pour un Français de penser à la Russie." In *Les écrits pour et contre. Les relations de la France avec les soviets russes,* edited by Marc Semenoff. Paris: Delpeuch 1923.

———. *Petit manuel de la Russie nouvelle*. Paris: Firmin-Didot 1931.

Mourin, Maxime. *Les relations franco-soviétiques, 1917–1967*. Paris: Payot 1967.

Muggeridge, Malcolm. *Chronicles of Wasted Time*. 2 vols. London: Fontana, Collins 1973.

Nabokov, Vladimir. *Nabokov's Dozen*. Garden City, NY: Doubleday 1958.

———. *The Gift*. Translated by Michael Scammell. London: Weidenfeld & Nicolson 1963.

———. *Speak, Memory. An Autobiography Revisited*. New York: Puttnam 1966.

Natsional'no-trudovoi soiuz (NTS), *Programma narodno-trudovogo soiuza (rossiiskikh solidaristov)*. Munich, 1975.

NTSNP vo Frantsii, *Molodezh' v bor'be za Rossiiu*. Paris, 1939.

Nazhivin, Ivan. *Glupost' ili izmena? (Otkritoe pis'mo Miliukovu)*. Brussels, 1930.

———. *Neglubokouvazhaemye*. Tientsin, 1935.

Nestyev, Israel. *Prokofiev*. Translated by Florence Jonas. Stanford: Stanford University Press 1960.

Nourissier, François. *Enracinement des immigrés*. Paris: Bloud & Gay 1951.

Ob'edinenie russkikh sinditsirovannykh rabochikh vo Frantsii. *General'naia konfederatsiia truda i sovremennye sobytiia. Zadachi trudovoi russkoi emigratsii*. Paris, 1937.

Office central des réfugiés russes. *Note sur l'activité de l'Office central des réfugiés russes depuis août 1944 à octobre 1946*. Paris, 1946.

Orwell, George. *Down and Out in Paris and London*. 1933. London: Penguin 1982.

Osorgin, Mikhail [Il'in]. *Pis'ma o neznachitel'nom, 1940–1942 gg*. New York: Chekhov 1952.

Pachmuss, Temira. *Zinaida Hippius, An Intellectual Profile*. Carbondale, IL: Southern Illinois University Press 1971.

Paon, Maurice. *L'immigration en France*. Paris: Payot 1926.

Parizhskie zavody: spravochnik-ocherk. Paris, 1924.

Pécoud, Jean. *L'étude et l'exercise de la médecine par les étrangers*. Paris: Sirey 1939.

Peshekhonov, A.V. *Pochemu ia ne emigriroval?* Berlin, 1923.

Pétchorine, D. *Questions concernant la condition des Russes en France et celle des étrangers (spécialement les Français) en URSS*. Paris: Sirey 1929.

Pipes, Richard. *Struve, Liberal on the Right, 1903–1944*. 2 vols. Cambridge, MA: Harvard University Press 1980.

Poltoratskii, N.P. ed., *Russkaia literatura v emigratsii: sbornik statei*. Pittsburgh: Center for International Studies, University of Pittsburgh 1972.

Pospielovsky, Dimitry. *The Russian Church under the Soviet Regime, 1917–1982*. 2 vols. Crestwood, N.Y.: St Vladimir's Seminary Press 1984.

Postnikov, S. *Russkie v Prage*. Prague, 1928.

Powell, Anthony. *To Keep the Ball Rolling*. Vol. 3, *Faces In My Time*. London: Penguin 1983.

Prost, Antoine. "L'éclatement du Front populaire" and "Le climat social." In *Edouard Daladier, chef du gouvernement, avril 1938 – septembre 1939*, edited by René Rémond and Janine Bourdin. Paris: Fondation nationale des sciences politiques 1977.

Ratz, Joseph. *La France que je cherchais, Les impressions d'un Russe engagé volontaire en France*. Limoges: Bontemps 1945.

Rimscha, Hans von. *Der russische Bürgerkrieg und die russische Emigration 1917–1921*. Jena: Frommann 1924.

———. *Russland jenseits der Grenzen 1921–1926. Ein Beitrag zur russischen Nachkriegsgeschichte*. Jena: Frommann 1927.

Romanov, Grand Duke Alexander. *Always A Grand Duke*. New York: Farrar & Rinehart 1933.

Romanov, Grand Duke Cyril. *My Life in Russia's Service: Then and Now*. London: Selwyn & Blount 1939.

Rosenberg, William. *Liberals in the Russian Revolution. The Constitutional Democratic Party, 1917–1921*. Princeton: Princeton University Press 1974.

Rossiiskii zemsko-gorodskoi komitet pomoshchi rossiiskim grazhdanam zagranitsei, ed., *Otchet po soveshchaniiu russkikh ispol'shchikov i aren-datorov na iugo-zapade Frantsii*. Paris, 1929.

———. *Mémorandum sur l'activité du comité des zemstvos et villes russes de secours aux citoyens russes à l'étranger*. Paris, 1937.

———. *Zarubezhnaia russkaia shkola*. Paris, 1924.

Rostand, Maurice. *Confession d'un demi-siècle*. Paris: Jeune Parque, 1948.

Rudnev, Vadim. *Usloviia zhizni detei emigratsii*. Prague, 1928.

Russian Committee in Turkey, ed., *Materials Concerning the Evacuation of Russian Refugees from Constantinople*. Constantinople, 1922.

Russkaia akademicheskaia gruppa, ed., *Russkii narodnyi universitet v Parizhe. Obzor deiatel'nosti za pervye desiat' let sushchestvovaniia*. Paris, 1931.

Russkaia armiia v izgnanii 1920–1923 gg n.p., n.d.

Russkii sovet, ed., *Russkii sovet*. Paris, 1921.

Russkoe studentcheskoe khristianskoe dvizhenie, ed., *R.S.Kh.D za rubezhom*. Paris, 1928.

Sarolea, Charles. *Impressions of Soviet Russia*. London: Nash & Grayson 1924.

Savitskii, Petr. *V bor'be za evraziistvo*. Paris, 1931.

Sedykh, Andrei [Iakov Tsvibak]. *Liudi z bortom*. Paris: Zeluk 1933.

———. *Doroga cherez okean*. New York: Novyi zhurnal? 1942.

Serafim, Metropolitan. *Vernye syny Rossii*. Paris, 1941.

Shakhovskaia, Zinaida. *Tel est mon siècle*. 4 vols. 1. *Lumières et ombres*; 2. *Une manière de vivre*; 3. *La folle Clio*; 4. *La drôle de paix*. Paris: Presses de la Cité 1964–7.

———. *Otrazheniia*. Paris: YMCA Press 1975.

Shcheglov, A.N. *Ostergaites' volkov v ovech'ei shkure!* Paris: "Doloi zlo" 1930?

Shkarenkov, L.K. *Agoniia beloi emigratsii*. Moscow, 1981.

Shostakovskii, Pavel. *Put' k pravde*. Minsk, 1960.

Shul'gin, V.V. *La résurrection de la Russie. Mon voyage sécret en Russie soviétique*. Translated from the Russian edition *Tri stolitsy* by P. Pouget. Paris: Payot 1927.

———. *Pis'ma k russkim emigrantam*. Moscow, 1961.

———. *The Years, Memoirs of a Member of the Russian Duma, 1906–1917*. Translated by Tanya Davis, introduced by Jonathan Sanders. New York: Hippocrene Books 1984.

Simpson, Sir John H. *The Refugee Problem: Report of a Survey.* Oxford & London: Oxford University Press 1939.

Snessarev, Nikolai. *Kirill pervyi, imperator ... koburgskii.* Berlin, 1925.

Société des Nations/League of Nations. *General Report on the Work Accomplished up to March 15, 1922 by Dr Fridtjof Nansen, High Commissioner of the League of Nations* (C.124.M74 1922).

——. *Rapport sur les travaux du Haut-Commissariat pour les réfugiés présenté à la 4ème Assemblée par le Dr Fridtjof Nansen* (4 Sept. 1923, A. 30 1923 XII).

——. *Rapports du Haut-Commissaire pour les réfugiés:* 10 March 1924 (C. 103 1924); 5 June 1926 (C. 327 1926); 5 September 1927 (A. 48 1927 VIII).

——. *Rapport du secrétaire-général sur l'organisation future de l'oeuvre des réfugiés.* (30 Aug. 1930, A. 28 1930 XIII).

Sokolov, B. *Le voyage de Cachin et de Frossard dans la Russie des Soviets.* Paris, 1921.

Solzhenitsyn, Alexander. *The Gulag Archipelago 1918–1956. An Experiment in Literary Investigation.* Translated by Thomas Whitney. 3 vols., Vol. 1. New York: Harper & Row 1973.

Sorel, Albert. *L'Europe et la Révolution française.* 8 vols. Vol. 2. *La chute de la royauté.* Paris: Plon, Nourrit 1903.

Soulié, Michel. *La vie politique d'Edouard Herriot.* Paris: Colin 1962.

Soyfer, Emmanuel. *40 ans après.* Monaco: Regain, Sylfa 1969.

Steenberg, Sven. *Vlasov.* New York: Knopf 1970.

Stephan, John. *The Russian Fascists: Tragedy and Farce in Exile, 1925–1945.* New York: Harper & Row 1978.

Stratton-Smith, T. *The Rebel Nun.* London: Souvenir Press 1965.

Struve, Gleb. *Russkaia literatura v izgnanii.* 1956. 2nd ed, Paris: YMCA Press 1984.

Tabori, Paul. *The Anatomy of Exile. A Semantic and Historical Study.* London: Harrap 1972.

Tchernavin, Tatiana. *Escape From The Soviets.* Translated by N. Alexander. New York: E.P. Dutton 1934.

Thompson, John. *Russia, Bolshevism and the Versailles Peace.* Princeton: Princeton University Press 1966.

Tolstoi, Aleksei. *Rukopis' naidennaia sredi musora pod krovat'iu.* Berlin, 1923.

Tolstoy, Nikolai. *Victims of Yalta.* London: Hodder & Stoughton 1977.

——. *The Tolstoys. Twenty-four Generations of Russian History, 1353–1983.* London: Hamish Hamilton 1983.

Trades Union Congress, ed., *Official Report of the British Trades Union Delegation to Russia and Caucasia in November – December 1924.* London, 1925.

Troyat, Henri. *Un si long chemin. Conversations avec Maurice Chavardès.* Paris: Stock 1976.

Tsentral'nyi komitet po obezpecheniiu vysshego obrazovaniia russkomu iunoshestvu zagranitsei, ed., *Russkaia molodezh' v vysshei shkole zagranitsei*. Paris, 1933.

United States Government. Office of Intelligence Research, External Research Staff. *N.T.S. The Russian Solidarist Movement.* Series 3, No. 76. Washington, 1951.

Varshavskii, Vladimir. *Sem' let. Povest' 1939–1945 gg.* Paris: YMCA Press 1950.

——. *Nezamechennoe pokolenie.* New York: Chekhov 1956.

Vernant, Jacques. *The Refugee in the Post-War World.* London: Allen & Unwin 1953.

Vishniak, Mark. *Dva puti (fevral' i oktiabr').* Paris, 1931.

——. *"Sovremennye zapiski": vospominaniia redaktora.* Bloomington: Indiana University Press 1957.

——. *Gody emigratsii: Parizh-N'iu Iork 1919–1969 gg.* Stanford: Hoover Institution Press 1970.

Vladislavlev [Kaminskii], S. *Iz zapisnoi knizhki bezhentsa.* Paris, 1963.

Volkmann, Hans-Erich. *Die russische Emigration in Deutschland, 1919–1929.* Würzburg: Holzner 1966.

Volkoff, Vladimir. *Le montage.* Paris: Julliard 1982.

Walpole, Hugh, ed., *Out of the Deep, Letters from Soviet Timber Camps.* London: G. Bles 1931.

Weidlé, Wladimir. *Russia Absent and Present.* Reprint. New York: Vintage 1961.

White, Stephen. *The Origins of Detente. The Genoa Conference and Soviet-Western Relations, 1921–1922.* Cambridge & London: Cambridge University Press 1985.

Williams, Robert. *Culture in Exile. Russian Émigrés in Germany, 1881–1941.* Ithaca: Cornell University Press 1972.

Wiser, William. *The Crazy Years: Paris in the Twenties.* London: Thames & Hudson 1983.

Yanovsky, Vassily. *Elysian Fields. A Book of Memory.* Translated by Isabella and Vassily Yanovsky. DeKalb: Northern Illinois University Press 1987.

Yousoupoff, Félix. *En exil, 1919–1953.* Paris: Plon, 1954.

Zaitseff, Cyrille. *Herriot en Russie.* Paris: Nouvelles éditions latines 1934.

Zeeler, V.F. *Indicateur. Les Russes en France/Spravochnik. Russkie vo Frantsii.* Paris, 1937.

Zernov, N.M. & M.V. *Za rubezhom: Belgrad-Parizh-Oksford 1921–1972 gg.* Paris: YMCA Press 1973.

ARTICLES

The abbreviation *SZ* is used in references in this section to the journal *Sovremenniia zapiski.*

Adamovich, Georgii. "O literature v emigratsii." *SZ* 50 (1932): 327–39.

Aldanov, Mark. "Pamiati A.I. Kuprina." *SZ* 67 (1938): 317–24.

Aleksinskaia, T. "Russkaia emigratsiia 1920–1939 gg." *Vozrozhdenie* 60 (December 1956): 33–41.

——. "Emigratsiia i ee molodoe pokolenie." *Vozrozhdenie* 65 (May 1957): 20–42.

Avksent'ev, N.D. "Front mira' i Rossiia." *SZ* 69 (1939): 318–28.

——. "Rossiia v voine." *Novyi zhurnal* 1 (1942): 203–13.

Berdiaev, Nikolai. "V zashchitu khristianskoi svobody (pis'mo v redaktsiiu)." *SZ* 24 (1925): 285–303.

Berlin, P. "Uroki moskovskikh protsessov." *SZ* 63 (1937): 398–404.

Bethea, David. "1944–1953: Ivan Bunin and the Time of Troubles in Russian Emigré Literature." *Slavic Review* 43, No. 1 (Spring 1984): 1–16.

Beucler, André. "Russes de France." *Revue de Paris* 44, No. 2 (1937): 866–96.

Bitsilli, P.M. "Dva lika evraziistva." *SZ* 31 (1927): 421–34.

Chalkhotin, S.S. "V Kanossu'," *Smena vekh* 1 (July 1921): 150–66.

Cullen, Robert et al. "Emigrés: Born in the USSR." *Newsweek*, 19 August 1985, 62–4.

Dan, Fedor. "Otechestvo v opasnosti'." *Novyi put'* 7 (23 July 1941): 81–3.

——. "Vozvrashcheniia domoi" and "Besslavnyi konets." *Novyi put'* 3 (49) (1 April 1945): 721–3, 729.

"Emigranty u Bogomolova." *Novyi zhurnal* 100 (1970): 269–79.

"Emigratsiia i sovetskaia vlast'." *Novyi zhurnal* 10 (1945): 340–60, 11 (1945): 350–74.

Fedotov, Georgii. "Problemy budushchei Rossii: politicheskaia problema diktatury." *SZ* 45 (1931): 475–90.

——. "Pravda pobezhdennykh." *SZ* 51 (1933): 360–85.

——. "Novyi idol." *SZ* 57 (1935): 397–411.

——. "Zachem my zdes'?". *SZ* 58 (1935): 433–44.

Fischer, George. "The Russian Archive in Prague." *The American Slavic and East European Review* 8 (1949): 289–95.

Fisher, Ralph. Obituary tribute to George Vernadsky. *Slavic Review* 33, No. 1 (March 1974): 206–8.

Gessain, Robert & Doré, Madeleine. "Facteurs comparés d'assimilation chez des Russes et des Arméniens." *Population* (Paris) 1 (January – March 1946): 99–116.

Gulevich, A.A. "Rôle et espoirs de l'émigration russe." *L'Indépendant de Paris*, 23 October 1937.

Halperin, Charles. "Russia and the Steppe: George Vernadsky and Eurasianism." *Forschungen zur osteuropäischen Geschichte* 36 (1985), 55–194.

Hayes, Nicholas. "Kazem-Bek and the Young Russians' Revolution." *Slavic Review* 39, No. 2 (June 1980): 255–68.

Ivanovich, St. [Portugeis]. "Edinyi front i krizis demokratii." *SZ* 56 (1934): 334–40.

——. "Puty svobody Rossii." *SZ* 60 (1936): 388–403.

——. "Tashkentsy zagranitsei." *SZ* 28 (1926): 308–423.

Izvol'skaia, E.A. "Velikoderzhavniki ili oprichniki?" *Novaia Rossiia* 70 (12 July 1939): 11–12.

Karpovich, M.M. "Kommentarii. 1. Emigratsiia i kul'tura. 2. Emigratsiia i politika." *Novyi zhurnal* 28 (1952): 272–84.

Kennan, George. Obituary tribute to Boris Nikolaevsky. *Slavic Review* 25, No. 2 (June 1966): 375–7.

Kerenskii, A.F. "Fevral' i oktiabr'." *SZ* 9 (1921): 269–93.

——. "Rossiia i voina." *Novaia Rossiia* 80–81 (22 March 1940): 1–4.

——. "Rossiia i Evropa." *Novaia Rossiia* 68 (30 May 1939): 1–2; 69 (15 June 1939): 1–2.

——. "O voine, o Kremle, o patriotizme." *Novaia Rossiia* 84 (10 May 1940): 1–4.

——. "Peredyshka." *Novyi zhurnal* 1 (1942): 183–202.

Kin, Tsetsiliia. "Stranitsy proshlogo." *Novyi mir*, 1969, nos. 5: 176–97, 6: 177–215.

Korzhavin, Naum. "Psikhologiia sovremennogo entuziazma." *Kontinent* 8 (1976): 161–200.

Krivoshein, I. "Russkie uchastniki soprotivleniia vo Frantsii." *Novosel'e* (New York) 35–36 (1947): 91–101.

Kuskova, E.D. "Chto imenno utverzhdaetsiia?" *Utverzhdeniia* 2 (August 1931): 125–9.

Lesure, Michel. ed. "Les réfugiés révolutionnaires russes à Paris." *Cahiers du monde russe et soviétique* 6, No. 3 (July – September 1965): 419–36.

Lifar, Sergei. "Russkii balet v Rossii, na zapade i v zarubezh'i." *Vozrozhdenie* 205 (January 1969): 71–83.

Liubimov, L.D. "Na chuzhbine." *Novyi mir*, 1957, nos. 2:177–206, 3:135–205, 4:153–194.

Maklakov, V.A. "Russkaia kul'tura i A.S. Pushkin." *SZ* 29 (1926): 228–39.

——. "Sovetskaia vlast' i emigratsiia." *Russkie novosti* 2, 25 May 1945.

Meir, Georgii. *Vozrozhdenie i belaia ideia.* *Vozrozhdenie* 42 (June 1955): 5–41.

Miliukov, P.N. "Kto zachinshchik?" *Posledniia novosti*, 19 April 1940.

——. "Prodolzhenie emigrantskikh razgovorov." *Posledniia novosti*, 6 June 1940.

——. "Pravda bol'shevizma." *Russkii patriot* 3 (16), 11 November 1944.

Mushkov, V. "Budushchee emigratsii." *Russkaia mysl'*, 13 January 1977.

Nabokov, Nicolas. "Under the Cranberry Tree." *New York Review of Books* 24, no. 3, 3 March 1977.

Nikitine, B. "L'émigration russe." *Revue des sciences politiques* 45 (1922): 190–216.

Nikulin, Lev. "Istoriia odnogo voiazha." *Nedelia* (Moscow) 11–17 October 1964, 10–11.

Novikov, V. "Vstrechi s sovetskimi poddannymi vo Frantsii." *Novyi zhurnal* 12 (1946): 207–22.

Obolenskii, P.A. "Na chuzhoi storone." *Moskva*, 1965, no. 8: 209–21.

Odinets, D. "Iz istorii emigrantskogo separatizma." *SZ* 68 (1939): 369–87.

Postnikov, S. "Literatura emigrantskogo separatizma." *SZ* 63 (1937): 450–7.

Rapoport, Iu. "Konets zarubezhia." *SZ* 69 (1939): 373–81.

Riasanovsky, Nicholas. "The Emergence of Eurasianism." *California Slavic Studies* 4 (1967): 39–72.

Rudnev, V.V. "Politicheskie zametki (eshche o 'Novom grade')." *SZ* 50 (1932): 438–55.

———. "K iubileiu 'Sovremennykh zapisok'." *SZ* 51 (1933): 431–53.

———. "Kommunizm i natsionalizm." *SZ* 57 (1935): 412–18.

Russell, John. "Farewell to Chagall, The Great Survivor." *New York Times*, 7 April 1985, Section 2:31.

Salisbury, Harrison. "The Russian Writer As World Conscience." *Saturday Review/World*, 27 July 1974, 18–20.

Schaufuss, T. "The White Russian Refugees." *The Annals of the American Academy of Political and Social Science* 203 (May 1939): 45–54.

Schoen, Elin. "The Russians Are Coming! The Russians Are Here!" *New York Times Book Review*, 7 September 1980, 20.

Sedykh, Andrei. "Zagadka V.A. Maklakova." *Novoe russkoe slovo*, 18 March 1945.

———. "25 – let so dnia pokhishcheniia generala A.P. Kutepova." *Novoe russkoe slovo*, 27 January 1955.

Shames, Laurence. "For Many Soviet Artists in Exile, These Are Lean Times." *New York Times*, 3 October 1982, Section 2:1.

Sirine, S.N. [V.V. Nabokov]. "La jeunesse de l'émigration russe." *Le Temps*, 2 November 1933.

Soloveichik, S. "Mezhdunarodnyi krizis i sssr." *Novaia Rossiia* 65 (15 April 1939): 4, 7.

Shkarenkov, L.K. "Belaia emigratsiia: agoniia kontrrevoliutsii." *Voprosy istorii*, 1976, no.5;100–20.

Sukhomlin, V. "Gitlerovtsy v Parizhe." *Novyi mir*, 1965, nos. 11:111–56; 12:96–138.

Tsederbaum-Dan, L.O. "Bukharin o Staline." *Novyi zhurnal* 75 (1964): 176–84.

Ul'ianov, Nikolai. "Kul'tura i emigratsiia." *Novyi zhurnal* 28 (1952): 261–72.

Vakar, N.P. "P.N. Miliukov v izgnanii." *Novyi zhurnal* 6 (1943): 369–78.

Veidle, V. "Granitsy Evropy." *SZ* 60 (1936): 304–18.

———. "Rossiia i zapad." *SZ* 67 (1938): 260–80.

Vertinskii, A. "Chetvert' veka bez rodiny." *Moskva*, 1962, nos. 3;211–20, 4:205–20, 5:209–20, 6;212–19.

Vishniak, Mark. "Priznanie." *SZ* 19 (1924): 334–50.

———. "Vozrozhdenie." *SZ* 25 (1925): 392–415.

———. "Mif oktiabria." *SZ* 33 (1927): 362–86.

——. "Geroi nashego vremeni." *SZ* 42 (1930): 428–68.

——. "Protiv techenii." *SZ* 52 (1933): 389–414.

——. "Narodnyi front." *SZ* 59 (1935): 338–53.

——. "Opyt Bliuma." *SZ* 62 (1936): 344–57.

——. "Pravda anti-bol'shevizma." *Novyi zhurnal* 2 (1942): 206–23.

Voronin, N. "O mladorossakh." *Nash soiuz* 70 (October 1935): 15–16.

——. "Eshche o mladorossakh i o natsional'noi revoliutsii." *Nash soiuz* 72 (December 1935): 10–15.

Vraga, R. "Test." *Vozrozhdenie* 7 (January – February 1950): 114–35.

"X". "Ottuda. Pis'ma starogo druga." *SZ* 61 (1936): 328–53, 63 (1937): 331–44.

NEWSPAPERS AND PERIODICALS

Emigré (published in Paris unless otherwise indicated)

Biulleten' rossiiskogo zemsko-gorodskogo komiteta pomoshchi rossiiskim grazhdanam zagranitsei. 1921–22.

Bodrost'. 1934–40. Organ of Kazem-Bek's Young Russians.

Dni. 1926–33. Edited by A.F. Kerenskii.

Dvuglavyi orel. 1926–31. Monarchist.

Evraziiskaia khronika. 1924–28. Eurasianist.

Evraziia. 1928–29. Eurasianist.

Nash soiuz. 1925–37. From 1937–39 *Nasha rodina.* Organ of the pro-Soviet Union of Return to the Motherland.

Novaia Rossiia. 1936–40. Edited by A.F. Kerenskii.

Novoe russkoe slovo (New York) 1910–. Leading Russian daily in the USA.

Novyi put' (New York). 1941–47. Edited by Fedor Dan.

Novyi zhurnal (New York). 1942–. Democratic. Principal "thick journal" of the post-World War II refugees.

Oboronicheskoe dvizhenie. 1936–37. From 1937–39 *Golos otechestva.* Pro-Soviet "defensist" organ.

Obshchee delo. 1918–22, 1928. Edited by V.L. Burtsev.

Parizhskii vestnik. 1942–44. Russian Nazi newspaper.

Posledniia novosti. 1920–40. Edited by P.N. Miliukov.

Russkaia mysl'. 1947–. Major Russian newspaper in post-World War II France.

Russkii patriot. 1944–45. From 1945–47 *Sovetskii patriot.* First of the pro-Soviet *émigré* newspapers to emerge from World War II. D.M. Odinets editor.

Russkii shofer. 1928–39? Democratic section of taxi-drivers union.

Russkie novosti. 1945–46. Second pro-Soviet *émigré* newspaper in liberated France. A.F. Stupnitskii editor.

Russkiia zapiski. 1937–40. Last "thick journal" founded before World War II by the first emigration. P.N. Miliukov editor.

Smena vekh (Prague & Paris). 1921–22.

Sotsialisticheskii vestnik. 1933–40. Menshevik.

Sovremenniia zapiski. 1920–40. Most important "thick journal" and cultural monument of the first emigration.

Ut'verzhdeniia. 1931–32. 3 issues. Iu.A. Shirinskii-Shikhmatov and postrevolutionary "affirmers" group.

Vestnik russkikh dobrovol'tsev, partizan i uchastnikov soprotivleniia vo Frantsii. January – February 1947.

Vozrozhdenie. 1925–40. In 1949 reappeared as a monthly periodical. Conservative.

Za rulem. 1933–35? Newssheet of the conservative section of the Russian taxi-drivers union.

French

L'Action française. Royalist.

Cahiers de la Quinzaine. (20e série, Vol. 5, 5 March 1930). Literary magazine.

L'Ere nouvelle. Organ of Herriot's Radical-Socialists.

L'Humanité. Communist party organ.

Je suis partout. Fascist.

La Liberté. Right-wing, bitterly anti-Soviet.

Le Matin. Centrist, very widely read.

Le National. Right-wing.

L'Oeuvre. Left of centre.

Le Populaire. Organ of the Socialist Party.

Le Temps. Right of centre. Authoritative.

Other

The New Republic
The New Statesman and Nation
New York Herald-Tribune
New York Times
The Times (including the *Times Literary Supplement*).

Index